D1438852

common-law doctrine. These judgements are printed in full.

The judgement in the last case, of Ali Ahmad Hussain Shah, is also given.

Both Tamizuddin Khan's Case and the Reference will have to be included in future standard works on constitutional law, and are here for the first time made conveniently accessible. Sir Ivor Jennings has added a long Introduction, giving the historical background to the controversy, a section on the Indian Independence Act, the traditional interpretation, the Royal Assent, emergency powers, and dissolution.

This is a work of the first importance for constitutional lawyers, historians of modern Asian politics, legislators and students of Commonwealth relations.

CONSTITUTIONAL PROBLEMS
IN PAKISTAN

CONSTITUTIONAL PROBLEMS IN PAKISTAN

BY

SIR IVOR JENNINGS
K.B.E., Q.C., LITT.D., LL.D., F.B.A.

Master of Trinity Hall and Hon. Fellow of St Catharine's College, Cambridge
Formerly Constitutional Adviser to the Government of Pakistan

CAMBRIDGE
AT THE UNIVERSITY PRESS
1957

PUBLISHED BY
THE SYNDICS OF THE CAMBRIDGE UNIVERSITY PRESS
London Office: Bentley House, N.W.1
American Branch: New York

Made and printed in Great Britain by
William Clowes and Sons, Limited, London and Beccles

JQ542
JA49c

CONTENTS

Preface   *page* vii

Table of Cases   ix

Table of Enactments   xi

Introduction:

    I. Preliminary   3

   II. The Historical Background   6

  III. The Indian Independence Act, 1947   11

  IV. The Traditional Interpretation   22

   V. The Royal Assent   25

  VI. Emergency Legislation   38

 VII. Dissolution   57

Judgment in the Case of *Federation of Pakistan and Others*
    v. *Moulvi Tamizuddin Khan*   77

Judgment in the Case of *Usif Patel and Two Others* v. *The*
    Crown   239

Report on the *Special Reference* made by His Excellency the
    Governor-General of Pakistan   257

Judgment in the Case of *Federation of Pakistan* v. *Ali Ahmad*
    Hussain Shah and the Union of India   351

Index   371

548861

PREFACE

THE litigation which followed the dissolution of the Constituent Assembly of Pakistan on 24 October 1954 dealt with fundamental principles of constitutional law of interest throughout the Commonwealth. The first case to reach the Federal Court, *Federation of Pakistan* v. *Moulvi Tamizuddin Khan*, showed that the Assembly had been misinterpreting for more than seven years the powers conferred upon it by the Indian Independence Act, 1947. It had passed forty-four Acts whose legal consequences were far-reaching, and all of them were believed to be invalid because they had not received the assent of the Governor-General. In the process of reaching the conclusion that such assent was required by section 6 of the Act of 1947, the Court found it necessary to examine the fundamental principles of democratic government as understood in the Commonwealth, the nature of Dominion status and the meaning of 'independent Dominion', the royal prerogatives in the Commonwealth and especially in territories acquired by cession or conquest, and the relations between statutory and prerogative powers.

If all the forty-four Acts were invalid, all the federal legislation passed by the Constituent Assembly since 1950 was also invalid, and so was all legislation enacted by the Governors of Provinces under section 92A of the Government of India Act and all legislation passed by the Provincial Legislatures since they had been reconstituted under legislation enacted by the Constituent Assembly; the operations of the State Bank of Pakistan had been unlawful from the beginning; and numerous decisions of the courts of law, including many of those of the Federal Court itself, were contrary to law. There was, in short, such legal chaos that a decision to suspend the Constitution and start again could have been defended politically. It was thought desirable, however, to maintain the Rule of Law so long as it was possible to discover some law to rule. Accordingly, an attempt was made to use the emergency powers of the Government of India Act, which had apparently been enlarged indirectly by those provisions of the Indian Independence Act which had been taken from the Statute of Westminster. This attempt was frustrated by the decision of the Federal Court in *Usif Patel* v. *The Crown*. Because the Government of Sind and not the Federation of Pakistan was the respondent in that case, the argument based upon the Statute of Westminster was not put, and accordingly the decision has no great intrinsic interest outside Pakistan. The decision is, however, a step in the process which led to the opinion of the Federal Court in the third case, which is usually known as the *Special Reference*.

The opinion of the Federal Court was sought in that case because it was still hoped, in spite of the decision in *Usif Patel's* case, that the Rule of Law could be maintained. Action had to be taken in advance of the Court's opinion, but it was made conditional upon approval by the Court, and the Court did in fact approve. In the process it was necessary for the Court to discuss the nature of the prerogative power to summon, prorogue and dissolve legislatures and—as in *Tamizuddin Khan's* case—the relations between statutory and prerogative powers. Of even wider interest, because it appears to be unique in the legal history of the Commonwealth, is the application of the common law doctrine of necessity to the conditions of emergency created by the decision in *Tamizuddin Khan's* case.

The final decision, *Federation of Pakistan* v. *Ali Ahmad Hussain Shah*, is something of an anticlimax, but it contains further discussion on the doctrine of necessity and in any case is part of the story.

This book contains the four cases mentioned, taken from the official copies supplied to me by the Ministry of Law. To provide the necessary background, including references to the legislation, a lengthy introduction has been supplied. It includes a summary of the decision of the Chief Court of Sind in *Tamizuddin Khan's* case and of the arguments in that case in both courts. Owing to my absence from Pakistan a similar treatment of the *Special Reference* was not practicable.

I am indebted to my learned friends the Advocate-General for Pakistan (Mr Fayaz Ali), the Secretary to the Ministry of Law (Sir Edward Snelson, K.B.E.), and my colleague in many unusual drafting adventures, Mr Justice Sheikh Abdul Hamid. They have not seen the Introduction, however, and bear no responsibility for its contents.

W. IVOR JENNINGS

TRINITY HALL
CAMBRIDGE
5 *October 1955*

TABLE OF CASES

Akbar Khan v. The Crown (1949), 36, 41, 46, 47, 178, 218
Akbar Khan v. The Crown (1956), 5
Anwar and Nawaz v. The Crown, 218
Athlumney, ex parte Wilson, In re, 252
Attorney-General v. De Keyser's Royal Hotel Co. Ltd., 64, 65, 68, 268, 300
Bateman's Trusts, In re, 237
Bates's Case, 301
Battersby v. Kirk, 213
Bonanza Creek Gold Mining Co. v. The King, 65
British Columbia Electric Rly. Co. Ltd. v. The King, 203
British Coal Corporation v. The King, 237
British Medical etc. Association v. Jones, 364
Burn v. Carvalho, 251, 252
Calvin's Case, 152
Campbell v. Hall, 29, 60, 121, 291
Commercial Cable Co. v. Government of Newfoundland, 65
Devi Ditta Mal v. Standard Bank of India, 364
Disallowance and Reservation References, In re, 238
Federation of Pakistan v. Ali Ahmad Hussain Shah, 6, 48, 351–70
Federation of Pakistan and Others v. Moulvi Tamizuddin Khan, 4, 5, 38, 40, 53, 57, 77–238, 242, 244, 247, 249, 253, 261, 262, 265, 266, 280, 281, 286, 288, 289, 295, 307, 309, 310, 329, 331, 336, 337, 339, 340, 353, 355, 356, 357, 358, 359, 360, 363, 365
Freeman v. Moyes, 251
Gagambol Ramalingam v. Ruku-ul-Mulk Syed Abdul Wajid, 66
Hawke v. Smith, 221
Hodge v. The Queen, 16
Hollingsworth v. Virginia, 221
Jamieson v. Attorney-General, 251
Julius v. Bishop of Oxford, 225, 228
Khan Iftikhar Hussain Khan of Mamdot v. Province of the Punjab, 36, 142, 148, 178, 217
Khuhro v. Federation of Pakistan, 32, 36, 141–2, 178, 216, 238
Lal Khan v. The Crown, 36
I. M. Lall's Case, 368, 369, 370
Liquidator of the Maritime Bank of Canada v. Receiver-General of New Brunswick, 169, 180, 197, 237
Moore v. Attorney-General for the Irish Free State, 65
Muhammad Umar Khan v. The Crown, 304

ix

Mulvenna *v.* The Admiralty, 369
Murray *v.* Parkes, 183
Musgrave *v.* Pulido, 65, 319
Ndlwana *v.* Hofmeyer, 120
Phillips *v.* Eyre, 304
R. *v.* Hampden, *see* Shipmoney, Case of
R. *v.* Middlesex Justices, 251
R. *v.* Pinney, 73
Ryan *v.* Lennon, 142
Saltpetre, Case of, 73, 300
Sammut *v.* Strickland, 65, 91, 224, 290
Sarfaraz Khan *v.* The Crown, 36, 156, 187, 229
Shankari Prasad Singh Deo *v.* Union of India, 35
Sharpe *v.* Wakefield, 238
Shipmoney, Case of, 45, 73, 300, 342
Shipton, Anderson & Co. and Harrison Bros. & Co., In re an Arbitration between, 299, 301
Special Reference No. 1 of 1955, 6, 48, 51, 75, 257–349, 353, 355, 357, 358
Stockdale *v.* Hansard, 120, 343
Stratton's Case, 305
Tamizuddin Khan *v.* Federation of Pakistan, 4, 29, 31–7, 43, 47, 55, 74, 271
Tilonko *v.* Attorney-General of Natal, 304
Usif Patel and Two Others *v.* The Crown, 5, 41, 46, 47, 48, 49, 51, 52, 54, 262, 264, 296, 297, 306, 307, 308, 315, 319, 322, 335, 337, 340, 345, 348, 357, 360

TABLE OF ENACTMENTS

Enactments are listed in alphabetical order within the calendar year. Those printed in bold type are quoted in full. Those marked * were invalid for want of assent. The enactment marked † was held invalid in *Usif Patel's* case.

Bill of Rights, 1689, 51, 302

Meeting of Parliament Act, 1694, 59

Act of Settlement, 1701, 51, 303

Union with Scotland Act, 1706, 19

Meeting of Parliament Act, 1715, 59

Regulatory Act, 1773, 101

Regulatory Act, 1781, 101

India Act, 1784, 101

India Act, 1793, 101

Charter Act, 1830, 101

Charter Act, 1833, 101
Judicial Committee Act, 1833, s. 4, 279

Defence Act, 1842, 268, 269

Colonial Evidence Act, 1843, s. 1, 132

New Zealand Constitution Act, 1852, s. 44, 271

Charter Act, 1858, 101

Indian Councils Act, 1861, 30

Companies Act, 1862, s. 67, 364

Colonial Laws Validity Act, 1865, 16, 94, 95, 96

British North America Act, 1867,   169, 197
  s. 9,   188, 191
  s. 11,   188
  s. 17,   188
  s. 50,   270
  s. 55,   189
  s. 56,   189
  s. 57,   189

Royal Titles Act, 1876,   101

Interpretation Act, 1889,   14
  s. 18,   89
  s. 18A,   14, 26, 31
  s. 32,   64, 266, 274, 275
  s. 36,   **250**

Colonial Courts of Admiralty Act, 1890,   17, 27, 37, 201
  s. 4,   27, 131

Merchant Shipping Act, 1894,   17, 27, 34, 45
  s. 735,   27, **130–1**, 162
  s. 736,   27, **131**, 162

General Clauses Act, 1897, s. 3,   360
  s. 5,   360

Constitution of Australia, 1900,
  s. 1,   189–90
  s. 2,   190
  s. 28,   270
  s. 58,   190
  s. 59,   190
  s. 60,   190

South Africa Act, 1909,
  s. 9,   182, 190
  s. 20,   271
  s. 64,   28, 182, 190–1
  s. 152,   182

Parliament Act, 1911,   59

Companies Act, 1913, s. 86,   364

British Nationality and Status of Aliens Act, 1914, s. 1,   19
Defence of the Realm Consolidation Act, 1914,   268

Government of India Act, 1915, 321
  s. 3, 101

Government of India Act, 1919, 101, 231

Irish Free State (Constitution) Act, 1922, 143
Irish Free State (Saorstat Eireann) Act, 1922, 142

Bombay City Municipalities Act, 1925, s. 57, 364

Royal and Parliamentary Titles Act, 1927, 19

Statute of Westminster, 1931, 13, 14–19, 89, 92–100, 120, 150, 151,
    152, 176, 180, 186, 194
  s. 2, 16, 17, 18, 95, 111, 120–1, 202
  s. 3, 15, 96, 111, **203**
  s. 4, 18, 50, 96, 111, 202
  s. 5, 17–18, 96, 111, 130
  s. 6, 17–18, 96, 111, 130
  s. 7, 96, 181
  s. 8, 96, 181
  s. 9, 181
  s. 11, 181

Status of the Union Act, 1934, 28

Government of India Act, 1935, 4, 11, 12, 19, 21, 22, 23, 26, 28, 33,
    35, 55, 60, 61, 80, 101–2, 114, 121, 123, 155, 156, 168, 175, 186,
    191, 204, 205, 206, 208, 215, 219, 224, 227, 233, 235, 244, 250,
    259, 267, 283, 291, 315, 320, 326, 328, 343
  s. 2, 29, 60, 102, 181, **191**, 197
  s. 3, **195**
  s. 5, 102
  s. 6, 102
  s. 7, 322
  s. 8, 102
  s. 9, 102
  s. 10, 4, 25, 82, 103, 165, 265
  s. 11, 103
  s. 12, 103
  s. 13, 103
  s. 14, 103
  s. 18, **193–4**, 271
  s. 19, 61, 62, 65, 66, 271, 272
  s. 23, 354, 363
  ss. 24–7, 267
  s. 32, 27, 32, 35, 37, 122, 126, 171, 176, **192**

Government of India Act, 1935—*(cont.)*

s. 42,   4, 5, 17, 41, **42**, 43, 44, 46, 47, 50, 54, 103, 244, 250, 253, 261, 262, 263, 264, 297, 306, 308, 335, 338, 344, 345, 348

s. 43,   103

s. 45,   71, 103, 330, 345

s. 48,   **197**

s. 60,   174, 193, **194**

s. 66,   354, 363

s. 75,   122, 126

s. 76,   122, 126

s. 91,   105

*s. 92A,   5, 39, 46, 48, 52, 242, 243, 252, 295, 337, 355

s. 93,   71

s. 99,   15, 105, 203

s. 102,   4, 17, 32, **41-2**, 43, 44, 47, 49, 54, 243, 244, 245, 247, 262, 336, 344, 345

s. 104,   247

s. 108,   16, 105, 192, 204, 247

s. 110,   16, 43, 105, 192, 204, 247

s. 176,   262

s. 205,   168, 243, 260

s. 212,   6, 159

s. 213,   5, 53, 259, 263, 265, 353

*s. 223A,   3, 25, 38, 43, 57, 71, 82, 116, 140, 160, **165-6**, 167, 178, 260, 261

ss. 232-9,   214

s. 262,   155

s. 295,   66, 196, 271

s. 298,   155

s. 306,   320

s. 316,   230

1st Sched.   267, 273

5th Sched.   39, 48, 57, 296

6th Sched.   39, 48, 57, 296

7th Sched.   245, 247

9th Sched.   15

Executive Authority (External Relations) Act, 1936,   183

Government of India (Provincial Legislative Assemblies) Order, 1936, 215

Ceylon (Constitution) Order in Council, 1946, s. 15,   271

India (Proclamations of Emergency) Act, 1946,   17, 32, 54, **246-7**

Burma Independence Act, 1947,   36, 153, 312

xiv

Ceylon Independence Act, 1947, 15, 16, 18, 271
  1st Sched. 16
Ceylon (Independence) Order in Council, 1947, 271
Indian Independence Act, 1947, 3, 7, 11–22, 32, 33, 55, 61, 62, 79,
  85, 86, 102, 116, 121, 139, 143, 156, 168, 175, 185, 186, 194–5,
  206, 208, 219, 224, 227, 235, 244, 250, 259, 268, 274, 282, 283,
  288, 289, 291, 315, 320, 343, 348
  s. 1, 13, 110
  s. 2, 13
  s. 3, 13
  s. 4, 13
  s. 5, 4, 12, **13**, 20, 29, 34, 40, 45, 54, 56, 63, 64, 65, 67, 68, 69, 70,
    71, 72, 74, 75, **107**, 110, 116, 134, 155, 171, 223, 227, 232, 237,
    261, 266, 273, 283, 315, 321, 322
  s. 6, 7, **13–14**, 15–19, 23, 25, 26, 29, 30, 31, 32, 35, 37, 43, 44, 47,
    49, 50, 54, 56, 58, 61, 68, 69, 74, **107–8**, 111, 112, 114, 115, 122,
    124, 125, 126, 127–30, 132, 133, 135, 136, 137, 138, 139, 141,
    142, 149, 157, 158, 159, 160, 161, 162, 167, 168, 169, 170, 175,
    177, 178, 179, 200, 202, 203, 205, 208, 223, 224, 225, 229, 231,
    232, 233, 234, 235, 236, 237, 238, 243, 266, 277, 316, 343
  s. 7, 19–20, 67, **108**, 113, 153
  s. 8, 6, 15, 19, **20–1**, 23, 25, 26, 29, 30, 31, 32, 35, 37, 43, 44, 49,
    52, 53, 54, 65, 67, 74, 75, **109–10**, 112, 113, 114–15, 125, 126, 127,
    133, 134, 136, 137, 138, 140, 142, 143, 148, 149, 158, 160, 161,
    162, 164, 171, 174, 177, **199–200**, 206, 208, 226, 230, 232, 235,
    242, 243, 245, 247, 249, 260, 261, 262, 264, 267, 270, 272, 273,
    277, 278, 283, 288, 290, 291, 295, 296, 306, 308, 316, 330, 332,
    339, 343, 354, 360
  s. 9, 15, 16, 21, 29, 30, 33, 36, 39, 42, 43, 55, 61, 67, **110**, 113, 195,
    198, 202, 242, 244, 273, 295, 337, 343, 345, 355
  s. 18, 14, 193
  s. 19, 54, 58, 63, 69, 74, 75, **110**, 211, 266, 274, 275, 276, 295, 308,
    334, 353, 354

British Nationality Act, 1948, s. 1, 155
*Indian Independence (Amendment) Act, 1948, 22, 39, 46, 242, 243,
  250, 252, 277, 295, 337

*Constituent Assembly for Pakistan (Increase and Redistribution of
    Seats) Act, 1949, 38, 57, 290, 353, 362
*Constituent Assembly for Pakistan (Increase and Redistribution of
    Seats) (Amendments) Act, 1949, 38, 57
India (Consequential Provisions) Act, 1949, 36, 143, 312
*Indian Independence (Amendment) Act, 1949, 38, 57
*Public and Representative Offices (Disqualification) Act, 1949, 142,
    148, 216, 217

Public Safety Act, 1949 (Punjab), 219
*Rawalpindi Conspiracy (Special Tribunal) Act, 1949, 41, 218

*Constitution (Amendment) Act, 1950, 25
*Government of India (Second Amendment) Act, 1950, 214
*Government of India (Third Amendment) Act, 1950, 39, 57
*Government of India (Fifth Amendment) Act, 1950, 39, 57
*Government of India (Sixth Amendment) Act, 1950, 39
*Privy Council (Abolition of Jurisdiction) Act, 1950, 6, 36, 40, 50,
    159, 243, 354, 357, 359, 362, 365, 366

*Constitution (Amendment) Act, 1951, 39, 57
*Constitution (Second Amendment) Act, 1951, 39, 57
*Delimitation of Constituencies (Adult Franchise) Act, 1951, 39, 57,
    214, 223, 356
*Delimitation of Constituencies (Adult Franchise) (Amendment) Act,
    1951, 39, 57
*Pakistan Citizenship Act, 1951, s. 2, 155

*Government of India (Second Amendment) Act, 1952, 215
*Government of India (Third Amendment) Act, 1952, 39, 57
*Security of Pakistan Act, 1952, 216

Royal Titles Act, 1953, 153

*Constitution (Amendment) Act, 1954, 19, 20
*Government of India (Amendment) Act, 1954, 4, 25, 38, 57, 82, 116,
    140, 165, 260
*Government of India (Fifth Amendment) Act, 1954, 4, 26, 40, 43,
    82, 165
Constituent Convention Order, 1955, 52, 75, 262, 294, 368
†Emergency Powers Ordinance, 1955, 19, 43–5, 47, 52, 53, 243, 250,
    261, 263, 297, 307, 309, 335, 337, 340, 348, 359, 360, 362
Validation of Laws Act, 1955, 6

INTRODUCTION

INTRODUCTION

I. PRELIMINARY

THE Constituent Assembly of Pakistan was set up by the Governor-General of India, Lord Mountbatten, by announcements of 22 July and 10 August 1947. Its powers were determined by the provisions of the Indian Independence Act, 1947, which had been enacted on 18 July 1947, and most of whose provisions came into operation on 15 August 1947. The main function of the Constituent Assembly was to prepare a Constitution for Pakistan, though it was defined rather more widely in the Act. For reasons which need not be explained, the Assembly failed to carry out that function within seven years. The defeat of the Muslim League at the elections for the East Bengal Legislative Assembly in April 1954 led to rapid acceleration of the process of constitution-making, but the proposals accepted by the Constituent Assembly were in many respects controversial. A Draft Constitution prepared on the instructions of the Drafting Committee would have been ready for signature on 25 October and would have been reported to the Assembly on 27 October. On 24 October, however, the Governor-General issued a proclamation asserting that 'the constitutional machinery has broken down'. He proclaimed a state of emergency and claimed that 'the Constituent Assembly as at present constituted has lost the confidence of the people and can no longer function'. Elections would be held as soon as possible. He had called upon the Prime Minister to reform the Cabinet 'with a view to giving the country a vigorous and stable administration'.

This Proclamation was read as an intimation that the Constituent Assembly had been dissolved, and administrative action was taken to prevent the meeting called for the 27 October. The President of the Assembly, Moulvi Tamizuddin Khan, denied that the Governor-General had power to dissolve the Assembly. He therefore petitioned the Sind Chief Court to issue a writ of mandamus under section 223A of the Government of India Act, 1935, which

3

had been inserted by the Government of India (Amendment) Act, 1954, and also a writ of quo warranto under the same section against the Ministers of the Central Government who, he claimed, were not qualified as Ministers under section 10 of the Government of India Act, 1935, as substituted by the Government of India (Fifth Amendment) Act, 1954.

In reply to what was in effect an order nisi, the Advocate-General for Pakistan, on behalf of all the respondents, made a return raising a number of important questions of constitutional law. In particular, he claimed that the Government of India (Amendment) Act, 1954, and the Government of India (Fifth Amendment) Act, 1954, were invalid because they had not received the Governor-General's assent and that the Governor-General, as representative of the Queen under section 5 of the Indian Independence Act, 1947, had power to dissolve the Constituent Assembly. A full bench of the Sind Chief Court found for Moulvi Tamizuddin Khan both on the mandamus and, so far as Ministers appointed on or after 24 October 1954 were concerned, on the quo warranto.[1] The Federation of Pakistan and the Ministers appealed to the Federal Court, which held (Cornelius, J., dissenting), without calling upon counsel for the appellants to reply to the arguments of the respondent, that the Sind Chief Court had acted without jurisdiction, in that section 223A, not having received the assent of the Governor-General, was not part of the law of Pakistan.[2]

In the view of the Government of Pakistan, this decision implied that all the 'Acts' passed by the Constituent Assembly, otherwise than in exercise of the powers of the Federal Legislature under the Government of India Act, 1935, were invalid because none of them had received the Governor-General's assent; that the Constituent Assembly itself, which had purported to amend its own composition by such 'Acts', had been unconstitutional since 1950; and that probably the Acts passed by the Constituent Assembly, acting as Federal Legislature, had also been invalid since 1950. The Governor-General therefore issued a proclamation of emergency under section 102 of the Government of India Act, 1935, and an Emergency Powers Ordinance under section 42 of the same

[1] *Moulvi Tamizuddin Khan* v. *Federation of Pakistan*, P.L.D. 1955 Sind 96.
[2] *Federation of Pakistan* v. *Moulvi Tamizuddin Khan*, *post*, pp. 77–238.

Act 'and all other powers in that behalf'. *Inter alia* the Emergency Powers Ordinance purported to validate thirty-five of the forty-four Acts deemed to have been invalidated by the decision in *Federation of Pakistan* v. *Moulvi Tamizuddin Khan*.

The validity of the Ordinance was at once challenged in the Lahore High Court in *Akbar Khan* v. *The Crown*, but before the argument was concluded the case of *Usif Patel* v. *The Crown*[1] was brought up in the Federal Court, where it was held that the Governor-General had no power under section 42 of the Government of India Act or otherwise to validate constitutional legislation retrospectively, and accordingly that the Ordinance was invalid.

The Governor-General then took the following steps:

(i) By ordinances under section 42 of the Government of India Act he validated retrospectively all the legislation enacted by the Provincial Legislatures and by the Governors of Provinces while section 92A of the Government of India Act was believed to be in force. Since no amendment of the Government of India Act or the Indian Independence Act was involved, the decision in *Usif Patel's* case did not apply.

(ii) He assented to the thirty-five Acts scheduled to the Emergency Powers Ordinance. It was appreciated that this assent could not have retrospective effect except (possibly) where the Act itself provided a date for its coming into force.

(iii) He issued a proclamation and an order summoning a Constituent Convention to exercise the constitution-making functions of the late Constituent Assembly.

(iv) He issued a proclamation purporting to validate the thirty-five Acts temporarily, subject to a reference to the Federal Court under section 213 of the Government of India Act and pending ratification by the Constituent Convention.

(v) He referred to the Federal Court for advisory opinion certain questions relating to his powers of dealing with the emergency and applied for an order stopping legal proceedings pending the issue of the opinion on the reference.

The Federal Court issued the stop order as requested, but at the same time suggested that the reference include questions as to the legal power of the Governor-General to dissolve the late Constituent Assembly and to summon a new Constituent Convention. After lengthy argument, the Court expressed the opinion

[1] *Post*, pp. 239–56.

5

in the *Special Reference*[1] that in the special circumstances set out
in the reference the Governor-General had power to dissolve the
Constituent Assembly, that he had power to summon another
Constituent Assembly (but not a Constituent Convention) which
could exercise all the powers under section 8 of the Indian
Independence Act, 1947, and that pending ratification by the Constituent Assembly he had power to validate temporarily the invalid
laws. The Court refused, however, to issue an order stopping
litigation in lower courts, asserting that it had no legal powers for
this purpose.

The *Special Reference*, being an advisory opinion, was not
binding on lower courts under section 212 of the Government of
India Act, 1935, and accordingly an appeal was brought up under
the Privy Council (Abolition of Jurisdiction) Act, 1950. In
Federation of Pakistan v. *Ali Ahmad Hussain Shah*[2] the Federal
Court held that the Act of 1950 was invalid because it had been
passed by the Constituent Assembly after its composition had
been changed by Acts which were invalid for want of assent, but
that it had been temporarily validated by the proclamation of 16
April 1955.

In accordance with the opinion in the *Special Reference*, the
Constituent Convention Orders were revoked by the Constituent
Assembly Order, 1955, and the new Constituent Assembly met
in Murree on 7 July 1955. Meanwhile the Governor-General had
assented to three of the nine Acts of the first Constituent Assembly
which had not previously received his assent. This brought up to
thirty-eight the number of Acts passed by that Assembly which
had received the assent. The Validation of Laws Bill, designed
to close the chapter, was referred to a select committee on 11 July,
and received the Governor-General's assent in October 1955.

II. THE HISTORICAL BACKGROUND

In argument before the Federal Court, counsel for Moulvi Tamizuddin Khan sought to show by reference to historical records
and the debates on the Indian Independence Bill that His Majesty's Government had accepted the position that the Constituent

[1] *Post*, pp. 257–349.
[2] *Post*, pp. 350–72.

6

Assemblies of India and Pakistan were 'sovereign bodies' not subject to any kind of legal control. Counsel for the Federation of Pakistan raised no objection because, not only were they prepared with references which showed, in their opinion, exactly the opposite, but also because they were anxious to quote from the *Parliamentary Debates* to show the meaning of the crucial section 6 of the Act of 1947. The Court refused to allow the quotations unless it were shown that section 6 was ambiguous.[1] To enable the reader to understand the nature of the problem, however, it is necessary to show how and why an interpretation was given to the Indian Independence Act which the Federation challenged for the first time in *Tamizuddin Khan's* case.

Pakistan came into existence on 15 August 1947 under the Indian Independence Act, 1947. To explain the background, however, it is necessary to go back to the Cabinet Mission of 1946, which issued its final statement on 16 May 1946.[2] The delegation recorded its inability to secure agreement between the Indian National Congress and the Muslim League, and set forth its own scheme which had had the approval of His Majesty's Government in the United Kingdom. The scheme put forward by the Indian National Congress for a united India was rejected. The proposal of the Muslim League to establish Pakistan was equally rejected. The scheme proposed by the Mission was that of a weak federation for the whole of India, with power vested in the Provinces to form groups with executives and legislatures, thus creating what would have been in effect a three-tiered federation. The scheme would be worked out by a Constituent Assembly, the members of which were to be elected by the members representing each of the three major communities—General (i.e. mainly Hindu), Muslim and Sikh—in each of the Provincial Assemblies. Representatives of the Chief Commissioners' provinces and of the Indian States were to be added. The elections were to be by proportional representation by means of a single transferable vote. The Assembly was to divide into three sections which were in effect the Hindu areas which ultimately formed (with East Punjab and West Bengal) the Union of India, West Pakistan (but including the whole of the Punjab) and East Pakistan (but including the whole of Bengal).

[1] Nevertheless, the Chief Justice quoted from the *Debates* in his judgment; see *post*, pp. 125, 126, 149–50.
[2] A. C. Banerjee, *The Making of the Indian Constitution*, I, pp. 137–50.

7

These sections would work out the Provincial Constitutions for their respective areas. Meanwhile the Governor-General would form an Interim Government. It was mentioned that there would have to be a 'treaty' between the Union Constituent Assembly and the United Kingdom 'to provide for certain matters arising out of the transfer of power'. Nothing was said about legislation, but clearly United Kingdom legislation would be required to repeal the Government of India Act and to bring the new Constitution into operation.

In a letter from Maulana Azad, on behalf of the Congress Working Committee, to Lord Pethick-Lawrence, dated 20 May 1946,[1] a question was raised which had some influence on Pakistan's constitutional problem:

As we understand the statement, it contains certain recommendations and procedure for the election and functioning of the Constituent Assembly. The Assembly itself, when formed, *will in my Committee's opinion be a sovereign body for the purpose of drafting the Constitution unhindered by any external authority*, as well as for entering into a treaty. Further that it will be open to the Assembly to vary in any way it likes the recommendations and the procedure suggested by the Cabinet Delegation. *The Constituent Assembly being a sovereign body for the purposes of the Constitution, its final decisions will automatically take effect.*

To this point Lord Pethick-Lawrence replied[2]:

We think the authority and the functions of the Constituent Assembly and the procedure which it is intended to follow are clear from the statement. Once the Constituent Assembly is formed and working on this basis, there is naturally no intention to interfere with its discretion or to question its decisions. When the Constituent Assembly has completed its labours, *His Majesty's Government will recommend to Parliament such action as may be necessary for the cession of sovereignty to the Indian people*, subject only to two provisos which are mentioned in the statement and which are not, we believe, controversial, namely, adequate provision for the protection of minorities and willingness to conclude a treaty to cover matters arising out of the transfer of power.

The resolution of the Congress Working Committee of 24 May 1946[3] raised the same point and received the same reply,[4] which was not acceptable to the Congress.[5] The attitude of the

[1] A. C. Banerjee, *The Making of the Indian Constitution*, p.162. The italic in all quotations is the present writer's.
[2] *Ibid.* p. 165.   [3] *Ibid.* p. 167.   [4] *Ibid.* p. 170.
[5] See speech of Jawaharlal Nehru, *ibid.* p. 242.

Muslim League to this particular question is not clear from the correspondence. No doubt there were, from the point of view of the League, two sides to the question. On the one hand the League did not object to 'external authority', by which it would mean His Majesty's Government being kept out of the picture; on the other hand it was not anxious to give complete discretion to a Congress-dominated Constituent Assembly. Muhammad Ali Jinnah refused to accept the scheme[1] and his action was endorsed by the Muslim League on 29 July 1946.[2] It should be said, however, that the principal reason for rejection was that the Interim Government proposed was not satisfactory to the League. The Congress, while reiterating its plea for the 'sovereignty' of the Constituent Assembly,[3] did its best to meet the contention of the Muslim League:

> *The Committee has emphasised the sovereign character of the Constituent Assembly, that is, its right to function and draw up the Constitution for India without external power or authority,* but the Assembly will naturally function within the internal limitations which are inherent in its task and will further seek the largest measure of cooperation in drawing up the Constitution of free India allowing the greatest measure of freedom and protection to all just claims and interests.

Both the Congress and the League were on the horns of a dilemma. If the Constituent Assembly was 'sovereign', its majority would necessarily decide the place of the Muslims in the new Constitution: if the Constituent Assembly was not 'sovereign', control for the protection of minorities would have to be exercised by the United Kingdom. The statement quoted was one of the statements to which M. A. Jinnah took exception on 12 August 1946, though he did not object to the statement of 'sovereignty' as against external authority.[4] Meanwhile the Muslim League had captured 95 per cent of the Muslim seats in the Constituent Assembly. After further correspondence the League decided on 13 October 1946 to refuse to join the Interim Government.[5]

There was a conference in London in December 1946 but it failed to reach agreement. The Union Constituent Assembly met in Delhi on 9 December, but the Muslim League members did not attend. An 'Objectives Resolution' was moved on 13 December and passed with acclamation on 13 January 1947. On

[1] *Ibid.* p. 246.   [2] *Ibid.* p. 260.   [3] *Ibid.* p. 268.
[4] *Ibid.* p. 271.   [5] *Ibid.* p. 298.

9

31 January the Working Committee of the Muslim League resolved that 'the continuation of the Constituent Assembly and its proceedings and decisions are *ultra vires*, invalid and illegal, and it should be forthwith dissolved'.[1]

The notion that His Majesty's Government was anxious to retain control of India is still prevalent on the sub-continent because of the Congress theory, propagated for a generation, that the conflict of Hindu and Muslim was a product of Britain's decision to 'divide and rule'. It is, however, plain from the published correspondence that the Labour Government (and, for that matter, its predecessor) was only too anxious to carry out Gandhi's advice to 'quit India'. Its problem was to quit in such a manner as not to leave chaos behind. Eventually the Government decided to take the risk. On 20 February 1947 the Prime Minister announced in the House of Commons[2] that it was the intention of His Majesty's Government 'to effect the transference of power to responsible Indian hands' by a date not later than June 1948. He added that Lord Mountbatten would supersede Lord Wavell as Governor-General. Lord Mountbatten worked out a scheme which was published on 3 June 1947[3] and which in effect provided for the creation of Pakistan. It provided that the Provincial Assemblies of Bengal and the Punjab (excluding the European members) would meet in two parts, the one representing the Muslim-majority districts and the other the rest of the Province. Each part would decide whether the Province should be partitioned, and a simple majority in either part could decide for partition. If partition was decided upon, each part would decide whether to join the existing Constituent Assembly or to join a new Constituent Assembly. The Legislative Assembly of Sind would decide the same question. In the North-West Frontier Province there would be a referendum. The representative of British Baluchistan would decide the same question. If Bengal were partitioned, there would be a referendum in the Sylhet district of Assam. The Governor-General reserved the right to make 'such further announcements as may be necessary in regard to procedure or any other matters for carrying out the above arrangements'.

There was in fact a partition. Sind, British Baluchistan, West

---

[1] Banerjee, *Making of the Ind. Const.* pp. 400–1.
[2] *Ibid.* pp. 401–5.   [3] *Ibid.* pp. 437–43.

Punjab, the North-West Frontier Province, East Bengal and the Sylhet district of Assam, all decided to join a new Constituent Assembly. This plan of 3 June 1947 was therefore the origin of the Constituent Assembly of Pakistan. The rump of the Union Constituent Assembly, which had been functioning since 9 December 1946, became the Constituent Assembly of India.

So far, no legal authority had been given for these actions. They were, however, not illegal but extra-legal. The government of India was being carried on more or less—it was pointed out that the law could not strictly be followed during the interim period—in accordance with the Government of India Act, 1935. There was nothing to prevent the King-Emperor or the Governor-General, or indeed anybody else, from setting up a constituent assembly or several such assemblies. Their decisions would have no legal effect unless and until they were validated by Act of the Parliament of the United Kingdom, which alone could repeal or amend the provisions of the Government of India Act. Meanwhile the Congress leaders were not concerned with the law. They wanted independence; and it was of no great interest to them whether it was obtained legally or illegally. As we have seen, they assumed that the Constituent Assembly would be 'a sovereign body for the purpose of drafting the Constitution unhindered by any external authority', though the Cabinet Mission had pointed out that under the plan of 1946 its decisions would have to be validated by Act of Parliament. Mr Jinnah and the Muslim League did not contest the principle of sovereignty, so long as it did not mean that the Union Constituent Assembly could by a majority bind the Muslims of India. They would not, therefore, contest the opinion that the Constituent Assembly of Pakistan should be a sovereign body. The questions were whether the Indian Independence Act, 1947, so provided and whether the Constituent Assembly was sovereign with or without the Governor-General.

III. THE INDIAN INDEPENDENCE ACT, 1947

The Mountbatten plan of 3 June 1947 announced[1] that 'His Majesty's Government propose to introduce legislation during the current session for the transfer of power this year on a Dominion

[1] *Ibid.* p. 442.

Status basis to one or two successor authorities according to the decisions taken as a result of this announcement'. In his broadcast address the same day,[1] Lord Mountbatten made plain that power was to be transferred to one or two *Governments*: it was not a transfer to one or two Constituent Assemblies. At his press conference next day the Governor-General explained[2] that until the new Constitutions were framed India would be governed under the Government of India Act, 1935.

The Mountbatten plan had already been agreed upon by the leaders of the Indian National Congress and the Muslim League. The Congress had at last come round to the view that they had to allow the Muslim areas to decide whether or not they should become part of Pakistan. The League had no doubt that the plan provided for the establishment of Pakistan. If, as seemed probable, Pakistan was created, power would be transferred in truncated India to a Congress Government headed by Jawaharlal Nehru and in Pakistan to a Muslim League Government headed by Muhammad Ali Jinnah. The Government of the United Kingdom hoped that Lord Mountbatten would remain Governor-General of both countries for a short transitional period, in the belief that a common armed force could be maintained and the danger of bloodshed avoided. This danger was not present to the minds of the Indian and Pakistani leaders because of the tradition that the whole conflict had been exaggerated by Britain for its own purposes. India agreed to the retention of Lord Mountbatten, but the League insisted that Jinnah become Governor-General of Pakistan. This fact was announced by the Prime Minister of the United Kingdom when he introduced the Indian Independence Bill. The argument used in the Federal Court of Pakistan, that the Parliament of the United Kingdom could not have intended that the Governor-General's assent should be needed for constitutional legislation because the Governor-General might have been a 'foreigner', was therefore beside the point.   Section 5 of the Act did allow the appointment of a joint Governor-General, but Parliament was aware that this power would not be used. It should be added that the terms of the Indian Independence Bill were discussed with the leaders of the two parties, and it is believed that the slight modifica-

[1] Banerjee, *Making of the Ind. Const.* p. 445.
[2] *Ibid.* p. 457.

tions of the language of the Statute of Westminster, 1931, which are to be found in sub-sections (2) and (4) of section 6 of the Act, were suggested by them. The first of these modifications was unnecessary and might have led to a misinterpretation of the powers of the Legislature of the Dominion. The second was unfortunate because it prevented recourse to the Parliament of the United Kingdom if the scheme broke down. The Government of the United Kingdom did not object to passing on the bath and the bath-water as well as the baby.

The Indian Independence Act, 1947, received the royal assent on 18 July 1947. The 'appointed day' on which 'two independent Dominions' should be set up was 15 August 1947.

Section 1 provided for the establishment of two 'independent Dominions', India and Pakistan, as from 15 August 1947. Counsel for Moulvi Tamizuddin Khan sought to show that there was a difference between a 'Dominion' and an 'independent Dominion', because the former had no right to change its own Constitution whereas India and Pakistan were provided with constituent assemblies so that they could provide, and from time to time alter, their own Constitutions.

Sections 2, 3 and 4 defined the territories of India and Pakistan and were not involved in the controversy.

Sections 5 and 6 were as follows:

5. For each of the new Dominions, there shall be a Governor-General who shall be appointed by His Majesty and shall represent His Majesty for the purposes of the government of the Dominion:
Provided that, unless and until provision to the contrary is made by a law of the Legislature of either of the new Dominions, the same person may be Governor-General of both the new Dominions.
6. (1) The Legislature of each of the new Dominions shall have full power to make laws for that Dominion, including laws having extra-territorial operation.
(2) No law and no provision of any law made by the Legislature of either of the new Dominions shall be void or inoperative on the ground that it is repugnant to the law of England, or to the provisions of this or any existing or future Act of Parliament of the United Kingdom, or to any order, rule or regulation made under any such Act, and the powers of the Legislature of each Dominion include the power to repeal or amend any such Act, order, rule or regulation in so far as it is part of the law of the Dominion.
(3) The Governor-General of each of the new Dominions shall have

13

full power to assent in His Majesty's name to any law of the Legislature of that Dominion and so much of any Act as relates to the disallowance of laws by His Majesty or the reservation of laws for the signification of His Majesty's pleasure thereon or the suspension of the operation of laws until the signification of His Majesty's pleasure thereon shall not apply to laws of the Legislature of either of the new Dominions.

(4) No Act of Parliament of the United Kingdom passed on or after the appointed day shall extend, or be deemed to extend, to either of the new Dominions as part of the law of that Dominion unless it is extended thereto by a law of the Legislature of the Dominion.

(5) No Order in Council made on or after the appointed day under any Act passed before the appointed day, and no order, rule or other instrument made on or after the appointed day under any such Act by any United Kingdom Minister or authority shall extend, or be deemed to extend, to either of the new Dominions as part of the law of that Dominion.

(6) The power referred to in sub-section (1) of this section extends to the making of laws limiting for the future the powers of the Legislature of the Dominion.

It will be convenient at this point to discuss the differences between the provisions of section 6 and those of the Statute of Westminster, 1931. It was unnecessary to provide that India and Pakistan should cease to be 'colonies' within the meaning of the Interpretation Act, 1889, because that definition had never applied to British India. There were, and still are, difficulties in finding out what Acts of the Parliament of the United Kingdom do apply to India and Pakistan, because many Acts apply to 'British possessions', a term now defined by section 18A of the Interpretation Act, 1889, which was inserted by the Schedule to the Government of India (Adaptation of Acts of Parliament) Order, 1937, as meaning 'British India as a whole'. These Acts continue to be part of the laws of India and Pakistan, or strictly speaking of those parts of India and Pakistan which were parts of British India, under section 18 (3) of the Indian Independence Act, 1947.[1]

[1] This is a perennial problem in Her Majesty's dominions overseas where (it should be remembered by learned parliamentary counsel) complete sets of United Kingdom legislation and delegated legislation rarely exist. In *Tamizuddin Khan's* case there was argument between the Chief Justice and counsel for the respondent as to whether Pakistani citizens were British subjects, and references were made to the British Nationality Act, 1948. Counsel for the appellants were waiting for an opportunity to point out that section 1 of the British Nationality and Status of Aliens Act, 1914, was still part of the law of Pakistan. The unofficial compilations of statute law help a little but can be misleading; for instance, they do not always include local adaptations such as those in the Government of India (Adaptation of Acts of Parliament) Order,

Section 6 (1) of the Independence Act contains a reference to extra-territorial legislation in somewhat different form from that of section 3 of the Statute of Westminster, 1931. The explanation, no doubt, is that extra-territorial legislation was covered by section 99 (2) of the Government of India Act, 1935. This provision was removed by Governor-General's Order under section 9 of the Independence Act, and the words 'including laws having extra-territorial operation' were included in the powers of the Federal Legislature under section 99 (1) of the Act of 1935. Incidentally this amendment showed that, in the opinion of Lord Mountbatten's advisers, the 'Federal Legislature' was part of the 'Legislature of the Dominion' for the purposes of section 6 (1).

The remainder of section 6 (1) has no parallel in the Statute of Westminster or in the Ceylon Independence Act, 1947. The 'Dominions' to which the statute applied had complete Constitutions in existence, and so had Ceylon in 1947. In each case the legislative powers of the 'legislature of the Dominion' were defined by Act of Parliament or prerogative instrument. Hence there was no need to define those powers in United Kingdom legislation. India and Pakistan had no legislatures on 15 August 1947 except the legislatures established under the Independence Act itself. British India was divided between India and Pakistan, and proviso (a) to section 8 (2) of the Independence Act provided for the abolition of the Indian Legislature which was, up to the appointed day, exercising legislative functions for British India under the Ninth Schedule to the Government of India Act, 1935, because chapter III of that Act, relating to the Federal Legislature, had not been brought into operation. It was therefore necessary in section 6 both to create and empower legislatures for the two Dominions. The two 'legislatures' were notional, in the sense that no composition was prescribed. The powers of the Legislatures of the Dominions were conferred in the first instance on the Constituent Assemblies by section 8; but, unless and until section 6 was repealed or amended by a Constituent Assembly, the

1937. In any case, the Adaptation of Acts by Order in Council is, from the point of view of a practising lawyer who may be called upon to give a reference in oral argument, an objectionable procedure. Not until the argument in *Tamizuddin Khan's* case was almost completed was it discovered that 'legislature' in section 8 (3) of the Independence Act was defined by an adaptation to the Interpretation Act; and, apparently, neither the court nor counsel for the respondent noticed it.

Legislature of the Dominion, including any legislature that might be established by a law of the Constituent Assembly, would have the wide powers conferred by that section.

Section 6 (1), read with section 6 (2), confers plenary powers upon the Legislature of the Dominion or, if Dicey's unfortunate phrase be preferred, 'sovereign' powers. The description in *Hodge* v. *The Queen*[1] is perhaps better: 'powers as plenary and as ample as the Imperial Parliament in the plenitude of its power, possessed and could bestow'. With section 6 (1), however, must be read section 6 (6), which again is peculiar to India and Pakistan. The 'Dominions' to which the Statute of Westminster applied, and also the parliament of Ceylon, had such constituent powers, if any, as their Constitutions provided. In India and Pakistan the Legislatures empowered by section 6 necessarily had constituent powers. Hence those Legislatures had to be empowered to 'limit their own sovereignty', if Dicey's phrase must be used. In other words, their plenary powers had to include a power to establish a legislature with limited legislative and constituent powers. This was not merely, as has sometimes been assumed, to enable either India or Pakistan (or both) to establish a federal Constitution; it also authorised the enactment of a Bill of Rights or other limitation upon the powers of the Legislature of the Dominion. It may be noted that in this case 'Legislature of the Dominion' quite clearly contemplates a legislature having constituent powers.

Section 6 (2) is in almost the same form as section 2 (2) of the Statute of Westminster and paragraph 1 (2) of the First Schedule to the Ceylon Independence Act, 1947. Section 2 (1) of the statute and paragraph 1 (1) of the First Schedule to the Ceylon Independence Act, 1947, were omitted because the Colonial Laws Validity Act, 1865, did not apply to British India. The provisions which had to be removed in India and Pakistan were those in sections 108 and 110 of the Government of India Act, 1935. It was assumed that those sections would be removed by Governor-General's Order under section 9 of the Independence Act—as was in fact done. This removal raised the interesting question, which need not be discussed at this point, whether the mere removal empowered the Federal Legislature under the Government of India Act to repeal or amend Acts of the Parliament of the United

[1] (1883), 9 App. Cas. 117.

Kingdom applying to India or Pakistan as part of its law. The question did not arise if the Federal Legislature was part of the 'Legislature of the Dominion' within the meaning of section 6 (2) of the Independence Act: but if it was not, it could be argued that under section 102 of the Government of India Act, as amended by the India (Proclamations of Emergency) Act, 1946, the Federal Legislature could in certain circumstances amend the Government of India Act itself. In that case, the Governor-General seemed to have the power under section 42 of the Act of 1935 to amend that Act.

Section 6 (2) of the Independence Act contains two words which are not to be found in section 2 (2) of the Statute of Westminster or the corresponding Ceylon provision. They are the words 'this or'. Clearly the intention was to enable the Legislature of the Dominion to repeal or amend the Independence Act itself. It is understood that these words were inserted at the request of the Indian advisers consulted by Lord Mountbatten. They seem, however, to be unnecessary. That the Statute of Westminster confers power upon the Parliament of a Dominion to repeal or amend that Act has certainly been generally accepted, and the power has been exercised in the Irish Free State and the Union of South Africa. There was no 'Legislature of the Dominion' until 15 August 1947, and the Independence Act was then 'an existing Act'. Incidentally, however, the insertion of the words made it plain that, for the purposes of this sub-section, 'Legislature of the Dominion' included the Constituent Assembly. Clearly the purpose was to enable the Constituent Assembly to provide for a republican Constitution or to make law for the secession of India or Pakistan from the Commonwealth.

Section 6 (3) is peculiar to India and Pakistan, though sections 5 and 6 of the Statute of Westminster applied to the Merchant Shipping Act, 1894, and the Colonial Courts of Admiralty Act, 1890, to which reference seems to be made by implication in the sub-section. Since the meaning of this sub-section was the main question in controversy in *Moulvi Tamizuddin Khan's* case, it would be inappropriate to analyse it at this point. The reason for the omission of any reference to assent in the Statute of Westminster is, however, plain. The Constitutions of all the Dominions contained provisions relating to assent, reservation and disallowance. There were, however, recognised methods of amending those Constitutions. In Canada (in 1931) an Act of the Parliament of the United Kingdom was required; in Australia a referendum was needed; in New Zealand there would be local legislation which would be reserved; in South Africa a local Act would suffice; in Newfoundland an Order in Council or Letters Patent would be required; in Ceylon (to which the provisions of the Statute were applied by the Ceylon Independence Act, 1947) a special majority would be needed. The Statute of Westminster and the Ceylon Independence Act carefully avoided the amendment of the respective Constitutions. In India and Pakistan some provision was needed because there Acts of Parliament provided for assent, reservation, suspension and disallowance.

Section 6 (4) is based upon section 4 of the Statute of Westminster. It specifically provides, however, that an Act of the Parliament of the United Kingdom shall apply to India or Pakistan only if it is extended thereto by a law of the Legislature of the Dominion. The leaders of the Indian National Congress in 1947 were still afraid that the United Kingdom would, by some means or other, find means to destroy the independence which seemed to them to be within their grasp. Whereas for Canada, for instance, the Parliament of the United Kingdom is a friendly legislature, always willing to help when its help is needed; for India it was a 'foreign' legislature whose gifts were to be regarded with suspicion. They were therefore prepared to ignore the difficulty that might arise if, for some reason or other, the scheme of the Independence Act broke down. It was an article of faith that everything would come right once responsibility was conferred upon the 'people of India'. It is reasonably certain that nobody contemplated that the Constituent Assembly of India or Pakistan would fail to carry out its moral duty of providing a Constitution. Everybody (in those days) was only too anxious to get on with the job.

Section 6 (5) of the Independence Act is peculiar to India and Pakistan. It was suggested in the Federal Court of Pakistan that this sub-section filled a lacuna in the Statute of Westminster. It may be doubted if that was the case. If there were any Acts of the Parliament of the United Kingdom empowering the Crown to legislate by Order in Council, they could be repealed or amended by legislation under section 2 of the Statute of Westminster; and, if they were useful provisions, they would be exercised on the advice of the Dominion Government concerned. In India and Pakistan, on the other hand, there were wide powers of legislation by Order in Council under the Government of India Act, and under the same Act the Secretary of State for India in Council also had wide powers. The necessity for removing these powers was obvious. Possibly there were other Acts containing similar powers, but these have not been studied.

Section 7 of the Independence Act contained provisions relating to the suzerainty of the Crown in the Indian States, tribal areas, etc. In India nobody seems to have bothered very much about the powers conferred on the Constituent Assembly in relation to these territories, which were not part of the territories of the Crown nor part of British India. The Constituent Assembly simply assumed the power to incorporate them into the territory of India. In Pakistan the delay in providing a Constitution and the intention to incorporate the Acceded States and the tribal areas into West Pakistan led to some discussion which resulted in an amendment to section 8 (1) of the Indian Independence Act by the Constitution (Amendment) Act, 1954, one of the 'Acts' of the Constituent Assembly which did not receive the assent of the Governor-General, but which was sought to be ratified by the Emergency Powers Ordinance, 1955.

Section 7 also authorised the omission of the words 'Emperor of India' from the royal style and titles. This was necessary because, since the Act of Union with Scotland, the royal style and titles have been governed by legislation. The sub-section authorising removal would seem to be a purely formal matter, but counsel for Tamizuddin Khan tried to make something of it. According to him, the King ceased to be Emperor of India and therefore he did not become King of Pakistan. The phrase 'Great Britain, Ireland and the British Dominions beyond the seas', which remained part of the title under the Royal and Parliamentary Titles Act, 1927, did not include Pakistan, which was an 'independent Dominion' not owing allegiance to the Crown. This led to a discussion whether citizens of Pakistan were 'British subjects', though no reference was made to section 1 of the British Nationality and Status of Aliens Act, 1914, which seems to answer the question. In any case a statement by the Chief Justice that he had somewhere read an assertion that Pakistan had asserted its common allegiance to the Crown enabled counsel for the Federation of Pakistan to read the decision of the Commonwealth Conference of April 1949, signed by Liaquat Ali Khan on behalf of Pakistan, to the effect that all the countries of the Commonwealth, including Pakistan but excluding India, owed a common allegiance to the Crown. It is, however, true that on the accession of Elizabeth II the United Kingdom, Canada, Australia, New Zealand, South Africa and Ceylon passed legislation authorising new titles. Pakistan did not, but proclaimed the Queen by title which did not include an assertion that the Queen was Queen of Pakistan. Counsel therefore asserted that 'her other realms and territories' did not include Pakistan. Besides, the Governor-General took an oath of allegiance to the Constitution of Pakistan and merely promised to be 'faithful' to the King. The Chief Justice made some caustic comments upon the attitude of the Constituent Assembly, which acted as the Constituent Assembly for a Dominion but did not accept the implications of Dominion status, and at the same time neglected to frame a Constitution by which Pakistan could cease to be a Dominion.

Finally, section 7 also provided that, as from the appointed day, 'His Majesty's Government in the United Kingdom have no responsibility as respects the government of any of the territories which, immediately before the appointed day, were included in British India'. In the argument in the Sind Chief Court some doubt was expressed as to whether Her Majesty was not included in 'Her Majesty's Government', and it was suggested that the Federation of Pakistan, by arguing that the Queen had prerogatives which were vested in the Governor-General by section 5 of the Act, was bringing the 'British Government' or simply 'the British' in by the back door after they had quietly and politely left by the front door. This misconception of the nature of Dominion status, which is by no means uncommon in Asia, had disappeared by the time the case came into the Federal Court.

Section 8 of the Act of 1947, excluding a proviso inserted in sub-section (1) by the Constitution (Amendment) Act, 1954, which had not received the assent of the Governor-General, was as follows:

8. (1) In the case of each of the new Dominions, the powers of the Legislature of the Dominion shall, for the purpose of making provision

as to the constitution of the Dominion, be exercisable in the first instance by the Constituent Assembly of that Dominion, and references in this Act to the Legislature of the Dominion shall be construed accordingly.

(2) Except in so far as provision is made by or in accordance with a law made by the Constituent Assembly of the Dominion under subsection (1) of this section, each of the new Dominions and all Provinces and other parts thereof shall be governed as nearly as may be in accordance with the Government of India Act, 1935; and the provisions of that Act, and of the Orders in Council, rules and other instruments made thereunder, shall, so far as applicable, and subject to any express provisions of this Act, and with such omissions, additions, adaptations and modifications as may be specified in orders of the Governor-General under the next succeeding section, have effect accordingly:

Provided that

(a) the said provisions shall apply separately in relation to each of the new Dominions and nothing in this sub-section shall be construed as continuing on or after the appointed day any Central Government or Legislature common to both the new Dominions;

(b) nothing in this sub-section shall be construed as continuing in force on or after the appointed day any form of control by His Majesty's Government in the United Kingdom over the affairs of the new Dominions or of any Province or other part thereof;

(c) so much of the said provisions as requires the Governor-General or any Governor to act in his discretion or exercise his individual judgment as respects any matter shall cease to have effect as from the appointed day;

(d) as from the appointed day, no Provincial Bill shall be reserved under the Government of India Act, 1935, for the signification of His Majesty's pleasure, and no Provincial Act shall be disallowed by His Majesty thereunder; and

(e) the powers of the Federal Legislature or Indian Legislature under that Act, as in force in relation to each Dominion, shall in the first instance be exercisable by the Constituent Assembly of the Dominion, in addition to the powers exercisable by that Assembly under sub-section (1) of this section.

(3) Any provision of the Government of India Act, 1935, which, as applied to either of the new Dominions by sub-section (2) of this section and the orders therein referred to, operates to limit the power of the legislature of that Dominion shall, unless and until other provision is made by or in accordance with a law made by the Constituent Assembly of the Dominion in accordance with the provisions of sub-section (1) of this section, have the like effect as a law of the Legislature of the Dominion limiting for the future the powers of that Legislature.

Section 9 of the Act contained very wide powers for the making of orders by the Governor-General, including orders 'for making omissions from, additions to, and adaptations and modifications of, the Government of India Act, 1935, and the Orders in Council, rules and other instruments made thereunder, in their application to the separate new Dominions'. The section was deemed to have had effect as from 3 June 1947, the date on which Lord Mountbatten made his announcement about the setting-up of two Constituent Assemblies, and any order made under the section might be made so as to be retrospective to any date not earlier than the said 3 June. The orders made under this section should, in the case of each Dominion, be subject to the same powers of repeal and amendment as laws of the Legislature of the Dominion (sub-section (4)). By sub-section (5) no order should be made by the Governor-General after 31 March 1948, or such earlier date as might be determined, in the case of either Dominion, by any law of the Legislature of that Dominion. The date had been altered to 31 March 1949 by the Indian Independence (Amendment) Act, 1948, which had not received the assent of the Governor-General.

In the main this section did not come into controversy. It was, however, argued by the Advocate-General in the Sind Chief Court that Lord Mountbatten's announcement of 3 June 1947, under which the composition of the Constituent Assembly of Pakistan had been determined, was an 'order' under this section.

IV. THE TRADITIONAL INTERPRETATION

The Constituent Assembly of India had begun its work early in 1948 and it 'enacted' the Constitution of India on 26 November 1949. The main principles of the Indian Independence Act, 1947, never came under the scrutiny of the Indian courts, but a traditional interpretation of the Act was adopted, based upon the concept laid down in the correspondence between the Indian National Congress and the Cabinet Mission that the Constituent Assembly was a 'sovereign body'. The same interpretation was adopted in Pakistan, but there the process of constitution-making proceeded in a desultory fashion for seven long years and had not been completed when the Assembly was 'dissolved' on 24 October 1954.

The traditional interpretation may be defined as follows:

(i) The Constituent Assembly was, in reality, two bodies, a constituent assembly exercising its powers of 'making provision as to the constitution' under section 8 (1) of the Indian Independence Act, which was sometimes called 'the Constituent Assembly as such' or even 'the Constituent Assembly' *tout court*; and an ordinary legislature called, in the Government of India Act as adapted for India, the 'Dominion Legislature', and in the Government of India Act as adapted for Pakistan, the 'Federal Legislature'. In other words, a distinction was drawn not, as section 8 specified, between constituent powers and legislative powers, but between the constituent body and the legislative body. In Pakistan the 'Constituent Assembly' and the 'Federal Legislature' were differently summoned, the Constituent Assembly by its President and the Federal Legislature by the Governor-General. There were, too, different rules of procedure for the 'Constituent Assembly' and the 'Constituent Assembly (Legislature)'. In part, this dichotomy was due to the manner in which the Government of India Act was adapted by Lord Mountbatten, acting on the advice of legal advisers drawn from the Indian National Congress and the Muslim League. A number of provisions in part II, chapter III, of the Government of India Act, which might have been omitted, were left in.

(ii) The 'Constituent Assembly as such' was a sovereign body. So far as is known, nobody explained whether this 'sovereignty' was obtained because it was exercising the powers of the Legislature of the Dominion under section 6, or whether it derived its powers independently from section 8. One of the counsel for Moulvi Tamizuddin Khan went so far as to assert that the Constituent Assembly derived its authority from the people, but generally the argument for the petitioner went on the basis that section 8 was the empowering clause, and that section 6 was put in merely because of the cherished wish of His Majesty's Government, which could be shown from the correspondence, that India and Pakistan would remain within the British Commonwealth. In other words, it was hoped that the Constituent Assembly, exercising its sovereign powers under section 8, would set up a Legislature of the Dominion: and, in order to show that a Dominion was—in spite of all appearances to the contrary—a free country, the wily draftsman had defined the powers which a Legislature of the Dominion would possess. This interpretation seems, however, to have been adopted after the petition was filed, and it is probable that none of the lawyer politicians really considered the matter. The Government of the United Kingdom was believed to have transferred 'power', in the case of Pakistan, to Muhammad Ali Jinnah on behalf of the people of Pakistan, who were represented by their Constituent Assembly. Indeed, Pakistan celebrates as 'Pakistan Day' the 14 August, the anniversary of the day on which Lord Mountbatten visited Karachi to 'transfer power' to Pakistan. The legal foundations of this claim to the *haereditas* were never thoroughly examined, at least in public.

One of the consequences of this interpretation was that, while the Governor-General's assent was clearly required for Bills passed by the 'Federal Legislature', because the Government of India Act so provided, it was assumed that the 'Constituent Assembly', being a sovereign body not bound by the Government of India Act, or (as Cornelius, J., put it in the course of argument in the Federal Court) 'above law', could pass Acts which did not need the assent of the Governor-General. In his judgment in the Sind Chief Court, Constantine, C.J., assumed that this interpretation had the authority of the law officers. This was not the case, and accordingly counsel for the Federation of Pakistan found it necessary to explain in the Federal Court that the Law Ministry had advised in 1948 that assent was required, and that it had consistently maintained that position. Why it was overruled has not been recorded, but it seems possible that the fact that the Qaid-i-Azam (a title conferred on Muhammad Ali Jinnah by resolution of the Constituent Assembly) was both Governor-General and President of the Constituent Assembly was a material factor. The same interpretation, however, had been adopted in India, where Lord Mountbatten was the first Governor-General, and where the conception of the 'sovereignty' of the Constituent Assembly was an article of faith, and indeed hope, with the Congress.

Politically speaking, the Indian National Congress intended to bring into operation the Constitution being drafted by the Constituent Assembly, whether it accorded with law or not. Lord Mountbatten had convinced Jawaharlal Nehru of his sincerity, but the tradition of *Albion perfide* was deep-seated. It was, too, part of that tradition that 'British imperialism' was an extremely cleverly administered policy, and that it was necessary to guard against some device or other which would enable the 'imperialists' to recover their position. In Ceylon, where there was no history of conflict, the left-wing groups found their theories completely destroyed, at least superficially, by the transfer of power by agreement. They made the facts conform with their theories by asserting that the 'white capitalists' had simply transferred power to the 'brown capitalists' to exercise on their behalf. In India, where most of the Congress leaders had been in gaol, suspicion of British intentions had been even more profound. The 'sovereignty' of the Constituent Assembly was the safeguard. Pakistan could have taken its own decision, but it would have been politically unwise to claim for the Constituent Assembly of Pakistan a less dominant position than that claimed for the Constituent Assembly of India. Anyhow it did not matter, except to a lawyer, whether or not the Qaid-i-Azam formally assented to a Bill. It would not pass the Constituent Assembly if he disapproved of it. In any case the Qaid-i-Azam disliked assenting to Bills 'in His Majesty's name', as section 6 (3) of the Independence Act provided, and he struck out the phrase when he assented to Bills under the Government of India Act. The Lahore High Court, in a judgment written by the present Chief Justice of Pakistan, held the assent to be valid, since the Governor-General assented in the King's name whether he so declared or not. To avoid the problem the phrase was struck out by an 'Act' which did not receive the assent, the Constitution (Amendment) Act, 1950. This rather petty punctilio indicates the political climate in which the question of assent was decided.

V. THE ROYAL ASSENT

The question of the royal assent to Bills (or laws) passed by the Constituent Assembly exercising powers in accordance with sub-section (1) of section 8 of the Indian Independence Act, 1947, was fundamental to the argument in *Moulvi Tamizuddin Khan* v. *Federation of Pakistan* because the Chief Court of Sind was asked to issue writs of mandamus and quo warranto under section 223 A of the Government of India Act, 1935. That section had been inserted by an 'Act' of the Constituent Assembly, the Government of India (Amendment) Act, 1954, which had not received the assent. It was therefore argued that the Chief Court had no power to issue the writs. Further, the claim for a quo warranto was based on the claim that the Ministers had not been appointed in accordance with section 10 of the Government of India Act, 1935, a section which had been substituted by the Government of India

25

(Fifth Amendment) Act, 1954, another 'Act' which had not received the assent.

The problem was purely a question of the interpretation of section 6 (3) of the Indian Independence Act, 1947, and this involved the meaning of a 'law of the Legislature of the Dominion'. In the Sind Chief Court the main argument for the Federation of Pakistan proceeded on the assumption that, in the first instance, a 'law of the Legislature of the Dominion' was a law passed by the Constituent Assembly under sub-section (1) of section 8, i.e. in the exercise of its constituent powers. It was, however, difficult to maintain this argument for the following reasons:

(i) The language of section 8 (2) is on all fours with that of section 8 (1). Under proviso (e) to the former sub-section, 'the powers of the Federal Legislature . . . shall, in the first instance, be exercisable by the Constituent Assembly in addition to the powers exercisable by that Assembly under sub-section (1) of this section'. The distinction between 'the Constituent Assembly as such' and the 'Federal Legislature', which was sought to be drawn by both sides, was not maintainable. There was one body, the Constituent Assembly, exercising both constituent and legislative powers. The distinction was drawn between legislative and constituent powers because, in the former respect, the Constituent Assembly was bound by the provisions of the Government of India Act, as adapted.

(ii) Proviso (d) of section 8 (2) was as follows: 'as from the appointed day, no Provincial Bill shall be reserved under the Government of India Act, 1935, for the signification of His Majesty's pleasure, and no Provincial Bill shall be disallowed by His Majesty thereunder'. There was no explanation of this limitation to Provincial Bills if Federal Bills under the Government of India Act did not come under section 6 (3) of the Indian Independence Act. It had to be admitted that that sub-section *included* laws made by the Constituent Assembly as 'Federal Legislature'.

(iii) Section 8 (3) provided that any provision of the Act of 1935 which operated to limit the power of 'the legislature of that Dominion' should, unless and until provision was made by law under section 8 (1), 'have the like effect as a law of the Legislature of the Dominion limiting for the future the powers of that Legislature'. Clearly (though Constantine, C.J., in the Sind Court said it made no difference), the 'legislature of the Dominion' was the Indian Legislature or the Federal Legislature under the Government of India Act, both as a matter of ordinary construction and by reference to section 18A of the Interpretation Act, 1889 (to which the attention of the Court had not been drawn): while 'Legislature of the Dominion' meant the Constituent Assembly exercising constituent powers. The cross-reference was to the powers of the Legislature of the Dominion under sub-section (1) and (6) of the Indian Independence Act. Thus, a 'law of the Legislature of the Dominion limiting for the future the powers of that Legislature' could, in the first instance, be translated as a 'law of the Constituent Assembly in the exercise of its constituent power limiting the powers of the Federal Legislature'. The 'Legislature of the Dominion' therefore included *both* the Constituent Assembly exercising constituent powers and the Constituent Assembly exercising the powers of the Federal Legislature.

(iv) Whatever might be the meaning of 'law of the Legislature of that Dominion' in the first part of section 6 (3), it was clear that 'laws of the Legislature of either of the new Dominions' in the second part included laws passed under the Government of India Act, 1935. Among the provisions which seemed to be included in 'so much of any Act' were: (*a*) section 32 of the Government of India Act, 1935; (*b*) sections 735 and 736 of the Merchant Shipping Act, 1894; and (*c*) section 4 of the Colonial Courts of Admiralty Act, 1890. Merchant shipping and Admiralty jurisdiction were within the powers of the Federal Legislature under entry 21 of the Federal List to the Government of India Act, 1935. Hence the second part of section 6 (3) applied to laws passed by the Constituent Assembly in exercise of the powers of the Federal Legislature.

The reason for arguing that 'Legislature of the Dominion' did not include the Constituent Assembly exercising the powers of the Federal Legislature was the fear that the whole sub-section might be interpreted to apply to the Constituent Assembly only in that capacity. Possibly this sought to prove too much, and in the Federal Court the Federation of Pakistan argued only that 'Legislature of the Dominion' meant 'Constituent Assembly' acting in either capacity. The distinction between 'Constituent Assembly as such' and 'Federal Legislature' was denied; and section 6 (3) was said to read:

The Governor-General of each of the new Dominions shall have full power to assent in His Majesty's name to any law of the Constituent Assembly and so much of any Act as relates to the disallowance of laws by His Majesty or the reservation of laws for the signification of His Majesty's pleasure thereon or the suspension of the operation of laws until the signification of His Majesty's pleasure thereon shall not apply to laws of the Constituent Assembly.

Counsel for Moulvi Tamizuddin Khan of course drew attention

to the peculiar language of the first clause: 'The Governor-General . . . shall have full power to assent . . . to any law'. The formulae used in the several Constitutions of the Commonwealth vary somewhat, but in Canada, Australia, New Zealand, South Africa and Ceylon, as well as in the Government of India Act, express power to withhold assent was conferred. Why, then, give only 'full power to assent' in the Indian Independence Act? Indeed, the Government of India Act went further. It provided that a Bill (and the Independence Act used 'law') *shall* be presented to the Governor-General, who *shall* declare whether he assents or withholds assent. Since this was the precedent before the draftsman, it was claimed that the change of language was deliberate, that the Governor-General had power to assent only where the law otherwise required assent, and that he was given 'full power' to assent because, under the law as it stood when the Independence Act was drafted, the power to assent was not full, but was subject to the powers of the King-Emperor. In other words, the whole subsection, like the rest of the section, was designed to remove fetters upon the powers of the Legislature of the Dominion and had no application to the constituent powers of the Constituent Assembly.

Counsel for the Federation of Pakistan was ready with the reply that in Canada, Australia, New Zealand and even in South Africa under section 64 of the South Africa Act, as substituted by the Status of the Union Act, 1934, the power to assent was not conferred but merely assumed. *When* a Bill was presented, the Governor-General was empowered to assent or withhold assent, but there was no statutory requirement that the Bill be presented, because that was a matter of fundamental common law. To this it could be answered that it was not fundamental common law, but that the requirement followed from the fact that the Queen (or, in New Zealand, the Governor-General) was part of the legislature of the Dominion, whereas nobody could allege that in Pakistan the Queen or the Governor-General was part of the Constituent Assembly. This argument was strongly pressed, and it seemed to convince the Sind Chief Court, though the different approaches of Constantine, C.J., and Vellani and Muhammad Bakhsh, JJ., weakened the effect of their unanimous decision. Counsel for the Federation could rely on the express words of the sub-section, which did not say that the Governor-General should have full power to assent to a law to which he had power to assent under some other law, but that he should have full power to assent to *any* law. Clearly, as Muhammad Bakhsh, J., himself admitted[1] full power to assent included power to refuse assent in proper cases. Besides, the position at common law was that, Pakistan being part of the dominions of the Crown acquired by cession or conquest, the Crown had complete power of legislation. How far had it lost that power under the rule in *Campbell* v. *Hall*?[2] There was no need to go into past history, because section 2 of the Government of India Act, 1935, as originally enacted, provided that:

All rights, authority and jurisdiction heretofore belonging to His Majesty the King, Emperor of India, which appertain to or are incident to the government of the territories in India for the time being vested in him, and all rights, authority and jurisdiction exercisable by him in or in relation to any other territories in India, are exercisable by His Majesty, except in so far as may be otherwise provided by or under this Act, or as may be otherwise directed by His Majesty.

This was one of the sections removed by Lord Mountbatten under section 9 of the Indian Independence Act, but all legislative powers in British India were removed simultaneously by reason of the partition and the express words of section 8 (2) (*a*). The Crown's right to legislate for Pakistan was therefore restored, subject to the express provisions of the Independence Act. The Governor-General was given full power to assent to all laws because otherwise the power would have been vested in the King personally. Section 2 of the Government of India Act was therefore correctly removed by Lord Mountbatten because the powers of the King-Emperor had been transferred to the Governor-General by sections 5 and 6 of the Indian Independence Act. Section 6 (3) did not expressly say that all Bills or laws should be submitted to him for his assent because, as in Canada, Australia, New Zealand and South Africa, the Crown's right to be a party to legislation was a matter of common law.

The use of the term 'law' in place of the term 'Bill' could easily be explained. It was, as the rest of the sub-section made plain, a generic term for any enactment of the legislature, whether or not it had received the assent. 'Disallowance of laws' clearly meant the disallowance of laws which had received the Governor-

[1] P.L.D. 1955 Sind 96 at p. 136.   [2] (1774), 20 St. Tr.

General's assent and therefore had full legal force and effect. 'Reservation of laws' meant the reservation of Bills which had not received the Governor-General's assent and which therefore had no legal force and effect. 'Suspension of the operation of laws' meant the suspension of the operation of laws which had received the Governor-General's assent, but which had no legal force and effect because of a suspending clause providing that they should not become laws until His Majesty's pleasure was known. Other cases could be produced of the use of the term 'law' to include a Bill or a law which had no legal force and effect: e.g. the Indian Councils Act, 1861, the Constitution of Southern Rhodesia (1921), and the laws of Jersey and the Isle of Man. It was therefore argued that all Bills had to be submitted to the Governor-General for his assent, and he could either assent or not assent. He could not reserve any Bill for the Queen's assent; nor was there any legal requirement that a suspending clause be inserted; nor could an Act be disallowed by the Queen.

As has already been mentioned, the principal argument for the petitioner was that the sub-section applied only to laws passed by the 'Federal Legislature', because the law required assent only in respect of those laws. The 'Constituent Assembly', i.e. the Constituent Assembly exercising constituent powers, was not a legislature but a constituent assembly, an entity *sui juris* whose sovereignty was recognised by section 8 (1) of the Indian Independence Act and whose actions were subject to no fetters whatsoever, whether external to Pakistan or inside Pakistan. There was no Legislature of the Dominion other than the Federal Legislature, though there might be a Legislature of the Dominion under the Constitution framed by the Constituent Assembly if that Assembly decided that Pakistan should remain a Dominion. Meanwhile the Constituent Assembly had all the powers which would be conferred upon the Legislature of the Dominion if such a Legislature were set up.[1]

---

[1] Had they been given opportunity to reply in the Federal Court, counsel for the Federation would have drawn attention to section 9 (5) of the Independence Act, which provided that no order should be made under that section after 31 March 1948 'or such earlier date as may be determined . . . by any law of the Legislature of that Dominion': and the Legislature of the Dominion was not the Federal Legislature because there was no power for this purpose under the Government of India Act. Hence there was a Legislature of the Dominion in existence between 15 August 1947 and 31 March 1948.

In studying the judgments in the Sind Chief Court it is necessary to remember the traditional distinction between the 'Constituent Assembly' exercising constituent powers and the 'Federal Legislature', which was the Constituent Assembly exercising legislative powers under the Government of India Act. It was only in the Federal Court that counsel for the Federation of Pakistan insisted that the distinction could not be drawn in such language. The 'Constituent Assembly' was the body which exercised both constituent and legislative powers, though it was proper to speak of the 'Federal Legislature' as meaning the Constituent Assembly exercising legislative powers subject to the limitations of the Government of India Act, as adapted.

Constantine, C.J.,[1] said that the purpose of section 6 of the Independence Act was to efface the supremacy of the Parliament of the United Kingdom and to confer power, unfettered by any control from the United Kingdom, upon the Legislature of the Dominion. 'The Legislature of the Dominion has not been defined but the wording in section 8 (1) shows that it is not restricted to the Constituent Assembly, but refers to future legislative bodies, and further that the legislature of the Dominion is not restricted to making provision as to the constitution. The Federal Legislature until other provision is made by the Assembly is also part of the Legislature of the Dominion. This is consistent with section 8 (3) which provides that any provision of the Government of India Act which limits the power of the legislature of the Dominion shall . . . have the like effect as a law of the Legislature of the Dominion limiting for the future the powers of that Legislature. I think that the use of a small or a capital letter in the word "legislature" is irrelevant.[2] Legislature of the Dominion appears thus to be a comprehensive term, embracing every legislature which has power to legislate for the Dominion as a whole whether its power is derived from the Independence Act or from the future legislation of the Constituent Assembly, and whether its power is restricted to or does not extend to the making of constitutional laws.' The purport of section 6 (3), in the view of the

[1] P.L.D. 1955 Sind 96 at pp. 103–4.
[2] The attention of the Court had not been drawn to section 18A of the Interpretation Act. It is, however, difficult to read 'legislature' as referring to anything other than the Federal Legislature or Indian Legislature in section 8 (2) (e) or 'Legislature' as referring to anything other than section 6.

Chief Judge, was 'to provide that the Governor-General's power of assent is not to be controlled by Her Majesty'. Agha, J., had held in *Khuhro* v. *Federation of Pakistan*[1] that the sub-section did not provide that assent was necessary but that if assent was necessary the Governor-General should have full power. The necessity of assent was retained in the Government of India Act in respect of the Federal Legislation (*sic* in the Federal Court brief as well as in P.L.D.): no corresponding provision necessitating consent in respect of the Constituent Assembly was inserted in the Independence Act.

This interpretation was criticised by counsel in the Federal Court not only because it drew a distinction between a legislature whose power was restricted to the making of constitutional laws and a legislature whose powers did not extend to the making of constitutional laws—a distinction which, it was said, was not to be found in the Independence Act—but also because it sought to interpret the Independence Act in the light of the adaptations to the Government of India Act. The Independence Act received the royal assent on 18 July and must be interpreted as at that day, when the Government of India Act had not been adapted or applied, and nobody knew whether or not Lord Mountbatten would leave section 32 in the Act. That section conferred a discretionary power which had to be removed under section 8 (2) (*c*) of the Independence Act. Sub-sections (2) and (3) had clearly to be removed under section 6 (3) of the Independence Act. Lord Mountbatten might have decided that section 6 (3) completely covered section 32, as indeed Moulvi Tamizuddin Khan claimed, and might thus have removed the whole section. In any case Lord Mountbatten's interpretation was not binding on the courts.

Vellani, J.,[2] began by asserting that 'The special task of the Constituent Assembly was to frame a Constitution of the Dominion, and till it had done so, it was to exercise the powers of the Federal Legislature as well. The function of the Federal Legislature was to make laws enumerated in the Federal and Concurrent Lists, and in emergency or by consent of the Provinces in the Provincial Legislative List.[3] It was a subordinate and not a sov-

---

[1] P.L.D. 1950 Sind 49.   [2] P.L.D. 1955 Sind 96 at pp. 108-9.
[3] It was not immediately relevant, though it became very important later: but Vellani, J., had apparently not noticed the amendment to section 102 of the 1935 Act made by the India (Proclamations of Emergency) Act, 1946.

32

ereign legislature, for its powers were limited, and it was subject to the legislation of the Westminster Parliament. The power and duty of framing a Constitution and bringing it into force, which are unmistakable attributes of sovereignty, were placed in the Constituent Assembly, and it was given the ancillary power which only the King and the Westminster Parliament had, of repealing or amending the Government of India Act and even the Indian Independence Act itself. The cession of these sovereign powers finally to the Constituent Assembly is confirmed by the prohibitions of sub-sections (4) and (5) of section 6 of the Indian Independence Act. In addition to these sovereign powers, the limited powers of the Federal Legislature were made exercisable by the Constituent Assembly of the Dominion. These two categories of powers, however, remained distinct, the powers of the Federal Legislature being governed by the Government of India Act, 1935, and the powers of the Constituent Assembly being governed by the Indian Independence Act.'

Even if the traditional distinction between the 'Constituent Assembly' exercising constituent powers and the 'Federal Legislature', were accepted it was difficult to follow this analysis. Politically, no doubt, it was admitted that the special task of the 'Constituent Assembly' was to frame a Constitution, but the Act did not say so. For the purpose of making provision as to the Constitution, the 'Constituent Assembly' had the powers of the Legislature of the Dominion. It might not frame a Constitution at all. Had the Government of India Act been suitably amended, either by Lord Mountbatten under section 9 or by the Constituent Assembly in the exercise of its powers under section 6, the Assembly might have been dissolved and the Government of India Act, as adapted, have become the permanent Constitution of the Dominion of Pakistan. The greatest difficulty, however, was in finding out where the 'sovereignty' of the 'Constituent Assembly' came from. If it was because it was, for the time being, endowed with the powers of the Legislature of the Dominion, the rest of the argument did not seem to follow. What is more, the phrase relating to the 'Federal Legislature', that 'it was a subordinate and not a sovereign legislature . . . *and its powers were subject to the legislation of the Westminster Parliament*' seemed rather odd: it was in fact subject to the powers of the 'Constituent Assembly'.

As counsel for Moulvi Tamizuddin Khan correctly pointed out in the Federal Court, the 'Constituent Assembly' could, under section 6 (6), limit the powers of the 'Federal Legislature'.

Vellani, J., next considered the general position of the Governor-General under sections 5 and 6 and then returned to the problem of assent.[1] In his view section 6 (3) of the Independence Act, which was a single sentence, must be read as a whole. Its intention was not to create the necessity of assent where none had been prescribed, but to remove the existing statutory requirements which derogated from the fullness of the power. The term 'Legislature of the Dominion' was but notional, because there was no Federal Legislature at the partition and the Constituent Assembly was improvised primarily to frame the Constitution. 'The function of legislation was two-fold, to exercise the powers of the Federal Legislature and those for the purpose of making provision as to the Constitution of the Dominion.' In section 8 (1) the words 'the powers of the Legislature of the Dominion' meant the powers of legislation of the Dominion.

This summary on this particular point may be inadequate because the analysis is difficult to follow. It perhaps implies that there was no Legislature of the Dominion because no such Legislature had yet been created, but there was a Constituent Assembly given the sovereign power of producing and enacting a Constitution and the ancillary power of exercising the functions of the Federal Legislature until it had enacted a Constitution. The Assembly therefore had complete powers of legislation for the Dominion. It this was so, however, how could section 6 (3) remove the personal powers of the Crown in respect of laws of the Legislature of the Dominion when that Legislature did not exist? One could not substitute 'legislation for the Dominion' for 'laws of the Legislature of the Dominion', for that would make nonsense of section 6 (1).

Vellani, J., then dealt with the argument based upon the prerogative powers of the Crown at common law. The prerogative powers of legislation for a conquered or ceded colony had been granted to the Constituent Assembly, and 'the Constituent Assembly can exercise it as fully as His Majesty could, that is to say, the exercise of it by the Constituent Assembly is as supreme and

[1] P.L.D. 1955 Sind 96 at pp. 115–19.

as unfettered as could be the exercise of it by His Majesty. When Parliament frames the Constitution it uses His Majesty's Prerogative by His Majesty's consent and the grant and the bringing into force of the Constitution is the act of the King. The true question is whether the exercise of the supreme Prerogative by the Constituent Assembly has been made subject to any limitation by the instrument making the grant. If it has, then to that extent the grant is not full.' The grant had been made by section 8 (1) of the Independence Act, and no limitation on the grant appeared. Outside the Government of India Act the Governor-General had no powers, and there was no express grant of powers, in clear and unmistakable terms, by the Independence Act. The powers of assent and dissolution were provisions relating to the Constitution. 'It follows, therefore, that there now resides in the Constituent Assembly the sovereign power and supreme prerogative to amend and repeal the existing, and frame and bring into force a new, Constitution, which was of the essence of His Majesty's sovereignty, and therefore, the Constituent Assembly being in the place of His Majesty is a sovereign body of no prescribed life or duration and subject to no agency or instrument outside itself to effect its dissolution or to give its laws validity, except such as it may itself choose to create.'

Muhammad Bakhsh, J.,[1] also insisted that section 6 (3) must be read as a whole and not in two parts. It clearly referred to the Government of India Act and laid down that all provisions of that Act relating to the reservation of Bills and disallowance of laws should disappear. Instead, the Governor-General would have full power to assent to Bills. Section 32 of the Government of India Act was adapted accordingly. The expression 'law' referred to the ordinary law which the Federal Legislature had to pass under the 1935 Act and not the law of the Constitution as provided by section 8 (1) of the Independence Act. 'Section 6 (3) read along with section 8 (2) (e) makes it quite clear that the assent of the Governor-General related only to the laws passed by the Constituent Assembly as Federal Legislature under (the) 1935 Act.' The distinction between ordinary law and constitutional law was drawn in *Shankari Prasad Singh Deo* v. *Union of India*.[2] 'The

[1] P.L.D. 1955 Sind 96 at pp. 137-45.
[2] A.I.R. (1951) S.C. 458, a case which drew a distinction between legislation

provisions of (the) Independence Act leave no room for doubt that the Constituent Assembly was a sovereign body and was not subject to any checks and balances, restraints and restrictions.' Having said that it could under section 6 (2) repeal the whole of the Independence Act, the learned judge added, 'it is impossible to think that an Act of the Constituent Assembly repealing or removing the provision regarding assent by [the] Governor-General would require the assent of [the] Governor-General'.[1] The fact that the orders of the Governor-General under section 9 were subject to amendment, variation or repeal by the Constituent Assembly clearly establishes the sovereignty and the overriding power of the Constituent Assembly with regard to the making of the Constitution of the country. The learned judge then pointed out that forty-six Acts (there had been a miscount, it was forty-four) had not received the assent, that the Governor-General had frequently acted under those Acts, that the Privy Council had referred to the Federal Court all appeals transferred to that Court under the Privy Council (Abolition of Jurisdiction) Act, 1950, which had not received assent, and the Federal Court had assumed jurisdiction under that Act, that the Parliament of the United Kingdom had passed the India (Consequential Provisions) Act, 1949, recognising the validity of the Constitution of India though it had not received the Governor-General's assent, and that the requirement of assent had been discussed in five cases in the courts of Pakistan.[2] 'All these facts clearly establish the theory that the Acts of the Constituent Assembly do not need the assent of the Governor-General. The question of the assent of the Governor-General arises under the 1935 Act only. The Constituent Assembly has no place in the 1935 Act. It was a special Chamber created by the Independence Act and possessed the sovereign power of

by the Parliament of India and an amendment of the Constitution of India under Article 368.

[1] This view, that it was impossible to conceive of the Crown assenting to a Bill depriving the Crown of its powers over a territory, was put more strongly by Cornelius, J., in the course of argument in the Federal Court. Counsel for the Federation promptly read out section 1 of the Burma Independence Act, 1947.

[2] *Khuhro* v. *Federation of Pakistan*, P.L.D. 1950 Sind 49, where Agha, J., decided that assent was not necessary; and *Khan Iftikhar Hussain Khan of Mamdot* v. *Province of the Punjab*, P.L.D. 1950 F.C. 15; *Sarfaraz Khan* v. *The Crown*, P.L.D. 1950 Lah. 384; *Akbar Khan* v. *The Crown*, P.L.D. 1954 F.C. 87; and *Lal Khan* v. *The Crown*, P.L.D. 1955 Lah. 215. In these last four cases the assent of the Governor-General was assumed not to be necessary for legislation of the 'Constituent Assembly' but the question was neither argued nor decided.

framing the Constitution by which this country was to be governed in future, and in the exercise of which power it could even repeal the whole of [the] 1935 Act. Therefore the question of the Governor-General's assent to its Acts does not arise at all.'

The characteristic of this judgment was its failure to meet the problems created by section 6 of the Independence Act. Presumably the 'Constituent Assembly' was a sovereign body because it had the powers of the Legislature of the Dominion under section 6 (1) and because it could repeal the Indian Independence Act and the Government of India Act in exercise of the powers of the Legislature of the Dominion in section 6 (2). But 'Legislature of the Dominion' in section 6 (3) meant only the 'Federal Legislature' because the purpose of that sub-section was to remove the Crown's powers under the unadapted section 32 of the Government of India Act—no reference was made to the Merchant Shipping Act or the Colonial Courts of Admiralty Act, though the 'Legislature of the Dominion' would still have been the 'Federal Legislature' because of entry 21 of the Federal List of the Government of India Act. Thus, section 6 (1) applied to the 'Constituent Assembly'; section 6 (2) applied to the 'Constituent Assembly'; and section 6 (3) applied to the 'Federal Legislature'; but in each case the section referred only to the 'Legislature of the Dominion'.

In the Federal Court counsel for Moulvi Tamizuddin Khan was clearly hampered by the desirability of keeping these diverse interpretations open. These interpretations seemed to be:

(i) Constantine, C.J.: The 'Legislature of the Dominion' included both the 'Constituent Assembly' and the 'Federal Legislature', but in section 6 (3) it meant the 'Federal Legislature' only.

(ii) Vellani, J.: The 'Legislature of the Dominion' was a mere notional body and did not exist until the Constituent Assembly made appropriate provision. The 'Constituent Assembly' was a sovereign body empowered by section 8 (1) and there were no limitations on its power.

(iii) Muhammad Bakhsh, J.: The 'Constituent Assembly' was a sovereign body because it had the powers of the 'Legislature of the Dominion' under sub-sections (1) and (2) of section 6, but sub-section (3) of section 6 applied only to the 'Federal Legislature'.

37

VI. EMERGENCY LEGISLATION

The decision of the Federal Court in *Federation of Pakistan* v. *Moulvi Tamizuddin Khan* related only to jurisdiction. Section 223 A of the Government of India Act, 1935, under which the Sind Chief Court had claimed jurisdiction to issue writs of mandamus and quo warranto, had been inserted by the Government of India (Amendment) Act, 1954, which had not received the assent of the Governor-General and therefore was not law. Counsel for the respondent had been stopped when he proposed to argue that the Governor-General had had no power to dissolve the Constituent Assembly, and accordingly only the case for the Federation was put before the court. The Federal Court did not decide that any other 'Act' of the Constituent Assembly was invalid, and indeed Munir, C.J., threw out the suggestion that, since no formality was prescribed in Pakistan for the Governor-General's assent, it might be possible to argue that in some cases in which he had exercised powers alleged to have been conferred by an 'Act' he had in fact assented by implication. Nevertheless, the legal advisers of the Government of Pakistan thought it necessary to assume that all the 'Acts' of the Constituent Assembly which had not received the Governor-General's assent—and there were forty-four of them going back to 1948—must be regarded as invalid.

The consequences which flowed from the decision, if this interpretation was correct, were far-reaching. The more important of them may be summarised as follows:

(i) The Constituent Assembly had been improperly composed since 1950. This conclusion arose from the fact that six members had been added to the Constituent Assembly under the Indian Independence (Amendment) Act, 1949, the Constituent Assembly for Pakistan (Increase and Redistribution of Seats) Act, 1949, and the Constituent Assembly for Pakistan (Increase and Redistribution of Seats) (Amendments) Act, 1949, none of which had received the Governor-General's assent.

(ii) Since the Constituent Assembly exercised the powers of the Federal Legislature in accordance with section 8 (2) of the Independence Act, it was possible that all the legislation passed in exercise of those powers since the Assembly became improperly composed in 1950 was invalid, though it had received the assent of the Governor-General.

(iii) The Provincial Legislatures were all improperly composed because they had been elected under laws enacted by the Constituent Assembly which had not received the Governor-General's assent and because their composition had been changed by similar laws.

The provisions applicable were the Fifth and Sixth Schedules to the Government of India Act, 1935, which had been amended by the Government of India (Third Amendment) Act, 1950, the Government of India (Fifth Amendment) Act, 1950, the Government of India (Sixth Amendment) Act, 1950, the Constitution (Amendment) Act, 1951, the Government of India (Amendment) Act, 1951, the Constitution (Second Amendment) Act, 1951, the Delimitation of Constituencies (Adult Franchise) Act, 1951, the amending Act of the same year, and the Government of India (Third Amendment) Act, 1952. There was also an Act of 1953 extending for one year the life of the East Bengal Legislature. None of these laws had received the Governor-General's assent.

(iv) Since the Provincial Legislatures of Sind, the Punjab (which ought to be called 'West Punjab', since the Act which changed its name had not received assent), and the North-West Frontier Province had enacted legislation since the re-election of the Legislative Assemblies under the above laws, all that legislation was invalid. There had been no legislation by the East Bengal Legislature since the election of 1954, but any legislation passed during its extended life would be invalid.

(v) All Orders issued by the Governor-General under section 9 of the Indian Independence Act, after the date originally fixed by that section, 31 March 1948, were invalid because the Act which purported to extend the period to 31 March 1949 was invalid. The Act was the Indian Independence (Amendment) Act, 1948.

There were twenty-one of these Orders issued before 31 March 1949, and twelve Orders issued after that date under powers conferred by Orders made before that date. The following were some of the more important consequences:

(a) Section 92A of the Government of India Act had been inserted and under it the Provincial Legislatures of Sind, the Punjab and East Bengal had been suspended. The respective Governors had issued 143 Acts, all of which were invalid.

(b) The State Bank of Pakistan had been constituted and empowered to regulate the currency, exercise exchange control, etc.: the exercise of these powers was invalid.

(c) The administration of Karachi as a Chief Commissioner's Province had been illegal since 1948.

(d) The application of the laws of Pakistan to the leased areas of Baluchistan had been invalid, and all persons convicted of offences against those laws had been unlawfully convicted.

(*e*) A great many Indian laws had been amended so as to apply to Pakistan: all the amendments were invalid.

(vi) The transfer of the jurisdiction of the Privy Council to the Federal Court and all decisions of the Court under the jurisdiction so transferred were invalid. The transfer was effected under the Privy Council (Abolition of Jurisdiction) Act, 1950, which had not received the Governor-General's assent.

These were by no means all the consequences to which attention had to be drawn, but the list is sufficiently long to justify the assumption that an emergency had been created requiring unusual constitutional measures. It would not be correct to say that the Constitution had completely broken down. The Governor-General had been validly appointed and had wide powers under the Government of India Act as it stood before the constitutional legislation, enacted by the Constituent Assembly, purported to amend it and also (according to the case for the Federation) under section 5 of the Indian Independence Act, 1947. Though the Sind Chief Court had held that most of the Central Ministers had been invalidly appointed, the decision of the Federal Court invalidated the Government of India (Fifth Amendment) Act, 1954, in accordance with which the Sind Court had ordered the issue of writs of quo warranto. The courts of law, too, were properly constituted, though the jurisdiction of the Federal Court as successor to the Privy Council was invalid. Even so, difficulties arose in practice. For instance, the hearing on the first day of *Federation of Pakistan* v. *Moulvi Tamizuddin Khan* was invalid because Rahman, J., had initially been appointed to the court under an invalid provision (the error was discovered within a few hours, and he was then appointed under a valid provision). The ordinary civil and criminal law was valid, though many amendments to it, actually administered by the courts, were invalid. On the other hand, there was no legislature in Pakistan properly constituted, though it might be possible to argue that the dissolution on 24 October 1954 was invalid and accordingly that the Assembly, without the six members elected under invalid legislation, could be summoned. The Federation had of course already argued in the Federal Court that the dissolution was valid, though no decision had been taken because the Court held that it had no jurisdiction.

Difficulties arose before action could be taken. As soon as the decision in *Tamizuddin Khan's* case was taken, counsel, instructed by Begum Akbar Khan, applied to a judge of the Lahore High Court in his private house for a writ of habeas corpus for the release of her husband, formerly Major-General, who had been sentenced to imprisonment under the Rawalpindi Conspiracy (Special Tribunal) Act, an Act of the Constituent Assembly which had not received the Governor-General's assent. Mr Akbar Khan was released on bail pending the hearing of the petition, was again arrested under a Punjab Act, and again released on bail. It was in this case, it was thought, that the validity of the emergency legislation would be questioned. As will be seen presently, *Usif Patel* v. *The Crown* came to the Federal Court before the Lahore High Court reached a decision in *Akbar Khan's* case.

Meanwhile, the Governor-General had issued a Proclamation of Emergency under section 102 of the Government of India Act, 1935, and an Emergency Powers Ordinance. The validity of the latter was placed upon section 42 of the Act of 1935 and all other powers in that behalf. These sections, omitting amendments which were invalid because they had not received the assent of the Governor-General, were:

102. (1) Notwithstanding anything in the preceding sections of this chapter, the Federal Legislature shall, if the Governor-General has declared by Proclamation (in this Act referred to as a 'Proclamation of Emergency') that a grave emergency exists whereby the security of Pakistan or any part thereof is threatened by war or internal disturbance, have power to make laws for a Province or any part thereof with respect to any of the matters enumerated in the Provincial Legislative List, or to make laws, whether or not for a Province or any part thereof, with respect to any matter not enumerated in any of the Lists in the Seventh Schedule to this Act:

Provided that no Bill or amendment for the purposes aforesaid shall be introduced or moved without the previous sanction of the Governor-General and the Governor-General shall not give his sanction unless it appears to him that the provision proposed to be made is a proper provision in view of the nature of the emergency.

(2) Nothing in this section shall restrict the power of a Provincial Legislature to make any law which under this Act it has power to make, but if any provision of a Provincial law is repugnant to any provision of a Federal law which the Federal Legislature has under this section power to make, the Federal law, whether passed before or after the Provincial law, shall prevail, and the Provincial law shall to the extent

41

of the repugnancy, but so long only as the Federal law continues to have effect, be void.

(3) A Proclamation of Emergency may be revoked by a subsequent Proclamation.

(4) A law made by the Federal Legislature which that Legislature would not but for the issue of a Proclamation of Emergency have been competent to make shall to the extent of the incompetency, cease to have effect on the expiration of a period of six months after the Proclamation has ceased to operate, except as respects things done or omitted to be done before the expiration of the said period.

42. (1) The Governor-General may, in cases of emergency, make and promulgate ordinances for the peace and good government of Pakistan or any part thereof, and any ordinance so made shall have the like force of law as an Act passed by the Federal Legislature, but the power of making ordinances under this section is subject to the like restrictions as the power of the Federal Legislature to make laws, and any ordinance made under this section may be controlled or superseded by any such Act.

(2) Notwithstanding any restrictions imposed by the previous subsection, an ordinance made under this section may authorise expenditure from the revenues of the Federation.

As has been mentioned above, large parts of the criminal law had been amended since 1948 by 'Acts' of the Constituent Assembly which appeared to be invalid, by legislation of the Provincial Legislatures which was presumably invalid because those Legislatures had been improperly constituted, and by the various authorities which had issued orders taking their validity from orders issued under section 9 of the Indian Independence Act after 31 March 1948. Since doubt existed about the validity of these parts of the criminal law, and since many of these provisions dealt with the maintenance of order, it was thought that there was a real danger of civil disturbance, and accordingly that the issue of a Proclamation of Emergency could be justified. In any event, it was believed that it was for the Governor-General to decide whether the threat existed and that the courts had no power to question his decision.

The Governor-General was also satisfied that it was necessary for the purposes of the Proclamation to validate *ab initio* thirty-five of the forty-four Acts which had been passed by the Constituent Assembly but which had not received his assent. It was not thought desirable to ratify the Acts which had amended the composition of the Constituent Assembly itself, in case this raised any argument against the exercise of the power of dissolution. The two Acts which had been in question in the Sind Chief Court—those which inserted section 223A into the Government of India Act and amended section 10 of that Act—also were omitted. In other words, it was not proposed to reverse the decision in *Tamizuddin Khan's* case and so to restore the decision of the Sind Chief Court in that case. An attempt was therefore made by the Emergency Powers Ordinance to validate these thirty-five Acts and at the same time to prevent any question arising as to the validity of legislation passed by the Constituent Assembly in exercise of the powers of the Federal Legislature.

The attempt to validate these Acts *ab initio* necessarily raised the question whether the Governor-General had power under section 42 to amend the Government of India Act and the Indian Independence Act. It was admitted that he had no such power before 15 August 1947, not only because of the common law rule that an authority exercising a delegated power under an Act of Parliament could not, except where the power had been delegated by express words, amend that Act, but also because of the express provisions of section 110 of the Government of India Act itself. That section had, however, been removed by order of the Governor-General under section 9 of the Indian Independence Act. The reason for that removal, it was believed, was that the Federal Legislature had received an enlarged power under section 6 of the Indian Independence Act.

In his argument before the Sind Chief Court in *Tamizuddin Khan's* case, the Advocate-General had asserted that 'Legislature of the Dominion' in section 6 of the Act of 1947 meant the Constituent Assembly exercising constituent powers under sub-section (1) of section 8 of that Act. Other counsel representing the Ministers in that case thought that this argument, while leading to judgment for the Federation if it could be sustained, could not for various reasons be regarded as persuasive. Mr Manzur Qadir had therefore argued that 'Legislature of the Dominion' meant the Constituent Assembly, whether it was exercising constituent powers under sub-section (1) of section 8 or whether it was exercising legislative powers under sub-section (2) of that section. In other words, he contended that the distinction drawn by counsel for Moulvi Tamizuddin Khan between the

Constituent Assembly 'acting as such' and the Federal Legislature was not justified by the section. There was one legislature, the Constituent Assembly, and it was 'in the first instance' the legislature of the Dominion. Counsel for Moulvi Tamizuddin Khan, on the other hand, argued that 'Legislature of the Dominion' meant the Federal Legislature, at least in section 6 (3). The decision of the Sind Chief Court seemed to imply that 'Legislature of the Dominion' in section 6 meant the Constituent Assembly, whether exercising powers under section 8 (1) or whether acting as Federal Legislature under section 8 (2), though the provision relating to assent in section 6 (3) applied only to legislation of the Federal Legislature. On this interpretation, the effect of section 6 (2) was to authorise the Federal Legislature to repeal or amend any Act of the Parliament of the United Kingdom extending to Pakistan as part of its law, including the Government of India Act and the Indian Independence Act. This was, of course, subject to the limitations imposed on the Federal Legislature by the Government of India Act itself, in accordance with section 8 (3) of the Indian Independence Act. There were, however, no such limitations when a Proclamation of Emergency was in operation, because section 102 of the Government of India Act, as amended by the Act of 1946, expressly conferred power on any matter in any of the lists or not in any of the lists. In other words, the Federal Legislature could, during the period of validity of a Proclamation, repeal or amend any provision of the Government of India Act or the Indian Independence Act. It is true that this gave the Constituent Assembly under section 8 (2) the same power as it possessed under section 8 (1) of the Act of 1947, but this seemed to be the cumulative effect of the amendments made by the Act of 1946, the Act of 1947, and the orders issued by the Governor-General under the Act of 1947. If this was so, the Governor-General had the same power under section 42 of the Act of 1935.

The decision of the Sind Chief Court had been reversed by the Federal Court, which specifically held that the Constituent Assembly, when exercising constituent powers in accordance with sub-section (1) of section 8, was acting as 'Legislature of the Dominion' under section 6 (3), and accordingly that constitutional legislation required the assent of the Governor-General. The

Federal Court did not say, however, that the Constituent Assembly was not the 'Legislature of the Dominion' when it was acting as Federal Legislature. On the contrary, section 6 (3) clearly applied to such matters as merchant shipping and Admiralty jurisdiction which could be enacted as federal legislation under the Government of India Act. In the view of the legal advisers of the Government, this applied equally to section 6 (2). For instance, though the Federal Legislature could not before 1947 have repealed the whole of the Merchant Shipping Act, 1894, it could do so afterwards, because that Act was an Act of the Parliament of the United Kingdom extending to Pakistan as part of its law. What is more, legislation on merchant shipping could not be regarded as 'making provision as to the constitution' under section 8 (1). Thus, the Constituent Assembly could repeal or amend the Government of India Act either under section 8 (1) or under section 8 (2), provided that the subject-matter came within the jurisdiction of the Federal Legislature under the Government of India Act; and it did come within that jurisdiction when a Proclamation of Emergency was in operation.

If that argument was not accepted, the Federation was prepared to fall back upon 'other powers in that behalf'. Those other powers were claimed by counsel for the Federation, Mr Diplock, in *Tamizuddin Khan's* case. *Salus populi suprema lex* stated good law during an emergency, and it did not require such an emergency as arose out of actual war or civil conflict. This argument was of course used to justify the dissolution of the Constituent Assembly if the Court held that power for that purpose could not be found in section 5 of the Indian Independence Act as a normal prerogative power. It was an exceptional power vested in the Crown for use in exceptional circumstances and had been delegated to the Governor-General by section 5. The decision of the Federal Court in *Tamizuddin Khan's* case had strengthened this argument. Conditions existed in which it was necessary for the Governor-General to issue a Proclamation of Emergency on account of a threat of civil disturbance. In such circumstances the prerogative powers recognised by counsel for Hampden and the minority against the Crown in the *Case of Shipmoney*[1] clearly existed. It had been held both in England and in Ireland that it was not

[1] (1637), 3 St. Tr. 825.

45

necessary to have a state of war in the place in which the act was committed. It was enough if there was such a threat to peace and order as to justify the exercise of exceptional powers. According to the Federation of Pakistan, a large part of what had been assumed to be criminal law had been declared invalid by the Federal Court, and there was no legislature in existence capable of dealing with the situation. If the Governor-General had no statutory power under section 42 of the Government of India Act or otherwise, there must be a prerogative power vested in the Crown to deal with the threat to public order, and this power had been vested in the Governor-General by section 5 of the Indian Independence Act.

It was anticipated that these arguments would be required for use in *Akbar Khan's* case. A memorandum was therefore drawn up for the use of counsel and was sent to Lahore by train. While it was still in the train, however, *Usif Patel* v. *The Crown* came before the Federal Court. In this case the Federation of Pakistan was not a party, because the respondent, the Crown, was the Government of Sind. It had come before the Federal Court on appeal from the Chief Court of Sind while the Federal Court was sitting in Karachi and the Chief Court was hearing argument for Moulvi Tamizuddin Khan. Counsel for the appellants had then raised the additional point, which had not been discussed in the court below, that the Act under which the appellants had been declared to be 'goondas' was invalid. It had been enacted by the Governor of Sind while section 92A of the Government of India Act had been in operation. In view of the pleadings in *Tamizuddin Khan's* case, it was argued for the appellants that the Indian Independence (Amendment) Act, 1948, under which section 92A had been inserted in the Government of India Act, was invalid because it had not received the Governor-General's assent. Exercising its powers under Rules of Court, the Federal Court summoned the Advocate-General of Pakistan, who admitted that, according to his view of the law, an Act of the Constituent Assembly which had not received the Governor-General's assent was invalid. The Court decided, however, that it could not deal with the matter in this manner. The question of the necessity for assent was being argued at length in the Chief Court, and would no doubt come to the Federal Court on appeal. There was nobody in the Federal Court prepared to argue the point, since the Advocate-General of Pakistan agreed with the appellants. It would be wrong to take a decision which would be binding on the Chief Court and so bring the argument in the Chief Court to an end. *Usif Patel's* case was therefore postponed to the Lahore session of the Federal Court, when it could be decided in the light of the decision in *Tamizuddin Khan's* case.

When the case was brought up on 12 April 1955, no notice was given to the Government of Pakistan, for the sufficient reason that it was not a party to the case. The Advocate-General, who was appearing in *Akbar Khan's* case, was summoned and was asked two questions, whether the Emergency Powers Act was constitutional legislation, and what powers other than those in section 42 of the Government of India Act were claimed by the Governor-General. The Advocate-General had received no instructions from his Government; since he had been in Lahore arguing in *Akbar Khan's* case he had not been made aware of the basis on which the Governor-General founded the validity of the Emergency Powers Ordinance; and the memorandum which would have given him the necessary information was in the train on the way to Lahore. In consequence, the case which the Federation of Pakistan had intended to make in court was never mentioned. The effect of section 6 of the Indian Independence Act upon the powers in sections 42 and 102 of the Government of India Act was not discussed, and there was no argument on the principle of necessity or the doctrine of *salus populi suprema lex*.

The court forthwith gave judgment against the Crown. The judgment assumed that the judgments in *Federation of Pakistan* v. *Moulvi Tamizuddin Khan* were available when the Emergency Powers Ordinance was approved. The Ordinance was, however, issued on 27 March. The judgments are dated 'April' and were apparently issued on 3 April, though printed copies were not available in Karachi until the following week. It is, however, unlikely that the action taken would have been different if it had been possible to delay the issue of the ordinance until the judgments were available. As mentioned above, it was proposed to defend the Ordinance on two grounds, neither of which was inconsistent with the judgments in *Tamizuddin Khan's* case, namely, the enlargement of the powers in section 102 of the Government

47

of India Act by section 6 of the Indian Independence Act, and the principle, ultimately accepted by the Federal Court in *Special Reference No. 1 of 1955* and in *Federation of Pakistan* v. *Ali Ahmad Hussain Shah*, that in an emergency of this character the Governor-General had special powers under the common law which were not to be found in the Acts of 1935 and 1947. The differences between the Ordinance declared invalid in *Usif Patel's* case and the instruments declared valid in the later cases were two. First, in the Ordinance the validation of the invalid Acts was not stated to be a temporary measure pending validation by a Constituent Assembly; and, secondly, there was no provision in the Ordinance for the summoning of a Constituent Assembly. In his judgment in *Usif Patel's* case, the Chief Justice drew pointed attention to this latter omission and quoted at length from the shorthand note of the argument for the Federation, in which Diplock, Q.C., in accordance with his instructions, stated that it had always been and still was the intention of the Government to summon a Constituent Assembly whose members would be elected by the Legislative Assemblies of the Provinces. The Chief Justice's statement that 'other counsels have since prevailed' would perhaps have been modified if the Government had been aware that the validity of the Ordinance was being challenged on 12 April and the Advocate-General had been instructed accordingly. At that time the whole question of the summoning of a Constituent Assembly had been postponed because of certain difficulties, legal and political. One difficulty was that, according to the interpretation given to *Tamizuddin Khan's* case by the Government's legal advisers, the Legislative Assemblies of the Provinces were unlawful bodies; they had not been elected and were not composed according to the provisions of the Fifth and Sixth Schedules of the Government of India Act because those provisions had been amended, and indeed radically amended, by Acts of the Constituent Assembly which had not received the Governor-General's assent. It was therefore at least doubtful whether the Governors had, or could be given, power to summon those Assemblies. Another difficulty was that section 92A of the Government of India Act had been put into operation in East Bengal. That section was invalid because it had been inserted under an Act which had not received the Governor-General's assent, but it was not at all clear

48

what sort of Government could supersede it. The election of the East Bengal Legislative Assembly in 1954 was invalid; and in any case efforts made by the Prime Minister to secure party agreement to the formation of a Government in the Province had not proved successful. The first step, in any event, was to validate the invalid laws, and this the Emergency Powers Ordinance had tried to do. It might then be possible to form a Government in East Bengal and summon the Provincial Legislature—or it might not. The whole question was therefore left for further discussion, and very general language was used in the Ordinance.

Examination of the judgment in *Usif Patel* v. *The Crown* did not alter the view of the Government's legal advisers that the validity of section 2 of the Emergency Powers Act could be defended. The Chief Justice drew attention in that case to his 'mathematical formula' in *Tamizuddin Khan's* case; but the Federation fully accepted that formula. Undoubtedly the Federal Legislature was subject to the 'fetters' of the Government of India Act and could not pass legislation on any matter unless power for that purpose could be found in the Act. It was, however, believed that the power was in section 102, during the operation of a Proclamation of Emergency, because of section 6 (2) of the Indian Independence Act. It might be argued that the insertion of 'making provision as to the constitution' in section 8 (1) of that Act prevented the Constituent Assembly from 'making provision as to the constitution' under section 8 (2): but section 8 (2), proviso, merely added powers to that in section 8 (1), while section 8 (3) made it plain that the 'fetters' were to be deemed to have been imposed by the Constituent Assembly itself, exercising the powers of the Legislature of the Dominion under section 8 (1). If the Assembly had not thought fit to impose a particular fetter while a Proclamation of Emergency was in force, so that it could amend the Government of India Act or the Indian Independence Act either under section 8 (1) or under section 8 (2), it could not be said that there was any inconsistency.

It was, however, difficult for the Federation to ask the Federal Court to reverse the decision in *Usif Patel's* case merely because a particular line of argument had not been put to the Court. It was therefore decided to proceed on the assumption that the

Government had been wrongly advised and to try to find some other means of solving the problem. It is of some interest to consider what steps, other than those eventually adopted, might have been taken. *First*, an application might have been made for special leave to appeal to the Privy Council. The Privy Council (Abolition of Jurisdiction) Act, 1950, which purported to transfer the jurisdiction of the Privy Council to the Federal Court, had not received the Governor-General's assent and was therefore invalid. It was of course by no means certain that leave would have been granted, for there was an evident intention that the Privy Council should not interfere with the decisions of the Federal Court, and possibly the Judicial Committee would have given effect to that intention even though it was expressed in an invalid law. In any case, the step was politically impracticable: already there were murmurs that the Government was betraying its trust by bringing the Queen back into the Constitution through claiming prerogative powers. *Secondly*, the problem arose because of a persistent misinterpretation by the Constituent Assembly of an Act of Parliament of the United Kingdom. Why not ask that Parliament to amend its own Act? The legal answer was that under section 6 (4) of the Indian Independence Act an Act of the Parliament of the United Kingdom could be extended to Pakistan as part of its law only if it was extended thereto by a 'law of the Legislature of the Dominion'. Here were two nice points. Was section 6 (4) (or, for that matter, section 4 of the Statute of Westminster) binding on the Parliament of the United Kingdom? During the operation of a Proclamation of Emergency was an ordinance made by the Governor-General under section 42 of the Government of India Act a 'law of the Legislature of the Dominion', particularly when there was no other Legislature of the Dominion in existence? Unfortunately these interesting questions could not be answered, for an appeal to Westminster was politically impracticable.

Thirdly, it was possible to leave the whole matter to the courts by taking no action at all. There would then have been a mass of litigation in every court in Pakistan, leading eventually to the Federal Court, where no doubt some indication would have been given to the lower courts as to how the unprecedented situation should be dealt with. This too was not a practicable solution, for no responsible Government could abdicate its responsibility for the maintenance of law and order.

Fourthly, it was possible for the Governor-General to suspend the Constitution by assuming to himself all the necessary powers, lawful or unlawful. This was much the easiest method, and it would have solved the political difficulties of getting a new Constitution into operation. There were, too, many historical precedents. In the course of the argument in *Tamizuddin Khan's* case the Chief Justice had referred counsel to the suspension of the French Constitution by Louis Napoleon in 1848. Even in England there were precedents between 1642 and 1660 and in 1688, though not all of them went so far. It is quite possible that public opinion would have supported any such action. Even so, the British tradition for the Rule of Law has been firmly established in Pakistan. In the long run, clearly, it was to Pakistan's advantage to follow the strait and narrow path of legal rectitude, rather than the broad and attractive highway that might, in the end, reach a dictatorship.

Finally, the old Constituent Assembly might have been summoned, told that it had been acting unlawfully for seven years and that it was illegally composed, but that the Government desired its concurrence in such measures as might be considered necessary to restore constitutional government. This was, theoretically, the best method, even though the Assembly could not, as an unlawful body, validate its own unlawful actions. There were, too, precedents in the 'Convention Parliaments' of 1660 and 1688: nobody now challenges the validity of the Bill of Rights and the Act of Settlement, though the non-jurors clearly had the law on their side. In view of the antagonisms which had developed among the political groups, however, this solution was politically impracticable.

To avoid misapprehension it must be emphasised that none of these remedies was either suggested to or, so far as is known, considered by the Government, though by way of precaution a draft of an instrument suspending the Constitution was prepared in case it was called for suddenly. In spite of *Usif Patel's* case, it was believed that a remedy could be found by lawful action in Pakistan, and such a remedy was indeed found, as the Federal Court made plain in the *Special Reference*. The first step was taken on 15 April 1955, when a Proclamation and an Order were issued for the summoning of a Constituent Convention. It was believed that this procedure could be justified under the prerogative, and accordingly the procedure adopted for the summoning of a Parliament of the United Kingdom was followed as closely as possible. The title 'Constituent Convention' was adopted for two reasons. First, it was believed to be desirable to draw a sharp distinction between the dissolved Assembly and the new Convention, so that the attitude of public opinion to the latter might be different. Secondly, the Order conferred powers under section 8 (1) of the Indian Independence Act only. It was not intended to delay the process of constitution-making by conferring the powers of the Federal Legislature, since the Governor-General had those powers under section 42 of the Government of India Act. Nor was it claimed, as a matter of law, that the Convention so established would be the Constituent Assembly to which the Indian Independence Act referred. That Assembly was to exercise the powers of the Legislature of the Dominion 'in the first instance'. In the second instance the Convention was to exercise those powers in so far as they were necessary for constitution-making, and it was to complete its task in six months so that there could be an appeal to the people, for the first time in the history of Pakistan, before the end of 1956.

On 16 April, ordinances were issued under section 42 to validate all the laws which could be validated under that section, as interpreted in *Usif Patel's* case. They included all the Acts issued by the Governors of Provinces while the Provincial Constitutions were suspended under section 92A of the Government of India Act, all the legislation enacted by the Provincial Legislatures, and all the laws enacted by the Federal Legislature. Further, the thirty-five Acts scheduled to the Emergency Powers Ordinance received the Governor-General's assent. This was something of a political demonstration, for the Acts which had altered the composition of the Constituent Assembly were not assented to, and in any case such assent would not have validated the composition of the Assembly retrospectively and all the laws passed since 1949, having been passed by an unlawful Assembly, could not become law even with the Governor-General's assent. Even if it were impossible to validate the laws retrospectively, however, it was desirable to give the impression that they were in force, in order to prevent (so far as might be possible) the commission of acts which would have been unlawful if the laws had been valid. In fact, however, another attempt was made to validate the laws, this time by Proclamation whose operative part was as follows:

(1) The Governor-General assumes to himself until other provision is made by the Constituent Convention such powers as are necessary to validate and enforce laws needed to avoid a possible breakdown in the constitutional and administrative machinery of the country and to preserve the State and maintain the government of the country in its existing condition.

(2) For the purposes aforesaid it is hereby declared that the laws mentioned in the Schedule to the Emergency Powers Ordinance, 1955, shall, subject to any report from the Federal Court of Pakistan, be regarded as having been valid and enforceable from the dates specified in that Schedule.

It was hoped that this Proclamation was valid under the common law, and the unusual form was adopted in order to make it easy for the Federal Court to hold it valid. Further, it was decided to make a reference to the Federal Court for an advisory opinion under section 213 of the Government of India Act. This reference asked two questions: a specific question about the Governor-General's power to validate the invalid laws temporarily, on the assumption that he could not validate them permanently without a legislature; and, in case the Court's opinion was in the negative, a general question designed to draw advice from the Court as to the action to be taken in the circumstances. At the same time an application was made to the Court for an interim order to lower courts so as to stop all litigation arising out of the invalid laws, pending the hearing of argument on the special reference.

When the application for the interim order came before the Federal Court, it was pointed out by the Court that two further questions should be submitted. The foundation of the reference was that the late Constituent Assembly had been lawfully dissolved, though the Court had expressly refused to decide this question in *Moulvi Tamizuddin Khan's* case. Accordingly, it was necessary to get that point decided. Secondly, the Constituent Convention which the Governor-General had decided to summon was to be empowered to exercise the powers conferred on the late Constituent Assembly by section 8 (1) of the Indian Independence

Act. The ratification of the invalid laws by that Convention would depend upon the question whether the Convention had the necessary powers under the sub-section, and accordingly it was necessary to ask the Court whether the Convention would indeed have those powers. After further examination of the case by counsel for the Federation it was thought to be safer to empower the Convention to exercise all the powers of the late Constituent Assembly, including the powers of the Federal Legislature conferred upon it by section 8 (2). The fourth question was then modified so as to ask the Court to pronounce whether the Constituent Convention could be given the powers of the late Constituent Assembly under section 8 as a whole. These changes represent a difference in approach to the problem. The line of action based upon sections 42 and 102 of the Government of India Act, as amended by the India (Proclamations of Emergency) Act, 1946, and (it was believed) section 6 of the Indian Independence Act, was stopped by the decisions in *Usif Patel's* case. The immediate reaction to that decision was to assume that illegal but constitutional action, not unlike that adopted in England in 1688, was necessary. Further discussion, however, led to the belief that such action could be legally justified on the ground of necessity; and the initial questions for opinion were framed on this assumption. The third and fourth questions show complete acceptance of this line of argument. The first question then became necessary only as a reserve, in case the Court was unable to agree that the Governor-General had the legal powers necessary to validate the invalid Acts in the interval before the meeting of the Constituent Convention.

The argument on the question of dissolution is discussed in the next section of this Introduction. Here it is necessary only to say a few words about the development of the argument *ex necessitate*. It was, in a sense, a by-product of the argument about dissolution, though its importance increased after the decision of the Federal Court in *Moulvi Tamizuddin Khan's* case.

As will be mentioned presently, the argument for dissolution rested partly upon section 19 of the Indian Independence Act, and partly upon section 5 of that Act. Section 19 was primarily (but not exclusively) a definition clause; and the express words of the definition of 'Constituent Assembly' did not encourage an interpretation that the original Constituent Assembly could be followed by a second, *authorised by that section.* The argument on section 5 was much stronger. It was of course necessary to argue that that section conferred not only a power of dissolution but also a power to constitute and summon another after dissolution. No Court was likely to agree that the section contained a power to destroy but not a power to replace, and in any case what the Governor-General wanted to do was not to destroy the Constitution but to carry it out as—so the Crown alleged—the Constituent Assembly had failed to do. This was not a difficult argument. In England Parliaments had originally been established and constituted under the authority of the Crown, and it could not be argued that the limitation of that authority by privilege and statute applied to Pakistan. What is more, the Crown had always claimed and exercised a prerogative to determine the form of government of a conquered or ceded territory; and if the slate had been clean there could have been no doubt whatever of its power to do so in Pakistan. The question to be decided, therefore, was whether the enactment of the Government of India Acts and the Indian Independence Act had totally deprived the Crown of that power, or whether the prerogative power had revived, within the limits of the Indian Independence Act and the Government of India Act, as adapted under section 9 of the Indian Independence Act, through the repeal of the provisions relating to the constitution and election of the Federal Legislature. It has to be noted, too, that what was claimed was not a power to summon a new Constituent Assembly, but a power to summon a new Legislature of the Dominion. There had to be a legislature of the Dominion, and the Constituent Assembly was the legislature of the Dominion in the first instance: did this not imply that, failing a statutory legislature, the Crown had power to establish one at common law?

The judgment of the Sind Chief Court in *Moulvi Tamizuddin Khan's* case did not seem substantially to weaken the case for the Federation on this point. On the other hand, it did not seem to be received by the Federal Court with very much favour. This was not conclusive, for it is the function of an appellate tribunal to bring out the weaknesses of any argument put before it. Had

55

counsel for Moulvi Tamizuddin Khan been called upon to argue against the validity of the dissolution the approach of the Federal Court would no doubt have been equally critical. The Court did, however, request counsel for the Federation to pursue an alternative argument based upon the necessities of the case. Assuming the allegation to be true that the Constituent Assembly, instead of proceeding with its proper function of providing Pakistan with a Constitution, had usurped a jurisdiction which it did not possess and had claimed a right to be a perpetual legislature, could not the Crown (i.e. the Governor-General under section 5) claim a right to dissolve the Constituent Assembly and establish a new one because of the circumstances of the case?

It may be noted that in 1642, when Charles I had, according to Parliament, broken the fundamental principles of the Constitution, the two Houses claimed a power of legislation without the king's assent. It is true that in 1660 the legislation was declared illegal: but there is no doubt that, had the Commonwealth been established permanently, it could not have been declared illegal merely because the legislation on which it was founded had not received the royal assent. In 1660, too, Charles II had been advised to summon as a Parliament the members who had sat in the Parliaments of James I and Charles I, though there was no common law or statute law under which this could be done. The precedent of 1688 was even stronger, for William of Orange, or William and Mary, had no lawful authority to summon a Parliament—and yet a Parliament was summoned because there was no other way of re-establishing the Constitution. These precedents seemed to lead to the conclusion that acts which would otherwise be illegal could become legal because of the special circumstances of the case. There were no recent examples from the colonies, because any difficulties were invariably overcome by an appeal to the sovereignty of the Parliament of the United Kingdom: but no such appeal could be made in Pakistan because of the provisions of section 6 (4) of the Indian Independence Act requiring that any legislation of the Parliament of the United Kingdom should not apply to Pakistan as part of its law unless extended thereto by an Act of the Legislature of the Dominion. It was believed that there were precedents from the North

American colonies, but the necessary material was not available in the libraries of Pakistan.

VII. DISSOLUTION

The decision of the Federal Court in *Federation of Pakistan* v. *Moulvi Tamizuddin Khan* related only to jurisdiction. Section 223 A of the Government of India Act, 1935, under which the Sind Chief Court had claimed jurisdiction to issue writs of mandamus and quo warranto, had been inserted by the Government of India (Amendment) Act, 1954, which had not received the assent of the Governor-General and therefore was not law. Counsel for the respondent had been stopped when he proposed to argue that the Governor-General had had no power to dissolve the Constituent Assembly, and accordingly only the case for the Federation was put before the Court. The Federal Court did not decide that any other 'Act' of the Constituent Assembly was invalid, and indeed Munir, C.J., threw out the suggestion that, since no formality was prescribed in Pakistan for the Governor-General's assent, it might be possible to argue that in some cases in which he had acted upon an 'Act' to which he had not expressly assented, he had in fact assented by implication. Nevertheless, the advisers of the Government of Pakistan assumed that all 'Acts' of the Constituent Assembly which had not received the Governor-General's assent—and there were forty-four of them—were invalid. Among other consequences,

(i) The members added to the Constituent Assembly (which also exercised the powers of the Federal Legislature) in 1950 under the Indian Independence (Amendment) Act, 1949, the Constituent Assembly for Pakistan (Increase and Redistribution of Seats) Act, 1949, and the Constituent Assembly for Pakistan (Increase and Redistribution of Seats) (Amendments) Act, 1949, had had no right to sit.

(ii) The amendments made to the Fifth and Sixth Schedules to the Government of India Act, 1935, by the Government of India (Third Amendment) Act, 1950, the Government of India (Fifth Amendment) Act, 1950, the Government of India (Sixth Amendment) Act, 1950, the Constitution (Amendment) Act, 1951, the Government of India (Amendment) Act, 1951, the Constitution (Second Amendment) Act, 1951, and the Government of India (Third Amendment) Act, 1952, were invalid; and so were the Delimitation of Constituencies (Adult Franchise) Act, 1951, and the amending Act of the same year. Since the Legislative Assemblies of the Provinces were elected under these provisions, they were and had been for some time unconstitutional bodies. The members elected by them to fill casual vacancies in the Constituent Assembly had no right to sit.

(iii) Some of the Rules of Procedure under which the Constituent Assembly had been operating since 1948 were inconsistent with the Indian Independence Act and were therefore invalid. These included Rules for the filling of casual vacancies which ought, if section 19 (3), proviso, of the Indian Independence Act was correctly interpreted, to have been provided for by legislation.

From these assumptions the conclusion was drawn that the Constituent Assembly had been an unconstitutional body since 1950, and accordingly that the legislation which it had purported to enact in exercise of the powers of the Federal Legislature under the Government of India Act was also invalid; that all the Provincial Assemblies were unconstitutional bodies and accordingly that all the legislation passed by them since re-election was invalid. In other words, the conclusion was that on the legislative side the Constitution had broken down.

If these conclusions were correct it could hardly be doubted that the Governor-General had not only the right but even the duty to order the unconstitutional Constituent Assembly to cease functioning. All parts of Pakistan within the Provincial limits had been part of British India, which had been acquired by cession or conquest. Though there are no quotable precedents, it cannot seriously be argued that, where the legislative machinery in conquered or ceded territory has completely broken down, the Queen has no power to reconstitute such machinery, even where the original machinery was established by Act of Parliament. There are no precedents because in such a case recourse would normally be had to the Parliament of the United Kingdom. Such recourse was not possible in Pakistan, not only because politically it would be undesirable for Parliament to be involved in the matter, but also because the authority of Parliament had been expressly excluded by section 6 (4) of the Indian Independence Act, 1947.

The question of dissolution had, however, been argued independently of the question of assent, in case the courts did not accept the case presented on the latter point. To prove that the

58

Governor-General had had a power of dissolution required proof of power to reconstitute either the Constituent Assembly or the Legislature of the Dominion, for it was not likely that the courts would admit a power to destroy unless there was also a power to re-create. In the Sind Chief Court and in the initial argument in the Federal Court it had been thought of as a problem of re-constituting the Constituent Assembly. In consequence of an acute cross-examination by the Federal Court, however, it became clear that the problem was not to re-constitute the Constituent Assembly but to establish another Legislature of the Dominion to exercise the powers under section 6 of the Indian Independence Act, which included constituent powers.

It cannot be doubted that in the United Kingdom the right to summon, prorogue and dissolve Parliament rests upon the pre-rogative. Counsel for Moulvi Tamizuddin Khan did indeed make an attempt, which persuaded Muhammad Bakhsh, J., to show that the prerogative power to dissolve Parliament had become statutory by reason of the Triennial Act (the Meeting of Parliament Act, 1694). It is, however, plain that the Triennial Act, 1694, the Septennial Act, 1715, and the Parliament Act, 1911, did not supersede the prerogative, but merely recognized and limited it. Unless sooner dissolved under the prerogative, a Parliament stands dissolved at the end of five years ; and unless it is sooner summoned under the prerogative, there is a statutory requirement that a new Parliament be summoned after three years. So far as could be ascertained, no Parliament had ever been summoned or dissolved under the statutory provisions, no doubt because for political convenience it was always desired to fix the dates under the pre-rogative.

It was contended for the Federation of Pakistan that not only were these powers matters of prerogative, but also that all matters relating to the composition of Parliament were, in their origin, matters of prerogative; and an analysis was made showing the dates on which Parliament began to cover such matters by legislation. The county franchise, for instance, was first regulated in 1430 and the borough franchise in 1832; though long before 1832 the House of Commons had claimed to control all matters relating to its own composition, it could hardly be contended that there was such a privilege in Pakistan, in the absence of legislation on the subject. The composition of the House of Lords was still, in principle, a matter of prerogative, since the Queen could create peers by letters patent; and though that House also had claimed the right to decide who should receive writs of summons, no such privilege could be claimed in Pakistan.

This prerogative, it was alleged, had become the prerogative of the Crown in all conquered and ceded territories, and that prerogative was regularly exercised by letters patent or Order in Council—the nearest example to Pakistan was Ceylon, where the Parliament was wholly regulated by Order in Council issued under the prerogative power. It was admitted that, in accordance with the principle in *Campbell* v. *Hall*,[1] the prerogative lapsed when a legislature had been established. The principle was, however, that the Queen could not derogate from her grant, and accordingly she could not establish another legislature unless she had reserved that power to herself. Suppose, however, that for some reason or other the legislature established by prerogative instrument failed to function: it was no derogation from the grant to replace it with a legislature which would function. The grant was, so to speak, a conditional grant, and the condition had not been fulfilled. The legislature established in Pakistan by the Indian Independence Act was a statutory creation, but it could hardly have been the intention of Parliament that the Constituent Assembly, which was to exercise the powers of the Legislature of the Dominion 'in the first instance', should continue in power permanently without making adequate provision as to the Constitution—and, of course, the Federation had already argued that it had made no provision at all, but had converted itself into an unconstitutional body by claiming a 'sovereignty' which did not exist. It was therefore urged that the grant by the King in Parliament had failed, that so long as that grant was outstanding the prerogative had been merged in the statute, and that on the failure of the grant—which would have to be decided by the Queen's representative—the prerogative was restored.

The King in Parliament had granted representative institutions to British India by the Government of India Act, 1935. It was unnecessary to go back beyond that Act because section 2 of that Act had specifically provided that 'all rights, authority and juris-

1 (1774), 20 St. Tr. 239.

diction heretofore belonging to His Majesty the King, Emperor of India, which appertain or are incidental to the government of the territories in India for the time being invested in him . . . are exercisable by His Majesty, except in so far as may be otherwise provided by or under this Act, or as may be otherwise directed by His Majesty'. That Act had ceased to operate on the partition of British India, and provision had been made in section 6 of the Indian Independence Act for a new Legislature for the Dominion of Pakistan, whose powers were to be exercised in the first instance by the Constituent Assembly. Subject to any laws made by the Constituent Assembly in the exercise of its constituent power, to the express provisions of the Independence Act, and to the omissions, additions, adaptations and modifications made in the Government of India Act under section 9 of the Independence Act, Pakistan was to be governed as nearly as may be in accordance with the Government of India Act, the powers of the Federal Legislature or Indian Legislature being exercisable in the first instance by the Constituent Assembly. Thus Pakistan had a Constitution consisting of the Indian Independence Act, which incorporated the Government of India Act, as adapted. Under it, as interpreted by the Federation of Pakistan, there was what came to be called, in the course of argument, a 'notional' Legislature of the Dominion, whose functions were exercisable in the first instance by the Constituent Assembly. If the Assembly failed to function or ceased to exist, there was no legislature, except of course the legislatures in the Provinces which had only the limited powers conferred on them by the Government of India Act, as adapted.

In section 19 of the Government of India Act, as originally enacted, the Governor-General had been empowered to summon the Chambers or either Chamber of the Federal Legislature, to prorogue the Chambers, and to dissolve the Federal Assembly. By reason of the adaptations made by Lord Mountbatten he had been empowered to summon or prorogue the Federal Legislature, but no reference was made to dissolution. The Independence Act itself contained no express provision relating to the summons, prorogation or dissolution either of the Legislature of the Dominion or of the Constituent Assembly. The case for Moulvi Tamizuddin Khan was that the Constituent Assembly would remain in being until it had enacted a Constitution and would then dissolve itself. But supposing that the Muslim League had boycotted the Constituent Assembly of Pakistan as they had boycotted the Union Constituent Assembly of India, or supposing that the members of the Constituent Assembly had passed a resolution dissolving themselves, without making provision for another Legislature of the Dominion?

It was argued for the Federation that section 19 of the Government of India Act had nothing to do with the problem. The Independence Act must be interpreted as it stood on 18 July 1947, when there was no Government of India Act in operation. In adapting section 19, Lord Mountbatten had presumably interpreted the Independence Act, but the interpretation might be right or wrong, and anyhow it could not bind the courts, who had to give the Independence Act the meaning which it bore on 18 July 1947. Presumably Lord Mountbatten had applied the power to summon and prorogue to the Federal Legislature because he thought it to be distinct from the Constituent Assembly in contemplation of law and he considered that it should be separately summoned and prorogued so as to sit in regular sessions for legislative business separately from the sittings of the Constituent Assembly for constituent business. Presumably he removed the power of dissolution because the Federal Legislature was in fact the Constituent Assembly, and one could not dissolve the one without dissolving the other, which clearly could not be done under the Government of India Act. He had had to remove the provisions relating to the election of the Federal Assembly, because there was no such Assembly, and therefore the Federal Assembly could be neither dissolved nor re-elected. This explanation was given, so to speak, to satisfy the curiosity of the Court: it was, according to the Federation, irrelevant to the question where the power of dissolution lay under the Indian Independence Act. There had to be some power of dissolution, because the Constituent Assembly was not intended to last for ever, and there was nothing in the Act to vest that power in the Assembly itself. Indeed, the Constituent Assembly had no powers except as 'Legislature of the Dominion' or (if there was a difference) 'Federal Legislature'; and, given the practice followed in the Commonwealth, it was impossible to assume that such a power had been vested in a legislature by implication. The power had to be vested in the Governor-General, and that power was to be found either in section 5 or in section 19 (3) (*b*) of the Independence Act, or in both provisions taken together.

Section 19 of the Indian Independence Act is mainly an interpretation clause, and it is well accepted that an interpretation clause cannot be so construed as to confer substantive powers. As the marginal note makes plain, however, the section is not merely an interpretation clause, because there are substantive powers in the proviso to sub-section (3) and in sub-section (5). It was therefore not impossible to read a substantive power into paragraph (*b*) of sub-section (3), though naturally such an attempt would be regarded with suspicion as an attempt to strain the statute.

Section 19 (3) (*a*) applied only to India after partition. Section 19 (3) (*b*) provided that 'References in this Act to the Constituent Assembly of a Dominion shall be construed as references . . . in relation to Pakistan, to the Constituent Assembly set up or about to be set up at the date of the passing of this Act under the authority of the Governor-General'. The date of the passing of the Act was 18 July 1947, and a Constituent Assembly was set up by announcements of the Governor-General of India (Lord Mountbatten) on 26 July and 10 August 1947. Did the paragraph authorise the Governor-General of Pakistan to dissolve the Constituent Assembly so set up and to establish another? The petitioner said it did not. The Constituent Assembly referred to in the Act was that set up in July and August. The Governor-General referred to was, in accordance with section 19 (2), the Governor-General within the meaning of the Government of India Act, who had disappeared at midnight on 14 August 1947. The Federation, on the other hand, argued that 'the authority of the Governor-General' was the authority conferred by the Statement of His Majesty's Government issued by Lord Mountbatten on 3 June 1947, to which legal effect was given by the section; and that authority, by paragraph 21, reserved to the Governor-General a right to make further announcements. After 14 August the Governor-General referred to was the Governor-General of Pakistan in accordance with section 19 (1). Reference was made to section 19 (5), which provided that any power conferred by the

Act to make an order included power to revoke or vary any order previously made in the exercise of that power: but reliance was placed on section 32 of the Interpretation Act, 1889, which provides that where an Act confers a power, it may be exercised from time to time, and by the holder for the time being of the office. It was therefore argued that the Governor-General of Pakistan had power to revoke Lord Mountbatten's order establishing the first Constituent Assembly, to dissolve that Assembly, and to summon a new Constituent Assembly in accordance with paragraph 21 of His Majesty's Government's Statement.

In the Sind Chief Court, Constantine, C.J., rejected this contention on the ground that the contrary intention appeared from the language of section 19 (3) (b). Vellani, J., said that the paragraph referred to a specific Constituent Assembly and a specific Governor-General, Lord Mountbatten. Muhammad Bakhsh, J., held that the 'Governor-General' referred to was, under section 19 (2), the Governor-General of India before partition.

In the main, however, the Federation rested its case on section 5 of the Independence Act, which counsel claimed to be a complete delegation of prerogative power to the Governor-General for the time being. It was argued that at common law the Crown had power to summon, prorogue and dissolve a representative legislature, that that power could be taken away only by express words or necessary intendment, and that there was nothing in the Act to take away that power, except of course section 5 itself, which vested it in the Governor-General.

The petitioner argued that the prerogative power had disappeared in the United Kingdom in 1694, and it would be strange to revive it in Pakistan in 1954. The Crown had lost any such power in India because legislatures had been established by Acts of Parliament and specific powers relating to dissolution had been conferred. *Attorney-General* v. *De Keyser's Royal Hotel Co.*,[1] which had been quoted for the Federation, was read as deciding that, when once a prerogative power had been covered by legislation it disappeared, and it was not revived when the legislation was repealed. In any case, section 5 of the Independence Act merely made the Governor-General the Queen's representative for the purpose of the 'government of the Dominion'. Subject to the

[1] [1920] A.C. 505.

grammatical variation, it had the same meaning as 'shall be governed' in section 8 (2) of the same Act. Accordingly, the phrase 'government of the Dominion' meant 'government under the Government of India Act': at least it did not include constitution-making or the constitution of the constitution-maker.

Constantine, C.J., admitted that nothing could be inferred from the repeal by Governor-General's order of the power to dissolve the Federal Assembly, because that power would have been repealed if an express power to dissolve the Constituent Assembly had been inserted in the Independence Act. He also agreed that in the United Kingdom dissolution was a matter of prerogative: but in the United Kingdom Parliament itself was a creation of prerogative. Where a legislature is created by statute, dissolution must be by statute.

Vellani, J., accepted the argument for the petitioner that 'government' in section 5 of the Independence Act was simply a grammatical variation of 'governed' in section 8 (2), and accordingly the Governor-General represented the Queen for the purposes of government under the Government of India Act only. The Governor of a colony is not a viceroy or a quasi-viceroy, but has only specific powers delegated to him.[1] When there is legislation covering a field of prerogative and it is desired to make the prerogative still available, it is necessary to reserve a power to exercise the prerogative.[2] The Act had defined the purposes for which the Governor-General represented the Crown, and so the prerogative of dissolution did not remain unaffected by the Independence Act. The removal of the power to dissolve the Federal Assembly from section 19 (2) (c) of the Government of India Act was a deliberate act, in consonance with the true meaning of section 5. It prohibits the dissolution of the Federal Legislature and therefore of the Constituent Assembly.

Muhammad Bakhsh, J., accepted the petitioner's argument in full. He agreed that the summoning, proroguing and dissolving of a legislature are prerogative powers: but if the power to dissolve

---

[1] *Musgrave v. Pulido* (1879), 5 App. Cas. 102; *Bonanza Creek Gold Mining Co. v. the King*, [1916] 1 A.C. 566; *Commercial Cable Co. v. Government of Newfoundland*, [1916] 2 A.C. 610.
[2] *Attorney-General v. De Keyser's Royal Hotel Co.*, [1920] A.C. 509; *Moore v. Attorney-General for the Irish Free State*, [1935] A.C. 484; *Sammut v. Strickland*, [1938] A.C. 678.

the Federal Assembly had to be removed, why did the Government of India Act retain a right to summon and prorogue the Federal Legislature? Section 19 (2) of that Act was a deliberate withdrawal of the prerogative of dissolution, which was merged in the statute. 'The Constituent Assembly being a sovereign body is summoned and prorogued by the President of the Constituent Assembly in accordance with the rules framed by the Constituent Assembly, while the Constituent Assembly sitting as Federal Legislature under the 1935 Act is summoned and prorogued by the Governor-General in accordance with the provisions of section 19 (2) (a) and (b). The Governor-General's power of dissolution of [the] Federal Legislature is withdrawn because the dissolution of [the] Federal Legislature will mean the dissolution of the Constituent Assembly, which is not permissible under the provisions of [the] Independence Act'. The words 'government of the Dominion' mean 'government of the Dominion as required by the Government of India Act, 1935': they have no reference to the constitution-making functions of the Constituent Assembly, which is a sovereign body under the Independence Act. The Governor-General was not a viceroy under the Government of India Act; he had only the powers conferred by the Act and such other powers as the Crown might assign to him. His position under the Independence Act was not better than this. The King gave away all his powers to Pakistan: *Gagambol Ramalingam* v. *Ruku-ul-Mulk Syed Abdul Wajid*.[1] The Governor-General cannot have more power than the Queen, who has renounced all power in Pakistan.[2] 'The representation is only a formal and symbolic representation of the Queen, who is the August and Beloved Head of the Commonwealth, who reigns but does not rule.' The Governor-General was a creature of the statute and his powers must be found in the statute or in his Commission. The only express delegation in the Commission is of the prerogative of pardon, in accordance with section 295 (2) of the Government of India Act. If the Governor-

[1] A.I.R. (1950) P.C. 64. This case related to the State of Mysore, which was not part of the dominions of the Crown, and in respect of which all the powers of the Crown lapsed by reason of the express provisions of section 7 (1) (b) of the Indian Independence Act. The relevance of the citation is therefore not appreciated.
[2] The authority quoted was Halsbury, *Laws of England* (3rd ed.), v, p. 463, para. 1025: 'In Pakistan, where the position may be regarded as transitional, the Queen is not designated as Queen of Pakistan'; a true statement, but apparently irrelevant.

General had all the prerogatives by section 5, why was section 295 (2) retained? The Constituent Assembly was a sovereign body specially created to frame the Constitution. The Governor-General had no power to dissolve it. If Parliament had wanted to give a power of dissolution they should have said so in clear terms. The Governor-General's only powers in connection with the Constitution are laid down in section 9 of the Independence Act. The prerogative was merged in the statute. Even in England it has ceased to be a prerogative since 1694, and it can hardly be revived in Pakistan after 1947. In the Dominions the right is always statutory.

Counsel for the Federation were prepared to challenge the foundations upon which these judgments rested:

(i) If the power to summon, prorogue and dissolve a legislature was a prerogative power, it could be taken away only by express words or necessary intendment. There were no express words, and there was nothing in the Independence Act about the Constituent Assembly being a sovereign body. For the purpose of making provision as to the constitution, the Assembly had all the legislative powers of the Legislature of the Dominion, which were virtually the same as those of the Parliament of the United Kingdom, but that Parliament is summoned, prorogued and dissolved under the prerogative.

(ii) The provisions left in or added to the Government of India Act by Lord Mountbatten—and it was he who applied section 19 to the 'Federal Legislature', because formerly it applied to the two Chambers—on 22 July 1947 could not be used to interpret an Act which received the royal assent on 18 July.

(iii) If the phrase 'government of the Dominion' in section 5 meant 'government under the Government of India Act' because the words 'governed . . . in accordance with the Government of India' were used in section 8, then presumably the words 'government of the Dominion' in section 7 had the same meaning, and Pakistan was not an independent Dominion because His Majesty's Government had not been deprived of responsibility for the government of Pakistan outside the Government of India Act. Muhammad Bakhsh, J., had actually quoted section 7 (1) (a), but for some reason unexplained he associated proviso (a) to section 8 (2) with it. That proviso merely enacted that the Government of India Act should apply separately to the Dominions and that there should be no Central Government or Legislature common to the two Dominions. Presumably he assumed that the dissolution of a legislature is a legislative power. It is, however, vested in the Queen or the Governor-General, not in Parliament or the Legislature of a Dominion. The only powers conferred on the Constituent Assembly were the powers of the Legislature of the Dominion, including the powers of the Federal Legislature under the Government of India Act. If the power to dissolve the Legislature of the Dominion was a prerogative power and was not delegated under section 5 of the Independence Act, it remained vested in the Queen.

(iv) The argument drawn from *Attorney-General* v. *De Keyser's Royal Hotel Co.* assumed that there was a prerogative power which had been dealt with by the Independence Act, with the result that the prerogative was in abeyance so long as the Act was in force: but there was no provision relating to dissolution in the Act. If, therefore, the prerogative was not delegated by section 5 it remained vested in the Queen. No doubt Muhammad Bakhsh, J., assumed that the power of dissolution was included in the 'sovereignty' of the Constituent Assembly; but the only powers conferred on that Assembly were legislative powers. No doubt the Queen's powers of *legislation* for Pakistan disappeared so long as the legislative powers of the Constituent Assembly existed. Alternatively, it might conceivably be argued that the Governor-General's power to dissolve the Federal Assembly had for all time abolished the Crown's power to dissolve any legislature in British India: but the Act did not say so, it merely gave a power to dissolve the Assembly set up by that Act.

(v) If section 5 conferred on the Governor-General only such powers as the King had had under the Government of India Act as it stood on 18 July 1947, or as the Queen now has under that Act as adapted, the Governor-General has no power to declare war or make peace or to enter into treaties or to accredit and receive diplomatic representatives. It may be that these powers remain with the Queen, as in other 'independent Dominions'; but in that case the power of dissolution also remains with the Queen; and this was not the line of argument which counsel for the petitioner followed.

(vi) The statement that in other Dominions the power of dissolution is always statutory is not quite correct. It is true that, as Constantine, C.J., pointed out, where there is a statutory legislature there is also a statutory power of dissolution. In Newfoundland in 1931 and in Ceylon after 1948 the legislature was created and the power of dissolution conferred by prerogative instruments. The difference in India and Pakistan was that only an interim Constitution was provided. Section 6 of the Independence Act provided for a notional Legislature whose composition and whose relations with other constitutional authorities were not set out, because it was assumed that the Constituent Assembly, exercising

68

the functions of the Legislature of the Dominion, would supply the necessary details, either by adapting the Government of India Act by the insertion of provisions relating to the legislature, or by repealing the Government of India Act and substituting new constitutional provisions. What the Federation of Pakistan alleged was that there had been a statutory delegation to the Governor-General of power to dissolve a statutory legislature, the Legislature of the Dominion, but the terms of the delegation could not be set out otherwise than in general terms, because the Parliament of the United Kingdom did not know what form the Legislature of the Dominion would take after the interim period, during which the Constituent Assembly was functioning: but there had to be a power to dissolve the Constituent Assembly in order that the permanent Legislature of the Dominion might take over. The Indian Constituent Assembly met the problem by repealing the Indian Independence Act *in toto*: that was a permissible solution because of the wide terms of section 6 of that Act, but it was not the solution expected by sections 5 and 6, which were drafted on the assumption that India and Pakistan would remain Dominions.

As the argument proceeded in the Federal Court, it became plain that the weakness of the Federation's case lay not in the arguments used by the Sind Chief Court but in the absence of any provisions in the Indian Independence Act for the reconstitution of the Legislature of the Dominion. The argument based on section 19 of that Act did not seem to appeal to the Court. It therefore became necessary to argue that the power in section 5 included not only power to dissolve the Constituent Assembly but also power to reconstitute the Legislature of the Dominion, which necessarily included power to determine its composition and mode of election. It seemed from observations which fell from the Bench during the initial argument—as has been mentioned, neither the argument for the respondent nor the reply of the appellants was heard by the Court because the decision on assent went to the root of the jurisdiction of the Sind Court—that the Court's *prima facie* view was that Parliament had assumed that the Constituent Assembly would proceed forthwith to the enactment of a new Constitution and that the law enacting the new Constitution would provide for the dissolution of the Constituent Assembly. On this view the failure to provide a Constitution left a lacuna which could be filled only by the application of general principles of law or by extra-legal action in which the courts should acquiesce. Certain observations of Munir, C.J., seem to support this view[1]:

It may incidentally be mentioned here that in the Act of 1947 there was no express provision for the dissolution of the Constituent Assembly, and it was alleged before us by Mr Chundrigar on behalf of the respondent that the only way to get rid of the Assembly, if it did not dissolve itself, was force or revolution, thus admitting that extra-legal acts like revolution, *coup d'état* and other unconstitutional acts become legal concepts where the people, deprived of political sovereignty which in a democracy is their birthright, seek to assert that right against an indissoluble Assembly.

There is, however, one obvious lacuna in the Indian Independence Act which is otherwise a masterpiece of draftsmanship—it contains no express provision as to what was to happen if the Constituent Assembly did not or was unable to make a constitution, or resigned *en bloc*, or converted itself into a perpetual legislature. It may be that any such contingency was beyond the imagination of the authors of the Act, but the more probable reason seems to be that they thought that any such contingency had ceased to be their headache and was purely a concern of the 'independent' Dominion. So long as the responsibility for the government of the country was that of the Government in London, a provision to meet such a situation appeared in the constitution, but the responsibility having been disclaimed by the Indian Independence Act, the necessity for retaining any such provision also disappeared from the constitution. If a breakdown came, it seems to have been thought, it was for the Dominion itself to reset the tumbled machinery. A third explanation has been suggested by the learned counsel for the appellants and that is that section 5, in view of its wide terms, was supposed to contain a solution of the difficulty by the exercise by the Governor-General of his prerogative powers as representative of the King.

If the result [of a decision for the Federation in respect of assent] is disaster, it will be merely another instance of how thoughtlessly the Constituent Assembly proceeded with its business and by assuming for itself the position of an irremovable legislature to what straits it has brought the country. Unless any rule of estoppel require us to pronounce merely purported legislation to be complete and valid legislation we have no option but to pronounce it to be void and to leave it to the relevant authorities under the Constitution or to the country to set right the position in any way it may be open to them. The question raised involves the rights of every citizen in Pakistan. . . .

[1] *Post*, pp. 85, 116, 140, 158.

70

Nor is there in any of the opinions delivered [in the Sind Chief Court] even a remote reference to the basic question, which I am not deciding because the respondent was not called upon to reply to it, but which must undoubtedly have stared the learned Judges in the face, namely, whether it is a wise exercise of discretion for the judiciary to re-install in power a deposed government by issuing enforceable writs against a *de facto* government.

The last quotation of course refers to the fact that the issue of prerogative writs under section 223A of the Government of India Act was clearly within the discretion of the Court, but the quotations generally suggested the possible interpretation that the actions of the Governor-General, on the advice of the Council of Ministers, if illegal, might still be necessary in the interests of Pakistan, and that it was not for the judiciary to decide that question. During the course of the argument, indeed, Munir, C.J., referred to the action of Louis Napoleon in 1848 and the decision of the courts in Rhode Island, after the American Revolution, that they could not decide between competing political authorities as to which of them was the lawful authority.

In the view of the Federation of Pakistan, it was not necessary to go so far. Their fundamental argument—with which the Federal Court eventually agreed—was that assent was needed for 'Acts' of the Constituent Assembly. Though they did not put the point because it was unnecessary for the case, they assumed that a favourable decision on that point would also decide the issue of dissolution, for in that case the Constituent Assembly would long since have become an unconstitutional body. If that failed, they relied upon section 5 of the Indian Independence Act. In their view, the question whether the breakdown of the constitutional machinery was within the contemplation of the draftsman did not matter. As a matter of history it probably was. Sections 45 and 93 of the Government of India Act, as originally enacted, dealt with that possibility. Moreover, the Muslim League had already boycotted the Union Constituent Assembly of India and had declared it to be an illegal body. It was therefore within the contemplation of 'Parliament' that some dispute—possibly a communal dispute—would result in one or both of the Constituent Assemblies failing to function. The obvious solution, of leaving the way open for the Government or the Parliament of the United Kingdom to reopen the matter in agreement with the Indian and Pakistani leaders, was politically impracticable. On the other hand, it was possible to define the powers of the Governor-General in sufficiently broad terms to enable him to take the necessary steps—and it will be remembered that the original intention was to continue Lord Mountbatten as Governor-General of both Dominions for a transitional period. It was not necessary, however, to make any such assumptions. It is a well-known rule, which has been applied both in Canada and in Australia, that the Constitution of a self-governing country must be regarded as containing all the powers necessary for self-government. One cannot, for instance, deny that Canada has power to regulate radio and aeronautics, merely because powers in those fields were not in the contemplation of Parliament in 1867. Accordingly, there can never be a lacuna in the Constitution of an independent country under the Crown. On the margin the powers of the Crown are deliciously vague, the draftsman's dream of the blanket clause that covers everything he has forgotten or cannot foresee. If all else fails the Queen is the Constitution, for every power that is not vested in somebody else must be vested in her.

Assuming that a power of dissolution could not be found in section 5 on the basis put forward by the Federation of Pakistan, it could not be urged that there was no remedy at all within the ambit of the Rule of Law. Acts otherwise illegal might have to be legalised by the logic of the case, as in 1641, 1688, and the insanity of George III, but only if the monarchy failed to function, as it did in those cases. In Pakistan the monarchy had not failed. Not only was there a Queen in London, no doubt anxious to be kept out of Pakistani politics if an internal solution could be found, but also she had a lawfully appointed representative in Karachi; and he in turn had appointed a Council of Ministers, including the Prime Minister, some of whose members had been lawfully appointed even if the intrigue of the night of the 20 September 1954, by which a bare quorum of the Constituent Assembly had sought, by a strained but (apparently) lawful interpretation of the Rules of Procedure, to take away the powers of the Governor-General while he was on the Frontier, had succeeded. The Queen or the Governor-General could therefore act on advice. It should here be mentioned that in the Federal Court there was a cross-fire of affidavits. On the one side it was urged, with a wealth of illustration, that the Constituent Assembly had abused its powers. On the other side it was sought to be shown that the Constituent Assembly had been about to produce the Constitution which would have ended the controversy, but was prevented from doing so by the action of the Governor-General. Such a question was obviously not justiciable, even on the basis of evidence, and clearly could not be decided by the courts on the basis of affidavits. What the affidavits showed, however, was that the newspaper term 'constitutional crisis' was, for once, not exaggerated. There was undoubtedly an emergency which must be solved eventually by an appeal to the people.

During the course of the argument in the Federal Court the Chief Justice referred to 'natural law', an unruly horse which counsel for the Federation hesitated to mount even with encouragement from the Court. The Advocate-General preferred the phrase 'justice, equity and good conscience', which appears in the Civil Procedure Code. Diplock, Q.C., for the Federation thought that *salus populi suprema lex* might solve the problem. Emergency powers begin in legal history with decisions that, when a town is on fire, any man may pull down houses and generally interfere with private rights for the benefit of the public. The *Case of Saltpetre*[1] shows that the principle may be extended to time of war, an extension admitted by counsel for John Hampden and by the minority of the judges in the *Case of Shipmoney*.[2] These cases have been used to justify 'martial law' in time not only of war but also of insurrection. The principle seemed to be that, if a court was satisfied that there was an emergency, the Crown had by prerogative the right and indeed the duty—as *R. v. Pinney*[3] suggested—to take such steps as might be necessary to meet the emergency. The case was stronger in Pakistan because it was ceded or conquered territory of the Crown, because the Constitution granted by the King in Parliament had, as the Federation of Pakistan alleged, broken down, and because Parliament had by its own act deprived itself of the power of intervening. It was therefore the duty of the Governor-General, as the Queen's

[1] (1607), 12 Co. Rep. 12.
[2] (1637), 3 St. Tr. 825.
[3] (1832), 5 Car. and P. 254.

73

representative, to take such steps as he thought necessary to overcome the emergency, and the courts were not competent bodies to assume the task of deciding whether he was right or wrong because this was a political controversy on which, very properly, the courts had no views.

These arguments produced no conclusion in *Tamizuddin Khan's* case. As soon as counsel for the respondent finished his argument on the question of assent the Court found for the appellants on that question. It was therefore unnecessary to argue whether the dissolution had been valid. The Government's legal advisers had, however, to reach conclusions of their own in order that consequential legislation might be drafted. These conclusions were as follows:

(i) Though it had been argued that section 19 (3) of the Indian Independence Act conferred a power to destroy the Constituent Assembly and to summon a new one, that interpretation was strained and was not likely to be acceptable. If counsel for the respondent had been given an opportunity to reply, he would no doubt have pointed out that there was no possible ambiguity in the reference to the Constituent Assembly of India. The power of the Governor-General had therefore to be founded on section 5.

(ii) The decision in *Tamizuddin Khan's* case showed that the Constituent Assembly had been an unlawful body for a long period because it had claimed to exercise powers which it did not possess, had altered its own composition by Acts which were invalid, and had operated under Rules of Procedure some of which could not be justified by the terms of the Indian Independence Act. Accordingly, 'dissolution' was not entirely an accurate phrase (which, incidentally, had not been used in the Proclamation of 24 October 1954). The Governor-General had dismissed an unlawful body.

(iii) There was no Legislature of the Dominion in existence. Section 8 of the Indian Independence Act had lapsed because the Constituent Assembly had destroyed itself as a lawful body.

(iv) The Crown's power to establish a representative legislature for Pakistan, which was conquered or ceded territory, had been restored by the disappearance of the legislature established by the Indian Independence Act. This representative legislature would be the Legislature of the Dominion within the meaning of section 6 of the Indian Independence Act. Since there were no other provisions relating to that Legislature, the Crown could determine its composition and functioning, so long as section 6 was observed.

74

The original Constituent Convention Order (No. 8 of 1955) was drafted on these assumptions. In the Federal Court, however, reliance was placed not only on this argument but also on the arguments which had been used in *Tamizuddin Khan's* case. As had been expected, the argument based on section 19 was rejected. The argument based on section 5 was accepted, but with an important modification; and the argument that the Constituent Assembly was an unlawful body was accepted without the logical consequences being drawn from it. It may be submitted, with deference, that there was nothing in the Indian Independence Act which required the Governor-General to follow the steps taken by Lord Mountbatten in 1947; nor does the Crown's power to set up a representative legislature imply that a minority of the members may not be nominated. The new Constituent Convention was not the Constituent Assembly contemplated by the Indian Independence Act, and it could be called an 'Assembly', a 'Convention', a 'Parliament', a 'Legislative Council', or anything else, so long as it was a representative legislature.

It need hardly be said, however, that the Government of Pakistan accepted the opinion of the Federal Court. Before the argument began the Constituent Convention Order (No. 8 of 1955) had been amended by Order 9 of 1955, so as to alter the method of election and the composition of the Convention. On 27 April, two days after argument began, the composition was again changed and the Convention was given all the powers under section 8 of the Indian Independence Act. Accordingly, the opinion of the Federal Court in the *Special Reference* relates to a Constituent Assembly having the same powers as the Assembly established by Lord Mountbatten. It is interesting to speculate whether the Court would have given the same welcome to the Convention contemplated by the Order No. 8 of 1955.

JUDGMENT

IN THE CASE OF

FEDERATION OF PAKISTAN AND OTHERS

v.

MOULVI TAMIZUDDIN KHAN

IN THE
FEDERAL COURT OF PAKISTAN
(APPELLATE JURISDICTION)

CONSTITUTIONAL CIVIL APPEAL
NO. 1 OF 1955

(On appeal from the judgment and order of the Chief Court of Sind at Karachi, dated 9 February 1955, in Writ Petition No. 43 of 1954)

Federation of Pakistan, Mohammed Ali, Chaudhri Muhammad Ali, Major-General Iskander Mirza, M. A. H. Ispahani, Dr A. M. Malik, Dr Khan Sahib, General Muhammad Ayub Khan, Ghyas-ud-din Pathan, and Mir Ghulam Ali Talpur, appellants, v. *Moulvi Tamizuddin Khan,* respondent.

Present: Muhammad Munir, C.J., A. S. M. Akram, A. R. Cornelius, Muhammad Sharif, and S. A. Rahman, JJ.

MUHAMMAD MUNIR, C.J.—This is a constitutional appeal Judgment from the judgment of the Chief Court of Sind, dated 9 February 1955, directing writs of mandamus and quo warranto to issue against the appellants, the Federation of Pakistan and certain Ministers of the Central Government, on the application of the respondent Mr Tamizuddin Khan. The application was heard by a Full Bench of five Judges of whom Mr Justice Hassanally Agha retired during the hearing and, therefore, gave no opinion. The remaining four Judges were unanimous in their findings. The leading judgment was written by Constantine, C.J., with which Muhammad Bachal, J., agreed, while Vellani and Muhammad Bakhsh A. Menon, JJ., delivered separate judgments.

Pakistan came into existence as an independent Dominion and a member of the British Commonwealth of Nations on 15 August 1947, with a provisional constitution of the federal pattern, under the Indian Independence Act, 1947 (10 & 11 Geo. VI, ch. 30) hereinafter also referred to as the Act of 1947. Under that Act, until a new Constitution was framed, the Government of Pakistan was to be carried on under the Government of India Act, 1935 (26 Geo. V, ch. 2), hereinafter referred to wherever necessary as the Act of 1935, subject to such adaptations and modifications as were consequential on her attaining the status of an independent Dominion. A Governor-General was to represent His Majesty for the purposes of the government of the Dominion. The functions of the Legislature of the Dominion, including the making of a constitution, were to be performed by a Constituent Assembly which had also to function as the Federal Legislature under the adapted Act of 1935. At the relevant time the respondent was the President of that Assembly. The Assembly had not made any constitution when, on 24 October 1954, it was dissolved by the following proclamation of His Excellency the Governor-General:

The Governor-General having considered the political crisis with which the country is faced, has with deep regret come to the conclusion that the constitutional machinery has broken down. He, therefore, has decided to declare a state of emergency throughout Pakistan. The Constituent Assembly as at present constituted has lost the confidence of the people and can no longer function.

The ultimate authority vests in the people who will decide all issues including constitutional issues through their representatives to be elected afresh. Elections will be held as early as possible.

Until such time as elections are held, the administration of the country will be carried on by a reconstituted Cabinet. He has called upon the Prime Minister to reform the Cabinet with a view to giving the country a vigorous and stable administration. The invitation has been accepted.

The security and stability of the country are of paramount importance. All personal, sectional and provincial interests must be subordinated to the supreme national interest.

The reconstituted Council of Ministers which was announced in an extraordinary issue of the *Gazette of Pakistan*, on 26 October 1954, consisted of Mr Mohammed Ali, Ch. Muhammad Ali, Major-General Iskander Mirza, Mr M. A. H. Ispahani, Dr A. M. Malik, General Muhammad Ayub Khan, Mr Ghyas-ud-din Pathan, and Mir Ghulam Ali Talpur. Dr Khan Sahib was included in the Council a few days later.

On 7 November 1954 the respondent put in an application, Writ Petition No. 43 of 1954 on the Extraordinary Special

Jurisdiction Side of the Chief Court of Sind. The respondents to this petition were the present appellants, namely, the Federation of Pakistan, the aforesaid members of the Council of Ministers, and the Estate Officer of the Government of Pakistan. After stating the facts leading to the setting up of the Constituent Assembly and the coming into force of the Act of 1947, the application alleged that the 4th appellant, Major-General Iskander Mirza, had informed the respondent on 26 October 1954, that the Constituent Assembly had been dissolved; that the respondent and members of the Constituent Assembly had been forcibly prevented from entering the premises of the Constituent Assembly Building in Karachi on 27 October 1954; that on 30 October 1954, the Estate Officer of the Government of Pakistan had addressed a letter to the respondent intimating to him that as he had ceased to be the President of the Constituent Assembly the allotment in his name of Bungalow No. 3, Bath Islands, had been cancelled with effect from 8 November 1954 and requesting him to vacate the said premises by 8 November 1954; that the appellants were contending that in pursuance of the alleged proclamation the Constituent Assembly had been dissolved and were interfering with the duties of the respondent as the President of the Assembly and preventing him from exercising his functions; that for the reasons stated in the application the alleged proclamation and the appointment of appellants (2 to 10)[1] as members of the Council of Ministers were unconstitutional, illegal, *ultra vires*, without jurisdiction, inoperative and void; that in any case the inclusion of appellants (4, 5, 7, 8 and 10)[2] in the Council was contrary to the provisions of the Act of 1935 inasmuch as they were not the members of the Federal Legislature; and that there resided in the respondent a legal right to the performance of legal duties by the appellants which was of a public nature. The application concluded with the prayer that a writ in the nature of mandamus be issued against the appellants, their agents, servants and all persons claiming and acting through or under them restraining them from implementing or otherwise giving effect to the proclamation of

[1] Mohammed Ali, Chaudhri Muhammad Ali, Major-General Iskander Mirza, M. A. H. Ispahani, Dr A. M. Malik, Dr Khan Sahib, General Muhammad Ayub Khan, Ghyas-ud-din Pathan, and Mir Ghulam Ali Talpur.
[2] Major-General Iskander Mirza, M. A. H. Ispahani, Dr Khan Sahib, General Muhammad Ayub Khan, and Mir Ghulam Ali Talpur.

24 October 1954, and from interfering, directly or indirectly, with the exercise of the respondent's functions and duties as the President of the Constituent Assembly; and that another writ in the nature of quo warranto be issued against appellants (4, 5, 7, 8 and 10)[1] with a view to determining the validity of their appointment as members of the Council of Ministers. A joint reply to this application was filed by the Advocate-General of Pakistan on behalf of the appellants, raising some preliminary objections and opposing the application on the merits. The reply alleged that the Sind Chief Court had no jurisdiction to issue either of the writs; that the dissolution of the Assembly was valid; that the writs prayed for could not, in any case should not, issue; and that the grounds mentioned in the proclamation for the dissolution of the Assembly were true, and if any proof was needed the appellants were prepared to show that the constitutional machinery had broken down, that the Constituent Assembly had lost the confidence of the people, and that it could no longer function in accordance with the provisions of the Act of 1947. In the arguments before the Chief Court several questions which the application and the reply gave rise to were debated, but the main points which received the attention of that Court and which were argued before us on behalf of the appellants were:

(i) that since the Government of India (Amendment) Act, 1954, by which on 16 July 1954, section 223A, which empowered the High Courts to issue writs of mandamus and of quo warranto, was inserted in the Act of 1935, had not received the assent of the Governor-General, it was not law, and that therefore the Sind Chief Court had no jurisdiction to issue the writs;

(ii) that the prayer for a writ of quo warranto must also fail on the ground that section 10A of the Act of 1935, which imposed on members of the Council of Ministers the qualification of being members of the Federal Legislature, and which was inserted in that Act by the Government of India (Fifth Amendment) Act, 1954, was not law because that Amendment Act also had not received the assent of the Governor-General;

(iii) that the Governor-General was competent to dissolve the Constituent Assembly and in the circumstances had rightly dissolved it; and

(iv) that the discretion to issue either of the writs should not be exercised in favour of the respondent.

[1] See p. 81, n. 2.

The Chief Court held that the Acts of the Constituent Assembly, when it did not function as the Federal Legislature, did not require the Governor-General's assent and that the dissolution of the Assembly was illegal. It, therefore, issued the writs prayed for.

In order to appreciate the nature of the issues raised and the implications flowing from their determination one way or the other it is necessary to preface this judgment with some observations of a general character before stating the precise constitutional position that the Act of 1947 brought about and deciding the main issue, the determination of which is in my opinion sufficient to dispose of this appeal.

The words democracy, democratic institutions, sovereignty, political sovereignty, legislative sovereignty, independent dominion, etc., have been freely used in the arguments before us. I, therefore, propose to give a general idea of these terms but only to the extent that it is necessary for the purposes of this judgment.

The word 'Democracy' is now used at least in three different senses. It is the name given to a philosophy of life, to the means requisite to live up to that philosophy and lastly to the principles which determine those means. In the first sense democracy is a subjective attitude by which the members of the community secure to every one his rights, look upon all fellow citizens without distinction of colour or race as brethren in a common enterprise and give spontaneous support to projects which enhance the civic excellence and promote the general welfare. It is thus a way of life, based contrary to the ancient Greek conception, upon the fundamental assumption of equality of all individuals and of their equal rights of life, liberty of action, thought and expression and pursuit of happiness. It is essentially an attitude towards life, and a definite conception of man's place in society, and of the ends of life. As a mode of government, democracy involves a study of the basic principles on which political institutions ought to be founded as well as of the actual mechanism to be employed in particular conditions. The basic idea on which such form of Government rests is that of self-rule of the people, of freely elected representative institutions and of an executive responsible to the people. The fundamental institution in modern democracy is the constitution, whether this be a written or an unwritten one. The constitution performs three functions: it expresses the consent by which the people actually establish the state itself; it sets up a definite form of Government; and it grants and at the same time limits the power which that Government possesses. It is the people who give the constitution and the appointed ruling agency is held in its administration within the rigid limits of its letter, subject to the right of the people at any time by appropriate means to enlarge or constrict the power it had granted. Since democracy is that form of government which represents the common will, political institutions under that form of government, whatever may be the form of the constitution, must be based on principles without which democratic ends cannot be realised. In no modern state can the people now, like the City States of ancient Greece, directly assume legislative functions, the number of population and size of the country making it impossible for them to meet in an assembly for purposes of legislation. Therefore in a nation of any size it is necessary to find some means by which people could rule without taking part in every immediate step of the process of authority. Thus the principle has now been firmly established of choosing a certain number of agents or representatives, who are numerous enough to speak for the whole people and few enough to meet at one place. The first essential of a democratic constitution therefore is that the entire people must be represented in the legislature by their nominees to be elected periodically by them. The object being that the popular will should be reflected in the legislature, the only means known to modern democracy of achieving this result is election of the people's representatives who on being elected constitute the popular assembly, whether it be called by the name of Parliament, the House of Commons, House of Representatives, the House of People or by any other name.

The second and by far the most important requirement of a democratic constitution is the need for periodic accountability of the representatives to their electors. In modern times within a few years political events of great and unanticipated importance may happen in a country and the mental horizon of the whole people may change by a sudden international or domestic event, the importance and implications of which may not have been present to the minds of the people when elections were held. It is, therefore, necessary that old representatives should seek re-election either because of their having ceased to reflect in the legislature the progressive or changing outlook of the people or because of their having ceased to represent the views of the people on a particular issue. The principle, therefore, is fundamental that in every democratic constitution there must exist a provision for holding elections after a few years, so that the House may continue to be representative of the varying aspirations and needs of the people. It is unnecessary to discuss here the position of a representative after he has been elected, whether he is an agent or trustee of the people or a mere messenger. The basic principle is that no representative body can continue indefinitely and that its composition must admit of change from time to time by means of an appeal to the people. An irremovable legislature is the very antithesis of democracy and no democratic constitution is known in the world where elections are for life or for an indefinitely long time.

It may incidentally be mentioned here that in the Act of 1947 there was no express provision for the dissolution of the Constituent Assembly, and it was alleged before us by Mr Chundrigar on behalf of the respondent that the only way to get rid of the Assembly, if it did not dissolve itself, was force or revolution, thus admitting that extra-legal acts like revolution, *coup d'état* and other unconstitutional acts become legal concepts where the people, deprived of political sovereignty which in a democracy is their birthright, seek to assert that right against an indissoluble Assembly.

This is what Sir William Blackstone said in 1765 about a perpetual legislature:

Lastly, a Parliament may be dissolved or expire by length of time. For if either the legislative body were perpetual; or might last for the life of the Prince who convened them, as formerly; and were so to be supplied, by occasionally filling the vacancies with new representatives; in these cases, if it were once corrupted, the evil would be past all remedy; but when different bodies succeed each other, if the people show cause to disapprove of the present, they may rectify its faults in the next (*Commentaries on the Laws of England*, book I, ch. 2, p. 189).

85

The requirement of periodic accountability of a representative Assembly to the electors is so basic that in the United Kingdom the Crown, which since long has ceased to exercise its discretion in opposition to the advice of the Ministry, will be considered to be justified in exercising its reserve powers of withholding assent or directing dissolution if Parliament ever attempted to prolong its own life indefinitely. The reason for it is that in a democratic constitution the ultimate or political sovereignty resides in the people, while the popular assembly, where the constitution does not impose any limitations on its powers, exercises legislative sovereignty only during its term. Since sovereignty as applied to States imports the supreme, absolute, uncontrollable power by which a State is governed, and democracy recognises all ultimate power as resting in the people, it is obvious that in the case of a conflict between the ultimate and legal sovereign, the latter must yield. An irremovable legislature, therefore, is not only a negation of democracy but is the worst calamity that can befall a nation because it tends to perpetuate an oligarchic rule which, while it has none of the advantages, has all the disadvantages of a dictatorial rule. An oligarchy, while it lacks the determination, the singleness of purpose and the clarity of vision of a dictator, is subject to all the temptations to which a dictator may be exposed. If, therefore, the Constituent Assembly was an irremovable legislature, it was a form of oligarchy and not a body of representatives subject to periodic accountability. The reason for it may be that the framers of the Act of 1947 expected that constitution would be framed within a reasonable time and that the Constituent Assembly would thus dissolve itself. They may not have imagined that the Assembly to which they were confiding all legislative powers would not complete the constitution even for seven years and, on the contrary, would assume the role of an irremovable and irresponsible legislature.

As Government is the responsibility of the executive in a constitution, it is an indisputable corollary of the democratic principle that the executive must be responsible to the legislature for its acts. The executive discharges its duty of day to day administration without the popular Assembly enquiring into it but there may come an occasion, and this sometimes does happen, when on some important issue, executive or legislative, there ensues a conflict between the executive and the Assembly. In such a case, if the Assembly does not support the executive, the Government must take it to mean that it has ceased to be the representative of the House, and on the principle of responsible government must make way for those who have the support of the Assembly. The same is the effect of a general vote of no confidence, which is intended to declare to the Government that it no longer enjoys the confidence of the House. In that case too, the Government, if it wishes to stay on, has one means of asserting its will against the will of the Assembly. If it is sure that the Assembly itself has ceased to be representative of the people and that in fact the Government has the popular support on that issue, it may ask for a dissolution of the House however recently the House might have been elected, though this course will constitutionally not be adopted where elections were held on the specific issue on which the Government insists on taking a particular stand. To meet such a situation and to enable the popular will to be reflected in the Assembly it is necessary that, apart from the provisions relating to periodic dissolution, there should exist in the constitution some power competent to dissolve the Assembly, if, before the expiry of its normal life, it adopts on a particular issue an attitude which is not the attitude of the electors. Every democratic constitution, therefore, written or unwritten, gives to the Head of the State the power to dissolve the Assembly in the contingency just mentioned.

The next basic fact in a democracy of the British pattern, which has a constitutional monarch at the head, is that of ministerial responsibility. This doctrine proceeds on the assumption that the sovereign himself belongs to no party, that he does nothing on his own individual responsibility, and that every act of his is backed by ministerial advice. If there be no clash between the Government and the Assembly, and a measure be brought up by Government which the Sovereign feels would be resented or disliked by the people, he is entitled to dismiss the Ministry, to form a Ministry from amongst the members of the opposition, and then on the advice of the new Ministry, to order dissolution. This power undoubtedly rests in the British Monarch, though it has not been exercised since the time of William IV, the established convention now being that by dismissing a Ministry, which represents the House of Commons whose life has not yet expired, the Monarch must be deemed to have taken active interest in party politics, and thus foregone his claim to the respect and affection which every one in the Realm owes to him because of his aloof and lofty position. It will have been noticed that the principles mentioned above can operate in full force only where there are organised parties in the country and at least two parties in the legislature, namely, the Treasury Benches and the Opposition, so that in case the existing Government be dismissed the Opposition may be called upon to form a new Government.

Another means possessed by the British Monarch of appealing to the electorate against the House of Commons and the Government which enjoys the confidence of that House is that of withholding his assent to a bill. This power was last exercised in the time of Queen Anne and is now stated to be as dead as the dodo. But as late as the reign of King George V there were suggestions, when the House of Commons twice passed the Irish Home Rule Bill, that the Sovereign could withhold his assent from the bill and appeal to the country. The King was himself inclined to accept this view and Sir William Harcourt had to tell him in a personal interview that, if he dissolved the House of Commons, in the ensuing elections Sir William would not mention the issue of Home Rule but that elections would be fought on the issue: 'Is the country governed by the King or by the people?' and that every Minister would then attack the King personally.

Thus the necessary mechanism in a normally functioning democratic constitution of the British principle consists of:

(i) a free and independent electorate, willing to give, when necessary, what is called an 'electoral mandate';
(ii) a popularly elected legislature;
(iii) an executive responsible to the legislature;
(iv) the Head of the State, with a legal right not only to dissolve the legislature but also to withhold assent to bills.

The question in what circumstances these powers of the King are to be exercised is an entirely different question and has nothing to do with the legal powers of the King, though clearly defined conventions have come to be recognised which the King can ignore only if he wishes to take the responsibility of ceasing to be a constitutional monarch. But these conventions cannot be enforced by the courts, though they will undoubtedly be taken cognisance

of in the interpretation of written constitutions. The only issue
that the court is required to determine in such cases is whether
the legal power existed or not, and not whether it was properly
and rightly exercised, which is a purely political issue.

As the principal argument which is to be found in the judgment
of the learned judges of the Chief Court of Sind and which has
been reiterated before us is founded on the conception of an
'independent dominion' and the alleged sovereignty of the Constituent Assembly, it becomes necessary to ascertain the meaning
of the words 'independent dominion' and to have a clear com-
prehension of the powers that the Governor-General of a Dominion exercised in 1947, when the Indian Independence Act was
passed. For that purpose we shall have to go far back in history
and to trace the origin and subsequent development of the British
Empire itself. Up to the date of the passing of the Statute of
Westminster in 1931 there was no distinction between a Colony
and a Dominion. Section 18 of the Interpretation Act, 1889, had
defined a colony as 'Any part of His Majesty's Dominions exclusive of the British Islands and of British India, and where
parts of such Dominions are both under a Central and a Local
legislature, all parts under the Central legislature shall, for the
purposes of this definition, be deemed to be one colony.' By
section 11 of the Statute of Westminster the definition of a
colony was not to include in any Act of the Parliament of the
United Kingdom passed after the commencement of the Statute, a
dominion or any province or state forming part of a 'dominion'
which was defined by section 1 of the Statute as meaning the
Dominion of Canada, the Commonwealth of Australia, the Dominion of New Zealand, the Union of South Africa, the Irish Free
State and Newfoundland.

Colonies in America and other parts of the globe were obtained
in three ways:

(i) by treaty of cession;
(ii) by conquest; and
(iii) by taking possession and peopling them where they were
found uninhabited.

On the well-recognised doctrine of Constitutional Law that all
acquisitions of sovereignty by a subject are on behalf of the Crown,

all ceded or conquered colonies were under the Common Law of England held of the Crown. The relationship between such colonies and countries which the King did not hold in right of his British Crown, as for instance, the German territories, was of a fundamentally different character because those territories during the union of the two Crowns had no connection with England or its laws.

Where a colony was acquired by treaty, the King could not legally disregard or violate the articles on which the country was ceded and such articles were sacred and inviolable according to their true intent and meaning. Subject to this qualification, there was hardly any distinction between a colony acquired by treaty or by conquest. Thus in the case of a territory, whether acquired by conquest or treaty, the King, subject to the terms of the treaty, possessed an exclusive prerogative power over it and could entirely change or new-model the whole or part of its laws and political form of government and govern it by Letters Patent or Orders-in-Council. But because a country acquired by British arms became a dominion of the King in right of his Crown, it was necessarily subject to the legislature of Great Britain and consequently the King's legislative powers over it, as conqueror, were subordinate to his own authority in Parliament, so that the King could not make any new change contrary to fundamental principles or exempt the inhabitants from the power of Parliament. The King could preclude himself from the exercise of his prerogative legislative authority in the first instance over a conquered or ceded territory by promising to vest it in an elected Assembly of the inhabitants and the Governor or by any other measure of a similar nature by which the King did not claim or reserve to himself that important prerogative. But the grant of representative institutions, without the reservation of a power of concurrent legislation, precluded the exercise of the prerogative only while the legislative institutions continued to exist.

If an uninhabited country was discovered and peopled by English subjects, they were supposed to possess themselves of it for the benefit of their Sovereign and such of the English laws then in force as were applicable and necessary to their situation were immediately enforced on the principle that wherever an Englishman goes he carries with him as much of English law and liberty as the nature of the situation will allow. In the case of such colonies the Crown never had the prerogative of legislation. The distinction between ceded or conquered territories and settled colonies was clearly brought out by the Privy Council in *Sammut v. Strickland*, [1938] A.C. 678, where Lord Maugham, L.C., delivering the judgment of the Board said:

> The line of distinction here has always been based on the circumstance that English settlers wherever they went carried with them the principles of English law, and that English common law necessarily applied in so far as such laws were applicable to the conditions of the new colony. The Crown clearly had no prerogative right to legislate in such a case. Where, however, the territory was acquired by cession or conquest, more particularly where there was an existing system of law, it has always been considered that there was an absolute power in the Crown, so far as was consistent with the terms of cession (if it was a case of that kind), to alter the existing system of law, though until such interference the laws remained as they were before the territory was acquired by the Crown.

But it was a common characteristic of all colonies, ceded, conquered or settled, that they were subject to the legislative sovereignty of Parliament.

I have already observed that the King cannot vary from any treaty which he has entered into on the acquisition of a country and may preclude himself from the exercise of his prerogative powers of legislation in the first instance over an acquired or ceded territory by vesting it in an elected Assembly of the inhabitants and a Governor. It is, therefore, the most important principle that though the King may keep in his own hands the power of regulating or governing inhabitants, he cannot infringe or depart from the provisions of the Charter by which he has, though voluntarily, granted them any liberties or privileges. Thus in every question which arises between the King and his colonies respecting the prerogative, the first consideration is the Charter granted to the inhabitants. If that be silent on the subject, it cannot be doubted that the King's prerogatives in the colony are precisely those prerogatives which he may exercise in the mother country. Where the Colonial Charter affords no criterion or rule of construction, the Common Law of England with respect to the rule or prerogative is the common law of the territory. But whether a colony was ceded or conquered territory to which representative legislative institutions were granted by Letters Patent or Order-in-Council or a settled colony governing itself under a constitution granted to it by Parliament, the King in no instance divested himself or was divested of the prerogative to withhold assent to colonial legislation. And this prerogative has always been considered to be so material to the existence of the King's real or formal sovereignty, that there can scarcely be imagined a case in which such power could not be exercised. True, the King did not exercise this power himself but only through his agent or representative, but that the power was exercised by the Governor or the Governor-General on the King's behalf has always remained undoubted. In every sense of the term the Governor-General has remained a constituent part of the local legislature.

Statute of Westminster Dominions   In exercise of its right to legislate for the colonies—settled, ceded or conquered—the British Parliament provided a constitution for the Dominion of Canada in 1867, for the Commonwealth of Australia in 1900, for South Africa in 1909, for New Zealand in 1852, and for Newfoundland in 1809. In the case of Ireland the Constitution framed by Dáil Eireann, sitting as a Constituent Assembly, was recognised by the Irish Free State Agreement to which statutory effect was given by the Irish Free State Constitution Act, 1922. These constitutions defined the legislative powers of the legislatures in these Dominions and worked under a Governor or a Governor-General who represented the King and exercised on behalf of the King the power of giving assent to or withholding assent from bills or of reserving them for the signification of His Majesty's pleasure. The Governor-General or the Governor had also the power to prorogue, adjourn or dissolve the legislature of which he himself as representative of the King was a necessary constituent. Though originally these Dominions were subject to British control through the Governor-General, and the British Parliament had the authority to legislate for them, the development of the system of responsible Government in them was so steady and consistent that they began to claim for themselves complete autonomy and an equal status with Great Britain. Accordingly, an Imperial Conference was held in London on 25 October 1926, in order to investigate some of the questions affecting inter-imperial relations. This Conference was attended by the representatives of Great Britain, Canada, Australia, New Zealand, Union of South Africa, Newfoundland, the Irish Free State and India. Among the resolutions passed at the Conference was one which defined the mutual position and relation of Great Britain and the Dominions. It stated:

They [Dominions] are autonomous communities within the British Empire, equal in status, in no way subordinate one to another in any respect of their domestic or external affairs, though united by a common allegiance to the Crown, and freely associated as members of the British Commonwealth of Nations.

It was recognised at the Conference that every self-governing member of the Empire was the master of its own destiny and that in fact, if not always in form, it was subject to no compulsion whatever. Regarding the position of the Governor-General it was declared:

In our opinion it is an essential consequence of the equality of status existing among the members of the British Commonwealth of Nations that the Governor-General of a Dominion is the representative of the Crown holding in all essential respects the same position in relation to the administration of public affairs in the Dominion as is held by His Majesty the King in Great Britain, and that he is not the representative or agent of His Majesty's Government in Great Britain or of any Department of that Government.

The attention of the Conference was also called to various points in connection with the operation of the Dominion Legislation which, it was suggested, required clarification, the particular points involved being:

(i) the practice under which Acts of the Dominion Parliaments were sent each year to London, and it was intimated, through the Secretary of State for Dominion Affairs, that 'His Majesty will not be advised to exercise his powers of disallowance' with regard to them;

(ii) the reservation of Dominion legislation, in certain circumstances, for the signification of His Majesty's pleasure which was signified on advice tendered by His Majesty's Government in Great Britain;

(iii) the difference between the legislative competence of the Parliament at Westminster and of the Dominion Parliament in that Acts passed by the latter operated, as a general rule, only within the territorial area of the Dominion concerned; and

(iv) the operation of legislation passed by the Parliament at Westminster in relation to the Dominions. In this connection special attention was called to such statutes as the Colonial Laws Validity Act. It was suggested that in future uniformity of legislation as between Great Britain and the Dominions could best be secured by the enactment of reciprocal statutes based upon consultation and agreement.

The Conference gave to these matters the best consideration possible but came to the conclusion that the issues involved were so complex that there would be grave danger in attempting any immediate pronouncement other than a statement of certain principles which underlay the whole question of the operation of the Dominion Legislation. It felt that for the rest it would be necessary to obtain expert guidance as preliminary to further consideration by the Governments in Great Britain and the Dominions. With regard to the disallowance and reservation of Dominion Legislation the Conference placed on record that, apart from the provisions embodied in the Constitutions or in specific statutes expressly providing for reservation, it was recognised that it was the right of the Government of each Dominion to advise the Crown in all matters relating to its own affairs. Secondly, that it would not be in accordance with constitutional practice that any advice should be tendered to His Majesty by His Majesty's Government in Great Britain in any matter appertaining to the affairs of the Dominion against the view of the Government of that Dominion.

On the question raised with regard to the legislative competence of members of the British Commonwealth of Nations other than Great Britain and in particular to the disability of those members to legislate with extra-territorial operation, the Conference thought that it should similarly be placed on record that the constitutional practice was that legislation by the Parliament at Westminster applying to a Dominion would only be passed with the consent of the Dominion concerned. The Conference recommended that steps should be taken by Great Britain and the Dominions to set up a committee to enquire into, report upon, and make recommendations concerning:

(i) the statutory provisions requiring reservation of Dominion Legislation for the assent of His Majesty or authorising the disallowance of such legislation;

(ii) (*a*) the position as to the competence of Dominion Parliaments to give their legislation extra-territorial operation;

(*b*) the practicability and most convenient method of giving effect to the principle that each Dominion Parliament should have power to give extra-territorial operation to its legislation in all cases where such operation is ancillary to provision for the peace, order and good government of the Dominion;

(iii) the principles embodied in or underlying the Colonial Laws Validity Act, 1869, and the extent to which any provisions of that Act ought to be repealed, amended, or modified in the light of the relations between the various members of the British Commonwealth of Nations.

At the Imperial Conference of 1930 the report of the Conference of 1929 on the operation of the Dominion legislation was considered and it was recommended that a statute be passed by the Parliament at Westminster embodying certain specific provisions. Accordingly in 1931 there was passed by the Parliament of the United Kingdom a statute called the Statute of Westminster which gave effect to the resolutions of the Imperial Conference of 1930. This Statute referred to the declarations and resolutions set forth in the report of the Imperial Conferences held in 1926 and 1930, and attended by the delegates of the Government in the United Kingdom, the Dominion of Canada, the Commonwealth of Australia, the Dominion of New Zealand, the Union of South Africa, the Irish Free State and Newfoundland, and considered it to be meet and proper to set out by way of Preamble that the Crown is the symbol of the free association of the members of the British Commonwealth of Nations, and that as they were united by a common allegiance to the Crown it would be in accordance with established constitutional position of all the members of the Commonwealth in relation to one another that any alteration in the law touching the succession to the throne or the Royal Style and Titles shall hereafter require the assent as well of the Parliaments of all the Dominions as of the Parliament of the United Kingdom, and enacted the resolutions of the Imperial Conferences in twelve sections. Section 2 of that Act declared that the Colonial Laws Validity Act, 1865, was not to apply to any law made after the commencement of the Act by the Parliament of a Dominion, that no law and no provision of any law made after the commencement of the Act by the Parliament of a Dominion shall be void or inoperative on the ground that it was repugnant to the law of England or to the provisions of any existing or future Act of the Parliament of the United Kingdom or to any order, rule or regulation made under any such Act and that the powers of the Parliament of a Dominion shall include the power to repeal or amend any such Act, order, rule or regulation in so far as the same was a part of the law of the Dominion. The Colonial Laws Validity Act which was declared by the Act not to be applicable to any law made by the Parliament of a Dominion had declared in section 2 that any Colonial Law which was or shall be in any respect repugnant to the provisions of any Act of Parliament extending to the colonies to which such law may relate or repugnant to any order or regulation made under the authority of such Act of Parliament, or having in the colony the force or effect of such Act, shall be read subject to such Act, order or regulation, and shall, to the extent of such repugnancy, but not otherwise, be and remain absolutely void and ineffective. Section 3 of the Statute gave to the Parliament of a Dominion full powers to make laws having extra-territorial operation. Section 4 declared that no Act of Parliament of the United Kingdom passed after the commencement of the Act should extend, or be deemed to extend, to a Dominion as part of the law of that Dominion unless it was expressly declared in that Act that that Dominion had requested, and consented to, the enactment thereof. Section 5 dealt with the powers of the Dominion Parliaments in relation to merchant shipping and section 6 with their powers in relation to Courts of Admiralty. Sections 7 and 8 enacted that nothing in the Act was to be deemed to apply to the repeal, amendment or alteration of the Constitutions of the Dominion of Canada, the Commonwealth of Australia and New Zealand or the distribution of legislative powers between the Parliament of Canada and the legislatures of the Provinces of that Dominion.

Some important constitutional practices which had been firmly established between the Dominions and the United Kingdom before the passing of the Statute of Westminster have to be fully understood with a view to appreciating the constitutional position existing at the time of the passing of that Statute. The first of these relates to the position of the Governor-General. Originally under the Constitution Acts of the Dominions the Governor-

General had substantial powers of interference in the administration of the Dominion. He was not a representative of the Dominion but a person appointed by the British Government who was responsible to that Government. Under the constitution he exercised his powers of control by withholding his assent from and reservation of bills or by dissolving the legislature, powers which were expressly vested in him. These powers could be exercised by him even in opposition to the advice of the Ministry. But by 1926, when the Imperial Conference met in London, his position had become that of a constitutional Governor-General; he had ceased to be an agent of the British Government and become a representative of the King, exercising in relation to the affairs of the Dominion the same powers as were exercised by the King in the United Kingdom. In other words, the principle of ministerial responsibility had been firmly established in the Dominions. This constitutional position was affirmed by the ruling of 3 December 1925, in the New South Wales constitutional crisis of 1926 when in reply to a request for instructions regarding some appointments to the Legislative Council, Mr Amery, the Secretary of State, informed the Governor that 'established constitutional principles require that the question should be settled between the Governor and the Ministry. Consequently I do not feel able to give you [i.e. the Governor] any instruction'. He re-affirmed this attitude in the House of Commons on 15 March 1926, and said:

Since there seems to be some misconception as to the position of the Secretary of State in relation to matters of this kind, I should like to take this opportunity of making it clear that, in my view, it would not be proper for the Secretary of State to issue instructions to the Governor with regard to the exercise of his constitutional duties.

Stating his final conclusion on the issue, which was conveyed by his letter, dated 14 July 1926, to the Attorney-General, he said that if Ministers at home purported to intervene in the internal affairs of New South Wales, that would be wholly incompatible with the status of New South Wales within the Empire, and that the matter in dispute as to the Legislative Council appointments was essentially one to be settled in New South Wales, and not in London (pp. 127 and 128 of Evatt's *The King and his Dominion Governors*, 1936 ed.).

After the post-Statute-of-Westminster controversy between Sir Philip Game and the Lang Ministry of New South Wales in 1932, Sir Alexander Hore-Ruthven, Sir Philip Game's successor, announced on his arrival that 'The Governor can advise his advisers. He can suggest. He can warn. But as long as Ministers are chosen representatives of the people, he must defer to their advice and assist them to the best of his ability in their deliberations, no matter what may be his private view or personal conviction' (Evatt, *The King and his Dominion Governors*, p. 152). These are only two of the several incidents in the history of Dominion Government which confirm the principle that the position of a Governor-General or a Governor *qua* a Dominion Government is precisely the same as that of the British Monarch *qua* the Government in London.

A much more important constitutional incident of the office of the Governor-General is that his appointment and dismissal actually rest with the Dominion Government and not with the Home Government, and that if he ever comes in conflict with the Government of the Dominion, that Government can successfully insist on his recall by the King. Speaking generally, he has ceased to possess the right of exercising the reserve powers of the King against the wishes of the Dominion Government. Stating the position as it exists after the Imperial Conferences of 1926 and 1930, Evatt at pp. 192 and 193 of his book *The King and his Dominion Governors* says:

Other aspects of these decisive declarations are of supreme importance, but, for present purposes, it has to be noted that the decisions of the two Conferences assert the general principle that the King proceeds upon the advice of responsible Ministers. Moreover, the general doctrine of Ministerial responsibility in its application to the affairs of a Dominion does not except from its operation, but definitely includes, the appointment of the King's representative therein. Such matter thus becomes a Dominion affair, and a very important and vital one. . . . The declarations of 1926 and 1930, despite their great significance in other respects, do not contain any final solution of the various problems of the reserve power, although it is recognised that the general principle of ministerial responsibility (illustrated by the Harcourt decision in the Tasmanian case of 1914) governs the actions of the King and Governors-General alike; and also that in the appointment of the latter the relevant Ministers are those of the Dominion concerned.

And Jenks states at p. 21 of the *Cambridge Law Journal* (1927), vol. III :

Who then is to advise the King upon the appointment of the Governor-General, say, of Canada, Australia, or New Zealand? The answer (I may be wrong) seems as a matter of principle to me to be reasonably plain, namely, that, just as the King in matters affecting the United Kingdom takes the advice of his Prime Minister in London, so in matters affecting Canada he will take the advice of his Prime Minister in the Dominion, and in the case of Australia that of his Prime Minister in the Commonwealth of Australia, and so forth. And I see no difficulty in applying the principle in that way.

Resuming the discussion at p. 196 of his book Evatt again says :

For paragraph VI of the Report of the 1930 Conference certainly secures to the Dominion Ministers direct access to the King himself for the purpose of the King's acting on their advice in relation to the appointment of the Governor-General, His Majesty's Government in Great Britain being neither interested nor concerned in such appointments. And the new method of appointing the Governor-General, exclusively upon the advice of Dominion Ministers, has been adopted in appointments since 1930.

The Strickland-Holman controversy of 1916 which resulted in the recall of Sir Gerald Strickland, the Governor of New South Wales, in something like disgrace is a very apt illustration of the power of the Dominion Government to insist on the recall of a Governor who does not act according to the advice of the Ministry. The implications of the Imperial Conference Resolutions and Declarations are thus stated by Evatt:

Now Jenks's logical inference from the 1926 Report, that the *appointment* of a Governor-General is exclusively a matter of Dominion concern, seems to justify the further inference—equally logical—that the *termination* of the appointment of a Governor-General is also a matter exclusively of local or Dominion concern. So far as the position of strict law is concerned, it is well-established that, in the absence of a controlling Statute, a person holding such a position as that of Governor or Governor-General holds it at the pleasure of the Crown. It would seem, therefore, that Dominion Ministers must possess sufficient constitutional authority to approach His Majesty directly, i.e. without any intervention by Ministers in Britain, for the purpose of advising the King that the appointment of the Governor-General should be terminated. This course was apparently the procedure adopted when the de Valera Government of the Irish Free State secured the termination of Mr McNeill's appointment as Governor-General in the year 1932 (*The King and his Dominion Governors*, p. 197).

Under the Constitutions of the Dominions the Governor-General had the power of withholding his assent from bills or reserving them for the signification of His Majesty's pleasure. But before the Imperial Conference of 1926 he had ceased to exercise these powers in opposition to the wishes of the Dominion Government, unless under some Act of the British Parliament he was bound to reserve a particular bill for the signification of His Majesty's pleasure. This was in consonance with the principle of ministerial responsibility, according to which his discretionary powers in all matters were to be exercised in accordance with the advice of the Dominion Ministry. His position had, therefore, become precisely that of a constitutional monarch in the United Kingdom, and this was recognised by the representatives of the United Kingdom who took part in the deliberations of the Imperial Conferences in 1926 and 1930. The resolutions of those Conferences relating to the position of the Dominions and the powers of the Governor-General were therefore a factual statement of the constitutional position. In fact, the position was so clearly understood by all concerned that the Statute of Westminster said nothing about it and took for granted the well recognised convention that the Governor-General was not in a position effectively to interfere with the administration of a Dominion contrary to the wishes of that Dominion. Thus, at the time the Statute of Westminster was passed there were only a few legal restrictions on the legislative sovereignty of the Dominion Parliaments. They could not pass laws having extra-territorial operations; any Dominion laws which were repugnant to the law of England were invalid; and the United Kingdom Parliament could still legislate for those Dominions. All these restrictions were removed by the Statute of Westminster.

Pre-independence India   Nowhere else is the common law principle that the acquisition of political power in a foreign land accrues for the benefit of the Crown better illustrated than by the history of the Government of India. By the Charter of A.D. 1600 granted to it by Queen Elizabeth, the East India Company was authorised to make reasonable laws, constitutions, orders and ordinances, not repugnant to English Law, for the good government of the Company and the management of its affairs. But when consequent on the grant of the 'Diwani' to the Company by the helpless Moghal Emperor, Shah Alam, on 12 August 1765, persistent scandals relating to the conduct of the officers of the Company began to reach England, the British Parliament stepped in and claiming the right to interfere with the exercise of political powers by the Company passed the Regulating Act of 1773. The subsequent Acts, namely, the Amending Act of 1781, Pitt's India Act of 1784, the Act of 1793, the Charter Acts of 1830 and 1833 and the Act of 1854, were all based on the claim that the Company held the Indian territories in trust for the Crown. By the Charter Act of 1858, the British Crown formally assumed responsibility for the Government of India and Lord Canning came to India as the first Viceroy and Governor-General. Eighteen years later Queen Victoria assumed the title of 'Empress of India' by the Royal Titles Act of 1876. This addition to the Royal Titles was indicative of the sovereignty of the Crown in India. The controversy between the Viceroy, Lord Northbrook, and the Secretary of State, Lord Salisbury, during Disraeli's Ministry resulted in an emphatic pronouncement by the latter that it was 'not open to question that Her Majesty's Government are as much responsible to the Parliament for the Government of India as they are for any of the Crown Colonies of the Empire', and section 33 of the Government of India Act, 1915, imposed upon the Governor-General in Council a constitutional obligation of paying true obedience to all such orders as he received from the Secretary of State, thus securing the supervision of British Parliament over Indian affairs.

The element of responsible government in the government of India was first introduced by the Act of 1919, which was passed on the recommendations contained in the Montague-Chelmsford Report. This Act introduced in the sphere of Provincial Government the system of Diarchy which was based on the principle that Ministers, without being answerable for the Reserved Departments or for the policy on the reserved side, were jointly responsible to the popularly elected legislature in respect of the Transferred Departments. The system was extended by the Act of 1935, so as to cover, with some important exceptions, the whole field of government. But though the element of responsibility had been considerably enlarged, the basic constitutional position still was that the ultimate responsibility for the administration of Indian affairs still vested in the United Kingdom Government. As the Indian Independence Act, 1947, brought about a complete change in the government and transferred all responsibility for the government of the Indo-Pakistan sub-continent to the two new Dominions, it is necessary to have a thorough grasp of the main principle which underlay the Act of 1935 in order to be able to appreciate the fundamental change that was effected by the Act of 1947.

Government of India Act, 1935

Section 2 of the Act of 1935 asserted that all rights, authority and jurisdiction heretofore belonging to His Majesty the King, Emperor of India, which appertained and were incidental to the government of the territories in India for the time being vested in him, and all rights, authority and jurisdiction exercisable by him in or in relation to any other territories in India, were exercisable by His Majesty, except in so far as it was otherwise provided by or under the Act, or as it was otherwise directed by His Majesty, provided that any powers connected with the exercise of the functions of the Crown in its relation with the Indian States was, if not exercised by His Majesty, to be exercised only by, or by persons acting under the authority of, His Majesty's representative for the exercise of those functions of the Crown. The said rights, authority and jurisdiction were to include any rights, authority or jurisdiction heretofore exercisable in, or in relation to, any territories in India by the Secretary of State, the Secretary of State-in-Council, the Governor-General, the Governor-General-in-Council, any Governor or any local Government, whether by any delegation from His Majesty or otherwise. Sections 5 and 6 of the Act contained provisions for the establishment of a Federation and the accession of the Indian States to that Federation. Section 8 defined the extent of the executive authority of the Federation and section 9 provided for the administration of the Federal affairs. The Council of Ministers to be set up under sub-section (1) of section 9 was to aid and advise the Governor-General in the exercise of his functions, except in so far as he was required by the Act to exercise those functions or any of them in his discretion and the proviso to the sub-section stated that nothing in that sub-section was to be construed as preventing the

102

Governor-General from exercising his individual judgment in any case whereby or under the Act he was required so to do. Subsection (3) of that section declared that if any question arose whether any matter was or was not a matter as respects which the Governor-General was under the Act required to act in his discretion or to exercise his individual judgment, the decision of the Governor-General in his discretion would be final and that the validity of anything done by the Governor-General was not to be called in question on the ground that he ought or ought not to have acted in his discretion or exercised his individual judgment. Under section 10 the Ministers were to be chosen or dismissed by the Governor-General in his discretion. Section 11 enumerated some of the functions of the Governor-General which were to be exercised by him in his discretion, while section 12 defined his special responsibilities in the discharge of which he was to exercise his individual judgment. Under section 13 the Secretary of State was, with the approval of Parliament, to issue an instrument of instructions to the Governor-General but the validity of anything done by the Governor-General was not to be called in question on the ground that it was done otherwise than in accordance with that instrument. Where the Governor-General acted in his discretion or in exercise of his individual judgment, he was placed by section 14 under the general control of the Secretary of State. Chapter III made provision for a Federal Legislature. The Governor-General had the power to summon, prorogue and dissolve the House of Assembly, one of the three constituents of the Federal Legislature. When a bill was passed by the chambers (the Council of State and the House of Assembly) it had to be presented to the Governor-General who was in his discretion to declare either that he assented in His Majesty's name to the bill or that he withheld assent therefrom or that he reserved the bill for the signification of His Majesty's pleasure, and a bill was not to become an Act unless and until within twelve months from the date on which it was presented to the Governor-General, he made known by public notification that His Majesty had assented thereto. An Act assented to by the Governor-General could be disallowed by His Majesty within twelve months from the date of the Governor-General's assent.

Under sections 42 and 43 the Governor-General had the power

to promulgate ordinances during the recess of the legislature, and with respect to certain subjects at any time. In any such case he acted either in his discretion or in exercise of his individual judgment. He could also enact Acts in relation to matters in which he was required to act in his discretion or in exercise of his individual judgment. By section 45 he had the power to assume to himself all or any of the powers vested in or exercisable by any Federal body or authority if he was satisfied that a situation had arisen in which the government of the Federation could not be carried on in accordance with the provisions of the Act, and in this matter he was to act in his discretion.

The position in the Provinces was similar to that at the Centre. The Governor was appointed, like the Governor-General, by His Majesty by a Commission under the Royal Sign Manual. He was also to have a Council of Ministers and in certain specified matters was required to act in his discretion or in exercise of his individual judgment, and when so acting he was subject to the general control of the Governor-General. He had the power to summon, prorogue or dissolve the Assembly. He could withhold assent to bills of the Provincial Legislature or reserve them for the consideration of the Governor-General, who could either assent to the bill or withhold his assent therefrom or reserve it for the signification of His Majesty's pleasure thereon. Apart from this, His Majesty had the power to disallow Acts passed by the Provincial Legislature. The Governor could either in his discretion or in exercise of his individual judgment promulgate ordinances during the recess of the legislature, and with respect to certain subjects at any time. He could also enact Acts concerning matters which were within his discretion or his individual judgment. If at any time he was satisfied that a situation had arisen in which the government of the Province could not be carried on in accordance with the provisions of the Act, he could by proclamation assume to himself all or any of the powers vested in or exercisable by any Provincial body or authority.

As the scheme underlying the Government of India Act was that of a federal pattern of government, the Act had defined in List I matters with respect to which the Federal Legislature could make laws, in List II matters with respect to which the Provincial Legislature could make laws and in List III matters in which the

Federation and the provinces, subject to certain restrictions, were both competent to make laws. Residual powers were to be assigned by the Governor-General to the Federal Legislature or to the Provincial Legislature by public notification. In the cases specified in section 99, the Federal Legislature could make laws having extra-territorial operation.

Under section 108, unless the Governor-General in his discretion thought fit to give his previous sanction, no bill or amendment could be introduced into or moved in either Chamber of the Federal Legislature which *inter alia*: (*a*) repealed, amended or was repugnant to any provision of any Act of Parliament extending to British India; (*b*) repealed, amended or was repugnant to any Governor-General's or Governor's Act or any ordinance promulgated in his discretion by the Governor-General or a Governor; and (*c*) affected matters as respects which the Governor-General was required by the Act to act in his discretion. There were similar restrictions on the chambers of the Provincial Legislature.

Section 110 enacted that nothing in the Act was to be taken to affect the power of Parliament to legislate for any part of British India; or to empower the Federal Legislature or any Provincial Legislature to make any law affecting the Sovereign or the Royal family or the sovereignty, dominion or suzerainty of the Crown in any part of India or the law of British nationality; or to make any law amending any provision of the Act.

Under section 91 His Majesty could at any time by Order-in-Council direct that a specified area shall be an excluded area or partially excluded area and on such direction no Act of the Federal Legislature or the Provincial Legislature was to apply to it unless the Governor by public notification so directed in his discretion.

To summarise, the position under the Act of 1935 was that, though in matters in which the Governor-General was not empowered to act in his discretion or in exercise of his individual judgment, the Ministers could take action, which as a matter of convention was not to be questioned by the Governor-General, there still remained a large sphere of action in which either the Governor-General did not consult the Ministers or he was not bound by their advice. In matters lying within that sphere he was responsible solely to the British Government through the Secretary of State. Though he was appointed by the King, he was a nominee of the British Government and subject to the control of the Secretary of State who was one of the members of the British Cabinet, which was ultimately responsible to Parliament for the government of India. The Indian Legislature was not a sovereign legislature and limitations on its powers were not only imposed by the Act but the Governor-General could withhold assent to its legislation. It was wholly incompetent to legislate on certain matters, and the United Kingdom Parliament had not only full authority specifically to legislate for British India but the laws made by that Parliament could extend to British India. It was in fact in exercise of this legislative sovereignty that the Indian Independence Act was passed. These restrictions on legislation and the external control on government had, therefore, to be removed if India was to become independent.

Now for a country to be independent it is necessary—

(i) that it should have a legislature with authority to legislate on all matters without any restriction, including matters relating to the making of a constitution;

(ii) no law made by it should be invalid by reason of its being repugnant to the law of any other country;

(iii) no other country should have any authority to legislate for it and no law made by any other country should extend to it;

(iv) its Government should be responsible only to its own people or to itself and not to any outside authority;

(v) if independence is to be granted by the law of a dominant country, that law must provide for the freed country a provisional constitution including a sovereign legislature and a Government so that the withdrawal of control may not be followed by chaos and confusion, and if the constitution with which the freed country starts its independence is a federal constitution, the legislature of the country must accept limitations on its powers if it has also to function as the federal legislature.

Limitations on the sovereignty of a legislature can be imposed by itself as well as by an external authority if it is the creation of such authority. Thus the dominant country, which grants the constitution of an independent country to a dominated country, can by that constitution impose limitations on the powers of the legislature of the independent country, provided it also leaves powers to that legislature to remove those limitations. Limitations on the powers of a legislature may also be imposed by itself, as for instance, where it has defined fundamental rights or has converted itself into a federal legislature with defined powers. Even in the case of a country with a unitary constitution, its legislature may impose future limitations on its power if it precludes itself from legislating on defined subjects or from making certain laws.

It is in the light of these principles that the Indian Independence Act has to be examined when it came into force on the midnight of 14 August 1947. The principles mentioned above underlie the whole scheme of that Act whose true scope and significance can be understood and appreciated only if those principles are borne in mind. The scheme of that Act for our present purposes will be apparent from the following sections of the Act:

The Governor-General of the new Dominions

5 For each of the new Dominions, there shall be a Governor-General who shall be appointed by His Majesty and shall represent His Majesty for the purposes of the government of the Dominion:

Legislation for the new Dominions

6 (1) The Legislature of each of the new Dominions shall have full power to make laws for that Dominion, including laws having extra-territorial operation.

(2) No law and no provision of any law made by the Legislature of either of the new Dominions shall be void or inoperative on the ground that it is repugnant to the law of England, or to the provisions of this or any existing or future Act of Parliament of the United Kingdom or to any order, rule or regulation made under any such Act, and the powers of the Legislature of each Dominion include the power to repeal or amend any such Act, order, rule or regulation in so far as it is part of the law of the Dominion.

(3) The Governor-General of each of the new Dominions shall have full power to assent to any law of the Legislature of that Dominion and so much of any Act as relates to the disallowance of laws by His Majesty or the reservation of laws for the signification of His Majesty's pleasure thereon or the suspension of the operation of laws until the signification of His Majesty's pleasure thereon shall not apply to laws of the Legislature of either of the new Dominions.

(4) No Act of Parliament of the United Kingdom passed on or after the appointed day shall extend, or be deemed to extend, to either of the new Dominions as part of the law of that Dominion unless it is extended thereto by a law of the Legislature of the Dominion.

(5) No Order in Council made on or after the appointed day under

any Act passed before the appointed day, and no order, rule or other instrument made on or after the appointed day under any such Act by any United Kingdom Minister or other authority, shall extend, or be deemed to extend, to either of the new Dominions as part of the law of that Dominion.

(6) The power referred to in sub-section (1) of this section extends to the making of laws limiting for the future the powers of the Legislature of the Dominion.

Consequences of the setting up of the new Dominions

7 (1) As from the appointed day

(a) His Majesty's Government in the United Kingdom have no responsibility as respects the government of any of the territories which, immediately before that day, were included in British India;

(b) the suzerainty of His Majesty over the Indian States lapses, and with it, all treaties and agreements in force at the date of the passing of this Act between His Majesty and the rulers of Indian States, all functions exercisable by His Majesty at that date with respect to Indian States, all obligations of His Majesty existing at that date towards Indian States or the rulers thereof, and all powers, rights, authority or jurisdiction exercisable by His Majesty at that date in or in relation to Indian States by treaty, grant, usage, sufferance or otherwise; and

(c) there lapse also any treaties or agreements in force at the date of the passing of this Act between His Majesty and any persons having authority in the tribal areas, any obligations of His Majesty existing at that date to any such persons or with respect to the tribal areas, and all powers, rights, authority or jurisdiction exercisable at that date by His Majesty in or in relation to the tribal areas by treaty, grant, usage, sufferance or otherwise:

Provided that, notwithstanding anything in paragraph (b) or paragraph (c) of this sub-section, effect shall, as nearly as may be, continue to be given to the provisions of any such agreement as is therein referred to which relate to customs, transit, and communications, posts and telegraphs, or other like matters, until the provisions in question are denounced by the ruler of the Indian State or person having authority in the tribal areas on the one hand, or by the Dominion or Province or other part thereof concerned on the other hand, or are superseded by subsequent agreements.

(2) The assent of the Parliament of the United Kingdom is hereby given to the omission from the Royal Style and Titles of the words 'Indiæ Imperator' and the words 'Emperor of India' and to the issue by His Majesty for that purpose of His Royal Proclamation under the Great Seal of the Realm.

Temporary provision as to government of each of the new Dominions

8 (1) In the case of each of the new Dominions, the powers of the Legislature of the Dominion shall, for the purpose of making provision as to the constitution of the Dominion, be exercisable in the first instance by the Constituent Assembly of that Dominion, and references in this Act to the Legislature of the Dominion shall be construed accordingly.

(2) Except in so far as other provision is made by or in accordance with a law made by the Constituent Assembly of the Dominion under sub-section (1) of this section, each of the new Dominions and all Provinces and other parts thereof shall be governed as nearly as may be in accordance with the Government of India Act, 1935; and the provisions of that Act, and of the Orders in Council, rules and other instruments made thereunder, shall, so far as applicable, and subject to any express provisions of this Act, and with such omissions, additions, adaptations and modifications as may be specified in orders of the Governor-General, under the next succeeding section, have effect accordingly:

Provided that

(*a*) the said provisions shall apply separately in relation to each of the new Dominions and nothing in this sub-section shall be construed as continuing on or after the appointed day any Central Government or Legislature common to both the new Dominions;

(*b*) nothing in this sub-section shall be construed as continuing in force on or after the appointed day any form of control by His Majesty's Government in the United Kingdom over the affairs of the new Dominions or of any Province or other part thereof;

(*c*) so much of the said provisions as requires the Governor-General or any Governor to act in his discretion or exercise his individual judgment as respects any matter shall cease to have effect as from the appointed day;

(*d*) as from the appointed day, no Provincial Bill shall be reserved under the Government of India Act, 1935, for the signification of His Majesty's pleasure, and no Provincial Act shall be disallowed by His Majesty thereunder; and

(*e*) the powers of the Federal Legislature or Indian Legislature under that Act, as in force in relation to each Dominion, shall, in the first instance, be exercisable by the Constituent Assembly of the Dominion in addition to the powers exercisable by that Assembly under sub-section (1) of this section.

(3) Any provision of the Government of India Act, 1935, which, as applied to either of the new Dominions by sub-section (2) of this section and the orders therein referred to, operates to limit the power of the legislature of that Dominion shall, unless and until other provision is made by or in accordance with a law made by the Constituent

Assembly of the Dominion in accordance with the provisions of sub-section (1) of this section, have the like effect as a law of the Legislature of the Dominion limiting for the future the powers of that Legislature.

Orders for bringing this Act into force

9 (1) The Governor-General shall by order make such provision as appears to him to be necessary or expedient—

· · ·   · · ·   · · ·

(*c*) for making omissions from, additions to, and adaptations and modifications of, the Government of India Act, 1935, and the Orders in Council, rules and other instruments made thereunder, in their application to the separate new Dominions.

Interpretations, etc.

19 (3) References in this Act to the Constituent Assembly of a Dominion shall be construed as references

· · ·   · · ·   · · ·

(*b*) in relation to Pakistan, to the Assembly set up or about to be set up at the date of the passing of this Act under the authority of the Governor-General as the Constituent Assembly for Pakistan:

Provided that nothing in this sub-section shall be construed as affecting the extent to which representatives of the Indian States take part in either of the said Assemblies, or as preventing the filling of casual vacancies in the said Assemblies, or as preventing the participation in either of the said Assemblies in accordance with such arrangements as may be made in that behalf of representatives of the tribal areas on the borders of the Dominion for which that Assembly sits, and the powers of the said Assemblies shall extend, and be deemed always to have extended, to the making of provision for the matters specified in this proviso.

Thus by section 1 Pakistan became an independent Dominion. Because it became a Dominion, it had to be connected by a legal link with the United Kingdom and the other Dominions. Section 5, therefore, provided that there shall be for the Dominion a Governor-General, who shall be appointed by His Majesty and who shall represent His Majesty for the purposes of the government of the Dominion. And because the status of Pakistan was that of an independent Dominion, its legislature should possess full power to make laws for that Dominion, including laws having extra-territorial operation, laws limiting for the future the powers of the Legislature of the Dominion, and laws making provision for its constitution. None of its laws should be void on the ground that it is repugnant to the past or future laws of another country; and it should have full power to alter any provision of the provisional constitution with which it started. There must also exist in that Dominion an authority competent to give assent to its laws and no law of the dominant country relating to disallowance, suspension or reservation of laws should be applicable to it. Nor should any law of the dominant country passed after the attainment of independence be applicable to it. These propositions were all recognised by section 6 of the Indian Independence Act which followed closely the scheme of the Statute of Westminster, sub-section (1) of the former corresponding to section 3 of the latter, sub-section (2) to sub-section (2) of section 2, sub-section (3) to sections 5 and 6, sub-section (4) to section 4 and sub-section (6) to sections 7 and 8. Thus section 6 of the Act of 1947 practically adopted every important provision of the Statute of Westminster. This section is the most important section in the Act because it gives to the Legislature of the Dominion full power to make any law that it likes, including laws making provision for the constitution, because laws having extra-territorial operation which this section mentions as being within the competence of the Legislature of the Dominion are often constitutional laws while laws repugnant to or repealing or amending the Government of India Act, 1935, or the Indian Independence Act itself, which are mentioned in sub-section (2) and laws limiting for the future the powers of the Legislature of the Dominion are necessarily constitutional laws. The words of the first sub-section 'the Legislature of each of the new Dominions shall have full power to make laws for that Dominion' are thus wide enough to include laws of every description. The exact meaning of the words 'Legislature of the Dominion' that occur in this section in several places has been the subject-matter of some discussion before us, counsel for the respondent contending that these words are used in the Act in several different senses. Any such possibility would, in my opinion, entirely take away the artistic value and destroy the underlying scheme of the Act, leaving it a jumble of confused ideas and full of inconsistencies and contradictions. Thus Mr Chundrigar's contention that the words 'Legislature of that Dominion' and 'Legislature of either of the new Dominions' that occur in sub-section (3) refer only to the Federal Legislature and not to the Legislature of the Dominion which is mentioned in sub-section (1) is entirely devoid of substance because, as I have pointed out, the laws which the Legislature of the Dominion may make include in three places expressly and in the whole of the section by necessary implication what are essentially constitutional laws. There can be no difficulty in understanding this section if it be borne in mind that the words 'Legislature of the Dominion' are used in this section to indicate the future Legislature which was to make all laws for the Dominion. When the Act was passed, the Legislature of the Dominion was an abstract conception which was to be applicable to the future sovereign Legislature of the Dominion, including the Legislature that came into existence on 15 August 1947, without any limitations on its power. The section is a power-giving section and must be read as such to be intelligible in all its implications. The power to make all laws was given to the Legislature of the Dominion while the power to give assent to those laws was given to the Governor-General, who thus became a constituent part of the legislature and was to occupy the same position as the Sovereign in the United Kingdom in respect of the prerogative of giving or withholding assent.

The next important provision in the Act is section 8 which makes temporary provision as to the government of each of the new Dominions. The first sub-section of that section provides that in the case of each of the new Dominions the powers of the Legislature of the Dominions shall, for the purpose of making provision as to the constitution of the Dominion, be exercisable, in the first instance, by the Constituent Assembly of that Dominion and that references in the Act to the Legislature of the Dominion shall be construed accordingly. The important point to remember about this sub-section is that it refers to the powers of the Legislature of the Dominion which had been defined in section 6 and which included the power to make constitutional laws. The sub-section, however, provides that so far as the powers for the purpose of making provision as to the Constitution of the Dominion are concerned, they shall be exercisable in the first instance by the Constituent Assembly which for the purposes of the Act shall be construed to be the first Legislature of the Dominion. The sub-section is a machinery provision as the words in the marginal note

112

to the section 'temporary provision as to government of each of the new Dominions' show and not a power-giving provision except in so far as it states that immediately on coming into force of the Act the Constituent Assembly shall, in the first instance, exercise the powers of the Legislature of the Dominion. Another important point not to be overlooked in construing sub-section (1) of section 8 is that the Constituent Assembly can make a provision as to the constitution of the Dominion only by 'law'. This is clear from the second sub-section which says that the dominion shall be governed in accordance with the Government of India Act, 1935, 'except in so far as other provision is made by or in accordance with a law made by the Constituent Assembly of the Dominion under sub-section (1) of this section'.

The second sub-section to section 8 also provides a provisional constitution for the new Dominions and that constitution is the Government of India Act, 1935, as adapted in exercise of the authority given to the Governor-General by section 9 of the Indian Independence Act. The sub-section has five provisos, of which proviso (c) declares that any provision of the Government of India Act which requires the Governor-General or any Governor to act in his discretion or exercise his individual judgment shall cease to have effect; and proviso (d) states that no Provincial Bill shall be reserved under the Government of India Act, 1935, for the signification of His Majesty's pleasure nor any Provincial Act disallowed by His Majesty thereunder. Both these provisos were necessary deductions from the main provision enacted in section 7, that from the appointed day His Majesty's Government in the United Kingdom shall have no responsibility as respects the government of any of the territories which immediately before that day were included in British India and from proviso (b) to sub-section (2) of section 8, that nothing in sub-section (2) shall be construed as continuing in force on or after the appointed day any form of control by His Majesty's Government in the United Kingdom over the affairs of the new Dominions or of any Province or other part thereof. The principle that His Majesty's Government in the United Kingdom had no responsibility for and had relinquished all control over the government of the Dominion made necessary the enactment of section 7 which declares that from the appointed day the suzerainty of His Majesty over the Indian

States lapses, as well as all treaties and agreements in force between His Majesty and any person having authority in the Tribal areas, and that the words 'Indiæ Imperator' and 'Emperor of India' which represented the sovereignty of the King over Indian territories shall be omitted from the Royal Style and Titles.

Under the temporary constitution provided by section 8 a Federal Legislature had to come into existence and some one from the appointed day had to exercise its functions under that constitution. Proviso (c) to sub-section (2) of section 8 therefore declares that the powers of the Federal Legislature or the Indian Legislature under the Government of India Act, 1935, as in force in relation to each of the Dominions, shall, in the first instance, be exercisable by the Constituent Assembly of the Dominion in addition to the powers exercisable by that Assembly under sub-section (1) of that section. Thus the Constituent Assembly became on 15 August 1947, not only the Legislature of the Dominion for the purposes of section 6, fully competent to make provision as to the constitution of the Dominion, but also the first Federal Legislature under the scheme outlined in the Government of India Act, 1935, which with necessary adaptation came into force on the same date. Accordingly the position of the Constituent Assembly is that it is the Legislature of the Dominion when it makes laws for the constitution of the Dominion and the Federal Legislature when it functions under the limitations imposed upon it by the Government of India Act, 1935. This position may be explained in the form of a mathematical proposition and that is this:

(i) Constituent Assembly *minus* the fetters to which it is subject as a Federal Legislature is equal to the Legislature of the Dominion; and

(ii) Constituent Assembly *plus* the fetters to which it is subject under the Government of India Act, 1935, is equal to the Federal Legislature.

This situation is clearly brought out in sub-section (3) of section 8 which says that any provision of the Government of India Act, 1935, which, as applied to either of the new Dominions by sub-section (2), operates to limit the powers of the Legislature of that Dominion shall, unless and until other provision is made by or in accordance with a law made by the Constituent Assembly

of the Dominion in accordance with the provisions of sub-section
(1) of the section, have the like effect as a law of the Legislature
of the Dominion limiting for the future the powers of that Legislature. Thus sub-section (3) recognises the principle I have mentioned earlier that the Legislature of a Dominion may impose
limitations on it for the future. The Constituent Assembly had
under sub-section (1) of section 8 the authority to exercise all the
powers given to the Legislature of the Dominion by section 6 but
because that Assembly had also to function as the Federal Legislature, the provisions of the Government of India Act which
operated to limit the powers of the Legislature of the Dominion
were to have the same effect as a law of the Legislature of the
Dominion limiting for the future the powers of that Legislature.
In other words, the Constituent Assembly by functioning as the
Federal Legislature had by law imposed future limits on its power,
but under section 6 it had full authority to remove those fetters
from itself at any time after the midnight of 14 August 1947, and
this position was recognised expressly both by sub-section (2) and
sub-section (3) of section 8, to indicate which the former uses the
words 'excepting in so far as other provision is made by or in
accordance with a law made by the Constituent Assembly of the
Dominion', and the latter the words 'unless and until other
provision is made by or in accordance with a law made by the
Constituent Assembly of the Dominion in accordance with the
provisions of sub-section (1) of this section'. Thus Pakistan
became independent because:

(i) in law, on the midnight of 14 August 1947, if the Constituent
Assembly made a law and the Governor-General assented to it, it
could secede from the Commonwealth and become a completely
independent State, its citizens owing no allegiance to the Crown
and not being British subjects; and

(ii) it was not subject, as Canada and Australia were, to any
disability to change its constitution. It could have any constitution
or form of government it liked, having no connection with the
Commonwealth or the Crown or the Governor-General as the
representative of the Crown.

But so long as it did not secede from the Commonwealth, it was
a Dominion because:

(a) it was linked with the Commonwealth by allegiance to a
common Crown;

(*b*) its citizens were internationally British subjects;

(*c*) its laws needed the assent of His Majesty or his representative, the Governor-General;

(*d*) the King's prerogative existed here except to the extent that it was utilised by Parliament in the Indian Independence Act because the King had placed his prerogatives and interests at the disposal of Parliament only 'so far as concerned the matters dealt with by the bill'; and

(iii) it could make any law it liked, constitutional or otherwise, and no law of the dominant country was to extend to it.

Lacuna   There is, however, one obvious lacuna in the Indian Independence Act which is otherwise a masterpiece of draftsmanship—it contains no express provision as to what was to happen if the Constituent Assembly did not or was not able to make a constitution, or resigned *en bloc*, or converted itself into a perpetual legislature. It may be that any such contingency was beyond the imagination of the authors of the Act, but the more probable reason seems to be that they thought that any such contingency had ceased to be their headache and was purely a concern of the 'independent' Dominion. So long as the responsibility for the government of the country was that of the Government in London, a provision to meet such a situation appeared in the constitution, but that responsibility having been disclaimed by the Indian Independence Act, the necessity for retaining any such provision also disappeared from the constitution. If a breakdown came, it seems to have been thought, it was for the Dominion itself to reset the tumbled machinery. A third explanation has been suggested by the learned counsel for the appellants and that is that section 5, in view of its wide terms, was supposed to contain a solution of the difficulty by the exercise by the Governor-General of his prerogative powers as representative of the King.

Royal assent   We are now in a position to approach the question whether the Sind Chief Court had the jurisdiction to issue the writs in question. The point sought to be made on behalf of the appellants is that section 223A of the Government of India Act, 1935, which gives to a High Court the power to issue writs in the nature of habeas corpus, mandamus, prohibition, quo warranto and certiorari and which was inserted in that Act by the Government of India

(Amendment) Act, 1954, is not a part of the law because the amending Act did not receive the assent of the Governor-General as required by sub-section (3) of section 6 of the Indian Independence Act. The answer to the question raised depends upon the true construction of that sub-section but before I come to that it is necessary briefly to refer to the English Constitutional Law and the law in force in the Dominions on the subject.

The necessity of the King's assent to all legislation in England has its origin in a remote period in British history. Not only was kingship the great central institution around which the English constitution grew, but monarchy has always been the most deeply rooted and enduring part of that constitution and the whole course of English constitutional history is a story of the ever varying concept of the King, the Crown, the Sovereign and His or Her Majesty. Though these words often represent a political abstraction and are not necessarily significant of any judgment or discretion to be exercised by the person who for the time being happens to occupy the throne, nevertheless they hide in themselves a political doctrine of profound practical importance which must be thoroughly understood in order to comprehend the essential characteristics of democratic institution of the British pattern. Kingship was not imported in Britain from the forests of Germany but is an essentially indigenous institution which first came into importance by the domination of the Heptarchy by Wessex. The emergence of a single kingship and his 'council of wise men' called the 'Witenagemot' lies at the root of present political institutions and the theory of the Royal Prerogative. The King issued his orders with the advice of the 'witen'; his acts were limited by the customs of the people; and though he was the supreme judge, the 'witen' sat with him when he held his supreme court of justice.

Though the British people were jealous of the power of the King—and they even beheaded one—except for a few brief periods they never ceased to associate his name with legislation, however strong and independent the Parliament became. He was always an integral part of Parliament and even now the enacting part of every Act begins with the words 'Be it enacted by the Queen's most Excellent Majesty by and with the advice and consent

117

of the Lords Spiritual and Temporal, and Commons, in this present Parliament assembled, and by the authority of the same.' The power to give assent to bills or withhold it therefrom continued to remain for a long time one of the personal prerogatives of the King which he could use to veto bills passed by Parliament, and though the last exercise of this power was in the time of Queen Anne, several eminent constitutional writers referred to this reserve power of the King to control legislation as recently as 1913 in the controversy that arose over the passing of the Irish Home Rule Bill. Professor Dicey, the celebrated constitutional writer, writing to *The Times* in the course of that controversy, declined to enter on the academic inquiry whether during that political crisis the King could rightly or wisely refuse assent to the Home Rule Bill after it should for a third time have been passed by the House of Commons and rejected by the House of Lords but he agreed with the following words of Burke:

The King's negative to bills is one of the most undisputed of the royal prerogatives, and it extends to all cases whatsoever. I am far from certain that if several laws which I know had fallen under the stroke of that sceptre the public would have had a very heavy loss, but it is not the propriety of the exercise which is in question. Its repose may be the preservation of its existence and its existence might be the means of saving the constitution itself on an occasion worthy of bringing it forth.

Mr Disraeli in 1852 expressed the view that the Crown's right to refuse assent to legislation was still outstanding and was not an empty form. 'It is not difficult', he said, 'to conceive an occasion when, supported by the sympathies of a loyal people, its exercise might defeat an unconstitutional ministry and a corrupt parliament'. Frederic Austin Ogg in his *English Government and Politics* asserts that the royal assent, though given indirectly and perfunctorily, is indispensable to legislation and then reproduces the following graphic account of the ceremony from Sir Courtenay Ilbert's book *Parliament*:

The assent is given periodically to batches of bills, as they are passed, the largest batch being usually at the end of the session. The ceremonial observed dates from Plantagenet times, and takes place in the House of Lords. The King is represented by Lords Commissioners who sit in front of the throne on a row of armchairs arrayed in scarlet robes and little cocked hats. . . . At the bar of the House stands the Speaker of the House of Commons who has been summoned from that House. Behind him stand such members of the House of Commons as have followed him through the lobbies. The Clerk of the House of Lords reads out, in sonorous voice, the commission which authorizes the assent to be given. The Clerk of the Crown at one side of the table reads out the title of each bill. The Clerk of the Parliament on the other side making profound obeisances, pronounces the Norman French formula by which the King's assent is signified: Little Peddington Electricity Supply Act. Le Roy le Veult. Between the two voices six centuries lie.

Mr Chundrigar in all seriousness raised what appeared to me to be a novel contention that the royal assent is not indispensable even in United Kingdom legislation, and in this connection he drew our attention to some episodes in English history when the country had to carry on the business of legislation without a King, and referred to the following passage from Anson's *Law and Custom of the Constitution* (5th ed. p. 333):

3. We have still to consider the action of the Crown as a party to legislation, and looking back at the history of this matter, and noting, as we have had to do, the large share of legislative power which the Crown once possessed, we are apt to forget that laws have been passed to which no royal assent was given; we are apt to forget the episode of the Commonwealth; the restoration of Charles II; the resolution of the Lords and Commons that the Crown should be offered, on the abdication of James II, to William and Mary; the strange conclusion at which Lord Chancellor Thurlow arrived during the insanity of George III, in 1788, that he could put the great seal to a Royal Commission empowering him to give the royal assent to Acts of Parliament.

He, however, omitted to read the very next passage at page 334 of the book which contains the following explanation of this anomalous position:

We may leave out of consideration the make-shifts to which constitutional lawyers may be reduced when the throne is vacant or its occupant insane. All that can be done under such circumstances is to supply, as soon as may be, the deficiency in the constitution. Apart from catastrophes which need to be dealt with as may best suit the circumstances of each case, we may safely join with the second Parliament of Charles II in holding that there is no truth in the 'opinion that both Houses of Parliament, or either of them, have a legislative power without the King', an opinion the expression of which rendered its holder liable, by the same statute, to the penalties of a *præmunire*.

119

As far therefore as English law is concerned, there has never been, and cannot be any doubt that a bill cannot become a law in the absence of the royal assent, and the House of Lords case of *Stockdale* v. *Hansard*[1] expressly rules that no resolution of the House of Commons is a law unless it is passed by the other House and receives the royal assent. There is a South African case, *Ndlwana* v. *Hofmeyer*[2], commenting upon which at page lii of his Introduction to Dicey's *Law of the Constitution* Wade says:

> The Court refused to regard the procedure of section 152 as binding and held that the legislature could pass any measure by joint or separate sessions at their option; provided that the bill received the royal assent, it was binding on the Courts who would accept the King's Printer's copy as conclusive evidence.

In that case Stratford, A.C.J., had thus stated the point:

> This is not a case where one of the constituent elements of Parliament has not functioned. The contrary is clearly to be inferred from the royal assent and promulgation. A resolution of one of the Houses of Parliament is an example of such a case: it is not an Act of Parliament, and a court of law would not enforce it.

The assent of the King is also necessary to all Dominion legislation, and before their independent status was recognised by the convention of non-interference, the Governors-General of the Dominions utilised their reserve powers to withhold assent if as representatives of the British Government they thought that the legislation in question was contrary to imperial interests. A similar power rested with the Governors of colonies and possessions. But before the Imperial Conference of 1926 the Governor-General's power to veto Dominion legislation had practically fallen into disuse and its removal was not therefore insisted upon at that conference. Thus the Statute of Westminster, 1931, which recognised the independent status of certain Dominions, did not, except in relation to Merchant Shipping and Colonial Admiralty Courts, contain any provision for the removal of this legal restriction; but this was not because these restrictions were not in law limitations on their sovereignty but because they had not since long been used and it was mutually understood that they shall not in future be used. Of course under sub-section (2) of section 2 of

[1] (1839), 9 Ad. & E. 1.   [2] 1937 A. D. 229.

that Statute these limitations could be removed by the Dominion concerned because under that sub-section no law and no provision of any law made after the commencement of the Statute by the Parliament of a Dominion could be void or inoperative on the ground that it was repugnant to the law of England or to the provisions of any existing or future Act of Parliament of the United Kingdom or to any order, rule or regulation made under any such Act, and the powers of the Parliament of a Dominion were to include the power to repeal or amend any such Act, order, rule or regulation in so far as the same was a part of the law of the Dominion; and the reason that they have not yet been so removed is that in practice they had become inoperative and no Governor-General who is appointed and is liable to dismissal at the instance of the Dominion concerned can now possibly think of bringing them into use, whatever his personal view or inclination may be.

Mr Mahmud Ali was obviously labouring under some misapprehension when he attempted to apply to the present case the principle that the right to withhold assent exists only where there is a power to legislate and that where the latter does not exist the former cannot. Stated as an abstract proposition, the principle is correct but I do not see how it is applicable here. Mr Mahmud Ali read long passages from Lord Mansfield's judgment in *Campbell* v. *Hall*[1] which lays down no more than that where the King has surrendered his prerogative of legislation to a popular Assembly in a conquered country, he himself cannot legislate. That case is considered by constitutional lawyers as an authority for the deduction that freedom once granted cannot be taken back. But how can that principle be applied to the present case? The Indian Independence Act does not take away anything which had been previously granted. On the contrary, it confers full freedom on the Dominion and gives to the legislature of the Dominion powers which under the Act of 1935 it was incompetent to exercise. If Mr Mahmud Ali assumes that the Crown had parted with the power to withhold its assent to legislation in India, he is clearly mistaken because under the Act of 1935 the Governor-General and the Governors were entitled not only to give assent to bills in His Majesty's name but also to withhold assent therefrom in their discretion. It is, therefore, wholly incorrect to suppose that

[1] (1774), 20 St. Tr. 239.

the right to control legislation by withholding assent did not exist before the Indian Independence Act came into force and that that Act, if it retains the Governor-General's power to withhold assent, has the effect of taking away something which had previously been granted. The Crown is a constituent part of Parliament in the United Kingdom and of all Dominion Legislatures either because it is expressly so stated in the constitutional statutes or because the Crown appoints the Governor-General who is empowered to give or withhold assent to the legislation of the Dominion. The same was the position under the Act of 1935, where the King's representative, i.e. the Governor-General, was a part of the Federal Legislature. It is this common restriction that exists on the Dominion legislation which sub-section (3) of section 6 intended to enact when it provided that the Governor-General of the Dominion shall have full power to assent in His Majesty's name (including the power to withhold assent) to the laws of the Legislature of the Dominion.

On this part of the case Mr Chundrigar's argument was that the right to withhold assent to bills was retained in the adapted Act of 1935 because it had existed in the original Act and that it was not a necessary deduction from the provisions of sub-section (3) of section 6 of the Act of 1947; but in adopting this position he contradicted his other proposition, vehemently urged, that the right to withhold assent to bills is an arbitrary control on legislation and therefore a restriction on the legislative sovereignty of the Constituent Assembly. If the power to withhold assent derogates from the legislative supremacy of the Legislature of the Dominion, i.e. the Constituent Assembly, it is obvious that sections 32, 75 and 76 of the adapted Act of 1935 which still retain for the Governor-General the right to withhold assent are incompatible with the otherwise limited legislative sovereignty of the Federal Legislature whose powers also are exercised by that Assembly, and that such restrictions being inconsistent with the conception of full freedom could only be retained or inserted if they were authorised by and followed from the provisions of sub-section (3). The restrictions are, therefore, illustrative of the constitutional position that assent to the Dominion legislation by the Crown or its representative is indispensable and has in no instance ever been dispensed with by the Crown. Elsewhere in this judgment I have pointed out that Mr Chundrigar's contention that the right to withhold assent is an effective restriction on the legislative activity of a Dominion Parliament is wholly unfounded and that no Governor-General or Governor of a Dominion can continue to occupy his office if he does not act on the advice of the Ministry to assent to any important legislation. This is certainly the position under the adapted Government of India Act because the appointment and dismissal of the Governor-General being a matter on which the advice of the Dominion Government would invariably be accepted by the Crown, it is impossible for the Governor-General to withhold assent from a bill to which the Ministry advises him to assent. Mr Chundrigar urges that in the case of the Constituent Assembly the position is different because the Assembly has no Cabinet and no Prime Minister, but he forgets the basic position that the Constituent Assembly is also the Federal Legislature and virtually chooses a Cabinet and a Prime Minister and that in case of a difference between the Governor-General and the Constituent Assembly, the Assembly as the Federal Legislature can always have the Governor-General recalled.

Equally incorrect is the contention of Mr Chundrigar that the requirement as to assent in the other constitutions is the creation of the statutes granting those constitutions. The true position is that the provisions of those statutes relating to assent do not create in the Crown or in its representative a new right, but confirm an existing right and merely provide the manner in which that right is to be exercised. Thus if the right to withhold assent to Dominion legislation is inherent in the Crown and the statute that legislates on that right merely says that a bill after it has been passed by the popularly elected House or Houses shall be presented for assent to the Governor-General, who will give assent to that bill or withhold it therefrom, the statute does not create the right to withhold assent but merely describes the manner in which that right is to be exercised. Similarly the provisions in the Government of India Act which give to the Governor-General the right to withhold assent from legislation do not confer on, or create a new right in, the Crown; on the contrary, they implicitly recognise such right and regulate the manner in which it is to be exercised. It is for this reason that the fiction of making the Crown a constituent of the legislature is resorted to, because neither the King nor his representative, the Governor-General, is a member of the legislature like other members. The King or the Governor-General is a part of the legislature only in the sense that all bills passed by the legislature are presented to him, so that he may exercise his right of giving or withholding assent. Thus sub-section (3) of section 6 produces the same result by giving to the Governor-General full power to assent in His Majesty's name to any law of the Legislature of the Dominion. It makes the Governor-General a constituent part of the legislature inasmuch as the right to give assent necessarily includes in it the right to withhold assent. Every bill must therefore be presented to him to provide him an occasion to exercise that right, and unless a bill is so presented a constituent part of the legislature does not function and the proposed legislation does not become law. There is, therefore, no distinction between those constitutions where the Crown is a constituent part of the legislature and the Legislature of the Dominion of Pakistan whose functions are being exercised by the Constituent Assembly and to whose legislation assent is enacted by sub-section (3) of section 6 as a necessary condition.

Let us now revert to sub-section (3) of section 6, the true question on which the decision of the case depends being whether the first part of that sub-section which says that the Governor-General of each of the new Dominions shall have full power to assent in His Majesty's name to any law of the legislature of that Dominion has the effect of enacting the necessity of assent of the Governor-General to all laws made by the Legislature of that Dominion and whether the Constituent Assembly when acting under sub-section (1) of section 8 is a Legislature of the Dominion within the meaning of sub-section (3) of section 6. It should be noticed that the marginal note to section 6 is 'Legislation for the new Dominions', which means that the provisions relating to the assent of the Governor-General relate to legislation by the legislature of the Dominion. If the power to assent includes in it the legal right to withhold assent, which it does as held by Muhammad Bakhsh, J., then the sub-section must be held to mean that the Governor-General has the right to withhold assent to any law of the Legislature of the Dominion. The plain meaning of this provision is that, as representative of His or Her Majesty, the Governor-General has full power of himself giving assent to laws which otherwise, on the common law doctrine that a law made by the legislature of a Dominion is not law unless it receives the royal assent, would require the royal assent. If the law gives to a person the power to do a thing, the necessary implication is that he need not exercise that power and that he has the right of refusing to exercise such power. A power is not a duty or an obligation and it is only if the words 'shall have full power to assent' are read to mean 'shall be under an obligation to assent', that the discretion to withhold assent can disappear, though even then the legal necessity of a formal assent would remain. Mr Chundrigar has referred to section 32 of the Interpretation Act, 1889, but that section in no way supports him because it not only draws the distinction between a power and a duty but also declares that where a power is given to a person to do a certain thing, that power may be exercised from time to time. In the debates on the Indian Independence Act in the House of Commons, Mr Molson speaking on clause (d) of the proviso to sub-section (2) of section 8 suggested that under that clause instead of His Majesty disallowing legislation on the advice of the Secretary of State for India, it would under the Act be done by the Governor-General. In replying to this, the Attorney-General said:

The second point raised by the Honourable Member was in regard to the provision in clause 8 (2) (d) as to reservation. That corresponds in the case of the Provincial Legislature with the provisions under clause 6 (3) with regard to the reservation of laws passed by the Central Legislature. That was dealing with reservation until His Majesty's pleasure was known and that was a form of reservation which enabled the Governor-General to withhold assent to a Bill until His Majesty could be advised by the Government of the United Kingdom about the matter. That provision would have been a wholly inappropriate one to retain and obviously would have involved a derogation from the sovereignty we are now giving to the Dominions. No doubt, the Governor-General will provide immediately, as the eventual Constitution will have to provide that there will be some sort of power of that kind vested in the Governor-General or provided for in the provisions of the new Constitution, but that will be a matter for the new Constituent Assembly (440 *H. C. Deb.*, 5th series, 1946–7, column 122).

It is quite clear from these observations of the Attorney-General that in place of the provisions which did away with reservation and disallowance by the insertion of clause (*d*) some sort of control on the Provincial Legislature was contemplated to be given to the Governor-General in the provisional constitution. Such control was actually given by providing in section 75 of the adapted Act of 1935 that the Governor shall declare either that he assents to a bill or that he withholds assent therefrom or that he reserves the bill for the consideration of the Governor-General, as well as by providing in section 76 that when a bill is reserved by a Governor for the consideration of the Governor-General, the Governor-General shall declare that he assents in His Majesty's name to the bill or that he withholds his assent therefrom. In the same way section 32 of the adapted Government of India Act gives to the Governor-General the power to withhold assent from a bill. This power to withhold assent could, however, be given only if it was implied in the provision in sub-section (3) of section 6 that the Governor-General of each of the new Dominions shall have full power to assent in His Majesty's name to any law of the Legislature of that Dominion. The position, therefore, is that the words of the provision in question give to the Governor-General the power to withhold assent; the sponsors of the Indian Independence Bill thought that this power was implied in this provision; and the experts who adapted the Government of India Act, 1935, took this provision to mean that the power to withhold assent is implied in the power to give assent. If the power to withhold assent had not been included in this provision, its insertion in sections 32, 75 and 76 of the adapted Government of India Act would have been entirely without authority.

I have already pointed out that the words 'the powers of the Legislature of the Dominion' in sub-section (1) of section 8 refer back to the powers of the Legislature of the Dominion defined in section 6, which the Constituent Assembly was to exercise in its capacity of Legislature of the Dominion. A pertinent reference to section 6 is to be found in the Attorney-General's speech in column 118 of 440 *H.C. Deb.*, 5th series, 1946-7; where referring to section 8 he said that that section was to provide for a temporary constitution and that sub-section (1) of section 8 gave the necessary legislative power to a Constituent Assembly and attracted the provisions of clause 6. This could only mean that section 6 was the power-giving section while sub-section (1) of section 8 made those powers exercisable by the Constituent Assembly. If this relation of the two provisions was correctly stated by the Attorney-General, as I think it was, it could only mean that the provisions of section 6 were applicable to the powers given to the Constituent Assembly by sub-section (1) of section 8 and that the restriction as to the Governor-General's assent to legislation by the Legislature of the Dominion, whatever may be the character of that legislation, was applicable when the Constituent Assembly exercised the powers of the Legislature of the Dominion under sub-section (1) of section 8. That sub-section does not say that the constitution of the Dominion shall be made by the Constituent Assembly. It assumes that the powers of the Legislature of the Dominion include the power to make provision as to the constitution of the Dominion, declares that those powers shall be exercisable in the first instance by the Constituent Assembly and directs that references in the Act to the Legislature of the Dominion shall be taken as references to the Constituent Assembly. It was contended both by Mr Chundrigar and Mr Mahmud Ali that the Constituent Assembly, though it exercises the powers of the Legislature of the Dominion, is not itself the Legislature of the Dominion. This to my mind is tantamount to a refusal to read sub-section (1) of section 8, the only purport of which can be that the Constituent Assembly shall be the first Legislature of the Dominion, competent to exercise all the powers given to that legislature by section 6 including the power to make laws as to the constitution of the Dominion. Learned counsel for the appellants therefore rightly contended that the plain words of sub-section (1) of section 8 that 'reference in this Act to the Legislature of the Dominion shall be construed accordingly' have the effect of substituting the Constituent Assembly for the words 'the Legislature of each of the new Dominions' in sub-sections (1) and (3) of section 6. That being the position, there can be no escape from the conclusion that the Governor-General's assent to the laws made by the Constituent Assembly is as necessary as his assent to any future Legislature of the Dominion brought into existence by the Constituent Assembly to replace itself. It was conceded before us that if the Constituent Assembly dissolved itself after creating another Legislature of the Dominion and everything else remained as it is today, the provisions of section 6 would be applicable to such Legislature, including the provision in sub-section (3) relating to the assent of the Governor-General, and if that be so, I do not see why the provisions of that sub-section should not have been applicable to the Constituent Assembly itself when under the express words of sub-section (1) of section 8 it became the Legislature of the Dominion on the coming into force of the Indian Independence Act.

The necessity for the Governor-General's assent to legislation is, as I have already said, based on a well-understood principle which is known to every constitutional lawyer conversant with constitutional practice in the United Kingdom and the Dominions. Legislation is the exercise of a high prerogative power and even where it is delegated by statute or charter to a legislature, in theory it is always subject to assent whether that assent be given by the King or by a person nominated by the King. In the British system there is not a single instance to the contrary. That necessity was enjoined in the case of Pakistan so long as it continued to be a Dominion, though it was open to that Dominion, if the Governor-General gave assent to a bill of secession, to repudiate its Dominion status. The force of the words 'full power to assent' would be realised if a situation arose where a bill of secession came up before the Governor-General for assent. So far as His Majesty was concerned he had given full powers to his Governor-General to assent to any legislation of the Dominion: but the Governor-General, though he was a representative of the King, was also the representative of the Dominion in the sense that he was a person in whom the majority party of the Assembly had confidence. He would, therefore, have no hesitation, and would also have the requisite authority to give assent. If, however, he withheld assent, his immediate recall by His Majesty would have been successfully insisted upon by the Assembly and the assent could then have been obtained from his successor.

Confused and clearly contradictory, though they are said to be alternative, arguments have been addressed to us as to the construction of this sub-section which consists of two distinct parts, the first declaring that the Governor-General of the Dominion shall have full power to assent in His Majesty's name to any law of the Legislature of the Dominion and the second saying that so much of any Act as relates to the disallowance of laws by His

Majesty or the reservation of laws for the signification of His Majesty's pleasure thereon or the suspension of the operation of laws until the signification of His Majesty's pleasure thereon shall not apply to the laws of the Legislature of the Dominion. I have already shown that if the power to assent includes, as in my opinion it does, the power to withhold assent, then the true import of the first part must be that the Governor-General, since he has the power to withhold assent, is a necessary part of the legislature in precisely the same sense as under the old Government of India Act he was a constituent part of the Federal Legislature because no bill could become law unless he gave his assent thereto. The argument of Mr Chundrigar and Mr Mahmud Ali is that the word 'law' as it first occurs in the sub-section means a bill to which the assent of the Governor-General has been given and which has thus become a law. In this connection the language of the sub-section is compared with clause (d) of the proviso to sub-section (2) which speaks of bills and not laws. No inference from this comparison can, however, be drawn because clause (d) uses the language of the Government of India Act when it refers to the reservation of the Provincial bills for the signification of His Majesty's pleasure, or when it refers to an assented bill as a 'Provincial Act'. The word 'law' in the sub-section has been used in a general sense, namely, any proposed legislation which has not as yet received the assent of the Governor-General; otherwise the sub-section would lead to this absurd result that a legislative proposal which has already received the assent of the Governor-General would need a second assent. The assent of the Governor-General in respect of a proposed legislation, which by the Government of India Act is described as a bill, is needed only once and it is ridiculous to say that the Governor-General of the new Dominion shall have full power to assent to any bill to which assent has already been given by him.

The second contention of Mr Chundrigar is that when this sub-section says that the Governor-General of the Dominion shall have full power to assent in His Majesty's name to any law of the Legislature of the Dominion, it empowers the Governor-General to give assent only in cases which are mentioned in the second part of the sub-section, namely, where a law may be disallowed by His Majesty or reserved for the signification of His Majesty's pleasure or suspended until the signification of such pleasure. This contention has to be rejected for several reasons. Firstly, on that construction the first part of the sub-section becomes wholly superfluous, because it is undoubtedly within the competence of the Legislature of the Dominion to say under sub-section (1) of section 6 that to a particular law the provisions of any Act of the Parliament of the United Kingdom relating to disallowance, reservation or suspension shall not apply; secondly, the plain terms of the first part of the sub-section do not limit its application to the cases specified in the second part; and thirdly, the words 'reservation of laws' cannot possibly relate to laws which have already received the assent of the Governor-General. When asked to paraphrase the first part of the sub-section in order to give to it the meaning contended for, Mr Chundrigar attempted the following substitution for it: the powers of the Governor-General to assent in His Majesty's name to any law of the Federal Legislature, which previously were not full, shall hereafter be full in the sense that the Governor-General shall be competent to give his assent in His Majesty's name in cases where a law could be disallowed by His Majesty or reserved for the signification of His Majesty's pleasure or suspended until the signification of such pleasure. Comment on this strained paraphrase is superfluous. There is no warrant for substituting 'Federal Legislature' for 'Legislature of the Dominion'; nor for limiting the operation of the first part only to cases contemplated in the second part; and the words used are clearly inapplicable to 'reservation' of laws.

Our attention was drawn to some Acts which provide for disallowance, reservation or suspension, but none of these Acts contemplates reservation after the proposed legislation has been assented to by the Governor-General or the Governor of a Dominion or a Colony. I have already pointed out that the second part of the sub-section corresponds to sections 5 and 6 of the Statute of Westminster which specifically refer to the Merchant Shipping Act and the Colonial Courts of Admiralty Act. Section 735 of the Merchant Shipping Act, 1894, enacts:

The Legislature of any British Possession may by any Act or Ordinance, confirmed by Her Majesty in Council, repeal wholly or in part, any provision of this Act relating to ships registered in that Possession; but any such Act or Ordinance shall not take effect until the approval of Her Majesty has been proclaimed in the Possession or until such time thereafter as may be fixed by the Act or Ordinance for the purpose.

It is obvious that the intention of this section is that even where an Act or Ordinance of any British Possession has received the assent of the Governor-General or the Governor, it shall not be law until it has been confirmed by Her Majesty in Council and Her Majesty's approval of that Act or Ordinance has been proclaimed in the Possession. Similarly, section 736 of that Act says:

The Legislature of a British Possession may, by any Act or Ordinance, regulate the coasting trade of that British Possession, subject *inter alia* to the condition that the Act or Ordinance shall contain a suspending clause providing that the Act or Ordinance shall not come into operation until Her Majesty's pleasure thereon has been publicly signified in the British Possession in which it has been passed.

Though the language used in this section is different from that of section 735, the principle underlying both of them is the same, inasmuch as section 736 instead of requiring confirmation and its proclamation enjoins on the legislature concerned that the Act or Ordinance itself shall contain a suspending clause providing that it shall not come into force until Her Majesty's pleasure thereon has been publicly signified. Thus though sub-section (3) of section 6 may apply to section 736, it does not in terms apply to confirmation or approval mentioned in section 735.

Section 4 of the Colonial Courts of Admiralty Act, 1890, relates to reservation of Colonial laws for Her Majesty's assent. It provides that certain Colonial laws shall, unless previously approved by Her Majesty through a Secretary of State, either be reserved for the signification of Her Majesty's pleasure thereon, or contain a suspending clause providing that such law shall not come into operation until Her Majesty's pleasure thereon has been publicly signified in the British Possession in which it has been passed. Here again the section relates to approval, reservation and suspension, and though the second part of sub-section (3) may be applicable to suspension, it does not apply to approval and is clearly inapplicable to reservation in the sense which Mr Chundrigar and Mr Mahmud Ali attach to it, because the section clearly enjoins the assenting authority not to assent to it but to reserve it for signification of Her Majesty's pleasure. Similarly the reference to section 1 of the Colonial Evidence Act, 1843, is beside the point because what that section enacts is:

No law or ordinance made or to be made by the legislature of any British colony for the admission of the evidence of any such persons as aforesaid in any court or before any magistrate within any such colony shall be or be deemed to have been null and void or invalid by reason of any repugnancy or supposed repugnancy of any such enactment to the law of England, but every law or ordinance made or to be made by any such legislature as aforesaid, for the admission before any such court or magistrate of the evidence of any such persons as aforesaid on any conditions thereby imposed, shall have such and the same effect, and shall be subject to the confirmation or disallowance of Her Majesty in such and the same manner, as any other law or ordinance enacted for any other purpose by any such colonial legislature,

but sub-section (3) of section 6 contains no reference to confirmation.

It will be apparent from what I have said above that it is a contradiction in terms to speak of the Governor-General as giving assent to a proposed legislation which has already received his assent, and unless this impossible position be accepted, the construction of this sub-section put forward for the respondent, namely, that the word 'law' where it first occurs in sub-section (3) refers to cases where the assent of the Governor-General has already been given, cannot be accepted. Again, the word 'law' has to be distinguished from the word 'Act' because while the first part of the sub-section says that the Governor-General shall have the power to assent to any law, the second part speaks of an Act relating to disallowance, reservation or suspension. This clearly means that the second part of the sub-section applies to Acts relating to disallowance, reservation or suspension and that the word 'Act' there is used in a sense different from that in which the word 'law' has been used in the first part, namely, in the sense of a bill or legislative proposal which has been passed by the Legislature but which has not received the assent of the Governor-General. Faced with this difficulty Mr Mahmud Ali shifted his position and asserted that the word 'law' in the first part of the sub-section means an Act or Ordinance. But any such construction would lead to the absurd result that an Ordinance or Act which has been passed by, or received the assent of the Governor-General would need a second assent by him. Thus none of the various

constructions suggested on behalf of the respondent fits in with
the plain language of the sub-section, which shows that the word
'law' in the first part of the sub-section is used in a general sense
and not in the sense of a bill which has already received the assent
of the Governor-General. Evidently the words 'so much of any
Act' used in the second part of the sub-section were intended to
refer not only to those provisions of the Act of 1935 which had
required the Governor-General to reserve bills for the signification of His Majesty's pleasure or enabled His Majesty to disallow
Acts, but also to those provisions of the other Acts of Parliament
of the United Kingdom which related to reservation, disallowance
or suspension of laws in the Dominions, Colonies or Possessions.
The power to withhold assent has not been specifically mentioned
in sub-section (3) and the sub-section, as it stands, cannot be
taken as enacting that the Governor-General shall not have the
power to withhold assent to legislation. The power to withhold
assent appeared in the Act of 1935, and has also been retained in
the adapted Act. Unless, therefore, the power to assent necessarily
included in it the power to withhold assent, and this result followed
from sub-section (3), it could not have found place in the adapted
Act either in regard to Federal legislation or in regard to Provincial
legislation, Mr Chundrigar's argument that it has been retained in
the adapted Act because it appeared in the original Act being based,
as already pointed out, on an obvious fallacy.

The argument seriously advanced on behalf of the respondent
and which was readily accepted in the Chief Court that the words
'Legislature of the Dominion' in sub-section (3) refer only to the
Federal Legislature must be rejected on the short ground that, as
already pointed out, the laws which the Legislature of the Dominion is empowered by section 6 to make may be constitutional
laws which are not within the competence of the Federal Legislature as, for instance, laws repealing or amending the Indian
Independence Act or the adapted Government of India Act, and
laws limiting for the future the powers of the Legislature of the
Dominion. If the reference in section 6 had been only to the
Federal Legislature, one would have expected for the present
phraseology of sub-section (3) some provision similar to proviso
(d) to sub-section (2) of section 8.

The next point taken by Mr Chundrigar was that sub-section

133

(3) of section 6 must be read with section 5 which says that the Governor-General represents the Crown only for the purposes of the government of the Dominion, the inference sought to be drawn being that because the Governor-General represents the Crown only for the purposes of the government of the Dominion he can have no say in constitutional legislation by the Constituent Assembly. This argument appeared to be unanswerable to one of the learned judges of the Sind Chief Court who thought that the words 'government of the Dominion' only meant government under the adapted Government of India Act as provided by sub-section (2) of section 8. When questioned whether government also includes the administration of constitutional laws Mr Chundrigar replied in the affirmative, but he asserted that so far as the making of constitutional laws is concerned it is not a part of the government of the Dominion and the Governor-General does not come in there. I do not understand how if the administration of constitutional laws is a part of the government of a Dominion, their making is not. The marginal note to section 8 'temporary provision as to the government of each of the new Dominions' shows that the legislation of the Constituent Assembly under sub-section (1) of section 8 is a part of the government of the Dominion and the whole scheme of the Government of India Act proceeds on the assumption that the Governor-General represents the Crown when he assents in Her Majesty's name to the laws of the Federal Legislature. Therefore it seems to me to be an impossible proposition to assert that the making of laws is not a part of the government of the Dominion, and that being so no reason whatsoever has been suggested why the making of constitutional laws should not be a part of the government of the Dominion. If the Governor-General represents the Crown for the purposes of the government of the Dominion when he gives assent to the laws passed by the Federal Legislature, it must *a fortiori* follow that he represents the Crown for the same purpose when he assents to constitutional laws, because in a State like ours it is impossible to conceive of a government without there being a constitution.

It is next contended on behalf of the respondent that rule 62 of the 'Rules of Procedure of the Constituent Assembly' which provides that when a bill is passed by the Assembly a copy thereof shall be signed by the President and it shall become law on being published in the official *Gazette* of Pakistan under the authority of the President, has the effect of validly dispensing with the Governor-General's assent. This rule has a history which should be mentioned. In its original form the Rule, when passed on 24 February 1948, in a meeting presided over by the Qaid-i-Azam who was then the President of the Constituent Assembly, was as follows: 'When a bill is passed by the Assembly a copy thereof shall be signed by the President.' In the meeting of 22 May 1948, under the presidentship of the respondent, Sardar Abdur Rab Khan Nishtar moved the following amendment:

That for rule 62 of the Constituent Assembly Rules, the following be substituted, namely:
'Assent to Bills,—When a Bill has been passed by the Assembly, it shall be presented to the President for his assent.'

Khan Sardar Bahadur Khan, however, moved the following amendment for that moved by Sardar Abdur Rab Khan Nishtar:

That for rule 62 of the Constituent Assembly Rules, the following be substituted:
'When a Bill is passed by the Assembly, a copy thereof shall be signed by the President and it shall become law on being published in the official Gazette of Pakistan under the authority of the President.'

This amendment was accepted by Sardar Abdur Rab Khan Nishtar and was adopted without discussion. The confusion as to the scope and nature of the rule is apparent from the two amendments. Sardar Abdur Rab Khan Nishtar's amendment related to assent to bills while that of Sardar Bahadur Khan related to their authentication. The former aimed at substituting the assent of the President for that of the Governor-General without an amendment of section 6 of the Indian Independence Act while the latter said nothing about assent and sought to provide for authentication of the bills and as to when they became law. The latter amendment succeeded and is now Rule 62 of the Rules of Procedure.

There is no specific provision in the Act of 1947 empowering the Constituent Assembly to make its own Rules of Procedure but that does not mean that it was incompetent to make such Rules. Such power is inherent to a Constituent Assembly and must be presumed to vest in it. The question, however, is whether Rule 62

135

is a mere rule of procedure or law in the sense that it overrides the provision in the constitution that every bill of the Legislature of the Dominion requires the Governor-General's assent. It will be noticed that the Rule says nothing about assent and relates only to authentication. It is, therefore, not inconsistent with the constitutional provision that a bill in order to become law must be assented to by the Governor-General, and is quite capable of the construction that it assumes a bill to have been assented to by the Governor-General before it is signed by the President and published in the *Gazette*. In the second place, it cannot be said to be a law governing the decision of the present question. It may be that if a legal right can be founded on a Rule of Procedure, the breach of that rule may provide to the person in whom that right vests a cause of action to come to Court, but no such rule can become law so long as the constitutional provision which conflicts with it is not repealed. Under the Assembly's own Rules, all amendments to the Constitution have to follow the procedure of bills which is prescribed by Rules 43 to 62 and it is admitted that the amendment which gives its present form to the Rule did not comply with that procedure. This shows that even the Constituent Assembly did not consider the Rule to be a constitutional provision, much less a provision overriding or repealing a specific constitutional provision. If the Assembly intended to change the law relating to assent, it was necessary for it to amend section 6 of the Indian Independence Act in such a manner as to dispense with the necessity of the Governor-General's assent. A mere Rule of Procedure cannot amend the Constitution Act any more than a resolution by the Assembly that a person named shall be stoned to death for an act that is not an offence under the substantive law of crimes and without his being tried in accordance with the law relating to criminal procedure. Lastly, even if this Rule be assumed to be a constitutional provision, it itself required the Governor-General's assent and, in the absence of such assent, is wholly invalid.

Contemporanea expositio and argument ab inconvenienti

I may notice here Mr Chundrigar's argument that because for several years no assent to an Act of the Constituent Assembly, while sitting as a constitution-making body under sub-section (1) of section 8, was ever obtained, and that some important Acts passed by the Assembly were treated as law by every one concerned, though they had not received the assent of the Governor-General, sub-section (3) of section 6 must be so interpreted as not to be applicable to the legislation passed by the Constituent Assembly under sub-section (1) of section 8. In this connection, he read to us some passages from pages 399–401 of Crawford's *Statutory Construction* (1940 ed.), and pages 144, 146, 147, 148 and 150 from Cooley's first volume of *Constitutional Limitations* (8th ed.). The rule enunciated in these passages is the principle of *contemporanea expositio* which also applies to the construction of documents. That principle as applied to documents may be stated to be as follows:

In order to explain, but not to contradict, ancient documents whose meaning is doubtful, the acts of the parties, even before the execution of the instrument, or the mode in which property has since been held and enjoyed thereunder, as well as constant modern user may be given in evidence. Such evidence, however, seems now admissible not only in the case of ancient, but also of modern, documents, and whether the ambiguity be a curable patent ambiguity or a latent ambiguity. On the other hand, where the meaning of the words is not ambiguous, the subsequent acts of the parties are not admissible to construe it, whether the document be ancient or modern.[1]

In its application to constitutional statutes, the rule is thus stated by Cooley at page 144 of his book:

Contemporaneous interpretation may indicate merely the understanding with which the people received it at the time, or it may be accompanied by acts done in putting the instrument in operation, and which necessarily assume that it is to be construed in a particular way. In the first case it can have very little force, because the evidences of the public understanding, when nothing has been done under the provision in question, must always of necessity be vague and indecisive. But where there has been a practical construction, which has been acquiesced in for a considerable period, considerations in favour of adhering to this construction sometimes present themselves to the courts with a plausibility and force which it is not easy to resist. Indeed, where a particular construction has been generally accepted as correct, and especially when this has occurred contemporaneously with the adoption of the constitution, and by those who had opportunity to understand the intention of the instrument, it is not to be denied that a strong presumption exists that the construction rightly interprets the intention.

[1] See Phipson's *Evidence* (7th ed.), 605, and Taylor, *Evidence*, sections 1204–5.

137

In all the cases where observations of this kind have been made, the true intention of the particular provision in the constitution was ambiguous or doubtful, and I know of no instance where the words of the constitution being clear and consistent with a reasonable interpretation, any court ever went to the extent of misconstruing its true purpose merely because somebody else had taken a mistaken view of it. There is no question of estoppel in such cases, the correct description of the reasoning employed being argument *ab inconvenienti*. This mode of construction of written constitutions is, therefore, subject to an overriding consideration which has thus been stated by Cooley himself at pages 149–50:

Contemporary construction . . . can never abrogate the text; it can never fritter away its obvious sense; it can never narrow down its true limitations; it can never enlarge its natural boundaries. While we conceive this to be the true and only safe rule, we shall be obliged to confess that some of the cases appear, on first reading, not to have observed these limitations. . . .

It is believed, however, that in each of these cases an examination of the Constitution left in the minds of the Judges sufficient doubt upon the question of its violation to warrant their looking elsewhere for aids in interpretation, and that the cases are not in conflict with the general rule as above laid down. Acquiescence for no length of time can legalise a clear usurpation of power, where the people have plainly expressed their will in the Constitution, and appointed judicial tribunals to enforce it. A power is frequently yielded to merely because it is claimed, and it may be exercised for a long period, in violation of the constitutional prohibition, without the mischief which the Constitution was designed to guard against appearing or without anyone being sufficiently interested in the subject to raise the question; but these circumstances cannot be allowed to sanction an infraction of the Constitution. We think we allow to contemporary and practical construction its full legitimate force when we suffer it, where it is clear and uniform, to solve in its own favour the doubts which arise on reading the instrument to be construed.

Therefore to apply the principle of contemporaneous and practical exposition to the present case, we shall first have to say that there is a doubt in our mind as to the true meaning of sections 6 and 8 as a whole, and particularly as to the meaning of sub-section (3) of section 6 and sub-section (1) of section 8. I think we should be mutilating the Act and misunderstanding its true purpose and scheme if we were to hold that the words of sub-section (1) of section 8 'for the purpose of making provision as to the constitution of the Dominion' do not refer to the power which section 6 gives to the Legislature of the Dominion, including the power to alter, repeal, or amend the two Constitution Acts themselves or that the power to give assent to which the third subsection of section 6 refers does not include the power to withhold assent. In my opinion, it is a mistake to suppose that sovereignty in its larger sense was conferred upon the Constituent Assembly, or that it could function outside the limits of the Indian Independence Act. The only power given to that Assembly was the power to make laws, constitutional or federal. In the former case, it exercised the power to make provision as to the constitution of the Dominion which had been included in the generality of the powers conferred by section 6 on the legislature of the Dominion, and in the latter it acted as the Federal Legislature with all the limitations to which that Legislature was subject. Apart from these powers, it had no other power and it lived in a fool's paradise if it was ever seized with the notion that it was the sovereign body in the State. It had, of course, legislative sovereignty as the legislature of the Dominion but then the Governor-General was a constituent part of the Legislature. Every Act passed by it required the Governor-General's assent, consistently with the position that prevails throughout the Dominions, the colonies and the possessions, settled or ceded or conquered, where the Crown still retains to itself or has delegated to its representative the high prerogative right of assenting to bills. If this basic position was misunderstood or misconstrued, there is neither any estoppel nor is the argument *ab inconvenienti* applicable. On its interpretation of the Indian Independence Act, the Constituent Assembly attempted to function outside the Constitution, and it was the right not only of the Governor-General to object to such unconstitutional activity, but the right of every citizen in the State to demand that the Assembly must function within its constitutional limits. The members of the Assembly before they undertake the duties of their office take the oath of allegiance to the Constitution of Pakistan, and they are subject to all the limitations of that Constitution. Having taken that oath, they cannot subsequently forswear themselves and assert that they are the only sovereign body in the State and that their will is the law whether the Governor-General endorses or does not endorse that will.

It has been suggested by the learned Judges of the Sind Chief Court and has also been vehemently urged before us that if the view that I take on the question of assent be correct, the result would be disastrous because the entire legislation passed by the Constituent Assembly, and the acts done and orders passed under it will in that case have to be held to be void. On this part of the case I do not wish to say anything more than that the sole question before us is whether the Governor-General's assent was obtained to the Government of India (Amendment) Act of 1954, which inserted section 223A to the Government of India Act, and nothing said here should be deemed to be applicable to any other Act. In England the assent is given by the King to a bill in person or by commission. It is a ceremonial act and has to be formally recorded. Mr Chundrigar is, however, right in the contention that in Pakistan no particular form for assent is prescribed, and that it need not be in writing. It may be that where the Governor-General has taken some action as, for example, where he has issued some rules in exercise of the authority given to him by the Act or taken some other step, his assent to the proposed legislation may be inferred. That question is not before us and I do not decide it. We are concerned in the present case only with the validity of the Government of India (Amendment) Act of 1954, and so far as that Act is concerned, it is common ground that it was not presented to the Governor-General for assent, and that he has not done anything under this Act which might be taken as indicative of his having assented to it. I am quite clear in my mind that we are not concerned with the consequences, however beneficial or disastrous they may be, if the undoubted legal position was that all legislation by the Legislature of the Dominion under sub-section (3) of section 8 needed the assent of the Governor-General. If the result is disaster, it will merely be another instance of how thoughtlessly the Constituent Assembly proceeded with its business and by assuming for itself the position of an irremovable legislature to what straits it has brought the country. Unless any rule of estoppel require us to pronounce merely purported legislation as complete and valid legislation, we have no option but to pronounce it to be void and to leave it to the relevant authorities under the Constitution or to the country to set right the position in any way it may be open to them. The question raised involves the rights of every citizen in Pakistan, and neither any rule of construction nor any rule of estoppel stands in the way of a clear pronouncement.

Consistently with the practice, that has grown up since his sad demise, of citing Qaid-i-Azam's alleged oral sayings as authority for a particular proposition, it has been alleged before us that the practice of not obtaining the assent of the Governor-General to Acts of the Constituent Assembly had come into existence during the Qaid's time and has his support. We have no record of any ruling having been given by him on this point, nor has any legal opinion obtained by the Assembly from anyone been produced before us. Reference has been made to two Acts which during the Qaid's Presidentship of the Assembly were published in the *Gazette* 'under the authority of the President of the Constituent Assembly' and it is alleged that they were never placed before the Qaid for purposes of assent. But during those days the Qaid was not only the President of the Assembly but also the Governor-General and it is quite possible that he might have thought that since the bills were passed under his own Presidentship it was unnecessary again to place them for his assent as Governor-General. Be this as it may, the conduct of one Governor-General in a matter like this does not relieve his successor of the duty of demanding compliance with the Constitution. Wheare, while discussing the efficacy of non-legal rules as a medium of constitutional change, says at page 18 of the fifth edition of his book *The Statute of Westminster and Dominion Status*: 'In the first place, they [non-legal rules] cannot always nullify or modify a rule of strict law. In the second place, though they may nullify a rule of strict law, they do not and cannot abolish it. They may paralyse a limb of the law but they cannot amputate it.' Can practices and conventions override an express statutory provision merely because nobody attempted or cared to understand it and its implication?

I now proceed to examine the cases on which Mr Chundrigar relied. The first of these is the Sind case, *M. A. Khuhro* v. *The Federation of Pakistan*[1] in which Hassanally Agha, J., held that the meaning of sub-section (3) of section 6 of the Indian Independence

[1] 1950 P.L.D. Sind, 49.

Act is that the assent of the Governor-General is required only where the assent of His Majesty is necessary under the Constitution. These, however, are not the words of the sub-section which speaks of the 'Legislature of the Dominion' in which expression sub-section (1) of section 8 expressly includes the Constituent Assembly, and says that the Governor-General of the Dominion shall have full power to assent in His Majesty's name to the laws of the Legislature of the Dominion, which power necessarily implies the power to withhold assent. In *Khan Iftikhar Hussain Khan of Mamdot* v. *The Crown*[1] the Crown was intervener, but there the sole question to be determined was whether the Public and Representative Offices (Disqualification) Act, 1949, fell within the powers of the Constituent Assembly as the Federal Legislature or within its powers of the Legislature of the Dominion competent to make constitutional provisions, it being assumed by every one concerned that the assent of the Governor-General was necessary only where the Constituent Assembly functioned as the Federal Legislature. The question whether when the Constituent Assembly acts under sub-section (1) of section 8 and exercises the powers of making provision as to the constitution of the Dominion, the assent of the Governor-General under sub-section (3) of section 6 is necessary for its legislation, was neither raised, nor discussed, nor decided. That case therefore is no authority for the proposition that the Governor-General's assent is not necessary under sub-section (3) of section 6 to legislation by the Constituent Assembly when it functions as the Legislature of the Dominion.

In the Irish case *Ryan* v. *Lennon*[2] extracts from which are reproduced at pages 377–83 of Sir Ivor Jennings' book *Constitutional Laws of the Commonwealth* (2nd ed.), the question involved was entirely different, namely, whether the amendment by the Oireachtas to the constitution set up by the Third Dáil, sitting as Constituent Assembly, was *ultra vires*, though there are some observations there in the arguments of counsel, Mr Gavan Duffy, that the constitution was proclaimed in the name of the people by Dáil Eireann (Third Dáil) as an act of supreme authority and that it did not require any assent. The all-important fact which must not be forgotten about the Irish instance is that the Constitution of the Irish Free State (Saorstát Eireann) Act, 1922, made by the

[1] 1951, F.C.R. 24.　　　　　　　　[2] [1935] I.R. 170.

Third Dáil (Dáil Eireann) was recognised by the Irish Free State (Constitution) Act, 1922, passed by the Parliament of the United Kingdom just as the Constitution of India made by the Constituent Assembly which, if the information supplied to us by Mr Chundrigar is correct, had not received the assent of the Governor-General, was recognised by the Parliament by the India (Consequential Provision) Act, 1949.[1]

Mr Chundrigar's next contention was that this interpretation of sub-section (3) should be rejected on the principle of *reductio ad absurdum* inasmuch as it affects the sovereignty of the Constituent Assembly by recognising outside that Assembly an authority which has the power to veto all legislation by it. He also relies on the omission of the words 'in his discretion' in the adapted Government of India Act by virtue of clause (*c*) to the Proviso to sub-section (2) of section 8 and the disappearance of the practice of issuing instructions to the Governor-General, as factors in favour of a contrary construction. Illustrating the point, he argues that on this construction of the sub-section the Crown may appoint any one it likes as the Governor-General of the Dominion and the person so appointed may be hostile to Pakistan, as, for instance, a retired officer of the old Civil Service with Congress sympathies and anti-Pakistan views who may not only refuse assent to all material legislation but also withhold assent from any legislation removing the office of the Governor-General himself or declaring Pakistan as an independent country. No construction of this sub-section, he says, should be accepted which would be completely incompatible with the independence of Pakistan as a Dominion and introduce into the legislation of the Dominion effective control by the Crown or by the Crown's representative. The argument proceeds on an obvious fallacy and a clearly mistaken assumption. In the first place, the Indian Independence Act nowhere says that the Constituent Assembly shall be the sovereign of the new Dominion. It gives to it only the power of the legislature of the Dominion and nothing more. The expression sovereignty of Constituent Assembly was repeated before us *ad nauseam* but as has been observed elsewhere when we pointedly asked Mr Chundrigar whether apart from legislative functions it had any other powers under the Indian Independence

Sovereignty of Constituent Assembly

[1] 12, 13 & 14 Geo. VI, ch. 92.

143

Act, the hesitating reply was, and rightly, in the negative. Now if it be held as a matter of construction that the Governor-General is assigned a necessary part in the legislation of the Dominion, the legal sovereignty of the Constituent Assembly is reduced to a myth, because on that construction the Assembly cannot effectively function alone. But that does not mean that its legislative sovereignty cannot be converted into an actuality in exactly the same way as in the other constitutions, namely, by having a Governor-General who is acceptable to the Assembly, who will not resist legislation by the Assembly, and who can be recalled if he goes against the advice of the Ministry. The rule has worked well for a long time in all self-governing Dominions. If, therefore, a similar provision has not in any way affected the independence of the other Dominions where well-established conventions have been responsible for a smooth working of the constitution, there is no reason why the Pakistan Constitution could not have been and should not have been worked in that manner. To illustrate the point, suppose that the Constituent Assembly decides to secede from the Commonwealth and to declare Pakistan as an independent republic. On my interpretation of sub-section (3), the Governor-General's assent to such legislation would be necessary. But there cannot be the slightest difficulty in obtaining his assent. If the Governor-General refuses assent a request for his recall addressed by the Prime Minister to the Secretary of Her Majesty would be sufficient for the purpose because the matter would not go to Her Majesty's Government in the United Kingdom, that Government having relinquished all responsibility for the government of this country, and Her Majesty the Queen in such matters normally acts on the advice of the Ministry of the Dominion provided that the ministry represents the people of the Dominion as ministries in other Dominions do. She herself takes no more part in the politics of a Dominion than she does in the United Kingdom and it is wholly erroneous to suppose that contrary to her attitude in home politics she would assume the role of a partisan in the internal politics of any of her Dominions. On having the Governor-General recalled, the Constituent Assembly can recommend for appointment another person who would be willing to give his assent to the bill of secession.

I have already pointed out that the necessity of the assent of the King to legislation by the House of Commons and the House of Lords was at one time one of the most important reserve powers and was actually used in Britain by the Crown in and before the reign of Queen Anne to veto objectionable legislation and in the Dominions by the Governor-General to defeat legislation which appeared to him adversely to affect the Imperial interests or to be otherwise unpopular. Now the generally accepted position in this respect, however, is that this power can be exercised in the United Kingdom only on the advice of the Ministry and in the Dominions on the advice of the Ministry of the Dominion. The issue has not actually arisen in recent times because the throwing out of an important Government bill by the House of Commons in England or by the legislature in a Dominion amounts to a vote of no-confidence in the Ministry and is thus a valid constitutional ground for the Ministry to resign or to ask for a dissolution and not for advising the King or the Governor-General to withhold assent. But whatever may be the position, it cannot possibly be said in the case of Dominions including Pakistan that the Governor-General is in a position to exercise this power in opposition to the wishes of a Ministry which represents the people of the Dominion. Though the Governor-General is supposed to be a representative of the King, in fact he is a representative of the Dominion concerned, because his appointment and dismissal depend on the advice of the Ministry of the Dominion which on the convention of non-intervention is always accepted by the Crown. If, therefore, the Governor-General withholds his assent to any legislative measure to which he is required to give his assent by the Ministry of the Dominion, the Ministry is generally in a position to have him immediately recalled or removed. He cannot, therefore, exercise the power of withholding assent contrary to the wishes of the Ministry or in order to veto legislation against the advice of the Ministry. It follows from this that the provisions empowering him to give his assent are in no sense a fetter on the sovereignty or the independence of the Dominion, and in Pakistan they certainly do not amount to an encroachment on the legislative sovereignty of the Legislature of the Dominion. Even in the case of Federal legislation the Governor-General has the power to give or withhold assent, but he cannot, if the Constitution is functioning in normal times and in its true spirit, withhold assent contrary to the wishes of the Ministry. And this is so, not because the words 'in his discretion' which occurred in the Act of 1935 have been omitted from the adapted relevant provisions but because the withholding of assent to such legislation, when the Ministry requires him to give his assent, can raise a constitutional issue which can only end in the recalling or removal of the Governor-General. Any attempt therefore to construe the Governor-General's power to withhold assent as a veto on legislation proceeds on a misapprehension and cannot be made a ground for the inference that that power is an infringement of the legislative sovereignty of the Legislature of the Dominion and thus of the Constituent Assembly.

Nodding automaton or autocrat From the fact that the Governor-General is the head of the State, it must not be inferred that in matters of legislation his position is either that of a nodding automaton or that of an autocrat. He is appointed by the King and represents the King for the purposes of the government of the Dominion, but that does not mean that he is an unrestrained autocrat, and purporting to act on behalf of the King, can in normal times take an active part in the actual administration of the country. Since the Imperial Conference of 1926 he has generally been a man of the Dominion and a representative of that Dominion just as the Prime Minister is. As a constitutional functionary, it is his duty to give his assent to all reasonable and necessary legislation by the legislature. But there may be occasions, however remote their conception may be, where the Governor-General would be entitled to withhold his assent from a particular legislation. In the United Kingdom, if the House of Commons passes a law which strikes at the very foundations of the constitution, as for instance, where Parliament indefinitely prolongs its life or trifles with the right of the electors to vote, the Sovereign may, and perhaps would, whether the Ministry advise it or not, exercise his reserve powers of withholding assent or dissolution. The same is the position of the Governor-General in the Dominions. Leslie Stephen, while illustrating the omnipotence of the legislature, says at page 143 of the 1882 edition of his *Science of Ethics*: 'If a legislature decided that blue-eyed babies should be murdered, the preservation of blue-eyed babies would be illegal; but legislators must go mad before they pass such a law and subjects be idiotic before they submit to it.' If a similar law were passed by the Constituent Assembly, and this of course is an extreme case which is being mentioned merely to explain the point, I have no doubt that it would be the duty of the Governor-General to withhold his assent from such legislation not because he has any instructions in the matter from the King, but because he represents the Dominion and in such matters he is supposed to be able rightly to gauge the public feelings and sentiments. Similarly, if the Constituent Assembly decided to make a law that all adults, shaven or unshaven as it chose to say, shall be deprived of the rights of citizenship in Pakistan, the Governor-General will undoubtedly withhold assent from such legislation. Or take the instances mentioned by Mr Faiyaz Ali before the learned Judges of the Chief Court to illustrate his theory of checks and balances. 'I have given your lordships', said Mr Faiyaz Ali,

one example of a possible misuse of these powers, namely, that the Constituent Assembly could, if absolutely uncontrolled, legislate that everyone of its members was to get a salary of one lac of rupees per month, enjoyable for life and heritable from generation to generation. What was there to prevent it from doing so? But let us take a more probable and less extravagant instance. Suppose the Constituent Assembly in the exercise of its absolute powers decided to impose a Soviet Constitution on Pakistan. Suppose they said: 'It is our will that there shall henceforth be no God in Pakistan and no Religion. Let Religion and God both be ejected from Pakistan and a Constitution based on the purely economic doctrine of Karl Marx be framed' and suppose they did all this against the will of the People and in open defiance of their views and sentiments. What would have happened in such a case? The Assembly, if it had absolute and uncontrolled powers, could very well impose such a Constitution on Pakistan. What could the People do? What could be their remedy?

And surprisingly enough the reply to it by one of the learned judges was, 'If the majority of the members are for it that means the people are for it'. Comment on this reply is unnecessary beyond saying that it overlooks the doctrine, which is a fundamental doctrine in democracy, that the mere fact that the majority of the members of a legislature are in favour of a measure does not necessarily mean that the people are for such measure. The second instance cited by Mr Faiyaz Ali was precisely the instance where

147

if the question arose in the United Kingdom the King would exercise his reserve powers of dissolution or of withholding assent. In the circumstances supposed, the Governor-General here will act in precisely the same way, namely, he will withhold his assent from such legislation, not because he represents the King but because he represents the people of the Dominion and in such matters acts on their behalf in the belief that his action will have their approval.

An instance may also be cited from the history of the Constituent Assembly itself. It is alleged before us in an affidavit put in by the attorney of the appellants that at the time the Constituent Assembly decided to repeal the Public and Representative Offices (Disqualification) Act, 1949, proceedings under that Act were contemplated against ten members of the Constituent Assembly itself. The law repealing the Act which is said to have been passed in undue haste could have been attributed by the Governor-General to a desire on the part of the Constituent Assembly to screen its own members from prosecution, and few people could have objected if he had withheld his assent from the repealing bill. It will, therefore, be seen that in this respect the Governor-General occupies a very important constitutional position. By withholding assent to an unpopular measure he can create a constitutional crisis of the first magnitude, and though eventually he himself may have to go, he can in appropriate cases rivet the attention of the country to the caprice, cupidity or folly of the legislature.

In the course of arguments before us, a question arose, similar to the one mooted before this Court in *Khan Iftikhar Hussain Khan of Mamdot* v. *The Crown*,[1] namely, whether if the Constituent Assembly passed a law, which was within its competence as the Federal Legislature, it could be held to be *ultra vires* on the ground that it did not receive the assent of the Governor-General. The point was not decided in that case, but Mr Chundrigar appeared to suggest before us that in such a case because the Constituent Assembly is a sovereign body, the Court could not inquire into the *ultra vires* of any law purporting to have been passed by it under sub-section (1) of section 8 of the Act of 1947. If Mr Chundrigar's claim is valid, does it not follow from it that the Constituent Assembly can dispense with the necessity

[1] 1951 F.C.R. 24

of all assent even in regard to laws which fall within the Federal List merely by purporting to pass such laws in exercise of the powers conferred on it by sub-section (1) of section 8? The question whether a law falls within the Federal List or relates to the constitution of the Dominion being one for the Constituent Assembly to determine and not for the courts to decide, the Assembly could at its will do away with the necessity of assent to all Federal legislation merely by not placing a bill before the Governor-General for his assent.

For the foregoing reasons I hold that so long as the provision in sub-section (3) of section 6, giving full powers to the Governor-General to assent to any law of the Legislature of the Dominion stands, every bill passed by the Legislature of the Dominion which has the effect of amending the existing constitution as contained in the Government of India Act and the Indian Independence Act must be presented for the assent of the Governor-General, and this assent is as necessary to the validity of legislation as the law which requires a document to be under seal or registered. It is a formality which cannot be dispensed with except by a proper amendment of the Constitution. In view of this it is wholly unnecessary to go into the other issues, and nothing said in this judgment is to be taken as an expression of opinion on any one of them.

I now proceed to notice some of the incidents of an independent Dominion which were referred to in the arguments before us by the parties. These incidents are connected with allegiance, Royal Style and Titles, nationality, assent to legislation and Prerogatives. 'Independent Dominion'

The words 'independent dominion' first received statutory recognition in the Act of 1947. The speakers in the House of Commons who took part in the debates on the bill had different conceptions of an independent dominion. There were also proposals that these words be substituted by some more expressive words. Thus Mr Godfrey Nicholson suggested the amendment 'two independent States within the British Commonwealth of Nations, hereinafter to be known for the purposes of this Act as the new Dominions', because he thought the word 'Dominion' was subject to several misconceptions. Mr Wilson Harris supported Mr Nicholson and said:

I think that we need the word 'Dominion' here and that it was a stroke of genius on the part of Lord Mountbatten to apply the possibility of Dominion Status to the two halves of India. I cannot help thinking, however, that the term 'Independent Dominion' involves a certain contradiction. Dominions as between themselves are interdependent and not independent. I would very much prefer the use of the word 'autonomous Dominions'. In the famous language of 1926, the Dominions are not subordinate one to another in any internal or external affairs, but they are not entirely independent. They do not stand completely apart from one another, indeed they have the right to secede from the Commonwealth in which case they would achieve complete independence. It seems to me the word 'independent' ought to be used for that status. It would be more desirable to speak of autonomy in this case and to use the words 'autonomous Dominions' rather than 'Independent Dominions'.

Replying to this criticism, the Prime Minister, Mr Attlee, said:

With regard to the term 'Independent Dominions', I think you need the word Dominions here. We do understand what Dominion Status means under the Statute of Westminster. Whatever alteration there may be in the future in the Statute of Westminster, that statute to-day does define this position. It does mean complete autonomy. With regard to the word 'Independence', that again one may quarrel over, but one has to consider both history and psychology in this matter and it is a fact that it is not generally realised throughout the world, that although it is quite properly said that there is interdependence there is complete independence in the Dominions from any control, whether from Whitehall or from Parliament. That is the important point that needs to be stressed. It is not perhaps quite the same as if this were being formed from some country adjoining, which had never been in the position of being under this Parliament and under Whitehall. I think that is what the Indians really want to have emphasised. I think they quite accept the position and they know the advantages of being in the Dominions. People, who have long been under the tutelage of Whitehall and under the control of this Parliament, feel that now, at last, they are independent of that control.

The essential characteristics of an independent Dominion were rightly brought out by Mr Attlee when he said that the independence of a Dominion implied freedom from all control by the Government in London and the British Parliament. If the Government of the United Kingdom has no right to interfere in the affairs of a Dominion and the Legislature of that Dominion can pass any law that it likes, including the law relating to its own future constitution, and the authority of the Parliament of the

United Kingdom to legislate for it comes to an end, we have a true conception of the independence that was intended to be conferred on the Dominions of India and Pakistan. In this sense the Dominions of Canada, Australia and New Zealand cannot be said to be independent because under the Statute of Westminster, their legislatures are incompetent to amend their Constitution Acts. India and Pakistan, however, could frame their own constitutions as independent countries and entirely secede from the Commonwealth.

But though independent in the sense just explained, Pakistan is a Dominion and therefore certain incidents attach to it by reason of that status. The first feature that is common to the Dominions which are members of the British Commonwealth of Nations is common allegiance to the Crown. This common feature, as pointed out by Wade and Phillips at page 443 of the fourth edition of their *Constitutional Law*, is the one legal link which joins members of the Commonwealth (except India) and Empire, though it is no longer regarded as indispensable for membership of the former. In the Commonwealth Declaration of April 1949 made by the Prime Ministers of the United Kingdom, Canada, Australia, New Zealand, South Africa, India, Pakistan and Ceylon and the Canadian Secretary of State for External Affairs, it was declared that their countries were united as members of the British Commonwealth of Nations and owed a common allegiance to the Crown which was also a symbol of their free association. The Declaration was made on the occasion of receiving India as a member of the Commonwealth in view of the new Republic Constitution she was about to adopt. In the resolutions of the Imperial Conference of 1926, common allegiance to the Crown was stated to be one of the bonds that united the participating Dominions. This position received a recognition by the Statute of Westminster, 1931, the preamble of which states that the Crown is the symbol of the free association of the members of the British Commonwealth of Nations and that they are all united by a common allegiance to the Crown. Halsbury describes common allegiance to the Crown as a common law doctrine (*Laws of England*, 3rd ed., vol. v, para. 1024). It is for this reason that the Statute of Westminster requires that any alteration in the law touching the succession to the Throne or the Royal Style and Titles must have the assent of the

Parliaments of the Dominions as well as the Parliament of the United Kingdom.

So important is the connection of a common Crown and common allegiance that in the case of Canada, Australia and New Zealand, it cannot be broken by local legislation, and General Smuts consistently maintained that even the King himself could not with due regard to his duty assent to a measure of a Dominion Parliament purporting to destroy the connection with the Crown. Writing in 1932, Keith, in his *Constitutional Law of the British Dominions* (page 61), thought that to effect a separation there would in law be necessary an Imperial as well as a Dominion measure and that under the principle enunciated by the Statute of Westminster the concurrence of the other Dominions would also be requisite. This relation is very different from the mere personal union between the United Kingdom and Hanover where the connection could be, and was, broken as a result of the different laws of descent of the Crowns of the two territories when Queen Victoria succeeded to the throne in 1837. He says at page 62 of the book:

Closely connected with the question of the common Crown is that of a common allegiance. The issue might rest, of course, on the old decision in *Calvin's Case*, after the union of the Crown of England and Scotland in the person of James I, that persons born in Scotland after the union were natural born English subjects, despite the absolutely distinct character of the two kingdoms. The same doctrine was applied during the period of the union of the Crown of England with the Electorate of Hanover. Even were each of the Dominions to be regarded as an absolutely distinct kingdom, the subjects of the King therein would on that doctrine be subjects in the United Kingdom.

These observations were of course not applicable to the two Dominions created by the Indian Independence Act because each of them was declared to be fully competent to secede. But so long as either of them remains a Dominion, assent to its legislation is necessary both under the common law doctrine and the statutory provision in sub-section (3) of section 6. So strict is this rule that even if a Dominion intended to secede from the Commonwealth and repudiate allegiance to the Crown, it could do so only by an extra-legal act. But if it intended to proceed constitutionally such secession would itself require the assent of the Queen or her representative, or legislation by the Parliament of the United

Kingdom. Such assent was given when Burma became independent under the Burma Independence Act, 1947. And though in the case of India no such assent seems to have been requested or given, the connection between India and the United Kingdom had to be recognised by a statute of the British Parliament, India (Consequential Provisions) Act, 1949, to retain India as a member of the Commonwealth.

Though by sub-section (2) of section 7 of the Act of 1947 the words 'Indiæ Imperator' and the words 'Emperor of India' were omitted from the Royal Style and Titles by a Royal Proclamation under the Great Seal of the Realm, the words 'of Great Britain, Ireland and British Dominions beyond the Seas, Queen' continued to be used. In December 1952, after consultation between the Governments of members of the Commonwealth it was agreed that in place of the existing Titles which had ceased to be fully appropriate each member should adopt for its own purpose a form of Title suitable to its particular circumstances but including a substantial common element. A separate Title has accordingly been adopted for use in the United Kingdom (including the territories for whose foreign relations the United Kingdom Government is responsible). This Title, which was adopted in pursuance of section 1 of the Royal Titles Act, 1953 (1 and 2 Eliz. II, ch. 9), is 'Elizabeth the Second, by the Grace of God of the United Kingdom of Great Britain and Northern Ireland and of Her other Realms and Territories, Queen, Head of the Commonwealth, Defender of the Faith'. In Canada, Australia and New Zealand, the Title adopted, in each case by a local enactment, is 'Elizabeth the Second, by the Grace of God, Queen of the United Kingdom (Canada or Australia or New Zealand) and Her other Realms and Territories, Head of the Commonwealth'. In South Africa the Title adopted by the Royal Style and Titles Act, 1953 (local), is 'Elizabeth the Second, Queen of South Africa and Her other Realms and Territories, Head of the Commonwealth'. In Ceylon the Title is the same as for South Africa with substitution of 'Ceylon' for 'South Africa'. A few days before her Coronation, the Queen received the Prime Ministers of the United Kingdom, Canada, Australia, New Zealand and Ceylon who submitted for her signature the proclamations relating to the Royal Style and Titles for their countries.

In Pakistan, the Title signed by the Governor-General, and published simultaneously in the Commonwealth capitals on 29 May 1953, was 'Elizabeth the Second, Queen of the United Kingdom and of Her other Realms and Territories, Head of the Commonwealth'. It should be noted that under sub-section (4) of section 6 of the Act of 1947 no Act of the United Kingdom passed on or after the appointed day was to extend or be deemed to extend to the Dominion of Pakistan as a part of the law of the Dominion unless it was extended thereto by a law of the Legislature of the Dominion. No such law adopting the Royal Title was passed by the Legislature of the Dominion and the Title was published by a proclamation signed by the Governor-General. The words 'Her other Realms and Territories' in the Title were evidently considered to embrace Pakistan because on the occasion of the Coronation of Her Majesty on 2 June 1953, the oath that was administered to her by the Archbishop of Canterbury was:

Will you solemnly promise and swear to govern the peoples of the United Kingdom of Great Britain and Northern Ireland, Canada, Australia, New Zealand, the Union of South Africa, Pakistan and Ceylon and of your possessions and the other Territories to any of them belonging or pertaining, according to their respective laws and customs?

The commission that was issued by His Majesty's command appointing the Governor-General of Pakistan described His Majesty as 'George VI, by the Grace of God of Great Britain and the British Dominions beyond the Seas, King, Defender of the Faith', and the oath that the Governor-General takes is: 'I do solemnly affirm true faith and allegiance to the Constitution of Pakistan as by Law established and I will be faithful to His Majesty (or Her Majesty), his heirs and successors in the Office of the Governor-General of Pakistan.'

The point sought to be made by Mr Chundrigar is that in this oath the allegiance that is sworn is to the Constitution of Pakistan and not to the Crown; but if allegiance to the Crown is a necessary incident of the Constitution of Pakistan, the allegiance to that Constitution obviously implies allegiance to the Crown. Further it does not make the slightest difference whether the Queen is described as the Queen of Pakistan or the Head of the Commonwealth of which Pakistan is a member.

From the common law doctrine of common allegiance it must follow that those who owe allegiance to the same Crown are common subjects. In United Kingdom law, citizens of the United Kingdom and the Colonies and citizens of other Commonwealth countries, including Pakistan, are British subjects and Commonwealth citizens, and by section 2 of the Pakistan Citizenship Act, 1951, read with section 1 of the British Nationality Act, 1948, a Commonwealth citizen, as for instance a citizen of Pakistan, is a British subject. Thus the second incident of Pakistan being a Dominion is that her citizens are for international purposes British subjects. Under section 262, sub-section (4) of the adapted Government of India Act, no person who is not a British subject is eligible to hold any office under the Crown in Pakistan, and under sub-section (1) of section 298 of that Act no subject of His Majesty domiciled in Pakistan shall, on grounds only of religion, place of birth, descent, colour or any of them be ineligible for office under the Crown in Pakistan.

The Governor-General of Pakistan is appointed by the King or Queen and represents him or her for the purposes of the Government of the Dominion (section 5 of the Indian Independence Act). The authority of the representative of the King extends to the exercise of the royal prerogative in so far as it is applicable to the internal affairs of the Member, State or Province, even without express delegation, subject to any contrary statutory or constitutional provisions. In Canada and the Union of South Africa the full external prerogatives are exercisable by the Governor-General, who is invariably invested with the duties of Commander-in-Chief of the armed forces, is authorised to appoint Judges, Ministers and other Crown servants, to summon, prorogue and dissolve Parliament, assent to legislation, and grant pardons on ministerial advice. Mr Mahmud Ali's contention that in Pakistan the Governor-General does not exercise any of the prerogatives of the King is clearly wrong because here, even under the adapted Act of 1935, the Governor-General appoints the Governors of Provinces, the Commanders-in-Chief of the Pakistan Army, Royal Pakistan Navy and the Royal Pakistan Air Force, and Judges of the Federal Court and the High Courts. Ambassadors to foreign countries are accredited and ambassadors from foreign countries are received by the Governor-General. The defence and civil services in Pakistan are services of the Crown and appointments to them are made by the Governor-General while in the Provinces the appointments to the services of the Province are made by the Governors. In defence services the Governor-General has the power to grant commissions. Every person who is a member of the Civil Service of the Crown in Pakistan or holds any post under the Crown holds office during His Majesty's pleasure. And assent to all legislation under the adapted Act of 1935 is given in His Majesty's name, in the case of bills of the Federal Legislature by the Governor-General, and in the case of Provincial bills by the Governor. Criminal prosecutions are initiated and conducted in the name of the Crown. In the face of these constitutional provisions I do not see how Mr Mahmud Ali finds it possible to assert that in Pakistan the Royal Prerogative is not exercised by the Governor-General.

I am conscious that in thus interpreting the Constitution of Pakistan and emphasising the incidents that attach to it as a Dominion I am going against a layman's idea of an 'independent dominion', the implications of which were not fully understood even by the wise and experienced members of the Constituent Assembly, though some of them were prominent members of the legal profession. But I am quite clear in my conscience what the duty of a Judge in such cases is. That duty is rightly to expound the law in complete indifference to any popular reaction. The status of which I have described the main incidents was accepted by our leaders under a gentlemen's agreement which received statutory recognition in the Act of 1947. If they had been so minded, they need not have accepted that status and like Burma could have complete independence. And if the legal incidents of association with the Commonwealth under a common head hurt their pride or were offensive to their susceptibilities, and the Constituent Assembly shared that feeling, it could have done away with all these so-called indicia of inferiority within a day. It is not that the Constituent Assembly was unaware of these incidents. I had drawn their attention to them by my judgment in the Full Bench case of *Sarfaraz Khan* v. *The Crown*[1] as far back as May 1950. But the only action taken by the Assembly on that judgment was to delete

[1] 1950 P.L.R. (Lahore) 658.

the words 'In His Majesty's name' from sub-section (3) of section 6 of the Act of 1947 and those provisions of the adapted Act of 1935 where these words occurred in respect of the Governor-General's assent to bills. This tinkering with the provisional constitution merely showed that the Constituent Assembly was unwilling to take big decisions, and they can hardly have any grievance if, on the present occasion, that position is restated to them. In this connection it will be interesting to mention here the history of an incident from a High Court file. In 1951 someone appears to have sent to the Prime Minister of Pakistan a High Court Notice which began with the words 'George VI, by the Grace of God of Great Britain and Northern Ireland and of the British Dominions beyond the Seas, King, Defender of the Faith'. The Prime Minister appears to have been surprised at the heading of this Notice and the Cabinet Secretariat, through the Secretary to the Governor, Punjab, drew the attention of the High Court to this Notice by a letter in which the view was expressed that while the inclusion of the name and Titles of the King in the Notice was constitutionally and legally correct, it did not appear to be legally necessary and was liable to misinterpretation. The letter also communicated the Prime Minister's desire to omit these words from the Court Notices if there was no objection. The matter was discussed in a meeting of the Judges of the Lahore High Court when I was the Chief Justice of that Court. In reply, the High Court pointed out that the Letters Patent Seal of the Court also contained the Royal Arms and suggested that the Seal of the Court be changed. That reply went from the High Court on 19 March 1952, but since an amendment of the Letters Patent, however simple it might appear to be, involves some study and thought, the matter is still under consideration, and the High Court writs, though they no longer run in the name of 'Elizabeth the Second, Queen of the United Kingdom and of her other Realms and Territories, Head of the Commonwealth', continue to issue under a seal containing the Royal Coat of Arms.

All that remains to notice now is the judgment of the Sind Chief Court. That judgment which was delivered after nineteen days of argument and twenty-five days of deliberation, is a disappointing document. In the lengthy arguments before us

Judgment of the Sind Chief Court

157

extending over three weeks, hardly any reference was made to it by either party. On the vital point in the case, repeatedly urged by Mr Faiyaz Ali before the learned Judges, namely, that the power of making provision as to the constitution of the Dominion which the Constituent Assembly was to exercise in the first instance under sub-section (1) section 8 was included in the powers conferred by section 6 on the Legislature of the Dominion, there is not one word in the judgment. Nor is there in any of the opinions delivered even a remote reference to the basic question, which I am not deciding because the respondent was not called upon to reply to it, but which must undoubtedly have stared the learned Judges in the face, namely, whether it is a wise exercise of discretion for the judiciary to re-install in power a deposed government by issuing enforceable writs against a *de facto* government.

On the question on which we are disposing of this appeal, Constantine, C.J., merely followed the opinion of Hassanally Agha, J., in a previous case and thought that the provision requiring the Governor-General's assent to legislation by the legislature of the Dominion was inconsistent with independence. He overlooked the obvious fact that if the Governor-General is a man from the Dominion and is appointed and dismissed on the advice of the Dominion Government, the legislative sovereignty of the legislature is not at all affected by the provision relating to assent. Nor, in the absence of a finding that some sort of estoppel operated or that there was an ambiguity in the Act, was he entitled to let his judgment be swayed by the consideration that the Law Officers of the Crown on previous occasions did not consider assent necessary, and that the objection was novel and, if accepted, would upset a consistent course of practice and understanding. I should incidentally mention here that it was stated before us by Mr Faiyaz Ali, Advocate-General of Pakistan, that on the point now raised the Law Ministry has consistently been taking the view that assent to constitutional legislation by the Constituent Assembly is necessary. As regards the point that assent is needed only with respect to legislation by the Federal legislature and that there is no corresponding provision in the Act of 1947 in respect of legislation by the Constituent Assembly as Legislature of the Dominion, it is sufficient to say that the argument begs the whole question because the essential question that has to be determined is whether sub-section (3) of section 6 does or does not have the effect of requiring assent to all legislation by the Constituent Assembly when it functions as the Legislature of the Dominion under sub-section (1) of section 8 to exercise the powers given to it by section 6. The ground on which Mr Justice Vellani's judgment proceeds is somewhat more remarkable inasmuch as that learned Judge merely contents himself by asserting that the Constituent Assembly was a supreme body, subject to no agency or instrument to give its laws validity, and that the provision requiring the Governor-General's assent to its legislation would make the Governor-General truly a Viceroy. He should have seen that other Dominions are independent, though similar provisions relating to assent exist in their constitutions, that the Governor-General, though a representative of the King, is a leading public man from the Dominion and certainly not the agent of the Government of the United Kingdom, and that the provision as to assent is not in the nature of a veto, because if the Constitution is properly worked as the constitutions of the other Dominions are, the Governor-General is not in a position to veto any legislation by the Legislature of the Dominion unless he withholds his assent from some outrageous legislation, in which case, whatever may be the legal position, the final law would be the will of the people and not the will of the Constituent Assembly. The finding of Mr Justice Muhammad Bakhsh Menon that the word 'law' occurring in sub-section (3) of section 6 of the Act of 1947 refers to laws made by the Federal Legislature amounts to a plain misreading of that provision and his view that the action of the Privy Council in transferring certain appeals to the Federal Court under the Privy Council (Abolition of Jurisdiction) Act, 1950, and their receipt by the Federal Court amounts to 'law declared' within the meaning of section 212 of the Act of 1935, amounts to a mis-understanding of how law is declared. He was not concerned with the consequences, if on a true construction of the Act, he had come to the conclusion that assent was necessary. The validity or otherwise of other Acts was not before him, the only question that he was called upon to decide being whether the impugned amendment to the Government of India Act was valid. He also begs the question when he finds that Rule 62 of the Constituent Assembly Rules is law, and whether that Rule did or did not receive the assent of the Governor-General, it can override the express provisions of sub-section (3) of section 6.

Conclusion   For the reasons given, I hold that the Constituent Assembly when it functions under sub-section (1) of section 8 of the Indian Independence Act, 1947, acts as the Legislature of the Dominion within the meaning of section 6 of that Act, that under sub-section (3) of the latter section the assent of the Governor-General is necessary to all legislation by the Legislature of the Dominion, that since section 223A of the Government of India Act under which the Chief Court of Sind assumed jurisdiction to issue the writs did not receive such assent, it is not yet law, and that, therefore, that Court had no jurisdiction to issue the writs. In view of this conclusion we cannot go into the other issues in the case whatever their general importance may be.

I would, therefore, accept the appeal, set aside the judgment of the Chief Court of Sind, and recall both the writs. Parties will bear their own costs throughout.

Before concluding I should like to express our appreciation of the assistance rendered by counsel in the decision of this case, of Mr Faiyaz Ali's vigorous all round argument, Mr Diplock's masterly analysis of the Acts of 1935 and 1947 and Mr Chundrigar's brave fight in defence of the sovereignty of the Constituent Assembly.

AKRAM, J.—I agree in the order allowing the appeal. I, however, desire to say a few words of my own in support of the order. The facts of the case are set out in detail in the judgment of my Lord the Chief Justice and need not be repeated. As regards the preliminary question: 'Whether the assent of the Governor-General is necessary before any constitutional legislation by the Constituent Assembly under section 8 (1) of the Independence Act, 1947, can pass into law?', the answer to it seems to me to depend upon a true construction of the relevant provisions of the Independence Act itself. Section 6 (3) and the first part of section 8 (1) of the Act are as follows:

6 (3) The Governor-General of each of the new Dominions shall have full power to assent to any law of the Legislature of that Dominion and so much of any Act as relates to the disallowance of laws by His Majesty or the reservation of laws for the signification of His Majesty's

pleasure thereon or the suspension of the operation of laws until the signification of His Majesty's pleasure thereon shall not apply to laws of the Legislature of either of the new Dominions.

8 (1) (First part) In the case of each of the new Dominions, the powers of the Legislature of the Dominion shall, for the purpose of making provision as to the constitution of the Dominion, be exercisable in the first instance by the Constituent Assembly of that Dominion, and references in this Act to the Legislature of the Dominion shall be construed accordingly.

Reading section 6 (3) and the first part of section 8 (1) together the conclusion which I am able to draw is that the Governor-General has full power to give assent to any kind of law proposed by the Legislature of the Dominion and that the Constituent Assembly which in the first instance is to make provision for the constitution of the Dominion is to exercise the power of the Legislature of the Dominion for that purpose. As a result, the assent of the Governor-General becomes necessary for the validity of even constitutional laws. In my opinion the words 'full power to assent' in the context carry with them full liberty to refuse assent as power conferred does not mean liability imposed or obligation created. I am unable to construe section 6 (3) in the manner suggested by counsel for the respondent and to hold that the assent of the Governor-General is not necessary so far as constitutional laws are concerned. I have carefully considered the arguments which he has advanced in its support, namely:

(i) That in case the assent of the Governor-General is regarded as essential to the validity of constitutional laws, then the result will be that the form of the Constitution will depend on the views of the Governor-General rather than those of the Constituent Assembly in contravention of section 8 (1) of the Independence Act.

(ii) That under section 5 of the same Act, the Governor-General is to represent His Majesty for the purposes of the Government of the Dominion, but this cannot confer on the Governor-General authority to nullify constitutional legislation by withholding assent.

(iii) That all along, the Government itself, the people and the Courts, proceeded on the same view as is now pressed for by the respondent, namely, that the assent of the Governor-General is not necessary for constitutional legislation under section 8 (1) of the Independence Act.

(iv) That in section 6 (3) reference to the Dominion Legislature is only notional as no Dominion Legislature exists or existed before; that in reality the reference is to the Federal Legislature functioning under section 8 (2) of the Independence Act; that 'law' in the sub-section (3) is used in a broad and comprehensive sense in order to cover not only proposed legislative bills but also enactments which require confirmation by His Majesty under section 736 of the Merchant Shipping Act and section 4 of the Colonial Courts of Admiralty Act; that the expression 'full power to assent' has been used because the power of disallowance, reservation or suspension which existed under section 32 of the old Government of India Act, 1935, is done away with; that the two parts of sub-section (3) are to be read in close conjunction with each other in order to bring out the real meaning of the sub-section; that 'full power to assent' cannot be interpreted as full option to refuse assent.

(v) That section 8 (1) is not to be read with section 6 (3); there is no connection between the two.

(vi) That there is no provision anywhere for the presentation of a constitutional legislation by the Constituent Assembly to the Governor-General for his assent.

But these arguments, though ingenious and interesting, do not seem to me to be so cogent and convincing as to prevail over the clear meaning of section 6 (3) read with section 8 (1) of the Independence Act. In the interpretation of laws and statutes plain words should, as a rule, be given their plain meaning and a laboured construction should not be put upon them to bring into prominence some kind of remote signification. I see no justification for any embroidery upon the plain and simple language of the sub-sections. Certain decisions in support of the respondent's contention were also cited but they do not appear to me to be precisely in point and need not be referred to. But apart from the reasons given by me, while interpreting sections 6 (3) and 8 (1) of the Independence Act, if we look to the Statement of His Majesty's Government, dated 3 June 1947, para. 20, and take into consideration the conditions and the circumstances existing at the time of the passing of the Independence Act, the plan and the purpose which the Legislature had in view will not, perhaps, be far to seek. Para. 20 of the Statement aforesaid runs as follows:

Accordingly, as the most expeditious, and indeed the only practicable way of meeting this desire, His Majesty's Government propose to introduce legislation during the current session for the transfer of power this year on a *Dominion Status* basis to one or two successor authorities according to the decisions taken as a result of this announcement. This will be without prejudice to the right of the Indian Constituent Assemblies to decide in due course whether or not the part of India, in respect of which they have authority, will remain within the British Commonwealth.

'Dominion Status', it appears, had already acquired a technical meaning; it implied, according to the declaration of the Imperial Conference held in London in 1926, 'autonomous communities within the British Empire, equal in status, in no way subordinate one to another in any respect of their domestic or external affairs, though united by a common allegiance to the Crown and freely associated as members of the British Commonwealth of Nations'. Indeed, the Dominions were virtually distinct kingdoms united by a common King and a common allegiance and their inter-Imperial relations were in no sense regarded as inter-national.

Thus the effect of conferring a Dominion Status was that certain rights and liabilities as between the Dominion and the United Kingdom came into existence; for instance, if the Dominion by its legislation negated allegiance to the Crown or severed connection with it, such legislation perhaps could not be considered as legally valid or justified. The expression 'Independent Dominion' has, therefore, been purposely used in the Independence Act in order to give to the Dominion a freedom of choice either to remain or to refuse to remain within the British Commonwealth of Nations as envisaged in para. 20 of the Statement of His Majesty's Government quoted above. It is clear that by the Independence Act the intention was to give a constitutional form of government modelled on the pattern of the British government pending the setting up of a final constitution by the Dominion itself. According to English constitutional theories, the Sovereign, who is the Executive Head of the State, is always a constituent part of the supreme legislative power and as such has the legal right not only of giving assent but also of refusing assent in case he considers a provision to be inexpedient or injurious. The power to give or to refuse assent is one of a great variety of royal prerogatives and cannot be abrogated or curtailed without clear statutory provision to that effect made with the royal concurrence. See:

(a) *Blackstone on the Laws of England*, 4th ed. vol. I, ch. VII, p. 221 :
He [the Sovereign] may reject what bills, may make what treaties, may create what peers, may pardon what offences he pleases : unless

where the constitution has expressly, or by evident consequence, laid down some exception or boundary: declaring, that thus far the prerogative shall go, and no further.

(b) Keith's *Constitutional Law*, 7th ed. (1946 reprint), p. 201:

The prerogative of the King is the privilege of his subjects; that is, the King must exercise his prerogative not for his own benefit but for the protection of his subjects in accordance with the advice of his constitutional legal advisers. The King in Council is the Executive; the King in Parliament is the Legislature; the King in his Courts administers justice; and thus the Crown binds together every department of the State.

(c) *Constitutional Law* by Wade and Phillips, 3rd ed. p. 95:

Parliament cannot legislate without the concurrence of all its parts, and therefore the assent of the King is required. The King not only summons Parliament and can dissolve Parliament, but must give his consent before any legislation can take effect.

(d) Stephen's *Commentaries on the Laws of England*, 18th ed. (by Edward Jenks), vol. i, p. 176:

In legal theory, the King is capable of refusing to give his assent to a Bill; and, if he did so refuse, the Bill, although it had passed both Commons and Lords, could not become law. But for over two centuries, no monarch has placed himself in opposition to the wishes of the people as expressed through their representatives. The spirit of the Constitution is, that the Government is carried on by the Houses of Parliament (since 1911 one may say by one House only), and that the King's functions in legislation are purely formal. The last occasion when the royal assent was refused was when Queen Anne rejected the Scotch Militia Bill in 1707; and it is unlikely that the words '*le roy s'avisera*' will ever be spoken in the House of Lords again.

Such being the English constitutional theories, it would be a strange supposition to make that the British Parliament, while framing an *interim* Constitutional Act for Pakistan, acted in a manner contrary to its own principles and traditions and deprived the Executive Head of the Dominion of power to give or to withhold assent as respects constitutional laws. For the reasons stated, I am of the view that in the absence of any express or implied provision in any enactment to the contrary, the assent of the Governor-General is necessary before any constitutional measure framed under section 8 (1) of the Independence Act, 1947, can pass into law.

CORNELIUS, J.—It is proper that, realising the grave issues which are involved in this case, I should commence with an expression of my sincere regret at being unable to agree with the view on one part of the case, which has commended itself to my Lord the Chief Justice and my learned brothers, in consequence of which, the appeal has been allowed. It will be my principal concern in this judgment to indicate with such clarity and brevity as may be possible to me, the reasons which have compelled me to come to a different conclusion. The resolution of a question affecting the interpretation of important provisions of the interim Constitution of Pakistan in relation to the very high matters which are involved, entails a responsibility going directly to the oath of office which the Constitution requires of a Judge, namely, to bear true faith and allegiance to the Constitution of Pakistan as by law established and faithfully to perform the duties of the office to the best of the incumbent's ability, knowledge and judgment. The reasons I am about to set out have the effect of determining my humble judgment in one way and one way only, namely, that in the given circumstances, there is nothing in the law which makes the grant of assent by the Governor-General to Acts of the Constituent Assembly, which make provision as to the Constitution of the country, a *sine qua non*, so that the absence of assent has the effect of invalidating all laws which have been passed in that mode, i.e. without the Governor-General's assent. Since the questions to be dealt with relate in essence to the period immediately prior to 24 October 1954 when the Proclamation was made by His Excellency the Governor-General, as a consequence of which the Constituent Assembly was deemed to have been dissolved, the argument will of necessity proceed upon the assumption that the Constituent Assembly is still in being. The assumption cannot of course affect the factual position.

A brief recital of the facts is necessary and may appropriately commence with the enactment by the Constituent Assembly of two Acts in the year 1954, amending the Government of India Act, 1935. The first of these Acts is described as the Government of India (Amendment) Act, 1954, and purported to insert a new section 223A in the Government of India Act, which reads as follows:

223A. Every High Court shall have power throughout the territories in relation to which it exercises jurisdiction to issue to any person or authority including in appropriate cases any government within those territories, writs including writs in the nature of *habeas corpus, mandamus,* prohibition, *quo warranto* and *certiorari* or any of them.

The second Act was described as the Government of India (Fifth Amendment) Act, 1954, which *inter alia* inserted a new section 10 to replace the existing sections 10, 10A and 10B. The relevant provision in the new section 10, for the purpose of the present case, is contained in sub-section (1) which reads as follows:

10 (1) The Governor-General shall appoint a Member of the Federal Legislature who commands the confidence of the majority of the Members of the Federal Legislature as Prime Minister. The other Ministers shall be appointed by the Governor-General, from amongst the Members of the Federal Legislature in accordance with the advice of the Prime Minister.

The previous provision on this subject was that 'the Governor-General's Ministers' were chosen and summoned by him, and that a Minister who for any period of ten consecutive months was not a member of the Federal Legislature, should at the expiration of that period, cease to be a Minister.

Both these Acts were passed by the Constituent Assembly and were signed by the President, by way of authentication and in the belief, based upon rule 62 of the Rules of Procedure of the Constituent Assembly of Pakistan which I reproduce below, that by such authentication and subsequent publication these Acts became law without the necessity of the Governor-General's assent. Rule 62 reads as below:

When a Bill is passed by the Assembly, a copy thereof shall be signed by the President and it shall become law on being published in the official Gazette of Pakistan under authority of the President.

Shortly after the making of the Proclamation, Moulvi Tamizuddin Khan, who was President of the Constituent Assembly, filed a writ petition in the Chief Court of Sind, citing as respondents the Federation of Pakistan and nine Ministers who had been sworn in as Ministers of the Federal Government. The reliefs claimed were *inter alia*, a writ of mandamus against all the respondents, their agents, etc., to prevent them from giving effect

166

to the Proclamation and from interfering with the exercise by Moulvi Tamizuddin Khan of his functions and duties as President of the Constituent Assembly, and a separate writ of quo warranto against each of the respondents who were Ministers in the newly constituted Government to determine the validity of their appointments. The respondents contested the petition raising preliminary objections as well as objections on the merits. The first preliminary objection was that section 223A (which has been reproduced above) had not yet become law in Pakistan by reason of absence of the Governor-General's assent, which was *sine qua non* for the purpose. The other preliminary objections were to the effect that, even if section 223A was held to be valid, in the existing circumstances, no writ as claimed could issue. The objections on the merits related to the dissolution of the Constituent Assembly and set out that in view of the fact that Pakistan is expressly constituted as 'one of the dominions of the Crown of the United Kingdom, a power to dissolve the Legislature was furnished by the common law and also lay in the prerogative which the Governor-General could exercise'. After lengthy arguments, a Bench of four Judges of the Sind Chief Court held unanimously that the conditions requisite for the issue of the writs claimed were shown to exist, and accordingly they directed that the writs should issue. Three of the learned Judges wrote separate judgments, the fourth learned Judge expressing agreement with the judgment written by the learned Chief Judge. It is not necessary to state in detail all the findings recorded by the learned Judges or the reasons which they have furnished in support of each finding, for the reason that in this Court the decision has been confined to the single question of necessity for the Governor-General's assent in relation to laws made by the Constituent Assembly containing provisions as to the Constitution of Pakistan. On the latter point, the reasons which guided the learned Judges of the Court below may be shortly stated as under:

(i) The key to the Indian Independence Act, 1947, is the independence of Pakistan, and the purpose of section 6 of that Act is to efface the supremacy of the British Parliament.

(ii) Sub-section (3) of section 6, which provides that 'the Governor-General shall have full power to assent to any law of the

Legislature of the Dominion' does not impose the requirement of assent for all laws made by the 'Legislature of the Dominion', but merely provides that if assent were necessary, the Governor-General should have full power in that respect. Express provision was retained in the Government of India Act, 1935, for the necessity of assent to Acts of the Federal Legislature only, and therefore section 6 (3) applies only to such Acts.

(iii) The Crown is not named in the relevant Constitutional Instruments, viz. the Indian Independence Act and the Government of India Act, 1935, as sharing in the power of legislation and the clear implication was that the Crown was excluded from such power.

(iv) On the Constitution-making side the Constituent Assembly had sovereign power, equal to that of the King, and therefore, no assent of the King was necessary.

(v) That the Constituent Assembly could have repealed section 6 (3) and even the whole of the Independence Act; it was impossible to think that such a law would require the assent of the Governor-General.

(vi) That all authorities in Pakistan, executive, legislative and judicial, had for many years past interpreted the Constitution in this way, i.e. that constitutional enactments by the Constituent Assembly became law without the assent of the Governor-General.

Accordingly, the learned Judges held that section 223A by which they were empowered to issue writs was good law, and proceeded thereafter to consider the question whether the Governor-General had the power to dissolve the Constituent Assembly, and whether in the given circumstances, the writs claimed could properly issue. They answered the first question in the negative and the second in the affirmative as against the Federation and five of the Ministers. The reasons for these findings have been given at great length, but do not require mention for the purpose of this judgment.

The respondents appealed in this Court against this decision under section 205 of the Government of India Act, on a certificate issued by the Court below as required by that section. In support of the appeal, the Court heard addresses from the Advocate-General of Pakistan who was followed by Mr Kenneth Diplock, Q.C., of the English Bar. On the question of assent, the argument of the learned Advocate-General was confined to showing that such a requirement could be construed out of the provisions of section 6, sub-section (3) of the Indian Independence Act, and that rule 62 made by the Constituent Assembly had no validity in law, through not having been made in the proper form, viz. by presentation as a Bill and consequential proceedings, and also through its lacking the assent of the Governor-General.

The learned Advocate-General urged that in order to produce the result which rule 62 was designed to achieve, the Constituent Assembly should have amended section 6 (3) of the Indian Independence Act, which they had full power to do, subject to the assent of the Governor-General. The argument presented by Mr Kenneth Diplock was lengthy and elaborate. The *résumé* which I proceed to attempt may, therefore, be incomplete in some respects. He started with the proposition that although when the King has once transferred legislative powers to representative institutions in one of his realms or territories, he cannot thereafter take back that power, yet, in every such realm or territory, at every stage of its development, the King remains an integral part of the law-making machinery. In this connection, he referred to the decision of the Privy Council in the case of *The Liquidator of the Maritime Bank of Canada* v. *The Receiver-General of New Brunswick*.[1] The question there raised was that the British Sovereign had no direct connection with a Province of the Dominion of Canada after the passing of the British North America Act, 1867. The Privy Council over-ruled the contention, having found that the Lieutenant-Governor of a Province was appointed by the Executive Government of the Dominion which was expressly vested in the Queen, that all public properties and revenues in the Province were also vested in the Queen, and that the Queen was part of the Legislature. The relevant observations, which relate to the last-mentioned finding, may be reproduced *verbatim*:

It would require very express language, such as is not to be found in the Act of 1867, to warrant the inference that the Imperial Legislature meant to vest in the provinces of Canada the right of exercising supreme legislative powers in which the British Sovereign was to have no share.

Next, Mr Diplock urged that the key to the Indian Independence Act was not the *independence* of Pakistan, as had been concluded by the learned Chief Judge of the Sind Chief Court, but the

[1] [1892] A.C. 437.

formation of an *independent Dominion* of Pakistan, and he argued that in all essential respects, Pakistan was on the same footing as any of the other Dominions. Dominion Status was virtually undistinguishable from independence, for it was recognised that the Dominions were Sovereign States in the eye of international law, since they enjoyed independent treaty-making powers, the right of separate representation in the United Nations, and the right to appoint their own ambassadors in foreign countries. Such was the degree of independence they enjoyed, that even a declaration of war against a foreign country by His Majesty's Government in the United Kingdom did not operate in relation to any Dominion of its own force. The Dominions were free to accept the British Sovereign in relation to themselves, with such royal titles as they might themselves determine. Yet, as is stated in the preamble to the Statute of Westminster, 1931, 'the Crown is the symbol of the free association of the members of the British Commonwealth of Nations and . . . they are united by a common allegiance to the Crown'. Both as a symbol of such free association and as recognition of the allegiance owed to the British Sovereign, it was the invariable practice in all Dominion countries to seek the assent of the Sovereign from his representative in the Dominion, namely, the Governor-General, in relation to Dominion laws. This was an inherent feature of Dominion Status, and could not be avoided unless by express words or necessary intendment. The right of assent was a prerogative right of the Sovereign and although it could be taken away either by the British Parliament, where it retained the capacity to legislate or by the 'Legislature of the Dominion' itself, following the rule applicable to prerogatives of the Crown, it could not be taken away except by express words or necessary intendment.

On this foundation it was argued that sub-section (3) of section 6 of the Indian Independence Act, so far from excluding the royal prerogative, was founded upon the assumption that the prerogative of assent was to apply in relation to all laws of the 'Legislature of the Dominion'. Although the 'Legislature of the Dominion' was not constituted by any provision in the Indian Independence Act, and the intention was that its constitution and powers should be settled by the Constitution to be drawn up by the Constituent Assembly, yet the provisions of the Indian Independence Act when read together could lead to only one conclusion, namely, that, pending the promulgation of a new Constitution, the Constituent Assembly was, to all legal intents and purposes, the 'Legislature of the Dominion'. Therefore, until such time as the country ceased to be a Dominion, or a new Constitution came into force which avoided the requirement, assent on behalf of the British Sovereign was a necessary requisite to validity of all laws made by the Constituent Assembly including laws of a constitutional nature. The latter conclusion was unavoidable in view of the provision in sub-section (6) of section 6, Indian Independence Act, that the 'Legislature of the Dominion' should have power to make laws limiting its own powers for the future, and such laws were undeniably constitutional in their nature.

Mr Diplock also argued at length that a power of dissolution of the Constituent Assembly could be found in favour of the Governor-General from the words of section 5 of the Indian Independence Act which provide that 'the Governor-General shall represent His Majesty for the purposes of the government of the Dominion', coupled with the proposition, firstly, that a power of dissolution vests in the Crown in the United Kingdom by virtue of the prerogative, and secondly, that after the grant of legislative institutions to an overseas possession, the Crown, acting through its Governor-General, stands in the same relation to the Legislature of that possession as it does to the British Parliament. The force of this argument was materially impeded by two powerful considerations, viz. that in the case of every other Dominion and possession, the power of dissolution was vested in the Governor or Governor-General by express provision in the Constitution, and secondly, by the circumstance that a power of dissolution of the Federal Legislature which was contained in section 32, Government of India Act, 1935, had been deliberately taken away in the course of adapting the Government of India Act to the conditions which were to obtain after the creation of the independent Dominions. By section 8 (2), proviso (e) of the Indian Independence Act, it was enacted that the powers of the Federal Legislature or the Indian Legislature, as set out in the Government of India Act, should be exercisable in the first instance by the Constituent Assembly, and it is all too plain that to allow the

Governor-General to dissolve the Federal Legislature, would in effect be to allow him to dissolve the Constituent Assembly. The second part of Mr Diplock's argument on this point was, to my mind, the more attractive, namely, that the Governor-General of Pakistan is the virtual head of the State and under the maxim *salus populi est suprema lex*, he has not only the power but also the duty to act, in face of any great national disaster, threatening the country, in such a way as to avert that disaster. His action, when purporting to be taken in exercise of this power and duty, would be above the law, and, consequently, not justiciable. I found it impossible, however, to accede to Mr Diplock's further claim that if, in such a threatening situation, the Governor-General should fail to act, the British Sovereign, by virtue of the relationship of allegiance, would have power to intervene and to take action for the safety and security of the country in accordance with the express wishes of the people of the country. Such a possibility has never so far as I am aware been present to the minds of any persons in Pakistan who have ever had occasion to examine the incidents of Dominion Status, and it is easy to imagine that any such action by the British Sovereign, as distinguished from the Government of the United Kingdom, would be beset by practical difficulties in relation to a country such as Pakistan, some of which would appear at first sight to be insuperable.

The main reply to these arguments on behalf of the petitioner was made by Mr Chundrigar. He stressed that the point for consideration was the validity of the practice of a sovereign Constitution-making body while engaged in making provision as to the Constitution. Both as to the practice as well as in relation to its validity, the right of decision vested in the Constitution-making body alone. In that view of the matter the expressed will of the Constituent Assembly as declared in Rule 62 of the Rules of Procedure must be regarded as final. The rule in its original shape merely provided for authentication of the Bill by the President. It was made at a meeting of the Constituent Assembly held on 24 February 1948, which was presided over by the late Qaid-i-Azam, who combined in himself the offices of first Governor-General of Pakistan and first President of the Constituent Assembly of Pakistan. The rule was amended and brought to its present shape at a meeting of the Constituent Assembly held on 22 May 1948, under the Chairmanship of Mr Tamizuddin Khan, then Deputy President of the Constituent Assembly of Pakistan, deputising for the Qaid-i-Azam in his absence. It must be assumed that the rule was made in its final shape to the knowledge of the then Governor-General.

On the point of assent, as a requisite derivable from the considerations (a) that the country possessed Dominion Status and (b) that it owed allegiance to the King, Mr Chundrigar argued that Pakistan and India were constituted not as mere Dominions, but as 'Independent Dominions' and the difference was very strong and very material. Each of these new Dominions was provided, at its very birth, with an apparatus, namely, the Constituent Assembly composed of elected representatives of the people for equipping itself with a Constitution of its own choice, even one which could take it out of the oversight of the British Sovereign altogether. No other case of the same kind was known in the history of development of the British Commonwealth. It was, he urged, in consequence of this enormous difference that a great change was brought about in the oath which the Governors-General of Pakistan are required to take upon assuming office. The previous oath was one to be 'faithful and bear true allegiance to His Majesty the King, etc.', but from the very inception of Pakistan the oath has been to bear true allegiance to the Constitution of Pakistan, and to be faithful to His Majesty the King, etc. Allegiance to a Constitution, which, although effective to create a Dominion, could have been changed by the Constituent Assembly at any time, could not be construed as acceptance by the Governor-General of the King as liege-lord, or to constitute the Governor-General as liege-man of the King. Between allegiance and faithfulness, as forms of human relationship, there was a vast difference. The position is further emphasised by the fact that, upon the accession of the present British Sovereign, Her Majesty Queen Elizabeth II, the title relevant to Pakistan which was accepted by Pakistan was not that of Queen of Pakistan but only that of 'Head of the Commonwealth'. The materiality of the difference appears from the fact that the other Independent Dominion created in 1947, namely, India, became by virtue of a Constitution passed by the Constituent Assembly of that country, which was set up in precisely the same circumstances, a Republic. That Constitution did not receive the assent of the then Governor-General, and in India also the practice throughout was that constitutional Acts of the Constituent Assembly were sufficiently passed into law by authentication of the President, and assent of the Governor-General was never obtained. India also, after becoming a Republic, has accepted the British Sovereign only in the capacity of 'Head of the Commonwealth'. Therefore, in the existing conditions, no bond of allegiance could be deemed to exist between the Governor-General of Pakistan as head of this State on the one side and the British Sovereign on the other. (It was emphasised that even the acceptance of the title 'Head of the Commonwealth' had been effected not by an expression of the will of the country's Legislature, but only by a proclamation made by the Governor-General, whose status under section 5 of the Indian Independence Act is that of representative of the British Sovereign.)

Mr Chundrigar then pointed out that the Constitutional Instruments relevant to Pakistan are devoid of any expression such as might have the effect of making the British Sovereign a part of any Legislature in Pakistan. This has been achieved by gradual steps. The provision in the Act that the Federal Legislature of India should consist of the British Sovereign represented by the Governor-General and two Chambers was radically altered in the course of adaptation to the new conditions which were expected to develop from the date of establishment of the new Dominions. The new section merely set out in different words the provisions of section 5, sub-section (2), proviso (*e*) of the Indian Independence Act, *viz.* that the powers of the Federal or Indian Legislature should be *exercisable* by the Constituent Assembly. The Constituent Assembly had thereafter been at pains, by amendment of the Indian Independence Act and the Government of India Act, to remove references to the grant of assent to legislation by the Governor-General and by Governors of Provinces *in His Majesty's name*, thereby emphasising the actual independence of the Governor-General and the Governors in respect of the grant of the assent. Where the interim Constitution provided that the head of the Government should be a part of the legislative machinery, it said so explicitly, e.g. in section 60 of the Government of India Act which declares that 'there shall for every Province be a Provincial Legislature, which shall consist of the Governor, and one Chamber'. This was in accordance with the practice in every other Dominion, and, therefore, since the Government of India Act and the Indian Independence Act are wholly devoid of any words which could make the Governor-General a part of the Constituent Assembly, either in the capacity of Federal Legislature or in its higher Constitution-making capacity, the conclusion must be that the Governor-General as such was not a part of the law-making machinery of the Dominion.

Next, Mr Chundrigar put forward the argument that assent is a form of control over legislation, and referred to the history of the grant of independence to the sub-continent of India for the purpose of showing that in relation to the preparation of new Constitutions for the two countries, it was impossible to suppose that any control was intended to be imposed. The constitutional documents relevant to the grant of independence showed a clear intention on the part of His Majesty's Government in the United Kingdom to fulfil the wish of the Indian people to attain freedom, and to assist the Indian people to achieve freedom in a form which they should freely decide for themselves, by helping to establish the necessary machinery. Although the hope was expressed that the new countries would remain within the Commonwealth, and emphasis was laid upon the advantages of such a position, contrasted with the perils of isolation in the modern world, it was nevertheless repeatedly stated that the Constitution would be settled by Indians for Indians. It was said that His Majesty's Government had 'no intention of attempting to frame any ultimate Constitution for India; this is a matter for the Indians themselves'. The argument for the appellants had been that the power of assent included necessarily the power to withhold assent and the implication was that insistence upon assent by the appellants was tantamount to insistence upon the acceptance of a control. The conditions which His Majesty's Government in the United Kingdom created in India and in Pakistan before they themselves relinquished all responsibility for the Government of these territories, clearly militated against the presence of any such control.

With reference to section 6 (3), Indian Independence Act, the contention was that its terms did not render assent to constitutional laws necessary, but, on the other hand, if the express terms imposing the necessity of assent which are contained in the Constitution of every other Dominion existing in 1947 be compared with this provision, the necessary conclusion must be that no provision, requiring assent to constitutional laws made by the Constituent Assembly, had been made by the British Parliament. The necessity for assent to Federal legislation arose out of the statutory provision under section 32, Government of India Act, 1935. The Constituent Assembly which in the interim period exercised the powers of the Federal Legislature could have amended section 32 to remove the requirement of assent, which was in the nature of a control, but it chose of its own free will, not to do so. The added powers of legislation which were to vest in the Dominions through the relinquishment of such power by the British Parliament were conveyed by the Indian Independence Act, and if it was the intention of Parliament, which was fully aware that such vested powers were being conveyed away, to impose upon the exercise of such powers the control implicit in assent, they would certainly have done so in explicit terms. That had been done by the same Parliament in the case of every other Dominion, and its omission from the Indian Independence Act could only lead to the conclusion that Parliament intentionally avoided making such a provision, and that it did so in view of the plenary powers which were being allowed in favour of the Constituent Assemblies of the Dominions, to prepare a wholly new Constitution for each Dominion. If there was to be any such control imposed upon the Constituent Assembly's power, that control must be left to the Constituent Assembly itself to impose; having declared the Constituent Assembly to be fully unfettered in this particular respect, the British Parliament could not thereafter concern itself with the imposition of control of any kind, whether exercisable from the United Kingdom or from within the new Dominion of Pakistan.

Consequently, section 6 (3), Indian Independence Act, was to be construed as a provision which broke down with one stroke all pre-existing restraints imposed from the United Kingdom, whether by virtue of His Majesty's prerogative, or by Act of the British Parliament, upon the Governor-General's power to grant assent to laws which might for the future be made so as to have effect throughout the new Dominion, supposing that it remained a Dominion. It had been made clear that this would depend upon the free choice of the Constituent Assembly, and therefore to suppose that section 6 (3) had the effect of making assent *sine qua non* was impossible, since that would be to fetter the powers of the Constituent Assembly.

It was next urged that the Indian Independence Act did not purport to set up a Legislature for either of the two independent Dominions that were to be formed. Here also, the Indian Independence Act furnishes a sharp contrast with every other law of the British Parliament, creating Dominions. No body of persons was specified which would constitute the 'Legislature of the Dominion'. The expression was indeed used in a completely abstract sense, as is clear from the fact that the only aid furnished by the Act to the formation of any idea as to the nature and quality of the 'Legislature of the Dominion' was by references to things which the 'Legislatures of the Dominions' might do, which were mentioned in a number of sections in the Act, notably sub-section (1) of section 8, which refers to 'the powers of the Legislature of the Dominion for the purpose of making provision as to the constitution of the Dominion'. On the other hand, the Constituent Assembly was referred to throughout as a specific body, and indeed on the appointed day, the Constituent Assembly of Pakistan was already in being. In section 8, Indian Independence Act, which has reference to the exercise of legislative powers of the Dominion, the Constituent Assembly is mentioned three times and each time as a distinct body, differentiated from the 'Legislature of the Dominion'. If the intention of the British Parliament had been that as from the appointed day, *viz.* 14 August 1947, the Constituent Assembly of Pakistan should be the 'Legislature of the Dominion', nothing could have been easier than to have said so expressly, and if that had been done, a considerable number of provisions, which were made necessary only because the conception of the 'Legislature of the Dominion' was to be kept distinct from the actuality of the Constituent Assembly, would have been rendered unnecessary, and the Act might have been greatly shortened and simplified. In fact, the Constituent Assembly could not conceivably be identified with the 'Legislature of the Dominion' for the simple reason that the Constituent Assembly was to be the parent and creator of the 'Legislature of the Dominion', whose shape and form the British Parliament could not presume to set, having once declared that this function was to be performed by the Constituent Assembly of Pakistan free of all control. It might have been that in the result the Constituent Assembly may have decided upon a Legislature to exercise the legislative powers of the Dominion, in which the Governor-General might have been an integral part, and in that case, that provision in section 6 (3), Indian Independence Act, would immediately come into play. But until that happened, the correct position was that the Constituent Assembly was not the 'Legislature of the Dominion', whether it was exercising Constitution-making powers or the powers of the Federal Legislature.

Lastly, Mr Chundrigar referred to the great number of constitutional laws which had been made by the Constituent Assembly in the same mode as the laws which were now being impugned, and emphasised that the addition of section 223A to the Government of India Act had been made by the Constituent Assembly upon motion of the then Law Minister, Mr A. K. Brohi. Being a provision relating to a highly important subject of great public interest, namely, the jurisdiction of the High Courts, it must be presumed to have been put forward after due consideration by the Federal Government. It did not lie in the mouth of that Government now to repudiate this provision, which it itself moved to obtain, presumably with the intention that it should be effective. Mr Chundrigar also referred to a number of judgments of superior Courts in Pakistan where, either directly or by implication, effect had been given to the view that a law of the Constituent Assembly making provision or containing a provision as to the Constitution of Pakistan did not require the assent of the Governor-General. These cases are firstly, *M. A. Khuhro* v. *The Federation of Pakistan*,[1] the *Mamdot* case[2] and *Ex-Major-General Akbar Khan's* case.[3] In the first case, a single Judge of the Sind Chief Court, in the year 1950, expressly accepted a contention advanced on behalf of the Federation of Pakistan, in respect of a law which the opponent was seeking to avoid, that that law, being a law making provision of a constitutional nature, was validly passed without the assent

[1] P.L.D. 1950 Sind. 49.   [2] 1950–1 F.C.R. 24.
[3] P.L.D. 1954 F.C. 87.

of the Governor-General. In the other two cases, which were subsequently decided in 1950 and 1954 respectively, in both of which the Federation of Pakistan was represented, the validity of the law in question in each case was challenged on the ground that it was not a law relating to the Constitution, and therefore required assent. In each case, this argument was negatived, but the absence of assent was the central and crucial fact in each of these cases and it was of the utmost significance that the eminent counsel who appeared did not challenge the validity of the legislation, even as constitutional legislation, on this ground. Nor did the learned Judges of the Federal Court themselves take notice of the matter, indicating clearly that the judicial view expressed in the Sind case was accepted as correct in this regard.

The issue between the parties on the point of necessity of assent may be stated somewhat as follows. For the Federation of Pakistan and the Ministers whose legal status has been held by the Sind Chief Court to be unsound, the contention is that the necessity of assent by the Governor-General, as a condition of the validity of all laws passed by any Legislature which has the capacity to make laws for the whole Dominion, including laws making provision as to the Constitution, is derivable from (a) the fact that Pakistan is a Dominion included in the British Commonwealth of Nations and (b) the following words contained in section 6 (3) of the Indian Independence Act, viz. 'The Governor-General of each of the new Dominions shall have full power to assent to any law of the Legislature of that Dominion'. On behalf of the petitioner, the contention is that no such condition or obligation can be construed out of Pakistan's membership of the British Commonwealth of Nations, even as a Dominion, in view of the present-day conception of such membership, of the deliberate avoidance by Pakistan of acceptance of allegiance to the British Crown, and the equally deliberate acceptance of the British Sovereign, not as Queen of Pakistan, but only as Head of the Commonwealth. The construction placed upon section 6 (3) of the Indian Independence Act is characterized as entirely incorrect, and it is contended that the words are only of enabling effect and cannot carry any connotation of duty. I shall examine first the question whether the necessity of assent by the Governor-General can be founded upon any consideration arising out of Pakistan's membership of the British Commonwealth of Nations.

As far back as 1926, following the Imperial Conference of that year (the British Empire being then a living reality), it was declared that the United Kingdom and the Dominions were 'autonomous communities within the British Empire, equal in status, in no way subordinate one to another in any aspect of their domestic or external affairs, though united by a common allegiance to the Crown, and freely associated as members of the British Commonwealth of Nations'. It was still possible at that time to describe the British Parliament as 'the Imperial Legislature', a term employed by the Privy Council in the *Maritime Bank of Canada* case which I have already cited. In 1931, 'the Imperial Legislature' passed what may be described, I hope without disrespect, as a self-denying enactment, viz. the Statute of Westminister, whose long title however was 'Act of the *Imperial Parliament* to give Effect to certain Resolutions passed by Imperial Conferences held in the years 1926 and 1930'.

The lengthy preamble to this Act is in six separate paragraphs of which the second contains an attempt at a definition of the position of members of the Commonwealth, couched in the following words:

It is meet and proper to set out by way of preamble to this Act that, inasmuch as the Crown is the symbol of the free association of the members of the British Commonwealth of Nations, and as they are united by a common allegiance to the Crown . . . .

It may be noted that the freedom was confined to the association of the countries among themselves; as against the Crown however there was not freedom but allegiance. It is, I think, entirely justifiable to give to the word 'allegiance', when used in respect of a high and mighty Prince, its full connotation, namely, that bond of servitude which a liege-man owes to his liege-lord. A liege-man is, in the feudal concept, from which it is not safe to depart when assessing at its full weight the power and authority of royalty, a sworn vassal, bound by an oath of fealty to his liege-lord, namely, a feudal superior or sovereign entitled to receive feudal service. It may be that by convention and also as a result of the devolution of power involved in the grant of representative institutions, the strict obligations, which words such as 'feudal sovereignty', 'feudal service' import, become inapplicable in course of time. In the case of the sub-continent of India, which was known as the Indian Empire in which the British Sovereign, as will appear from section 2 of the Government of India Act, 1935, enjoyed and possessed every kind of royal power and authority, being also sovereign of all the territories thereof, it would be possible, in my view, to place a meaning upon the word 'allegiance' not far removed from that which might be thought to convey the maximum obligations arising out of the relationship. At that time, however, i.e. in the year 1931, India was not a Dominion.

As a result of the Statute of Westminster, the conception of an 'Imperial Parliament' was swept away in relation to the Dominions of Canada, Australia, New Zealand, South Africa, the Irish Free State and Newfoundland. Yet, allegiance to the British Crown was retained on the one side, and while it was declared that no future Act of the British Parliament would extend to any of these Dominions (subject to acceptance of this provision by Australia, New Zealand and Newfoundland) and that the Parliaments of these Dominions should be free to make any law they pleased, even a law repugnant to any United Kingdom law having effect in the Dominion so that the power to repeal any such law of England was included, yet the Parliaments of Canada, Australia and New Zealand were expressly debarred by sections 7 and 8 from amending or repealing their respective constitutional Acts, being Acts of the erstwhile 'Imperial Parliament'. In the case of Australia, a further limitation upon the fullness of the legislative power of the Dominion was provided by section 9, namely, that the British Parliament retained power to make laws 'with respect to any matter within the authority of the States of Australia, not being a matter within the authority of the Parliament or Government of the Commonwealth of Australia', where the making of such a law without the concurrence of the Parliament of the Dominion was in accordance with the previous constitutional practice. These provisions are still substantially in operation as law, and, in my opinion, they detract very greatly from the nature of the sovereignty which was received by these Dominions in consequence of the Statute of Westminster. It was argued for the appellants that by convention the stringency of these powerful controls was susceptible of relaxation, but at this point, it is useful, in my opinion, to repeat one of the basic propositions which Mr Kenneth Diplock advanced as the foundation of his argument, viz. that in construing any constitutional enactment the Courts are concerned only with legal powers. In my opinion, the existence of these restraints clearly, and forcefully, stands in the way of acceptance of Mr Diplock's assertion that all the Dominions were *independent* Dominions in exactly the same sense as India and Pakistan became independent Dominions in August 1947. It is true that Mr Diplock did not rely to the greatest extent for this assertion on the case of Canada, Australia and New Zealand. His strongest card was the South Africa Act, 1909, which, by section 152, gave power to the Parliament of the Dominion to repeal or alter any of the provisions of that Act. Yet that Act imposed specific restrictions of a very real kind which exist to this day, as is evident from section 9 providing that the Governor-General shall be appointed by the King and section 64 which lays down that a Bill passed by the two Houses should be presented to the Governor-General for the King's assent, and the Governor-General shall declare 'according to his discretion, but subject to the provisions of this Act, and *to such instructions as may from time to time be given in that behalf by the King*, that he assents in the King's name, or that he withholds assent'. The power of this strong legal provision was sought to be minimised in argument by reference to conventions, but again, I repeat that the Court is not concerned with conventions but only with legal provisions.

The conclusions which I reach on the basis of this brief examination regarding the effect of the Statute of Westminster are as follows. In respect of the specified Dominions, for the future, the British Parliament, altogether, lost the status of 'Imperial Legislature'. In the case of each Dominion, the duty of allegiance to the British Crown was asserted, and in the case of three of them, the power to alter their own Constitutions, which had been conferred upon them by Act of the 'Imperial Legislature', was expressly withheld. The idea of *independence* is certainly not the first or the strongest impression conveyed by these stipulations. In only one respect was a word of liberation employed, viz. these countries, enjoying a mitigated form of legislative power, approximating to but distinctly different from legal sovereignty, were described as being 'freely associated' with each other, as well as with His Majesty's Government in the United Kingdom.

After the year 1931, a number of rapid developments took place, particularly in relation to the Irish Free State, which are of great importance to a proper understanding of the position occupied by Pakistan and the obligations arising out of that position, when it was admitted to the community of the Dominions in 1947. The history of the developments affecting the Irish Free State may be conveniently extracted from a footnote to para. 1022 on page 458 of vol. v of Halsbury's *Laws of England* (3rd ed.), which reads as follows, the unnecessary matter being excised:

The Irish Free State was one of the Dominions specified in the Statute of Westminster, 1931. In 1933 she abolished the oath of allegiance; in 1935 she purported to exclude her citizens from the definition of British subjects; in 1936 she abolished the office of Governor-General; in 1937 she adopted what was in effect a republican Constitution, in which the only reference to the Crown related to the Executive Authority (External Relations) Act, 1936, which provided that so long as the Free State was associated with the Commonwealth the King could act on her behalf and on the advice of her Government for the appointment of diplomatic and consular representatives. The adoption of the 1936 Constitution was not accepted by the United Kingdom as effecting a fundamental change in Eire's relations with the Commonwealth, and an argument that the adoption of the 1937 Constitution was an act of secession was rejected in *Murray* v. *Parkes*, [1942] 2 K.B. 123.

The final steps were, however, not taken until 1949, and these may be conveniently set out in the words of paragraph 1022 mentioned above:

In 1949 Eire, which, regarding herself as being externally associated within the Commonwealth, had for long occupied an equivocal and anomalous constitutional position, seceded from the Commonwealth by her own action. By an Act of the Oireachtas her remaining formal links with the Crown were severed and she was declared to be the Republic of Ireland; this measure was accompanied by an announcement by the Government of Eire of intention to terminate the association with the Commonwealth. The United Kingdom Parliament by statute recognised and declared that Eire had ceased as from 18 April 1949 (the date fixed by Eire) to be part of His Majesty's dominions.

From footnote (*o*) at page 459, however, it appears quite clearly that even these acts are not construed in the United Kingdom as determining finally the traditional relationship between Eire and the United Kingdom.

Accordingly it would appear to be perfectly clear that in August 1947, when India and Pakistan entered the community of the Dominions, there was in existence one Dominion accepted as such by His Majesty, and by His Majesty's Government in the United Kingdom as well as by the other Dominions, which did not owe allegiance to the British Crown, which by law had declared that her citizens were not British subjects, and had by law abolished the office of Governor-General hitherto within the power of the British sovereign to fill, replacing him by an elected President. These several acts, which might be thought to be unequivocal acts of dissociation and severance from the purview of the British Sovereign, were not regarded by any of the other parties interested to maintain the position of Eire as a country within the community of the British Commonwealth of Nations, to have the effect of excluding Eire from that community. The same view was apparently taken by Eire herself, for she delayed her final act of severance from the Commonwealth for another twelve years. Nothing can indicate more clearly the interest which the United Kingdom displayed in retaining Ireland within the Commonwealth, despite its denial of every kind of obligation which might be thought to stem from a 'common allegiance to the Crown', than the fact that even after 1949, it continued to be assumed in the United Kingdom that citizens of Eire and Eire herself were not yet wholly free of the character which they had earlier possessed.

It is, therefore, not surprising to find the learned author of the monograph on 'Commonwealth and Dependencies' in the latest edition of Halsbury's *Laws* declaring at page 431 of the volume already cited that: 'Having regard to the variant conceptions of the Commonwealth association held by different members, no attempt has been made or is likely to be made to prescribe a uniform terminology to designate the association'.

By the year 1947, the clear-cut conception of 'a common allegiance to the Crown' as a necessary incident of membership of the Commonwealth had, as a result of the studied defection therefrom of a valued and apparently still-cherished member, become obscured to vanishing point. Consequently, any new entrants into the Commonwealth might reasonably consider that they were under no obligation to accept any ties or bonds in excess of the minimum which the existing members, being, of course, freely associated with each other, were content to regard as sufficient in relation to any one of their number. The point is of crucial importance for determining the obligations of India and Pakistan when they entered the Commonwealth in 1947, that Ireland had completely renounced all allegiance to the British Crown at that time, and was being governed under a republican constitution, according to which the head of the State was an elected President, whose powers of all kinds were derived from the Constitution of the country and not in any way from or through the British Sovereign. When it is borne in mind, as a matter of public general knowledge of which judicial notice may properly be taken, that the Indian Independence Act was passed by the British Parliament as a result of an insistent public demand throughout the sub-continent of India for independence from what used to be described as the 'British yoke', a fair idea may be formed of the sense in which entry into the Commonwealth was regarded by those to whom, on their departure from the sub-continent, the British transferred power of every kind. The temper of the people may be gauged with a high degree of accuracy from the last of the popular political slogans which preceded the transfer of power. It was contained in two words, namely, 'Quit India'. Further proof of that temper, if proof be needed, is provided by the rapidity with which the Indian people proceeded to frame a new Constitution for themselves and proclaimed a Republic under an elected President in January 1950. It is true that this did not lead to dissociation of India from the Commonwealth, any more than a similar declaration some thirteen years earlier by Eire had been thought either by Eire or by the United Kingdom or by any of the other then existing Dominions to have caused such a severance. But *allegiance* to the British Crown of necessity disappeared and India accepted the British Sovereign only as Head of the Commonwealth.

Again, as a matter of public general knowledge, judicial notice may be taken of the fact that in material respects, the attitude in Pakistan was no different from that displayed in the other 'Independent Dominion' towards the British connection. By way of evidence, one may cite the several occasions upon which the

185

Constituent Assembly has acted to remove from the instruments which formed the interim Constitution of the country, namely, the Indian Independence Act, 1947, and the Government of India Act, 1935 (as adapted to come into effect on 14 August 1947), various residual references to the British Sovereign which were taken as imposing restraints upon legislative freedom. Another indication of the same intention is to be found in the official declaration by Pakistan that the country is to be, under its new Constitution, an Islamic Republic. I am not aware that any later declaration has been made on this subject by any competent authority.

There are, however, two very precise acts of the Pakistan Governor-General which cannot be interpreted otherwise than as acts of denial of allegiance to the British Sovereign. The first such act was performed by the first Governor-General of Pakistan, the late Qaid-i-Azam Muhammad Ali Jinnah. When the time came for him to take the oath upon assuming office as Governor-General of Pakistan, he refused to accept the earlier form which required the Governor-General to bear 'true faith and allegiance to His Majesty' and thereupon, by agreement with the British Sovereign, the oath which he took and which his successors after him have taken requires that he should bear true allegiance to the Constitution and *be faithful to His Majesty*. Nothing can indicate more clearly that appointment at the hands of the British Sovereign to the office of the Governor-General of Pakistan is accepted by the Governors-General of this country in a form vastly different from that which the Governors-General of the other Dominions are required to accept. In the case of these latter Governors-General, they swear 'true faith and allegiance to the British Sovereign'. That imports of necessity a disparity of position and acceptance of servitude. The Governor-General of Pakistan, when he swears to be faithful to the British Sovereign, cannot be thought to accept any inferiority of position, much less of servitude in the feudal sense appropriate to the conception of royalty. At the highest it is an undertaking of loyalty on equal terms and entirely appropriate to acceptance of the British Sovereign not as a Queen, but as a symbolic Head of the Commonwealth.

The second such act was performed by the present Governor-General, His Excellency Mr Ghulam Muhammad. By the preamble to the Statute of Westminster, it is set out that, through the

186

Crown being the symbol of free association within the Commonwealth, and as the members are united by a common allegiance to the Crown, constitutional practice requires that the royal styles and titles should, after the Act, require the assent 'as well of the Parliaments of the Dominions as of the Parliament of the United Kingdom'. Such a question arose upon the accession of the present occupant of the British Throne, Her Majesty Queen Elizabeth II. Although the Constituent Assembly met on numerous occasions after June 1953, when Her Majesty was crowned, it does not appear that the matter of acceptance or otherwise of the royal styles and titles appropriate to Her Majesty, in relation to Pakistan, was ever brought before the Constituent Assembly. On the other hand, and perhaps by way of substitution, a proclamation was made by the Governor-General accepting Her Majesty Queen Elizabeth II as 'Head of the Commonwealth', which expression, so far as I can gather, includes every Dominion and may also include other realms and territories. It seems to me quite clear from this single act that the position which has been accepted by Pakistan, as being occupied by Her Majesty in relation to this country, is in no way different from that which has been accepted by the neighbouring Republic of India. Despite the apparently constant activity of well-informed persons, in unravelling the legal incidents of the various terms employed in British constitutional law with reference to the Commonwealth, no authority has yet chosen to derive from the description 'Head of the Commonwealth' anything importing the exercise either directly or by a delegate of royal prerogatives or powers. A passage from a notable judgment by My Lord the Chief Justice delivered as Chief Justice of the Lahore High Court in the case of *Sarfaraz Khan* v. *The Crown*[1] may assist materially in elucidating the position. That judgment was delivered at a time when the declaration of the Governor-General in relation to the status of Her Majesty Queen Elizabeth II *qua* Pakistan had not yet been made. The passage reads as follows:

The assent to the Bills, however, is still given by the Governor-General and the Governors in the name of His Majesty but that is because the Crown is the symbol of the free association of the members of the British Commonwealth of Nations and not because His Majesty

[1] P.L.R. 1950 Lahore 658.

exercises any control over it in the form of revoking the assent or the authority of the Governor-General or disallowing the Act. The Governor-General is the head of the Government of the Dominion, and he is there by reason of the will of that Government and not by the will of the British Government or that of His Majesty, His Majesty in such matters having no will at all.

True he represents His Majesty for the purposes of the government of the Dominion but that does not mean that he is an agent of His Majesty in the sense that His Majesty has delegated any authority to him which His Majesty can revoke at will.

Having regard to the change brought about by the Governor-General's proclamation in respect of the present occupant of the British Throne *qua* Pakistan, the view expressed in this passage gains enormous emphasis from the circumstance that, as Head of the Commonwealth, Her Majesty is indeed a mere symbol, although as Queen of Pakistan a more substantial position might perhaps have been claimed.

The next question to which I propose to address myself is what was the nature of the freedom which the Indian Independence Act, 1947, was intended to convey? I use the expression 'freedom' advisedly, for it is sufficiently clear from the foregoing that in the description 'free association of free peoples', so often applied to the Dominions, the words 'free peoples' must necessarily be understood in a qualified sense. I conceive that they are meant in the sense of peoples enjoying the advantage of representative institutions according to the British pattern, and that fullness of legislative competence does not necessarily follow from the application of these words. In order to confirm this view, I propose at this stage to reproduce verbatim from the Constitutions of the three principal Dominions, namely, Canada, Australia and South Africa, provisions relating to the powers still reserved in His Majesty to control legislation in these Dominions.

In Canada, by section 17 of the British North America Act, 1867, it is provided that: 'There shall be one Parliament for Canada, consisting of the Queen, an Upper House styled "the Senate", and the House of Commons'. By section 9 of the same Act, it is provided that: 'The Executive Government and authority of and over Canada is hereby declared to continue and be vested in the Queen'.

Provision under section 11 is made for the Governor-General

who is to be aided and advised by a Council composed of members to be chosen and summoned by him, this Council being described as 'The Queen's Privy Council for Canada'. Section 55 of the Act relating to Royal assent is of the utmost significance. I reproduce it below along with sections 56 and 57, as these form a self-contained legal code, which visibly and expressly reserves power in the Queen to veto legislation by the Parliament of Canada:

55. Where a bill passed by the Houses of the Parliament is presented to the Governor-General for the Queen's assent, he shall declare, according to his discretion, but subject to the provisions of this Act and to Her Majesty's instructions, either that he assents thereto in the Queen's name, or that he withholds the Queen's assent, or that he reserves the bill for the signification of the Queen's pleasure.

56. Where the Governor-General assents to a bill in the Queen's name, he shall by the first convenient opportunity send an authentic copy of the Act to one of Her Majesty's Principal Secretaries of State, and if the Queen in Council within 2 years after receipt thereof by the Secretary of State thinks fit to disallow the Act, such disallowance (with a certificate of the Secretary of State of the day on which the Act was received by him) being signified by the Governor-General, by speech or message to each of the Houses of the Parliament or by proclamation, shall annul the Act from and after the day of such signification.

57. A bill reserved for the signification of the Queen's pleasure shall not have any force unless and until, within 2 years from the day on which it was presented to the Governor-General for the Queen's assent, the Governor-General signifies, by speech or message to each of the Houses of the Parliament or by proclamation, that it has received the assent of the Queen in Council.

In a judgment of this character it may, I think, be presumed that where a Governor-General reserves a bill for the signification of the Royal pleasure, he does so in accordance with general instructions received in that behalf from the British Sovereign. In each of the three sections which are reproduced above the assent of the British Sovereign in person therefore appears with absolute clearness, as a final controlling force applicable to legislation of the Canadian Parliament.

The corresponding provisions in the Australian Constitution are as follows. In the Commonwealth of Australia Constitution Act, 1900, it is provided by section 1 of chapter 1 as follows:

The legislative power of the Commonwealth shall be vested in a Federal Parliament, which shall consist of the Queen, a Senate, and a

House of Representatives, and which is hereinafter called 'the Parliament', or 'the Parliament of the Commonwealth'.

By section 2 provision is made for appointment by the British Sovereign of a Governor-General to be the Sovereign's representative in the Commonwealth. Sections 58, 59 and 60 give effect to the control provided by the requirement of Royal assent and are in the following terms:

58. When a proposed law passed by both Houses of the Parliament is presented to the Governor-General for the Queen's assent, he shall declare, according to his discretion, but subject to this constitution, that he assents in the Queen's name, or that he withholds assent, or that he reserves the law for the Queen's pleasure.

The Governor-General may return to the House in which it originated any proposed law so presented to him, and may transmit therewith any amendments which he may recommend, and the Houses may deal with the recommendation.

59. The Queen may disallow any law within one year from the Governor-General's assent, and such disallowance on being made known by the Governor-General by speech or message to each of the Houses of the Parliament, or by proclamation, shall annul the law from the day when the disallowance is so made known.

60. A proposed law reserved for the Queen's pleasure shall not have any force unless and until within 2 years from the day on which it was presented to the Governor-General for the Queen's assent the Governor-General makes known, by speech or message to each of the Houses of the Parliament, or by proclamation, that it has received the Queen's assent.

The same observations as have been made above with reference to the Canadian Constitution are fully applicable to the restraints so specifically imposed upon the legislative power of 'the Parliament of the Commonwealth'.

In the South Africa Act, 1909, section 19, by which the Parliament of the Union was constituted, reads as under: 'The legislative powers of the Union shall be vested in the Parliament of the Union, herein called "Parliament", which shall consist of the King, a Senate and a House of Assembly.'

By section 9 it is provided that the Governor-General shall be appointed by the King. Section 64 to which reference has already been made may here be reproduced in full with advantage:

64. When a bill is presented to the Governor-General for the King's assent, he shall declare according to his discretion, *but subject to the*

provisions of this Act, and to such instructions as may from time to time be given in that behalf by the King, that he assents in the King's name, or that he withholds assent. The Governor-General may return to the House in which it originated any bill so presented to him, and may transmit therewith any amendments which he may recommend, and the House may deal with the recommendation.

In the face of these provisions it is obvious that these great countries can hardly be called 'Independent Dominions'. Their principal legislatures work under controls imposed from without, by force of law.

The Indian Empire, as it was till the grant of independence in 1947, did not enjoy Dominion Status, but it had been provided by the British Parliament with a series of constitutions, progressively liberal in character, under which the Government of the country with its vast population and extremely complex administrative problems, had been successfully carried on for a great many years. The last of these constitutions was that contained in the Government of India Act, 1935 and it falls to be observed that in many essential respects, it provided a degree of freedom not far removed from that enjoyed by the recognised Dominions. True, by section 2 of the Government of India Act, it was stated, in words of high import, that:

All rights, authority and jurisdiction heretofore belonging to His Majesty the King, Emperor of India, which appertain or are incidental to the Government of the territories in India for the time being vested in him, and all rights, authority and jurisdiction exercisable by him in or in relation to any other territories in India, are exercisable by His Majesty, except in so far as may be otherwise provided by or under this Act, or as may be otherwise directed by His Majesty.

The words, perhaps by design, convey a vast sense of majesty and authority, which despite the generous distribution effected by the Act could yet be exercised by the Sovereign, free of all control. Nevertheless, in their effect, they are scarcely to be distinguished from the simpler words of section 9 of the British North America Act, 1867, relating to Canada. Indeed, if distinction be sought, in relation to imposition of legal limitations upon the exercise of royal power, that distinction would appear to lie clearly in favour of the then Indian Empire. But Canada as a country within the purview of the Statute of Westminster, 1931, enjoyed one advantage, namely that the British Parliament could no longer legislate for Canada, except with the consent of the Dominion. The condition in India was entirely different. Although very wide legislative powers had been expressly conveyed to the Indian people by numerous provisions in the Government of India Act and intricate provisions were made for exercise of these powers in a harmonious manner by the Centre and the Provinces among whom those powers had been distributed, yet, by section 110, the following over-riding provision was made, viz.: 'Nothing in this Act shall be taken to affect the power of Parliament to legislate for British India, or any part thereof.'

There were other limitations also contained in this section, but these are of minor importance compared with that appearing from the words reproduced above. Restrictions on the exercise of legislative power were spread all over the Government of India Act, in several different forms, but as regards reservation and disallowance, the main provisions relating to the Central Legislature were contained in a single section, viz. section 32, which is reproduced below:

32 (1) When a Bill has been passed by the Chambers, it shall be presented to the Governor-General, and the Governor-General shall in his discretion declare either that he assents in His Majesty's name to the Bill, or that he withholds assent therefrom, or that he reserves the Bill for the signification of His Majesty's pleasure:
Provided that the Governor-General may in his discretion return the Bill to the Chambers with a message requesting that they will reconsider the Bill or any specified provisions thereof and, in particular, will consider the desirability of introducing any such amendments as he may recommend in his message, and the Chambers shall reconsider the Bill accordingly.
(2) A Bill reserved for the signification of His Majesty's pleasure shall not become an Act of the Federal Legislature unless and until, within twelve months from the day on which it was presented to the Governor-General, the Governor-General makes known by public notification that His Majesty has assented thereto.
(3) Any Act assented to by the Governor-General may be disallowed by His Majesty within twelve months from the day of the Governor-General's assent, and where any Act is so disallowed the Governor-General shall forthwith make the disallowance known by public notification, and as from the date of the notification the Act shall become void.

The terms of this section do not vary materially from those which are still in operation in the senior Dominions of Canada and Australia. In the case of laws made by the Provincial Legislatures, which had their own independent powers of legislation, it was laid down that the assent of the Governor should be necessary and the Governor should either accord assent, or reserve the bill for the consideration of the Governor-General, who might in his discretion either grant or withhold the assent or reserve the bill for the signification of His Majesty's pleasure. A time limit was fixed within which a reserved bill could become law by proclamation of His Majesty's assent, as in the case of Federal laws. Finally, there was a specific provision enabling His Majesty to disallow Provincial Acts within twelve months of the giving of the assent by the Governor or the Governor-General.

Here again, it seems evident that the position in the Indian Empire was not materially different from that which the great self-governing Dominions were enjoying. The Governor-General and the Governors were required to observe Instruments of Instructions issued to them after approval by the British Parliament in the name of His Majesty, and these contained, *inter alia*, very precise directions regarding the kind of legislation which must be submitted for signification of His Majesty's pleasure. (These Instruments of Instructions were declared by sub-section (4) of section 18, Indian Independence Act, to 'lapse as from the appointed day'.)

A distinction might perhaps appear at this point, in favour of the older Dominions, viz. that His Majesty, when exercising the power of granting or withholding Royal assent, or disallowing Acts, would not be advised by His Majesty's Government in the United Kingdom, as was the case in relation to the Indian Empire. In this respect the position of the Indian Empire approximated to that of a British Colony or Possession, for the government of which the British Parliament was directly responsible.

It will be of advantage, if at this stage, two sections from the Government of India Act, 1935, relating to the constitution of Legislatures under the Act, are reproduced, *viz.* section 18 relating to the Federal Legislature and section 60 relating to Provincial Legislatures:

18 (1) There shall be a Federal Legislature which shall consist of His Majesty, represented by the Governor-General, and two Chambers, to be known respectively as the Council of State and the House of Assembly (in this Act referred to as 'the Federal Assembly').

(2) The Council of State shall consist of one hundred and fifty-six representatives of British India and not more than one hundred and four representatives of the Indian States, and the Federal Assembly shall consist of two hundred and fifty representatives of British India and not more than one hundred and twenty-five representatives of the Indian States.

(3) The said representatives shall be chosen in accordance with the provisions in that behalf contained in the First Schedule to this Act.

(4) The Council of State shall be a permanent body not subject to dissolution, but as near as may be one-third of the members thereof shall retire in every third year in accordance with the provisions in that behalf contained in the said First Schedule.

(5) Every Federal Assembly, unless sooner dissolved, shall continue for five years from the date appointed for their first meeting and no longer, and the expiration of the said period of five years shall operate as a dissolution of the Assembly.

60 (1) There shall for every Province be a Provincial Legislature which shall consist of His Majesty, represented by the Governor, and
    (a) in the Provinces of Madras, Bombay, Bengal, the United Provinces, Bihar and Assam, two Chambers;
    (b) in other Provinces one Chamber.

(2) Where there are two Chambers of a Provincial Legislature, they shall be known respectively as the Legislative Council and the Legislative Assembly, and where there is only one Chamber, the Chamber shall be known as the Legislative Assembly.

It is particularly to be noted that as in the case of each of the Dominions, the sections expressly declared His Majesty represented by the Governor-General or the Governor to be a part of the relevant Legislature.

I now proceed to consider the impact of the Indian Independence Act in relation to the matters appearing from the Government of India Act to which I have referred above, all of which were materially altered in the course of adaptation by the Governor-General of the Indian Empire in the exercise of the powers conferred upon him by section 9 of the Indian Independence Act. It should be fairly clear from the preceding discussion that the Indian Independence Act, 1947, possessed in several respects the same character as the Statute of Westminster, 1931, but with one major difference. It will, I think, be clear from the analysis I am about to attempt, that the extent of freedom accorded to the countries which, as Dominions, were to replace the Indian Empire, was in a very material degree greater than that which the older Dominions had gained in 1931. That, in my view, is the circumstance which justifies the application of the special description 'Independent Dominions' to the two new States which were brought into existence by means of this highly effective instrument.

Firstly, I take up the provisions for appointment of the Governor-General and the Provincial Governors. The original Government of India Act provision relating to the Governor-General read as follows:

3. (1) The Governor-General of India is appointed by His Majesty by a Commission under the Royal Sign Manual and has—
    (a) all such powers and duties as are conferred or imposed on him by or under this Act; and
    (b) such other powers of His Majesty, not being powers connected with the exercise of the functions of the Crown in its relations with Indian States, as His Majesty may be pleased to assign to him.

In the adapted Government of India Act, 1935, which was in force when Pakistan came into existence, section 3 reads simply as follows: 'The Governor-General of Pakistan is appointed by His Majesty by a Commission under the Royal Sign Manual'.

This, however, is not to be regarded as divesting him of all power, for by section 5 of the Indian Independence Act, 1947, it was provided that: 'For each of the new Dominions, there shall be a Governor-General who shall be appointed by His Majesty and shall represent His Majesty for the purposes of the government of the Dominion.'

The Royal Commission which issues under His Majesty's signature contains the following significant provisions. Firstly, the appointment is 'during our pleasure'. Secondly, the Governor-General is to have 'all the powers, rights, privileges and advantages to the said office belonging or appertaining' and it would appear that neither the British Sovereign nor the British Parliament possesses any longer the authority to vary these powers, rights, privileges and advantages. On the date of the creation of Pakistan, and at least until just before 24 October 1954, such a power could be regarded as belonging to no person or body, other than the Constituent Assembly of Pakistan. Next, the Governor-General is authorised, empowered and commanded to perform the powers and duties conferred and imposed upon him by and under the Indian Independence Act, 1947. These powers and duties also are no longer subject to regulation by either the British Sovereign or the British Parliament. Only one of the Royal prerogatives is specifically conveyed to the Governor-General, namely, that of pardon, and is conferred in the following terms:

> We do hereby authorise and empower you in our name and on our behalf to grant to any offender convicted in the exercise of its criminal jurisdiction by any Court of Justice within our territories in Pakistan a pardon, either free or subject to such lawful conditions as you may deem fit.

There are no instructions or authorisations in relation to legislation, e.g. with respect to grant of assent, and even the prerogative of summoning, proroguing and dissolving the Legislature is not conveyed.

The contrast with the case of Governors-General of the older Dominions is almost startling. In South Africa which Mr Diplock urged was as 'independent' as Pakistan, the following authorisations are found in the Letters Patent, viz. (a) to fulfil his duties 'according to our instructions'; (b) to keep and use the Great Seal; (c) to summon, prorogue and dissolve the Union Parliament; (d) to appoint deputies to himself; and (e) to exercise the prerogative of mercy. In Canada and Australia, the Governor-General is authorised to appoint Judges, commissioners, justices of the peace, Ministers, and other officers 'in our name and on our behalf', and also to suspend and remove such persons, under instructions given by, or under the authority of, the King. In each case, the Governor-General is forbidden to quit the Dominion on any pretence whatsoever, except under the Sign Manual of the King, on the ground, expressed in the Canada Royal Instructions, 1931, that 'great prejudice may happen to our service and to the security of our said Dominion' otherwise.

One cannot fail to observe that the formal order made by the British Sovereign in relation to the Pakistan Governor-General contains no instructions or prohibition at all. He is merely enjoined to perform his duties under the interim Constitution, which itself provides for the grant of the Royal prerogative of mercy in section 295, Government of India Act, 1935. It could hardly appear more clearly that the Governor-General owes nothing to the British Sovereign except his warrant of appointment, issued upon the recommendation of the Government of Pakistan. No duty of any kind is prescribed which he owes to Her Majesty, except that of being 'faithful', appearing in the oath which Her Majesty is pleased to accept. The appointment, by its terms, affirms and emphasises that the Governor-General's duty, or as it might be termed 'allegiance', is to the Constitution, as in existence from time to time.

With respect to Governors, the earlier position was that each Governor was appointed by His Majesty by a Commission under the Royal Sign Manual, but under the adapted Government of India Act, 1935, the new provision reads as follows:

48. The Governor of a Province holding office as from the date of the establishment of the Federation is appointed by His Majesty by a Commission under the Royal Sign Manual but any person appointed thereafter to be the Governor of a Province shall be appointed by the Governor-General and shall hold office at the Governor-General's pleasure.

A provision similar to the latter part of the section cited above was also included in the British North America Act, 1867, but as has been seen in the *Maritime Bank* case cited above, such a provision was not regarded as sufficient for holding that the Lieutenant-Governor of a province in Canada was not a representative of His Majesty, because the same Act expressly vested the Executive Government of Canada in the Queen. The corresponding provision in section 2 of the Government of India Act, 1935 (cited above), was entirely omitted, in advance of the creation of Pakistan in the course of adaptation and, consequently, it would appear difficult to suppose, under the existing provisions, that Governors of Provinces other than those who were holding office at the time when Pakistan came into being, are appointees of or owe their position in any respect to, the British Sovereign.

The impression is thus clearly gained that the effective presence of the British Sovereign in the new State of Pakistan was confined to the connection still retained by virtue of the power of appointment of the Governor-General being by law vested in Her Majesty. That furnishes, in my opinion, a precise indication of the measure of freedom which Pakistan possessed, at its creation, by virtue of the legislative and other actions taken by the King and the British Parliament. In all but name, the Governor-General was free of all connection with the British Sovereign; and in point of control, he was altogether free.

At this stage it will be convenient for me to state my opinion regarding an argument raised by Mr Diplock concerning the use to be made of adaptations of the Government of India Act effected by the then Governor-General, in advance of the creation of the new Dominions, under the powers given by section 9 of the Indian Independence Act. I am unable to agree with Mr Diplock that these are acts of a subordinate or delegated character and therefore cannot be called in aid for the purpose of interpreting the meaning of words contained in the Indian Independence Act and the intention underlying those words. This is a proposition which may be appropriate to many types of legislation but it cannot, in my view, be sustained in relation to an organic document such as the Indian Independence Act. By section 9 of that Act, the Governor-General was given power equivalent to that of the British Parliament to make all changes in the Government of India Act which were necessary for the purpose of carrying out the intentions underlying the specific provisions of that Act. The Governor-General of that time, namely, Lord Mountbatten, was not a mere statutory authority, working within the four corners of the Government of India Act, 1935, as a number of his predecessors had been. He acted, for instance, as a plenipotentiary of His Majesty's Government in the United Kingdom, for the purpose of carrying out the design of that Government to provide the peoples of the Indian Empire with machinery appropriate for the purpose of enabling them to draw up a new Constitution for themselves, and to decide at the same time whether or not they would remain within the British Empire. Similarly, under section 9 of the Indian Independence Act, the power which the Governor-General exercised was not exercised by him as merely an instructed agent, for it is a matter of public general knowledge that Lord Mountbatten had been most intimately associated with both the peoples of the Indian Empire as well as the members of His Majesty's Government in the United Kingdom, in settling details of the great compromise which was eventually found acceptable to both parties. Any action taken by a person in that position, which in its nature is susceptible of only one explanation in point of intention, must, in my view, be regarded

as furnishing a very powerful indication of the intention underlying the provision in the Indian Independence Act, which was
thereby carried into effect. Exactly the same holds good in the
case of the first Governor-General of Pakistan, the late Qaid-i-
Azam Muhammad Ali Jinnah, for he too had been associated in
the closest manner with the negotiations of 1946–7 which preceded the elimination of the British power in the sub-continent
of India, and having been designated as the first Governor-
General of Pakistan well in advance of that event, may be assumed
to have been directly concerned in the decisions relevant to the
adaptations which were necessary in the case of Pakistan.

The important changes in the Government of India Act
relating to the exercise of the legislative power in respect of the
future Dominion as a whole may now be considered. The Government of India Act provided, as has already been stated, a very
precise distribution of legislative powers between the Centre and
the Provinces, and as section 8, sub-section (2) of the Indian
Independence Act clearly shows, it had been agreed that each of
the Dominions should continue, during the interim period, to be
governed in all respects according to that Act as adapted, and
subject to any alterations therein which might be subsequently
effected by the Constituent Assembly. The wording of this
provision is important and it is accordingly reproduced below in
full :

8 (2) Except in so far as other provision is made by or in accordance
with a law made by the Constituent Assembly of the Dominion under
sub-section (1) of this section, each of the new Dominions and all
Provinces and other parts thereof shall be governed as nearly as may be
in accordance with the Government of India Act, 1935; and the
provisions of that Act, and of the Orders in Council, rules and other
instruments made thereunder, shall, so far as applicable, and subject
to any express provisions of this Act, and with such omissions, additions, adaptations and modifications as may be specified in orders of the
Governor-General under the next succeeding section, have effect
accordingly :

Provided that—

(a) the said provisions shall apply separately in relation to each of
the new Dominions and nothing in this sub-section shall be construed
as continuing on or after the appointed day any Central Government
or Legislature common to both the new Dominions;

(*b*) nothing in this sub-section shall be construed as continuing in force on or after the appointed day any form of control by His Majesty's Government in the United Kingdom over the affairs of the new Dominions or of any Province or other part thereof;

(*c*) so much of the said provisions as requires the Governor-General or any Governor to act in his discretion or exercise his individual judgment as respects any matter shall cease to have effect as from the appointed day;

(*d*) as from the appointed day, no Provincial Bill shall be reserved under the Government of India Act, 1935, for the signification of His Majesty's pleasure and no Provincial Act shall be disallowed by His Majesty thereunder; and

(*e*) the powers of the Federal Legislature or Indian Legislature under that Act, as in force in relation to each Dominion, shall, in the first instance, be exercisable by the Constituent Assembly of the Dominion, in addition to the powers exercisable by that Assembly under sub-section (1) of this section.

At this stage I invite particular reference to provisos (*b*), (*c*) and (*d*) in this sub-section. By these provisos, the power of His Majesty's Government in the United Kingdom over the affairs of Pakistan and its Provinces was completely eliminated. The pre-existing requirement that the Governor-General and the Governors should in certain respects act in their discretion (i.e. independently of the elected Ministers) or in their individual judgments (i.e. according to their own judgment although after consultation with the elected Ministers) were also removed and the removal is significant in this respect that by specific provisions in the Government of India Act and the instructions issued to the Governor-General and the Governors, these powers were to be exercised in consultation with the Secretary of State for India in London, who was in the last resort to be the deciding authority. Thirdly, there was an express prohibition against reservation of Provincial laws for signification of His Majesty's pleasure, and equally express withdrawal of His Majesty's power to disallow such laws, both to take effect upon a date in the future, which in the case of Pakistan was fixed as 14 August 1947.

The terms of the last-mentioned provision are, in my opinion, of high significance. In respect of the laws applicable in the whole of the Dominions, the corresponding provision was in sub-section (3) of section 6, and is contained in the following words:

so much of any Act as relates to the disallowance of laws by His Majesty or the reservation of laws for the signification of His Majesty's pleasure thereon or the suspension of the operation of laws until the signification of His Majesty's pleasure thereon shall not apply to laws of the Legislature of either of the new Dominions.

As has been seen, provisions for disallowance and reservation of Central laws were contained in the Government of India Act, 1935, and it appears that such provisions might also be found in other Acts of the British Parliament. As regards suspension, the only example brought to the notice of the Court was a provision contained in the Colonial Courts of Admiralty Act, 1890, which did apply to the Indian Empire. The point which emerges, and which is, to my mind, of the greatest importance, is that whereas the wording in relation to Provincial laws is in absolute and peremptory terms of immediate application on the appointed date, the provision relating to the 'Legislature of the Dominions' is expressed in terms of simple futurity. This is relevant, and in my opinion appreciably so, to the contention raised on behalf of the petitioner in the present case that the British Parliament in the Indian Independence Act having indicated some forms of legislative activity appropriate to a Legislature whose Acts were to have force throughout the Dominion, designedly refrained from constituting such a Legislature. Since it was concerned only to make provision for an interim period to precede the establishment of the new Constitution which was to be drawn up by the Constituent Assembly, the British Parliament was content to provide for *exercise* of those legislative powers only—section 8, sub-section (1) and proviso (e) to sub-section (2), Indian Independence Act. Therefore, the 'Legislature of the Dominion' being intended to assume concrete form at a date in the future, under and in accordance with the decision of the Constituent Assembly it was deemed sufficient to provide that the laws of such a Legislature, *assuming that the country still remained a Dominion*, would not be subject to the restrictions and controls which were part of the heritage of the other Dominions and had also by statute been imposed upon the pre-existing Indian Empire. As for laws of the Constituent Assembly made in the interim period, that Assembly being a sovereign body, it was unnecessary and might have been thought derogatory to its position, for a Legislature not superior in status, to provide that such laws should be not subject to controls exercisable by the British Sovereign. But as for the Provincial Legislatures, they were either in being, or were to be constituted for newly-created Provinces by the Governor-General under section 9 (1) (*i*), Indian Independence Act, and they were to act under the terms of the adapted Government of India Act, 1935, as from the appointed day. Their existence and powers being *actual* on the appointed day, the words used to free those powers from all control by His Majesty needed to be absolute and peremptory in their effect.

In my opinion, the language in which the relevant controls were sought to be eliminated in relation to laws of 'the Legislature of the Dominion' furnishes a strong clue to the time when the words were to take effect, and the nature of that effect. Putting the matter in a single sentence, I would say that these words constituted a promise that, should the country remain a Dominion, and should it have, as of course could be more confidently expected, a Union Legislature, then unlike the great self-governing Dominions of Canada, Australia and South Africa, Pakistan would be wholly free of any control of any kind exercisable over the laws of the Union Legislature by His Majesty. But the difference of language also inclines me to think that section 6 (3) of the Indian Independence Act was not drafted on the assumption that on the appointed date there would be a 'Legislature of the Dominion' in existence in Pakistan.

Section 6 of the Indian Independence Act contains provisions of the highest significance, couched in language of subtle and comprehensive nature, whose interpretation is a task, as the lengthy arguments in the present case clearly show, of no mean magnitude. Sub-section (2) of section 6 is in almost precisely the same terms as sub-section (2) of section 2 of the Statute of Westminster. Taken by itself, this provision would necessarily be understood as constituting the people of Pakistan a 'free people' in a sense no higher than that which, as has already been seen, must be accepted in relation to the 'free peoples' of Canada, Australia and New Zealand. Sub-section (4) of section 6 of the Independence Act corresponds to section 4 of the Statute of Westminster. It provides that Acts of the British Parliament passed after the transfer of power should not extend or be deemed to extend to Pakistan, unless extended to Pakistan 'by a law of the Legislature of the Dominion'. (In the Statute of Westminster, the condition is differently expressed as follows, *viz.* 'unless it is expressly declared in that Act that that Dominion has requested, and consented to, the enactment thereof'.) Sub-section (5) provides similar immunity from the operation of Orders in Council, and other orders, rules and instruments made under Acts of the British Parliament, passed after the transfer of power. Sub-section (1) of section 6 is in the following terms: 'The Legislature of each of the new Dominions shall have full power to make laws for that Dominion, including laws having extra-territorial operation'.

This may be compared with section 3 of the Statute of Westminster which reads as follows: 'It is hereby declared and enacted that the Parliament of a Dominion has full power to make laws having extra-territorial operation'.

This provision was interpreted in *The British Columbia Electric Rly. Co., Ltd.* v. *The King*[1] in the following terms:

The specific investment of extra-territorial power by section 3 of the Statute of 1931 was designed no doubt to remove the generally accepted limitation of colonial legislative jurisdiction, a limitation which the Courts of the colony itself were bound to recognise.

It may be pointed out that in the original Government of India Act by section 99 (2), extra-territorial operation had been allowed within specified limits to laws of the Federal Legislature of India. The effect of the relevant clause in section 6 of the Indian Independence Act would naturally be to remove these limitations, and accordingly it is found that section 99 was adapted, before the transfer of power, so as to eliminate the sub-section making this provision.

It yet remains to consider why it was thought necessary by the British Parliament to declare, in the clear language of futurity, that 'the Legislature of the Dominion' should have 'full power to make laws for that Dominion'. Having equipped the Dominion at its very birth with a Constituent Assembly whose function would be to make provision for exercise of legislative powers including the legislative power which was to vest in the Union or Federation, it might have been thought sufficient for the British Parliament to

[1] [1946] 4 D. L. R. 81.

203

remove by express words, all the controls of any kind which had previously operated on such laws, through operation of laws of the British Parliament or through the exercise of the Royal prerogative.

The Government of India Act, 1935, as originally enacted contained a number of scattered provisions operating in restraint of the power of the Federal Legislature to pass laws within the sphere allotted to it in the distribution of the powers effected by that Act. Thus, under section 110, which has been referred to already, there are words which clearly debar the Federal Legislature or any Provincial Legislature from making laws, *inter alia*, affecting the British Sovereign or the Royal Family, Succession to the Crown, the sovereignty of the Crown in any part of India, the law of British nationality, the Army Act, the Air Force Act, the Naval Discipline Act, or the law of prize or prize courts; it was forbidden also for these Legislatures to make any laws amending any provision of the Government of India Act, 1935, or any subordinate legislation thereunder, except to the extent permitted expressly by the Act; and finally subject to the same condition, they were forbidden to legislate so as to take away the prerogative right of His Majesty to grant special leave to appeal from any court (i.e. to the Privy Council). Another mode of restraint appears in section 108 which contains a lengthy list of subjects in regard to which the introduction of any bill in the Federal Legislature would require the previous sanction of the Governor-General *in his discretion*, i.e. acting within that sphere of his executive power which was controlled by His Majesty's Government in the United Kingdom.

It should be remembered that the Indian Independence Act was passed in advance of the adaptations which were made in the stage immediately prior to the transfer of power. Two of these adaptations were the entire elimination of section 108 and section 110 and it may safely be said that all other provisions of a similarly restraining nature were also removed in the same process. The conclusion would appear to be plain that the complete removal of these powerful restraints was a necessary consequence of the employment by the British Parliament, whose intention was being carried out in the course of the adaptations, of the expression 'full power to make laws'. The word 'full' in that aspect would perhaps be completely translated as 'unrestrained'.

It was stated from time to time in the course of arguments that the Constituent Assembly derives power to make laws for the Dominion from section 6 (1), but with great respect, it seems to me that the interpretation overlooks the fact that the Constituent Assembly was, as a body, not a creation of the British Parliament. It is, in my opinion, to be regarded as a body created by a supra-legal power to discharge the supra-legal function of preparing a Constitution for Pakistan. Its powers in this respect belonged to itself inherently, by virtue of its being a body representative of the will of the people in relation to their future mode of Government. The will of the people had, up to that time, been denied expression in this respect, through the presence, by virtue of conquest and cession, of the undisputed and plenary executive power in India of the British Sovereign, which was being withdrawn by unilateral act. That power did not owe its existence to any law, though its exercise may have, from time to time, progressively been reduced to regulation by laws of the British Parliament and of the Indian Empire.

I draw a sharp distinction between the function of providing for the government of the Indian Empire and the function of governing the Indian Empire. The latter function was to be carried out by the Governor-General of India and his subordinates acting in accordance with instructions received from His Majesty's Government in the United Kingdom in certain respects, and in other respects in accordance with the provisions of the statutory instrument then in force, viz. the Government of India Act, 1935. That Act, however, must not itself be included in the complex which may be described as the 'Government of India'. It was set apart from and above that complex, the whole of which was conducted in accordance with the strict terms of that Act. The making of that Act, and the replacement and amendment of that Act, on the other hand, belong to the sphere of making provision for the government of the Indian Empire, and that was, until 14 August 1947, a function exclusively to be discharged by the British Parliament of which the British Sovereign is an integral part. For the purpose of making such provision, the British Sovereign has invariably made the Royal prerogatives available to the British Parliament so that their operation might be provided for, so far as necessary, in the constitutional instrument to be enacted. It is quite clear that the latter function, which is obviously the higher of the two functions, was entrusted to the Constituent Assembly of Pakistan.

The nature of the freedom from external control of the Governor-General having already been considered, and found to be absolute, so long as he remained 'faithful to His Majesty', it is now possible to answer the question posed at the commencement of this discussion. That answer may be considered under three heads:

(i) What was the nature of the autonomy, in the legislative sphere, which the British Parliament intended to convey by means of the Indian Independence Act, 1947, and the adapted Government of India Act, 1935?

(ii) Did the autonomy include power to interpret and apply the provisions in these constitutional instruments as the successor authorities thought best?

(iii) How did these successor authorities interpret and apply the provisions, in respect of the matter now in dispute, and what weight is to be allowed to the interpretations as they appear from the actions of these persons or bodies?

It should be quite clear from the foregoing discussion that, in a legal sense, the older Dominions to which in 1926 the description 'autonomous communities within the British Empire, equal in status, in no way subordinate one to another in any aspect of their domestic or external affairs', had been applied, were, in respect of legislation at least, not so blessed as was Pakistan when it emerged as an 'independent Dominion'. In the case of Pakistan, the statute which created the new State was prepared with meticulous attention to the elimination in detail of every provision of law which had hitherto operated to impose controls upon the Executive Government and Legislatures in the territory. Existing laws were retained, whether they operated as part of the law of the territory or as part of the law of the United Kingdom, but there was provided a Constituent Assembly which, being empowered to furnish, if it so chose, a completely new Constitution for the country, was not to be regarded as bound by any law in existence unless it chose to be so bound. In relation to constitutional provisions, it exercised the powers of the British Parliament, which were in that respect untrammelled by any laws. By way of a practical expedient, it was declared in section 8, Indian Indepen-

206

dence Act, that (*a*) 'the powers of the Legislature of the Dominion shall for the purpose of making provision as to the Constitution of the Dominion, be *exercisable* in the first instance by the Constituent Assembly', and (*b*) 'the powers of the Federal Legislature or Indian Legislature under [the Government of India] Act, as in force in relation to each Dominion, shall, in the first instant, be *exercisable* by the Constituent Assembly'.

It will be necessary, in connection with an argument to be dealt with later, to decide whether these provisions have the effect contended for by the appellants of (*a*) prescribing the powers of the 'Legislature of the Dominion' as being the aggregate of 'powers for the purpose of making provision for the Constitution of the Dominion' and 'powers of the Federal or Indian Legislature under the Government of India Act' and (*b*) making the Constituent Assembly, since these powers were *exercisable* by it, identical with the 'Legislature of the Dominion' as so composed. It may save discussion at a later stage if I utilise this occasion to say that proposition (*a*) involves usurpation by the British Parliament of a very essential part of the power which had expressly been delivered over to the Constituent Assembly, namely to provide a Constitution for Pakistan, in which there might or might not be a 'Legislature of the Dominion', and if there were such a Legislature, to prescribe its powers and functions. To my mind, such an inference is obnoxious to the entire plan which His Majesty's Government in the United Kingdom implemented through the enactment by the British Parliament of the Indian Independence Act. And it seems to me that to identify an existing body of persons such as the Constituent Assembly, clothed with sovereign power to provide a new Constitution for the country, with an entirely different and as yet notional body, whose constitution and powers were yet to be shaped by the Constituent Assembly, involves an operation in thought of extreme difficulty. It stands out most prominently, in this context, that the Indian Independence Act uses no words to relate 'the powers of the Federal Legislature or the Indian Legislature under the Government of India Act' with any future power of the 'Legislature of the Dominion'. The reason seems obvious, namely, that it was for the Constituent Assembly to say what should be the powers of the 'Union Legislature', and they were in no way bound to follow

207

the pattern provided by the Government of India Act, 1935. In marked contrast with the Constitutions of other Dominions, all of which have been enacted by the same British Parliament, the Indian Independence Act refrains from constituting any 'Legislature of the Dominion'. The references to it are confined to mentioning, in scattered sections, certain powers which it could exercise, and certain matters with which it might deal. There are only eleven such provisions and, putting all these together, they cannot in the remotest degree be thought to meet the enormous complexities involved in a distribution of legislative powers between the Centre (or Dominion) and the Provinces. Therefore, to refer to the expression 'full power to make laws for the Dominion' as conferring plenitude of power is not helpful, and the deliberate avoidance of any words to suggest that, on the appointed day, the 'Federal Legislature or the Indian Legislature' was to be replaced by the 'Legislature of the Dominion' makes it clear beyond doubt that no definition of the 'Legislature of the Dominion' by reference to the powers which it was to exercise was attempted in the Indian Independence Act. For that, the plain reason is that it was for the Constituent Assembly to provide for (a) the Constitution, and (b) the powers of the Union Legislature, or the 'Legislature of the Dominion'.

But to return to the question of the legislative autonomy which can be construed out of the Indian Independence Act, I think I can safely predicate on the basis of what I have already said, that it was intended to be *absolute*, the existing laws as adapted being retained only for the purpose of continuing the government of the country on a stable and uniform basis, pending the preparation and promulgation of a new Constitution. The British Parliament was so meticulous in this regard that it was even at pains to include in the Indian Independence Act two provisions designed to produce the effect that the limitations upon legislative powers which were contained in the Government of India Act, 1935, should be *deemed to be of Dominion origin*. By sub-section (6) of section 6, the following provision was made: 'The power referred to in sub-section (1) of this section (i.e. full power to make laws for the Dominion) extends to the making of laws limiting for the future the powers of the Legislature of the Dominion.'

Learned counsel on the two sides were at a loss to explain the purpose of this provision. It was referred to for the appellants as conveying indubitably a power of making constitutional laws, to the 'Legislature of the Dominion', but that appears in clearer terms from section 8 (1) of the same Act. It might have been thought that an autonomous Legislature, such as was intended by sub-sections (1) and (2) of the same section, would possess the capacity to limit its own legislative competence, e.g. in the interest of a harmonious operation of legislative powers distributed between the Centre and the Provinces. Such a distribution already existed, and might conceivably have been thought to be likely to continue under the future arrangements.

In my opinion, the true explanation of section 6 (6) is to be found in the presence of section 8 (3) of the Indian Independence Act, which reads as follows:

(3) Any provision of the Government of India Act, 1935, which, as applied to either of the new Dominions by sub-section (2) of this section and the orders therein referred to, operates to limit the power of the legislature of that Dominion shall, unless and until other provision is made by or in accordance with a law made by the Constituent Assembly of the Dominion in accordance with the provisions of sub-section (1) of this section, have the like effect as a law of the Legislature of the Dominion limiting for the future the powers of that Legislature.

The operation of 'deeming' involves the supposition that a thing is that which it is not. All the limitations on the powers of the 'legislature of the Dominion' with a small 'l', indicating as Mr Diplock thought, that the reference might be to the legislature, which had power to legislate for the whole of British India before the transfer of power—were limitations imposed upon it by the British Parliament. The delicate design and intention of section 6 (6) and section 8 (3) seems clearly enough to be to cause it to appear, for the satisfaction of all those who were sensitive to controls from outside the country, that the limitations were of local origin, and for the time being only, until the Constituent Assembly should see fit to remove or alter them.

As the Governor-General's power of granting assent to laws of the 'Legislature of the Dominion' was uncontrolled from without, complete autonomy was secured to the new Dominion in the legislative sphere, by virtue of the terms employed in the relevant documents, if and when it should be equipped with a 'Legislature of the Dominion'. In the interim period, the position was, if anything, superior in point of freedom, for the Constituent Assembly, which was to legislate in place both of the self-effaced British Parliament as well as of the dissolved Federal or Indian Legislature, was a body which *ex hypothesi* was free of all forms of legal or other control.

But, in the operation of a Constitution, there frequently arise occasions where the meaning of one or more of its provisions, or the intention in a particular respect of the instrument as a whole, gives rise to doubt. With respect to the necessity of assent by the Governor-General to laws of a constitutional nature passed by the Constituent Assembly, this doubt arose at a very early stage. The Court is indebted to the learned Advocate-General of Pakistan for the assertion, made on more than one occasion, that the Law Ministry of the Government of Pakistan (by which was meant the body of permanent officials constituting the staff of the Ministry under the Law Minister) had consistently advised the Minister that such assent was *sine qua non*. On the other hand, the Constituent Assembly had throughout maintained the view that assent was not necessary, and acting on that view had made and promulgated a rule, No 62 in the Rules of the Constituent Assembly, to give formal expression to that view. This rule, as originally framed on 24 February 1948, at a meeting presided over by the President, the late Qaid-i-Azam Muhammad Ali Jinnah, merely provided that when a Bill had been passed by the Assembly, a copy of it should be signed by the President. As this was not followed by any provision for submission to the Governor-General for his assent, it was understood to provide a sufficient formal act to give validity as law to the Bill as passed, but it appears that doubts were felt on this subject, and the rule was amended at a meeting presided over by the Deputy President, Mr Tamizuddin Khan, and held on 22 May 1948, to read as follows: 'When a Bill is passed by the Assembly, a copy thereof shall be signed by the President, and it shall become law on being published in the official *Gazette* of Pakistan under authority of the President.'

No words could express more clearly the opinion of the Constituent Assembly, passed nearly seven years ago, on the question

210

which is now before the Court. I quote here from Craies on Statute Law, 5th ed. at p. 11:

> Parliament is the supreme authority for interpretation of Statutes. . . . Parliament has power to declare by statute the common law or the meaning of any prior statute, and may declare wrong and repeal any judicial legislation effected by interpretation or misinterpretation of statutes, and may make the declaratory or repealing statute retrospective.

It is argued, however, for the appellants that a rule of the Constituent Assembly is not a law. The proposition, on the face of it, seems valid, but it is permissible to observe that there are several other rules made by the Constituent Assembly which it alone was competent to make, which have been acted upon, and which in their character and essence are not only laws in the most thorough-going sense, but must also be placed in the very highest category of laws, *viz.* constitutional laws. I cite three instances below. Rule 6 of the Rules makes elaborate provision for filling of 'casual vacancies' in the membership of the Assembly. By the first proviso to sub-section (3) of section 19, Indian Independence Act, 1947, it was declared that 'nothing in this sub-section shall be construed as preventing the filling of casual vacancies in the (Constituent Assembly of Pakistan) . . . and the powers of the said (Assembly) shall extend, and be deemed always to have extended, to the making of provision for the matters specified in this proviso'.

I do not construe this proviso as conferring any power upon the Constituent Assembly which it did not inherently possess; it is obviously intended for the avoidance of doubts which might have been founded on the wording of sub-section (3). But it would seem clear enough that, in the eye of the British Parliament, the matter was one of 'powers', and not merely of administrative or incidental or ancillary nature so that the exercise of the power in question would, I apprehend, lead to the creation of law.

Next, I refer to Rule 6B which provides for 'Disqualification from membership', and lays down a large number of conditions which individually shall be sufficient to cause vacation of his seat by a member. In one case, the President is enjoined to direct, upon being satisfied of the conditions, that the disqualified member ceases to be a member and to declare his seat vacant; and it is further provided that the President's decision shall be final and shall not be questioned in any court of law or before any other authority. A fine of five hundred rupees per day, recoverable as a debt to the Federation, is prescribed for any person who sits or votes as a member of the Constituent Assembly while under disqualification or prohibition. There cannot be the slightest doubt that by this rule, the Constituent Assembly purported to make law.

Rules 75 to 86 of the Rules relate to 'Doubts and Disputes as to Elections' to membership of the Constituent Assembly. No possible doubt can be entertained regarding these rules that they constitute law. It is true that they were not made in the form prescribed for a statute, but there is authority for the view that in the case of a sovereign body, like the Constituent Assembly, it is the substance and not the form which determines whether the expressed will of such a body constitutes law. I reproduce below the observations of a learned and much respected American authority on Constitutional Law. In Cooley's *Constitutional Limitations*, 8th ed. at page 266, at the commencement of the chapter entitled 'On the Enactment of Laws', there occurs the following passage, which is deserving of careful study:

When the supreme power of a country is wielded by a single man, or by a single body of men, any discussion, in the courts, of the rules which should be observed in the enactment of laws must generally be without practical value, and in fact impertinent; for, whenever the unfettered sovereign power of any country expresses its will in the promulgation of a rule of law, the expression must be conclusive, though proper and suitable forms may have been wholly omitted in declaring it. It is a necessary attribute of sovereignty that the expressed will of the sovereign is law; and while we may question and cross-question the words employed, to make certain of the real meaning, and may hesitate and doubt concerning it, yet, when the intent is made out, it must govern, and it is idle to talk of forms that should have surrounded the expression, but do not.

But even if statutory authority be not conceded in favour of Rule 62, on the grounds discussed above it cannot be denied that it embodies a 'parliamentary exposition' of the highest importance. I quote again from Craies on Statute Law, p. 137:

But Acts of Parliament, without having been passed for the express purpose of explaining previous Acts, are sometimes spoken of as being 'legislative declarations' or 'parliamentary expositions' of the meaning of some earlier Act. Thus in *Battersby* v. *Kirk*,[1] Tindal, C.J., said, 'We cannot but consider these legislative enactments as forming a glossary for the proper interpretation of the expressions in the Bristol Dock Act which are considered to be left in doubt'. . . . But, as has been pointed out, it is the Courts of law and not the Legislature, who are the authorised expositors of the statute law of the land, so that anything in the nature of a 'parliamentary exposition' of an Act of Parliament is only an argument that may be prayed in aid of attaching some certain meaning to a statute, and cannot be treated as *per se* conclusive.

If the matter related to the meaning of a doubtful expression in some Act making a substantive provision, so clear an expression of opinion by the Constituent Assembly would carry very great weight. The question here is of the mode of enactment of constitutional laws. Here I am concerned to point out that the major limb of the three great limbs of the autonomous State of Pakistan had clearly expressed in 1948 its view on this question, which has now assumed so high an importance. I place the Constituent Assembly above the Governor-General, the chief Executive of the State, for two reasons; firstly that the Constituent Assembly was a sovereign body, and secondly because the statutes under and in accordance with which the Governor-General was required to function were within the competence of the Constituent Assembly to amend.

The second great limb of the State, namely the Executive Government of the Federation, has never, until after the event of 24 October 1954, shown any sign of doubt on this point. This was in the highest degree natural, for not only the three successive Governors-General of Pakistan, but with a few exceptions, mostly of very recent date, every Minister of the Federal Government has been a member of the Constituent Assembly. The first Governor-General, the late Qaid-i-Azam Muhammad Ali Jinnah, and the second Governor-General, Khwaja Nazimuddin, were original members of the Constituent Assembly, as appears from the notification on the subject in the Gazette of India of 26 July 1947. The third Governor-General, H.E. Mr Ghulam Muhammad, was elected as a member of the Constituent Assembly from East Bengal in June 1948, and retained his membership until July, 1953. The requirement that Ministers of the Federation should be members of the 'Federal Legislature' was contained in the Government of India Act, 1935, and has already been cited. Thus

[1] (1836), 2 Bing. N.C. 584, 609.

213

it is possible to declare that the Government of Pakistan, composed of the Governor-General and his Ministers, have, throughout the relevant period, been aware that the Constituent Assembly had formally declared that its constitutional laws became law under its own Rule 62, without the need of the Governor-General's assent. The knowledge was not passively possessed, for occasions when the Federal Government was under the necessity of obtaining enactment of laws of a constitutional nature arose from a very early stage in the history of the country, and continued to arise with increasing frequency as it progressed. Not all these laws were of the same importance, and I shall therefore select for mention those which, in my humble opinion, are connected with matters of the highest importance to the State.

From the very inception of Pakistan, matters connected with defence have been germane to its very existence. It might reasonably be assumed that in obtaining a necessary law relating to the Defence Services, the Federal Government would exercise the utmost care to ensure that the mode of enactment was fully effective. Chapter I in Part X of the Government of India Act, 1935, originally contained sections 232 to 239, which empowered His Majesty-in-Council in all necessary respects, and contained numerous references to 'His Majesty's Forces'. These sections were deleted at the adaptation prior to the transfer of power in 1947, and were not replaced until 1950, when two new sections, *viz.* nos. 232 and 233, were inserted in the Act, empowering the Governor-General to raise and maintain Forces and Reserves, to grant Commissions in the Forces and Reserves, to appoint Commanders-in-Chief of the three Services, and to fix their emoluments, etc. These powers, which of necessity are frequently exercised, thus derive from an Act of the Constituent Assembly, *viz.* the Government of India (Second Amendment) Act, 1950, which was passed into law without the assent of the Governor-General.

The second instance I propose to cite is the delimitation of Constituencies (Adult Franchise) Act, 1951, which was passed by the Constituent Assembly in the same form. This Act was designed to extend adult franchise to the Provinces of Pakistan, and provided for the necessary increase of seats and readjustment of constituencies, on the basis of a report to be submitted by a

Committee to be appointed in each Province where an election was to be held, which Committee would be appointed by the Central Government. That Government was empowered to amend and modify the scheme of delimitation proposed by the Committee, and the Governor-General was empowered, by order, to make consequential amendments in the Government of India (Provincial Legislative Assemblies) Order, 1936. So far as I am aware, action has been taken in regard to three Provinces, under powers derived from this Act, and consequential amendments have also been made in the appropriate schedule of the Government of India Act. As a consequence, these Provinces, namely East Bengal, Sind and the North-West Frontier Province are today equipped with Legislative Assemblies elected on the basis of adult franchise, and so far as I am aware, these Assemblies have during their term already passed numerous laws of far-reaching effect, touching great numbers of citizens and a great many rights, in property and otherwise. All concerned, including the Provincial executive authorities, and the newly elected Legislatures themselves have acted throughout in the firm belief that they were doing so effectively.

I shall mention the third instance very briefly. Under the original Government of India Act, the Federation had power under List I, Item I of the Legislative Lists, to legislate on 'preventive detention for reasons of State connected with defence or external affairs', while the Provinces had power under List II, Item I, to legislate on 'preventive detention for reasons connected with the maintenance of public order'. The division of powers being found inconvenient, the Government of India (Second Amendment) Act, 1952, was passed by the Constituent Assembly whereby in List I, Item I, the relevant entry was altered so as to read 'preventive detention for reasons of state connected with defence, external affairs, or the security of Pakistan or any part thereof', the relevant words in List II, Item I were deleted, and in their place, a new entry was added in List III as Item I A, so as to come within the legislative competence of the Federation as well as the Provinces, which reads as follows: 'Preventive detention for reasons connected with the maintenance of public order, or the maintenance of supplies and services essential to the community'. The law did not receive the assent of the Governor-General, but that it was initiated by the Federal Government is evident from the fact that in the same year, a comprehensive measure entitled the Security of Pakistan Act, 1952, was moved by that Government in the Federal Legislature, which took advantage of the access of power derived from the amendment of the Lists, to make necessary provisions 'to deal with persons acting in a manner prejudicial to the defence, external affairs and security of Pakistan, or the maintenance of supplies and services essential for the community, or for the maintenance of public order'. Here again was a matter touching the safety of Pakistan, on which the Federal Government might have been expected to act with the utmost circumspection. There can be no doubt that they did so, and the Court is indebted to the learned Advocate-General of Pakistan for the assurance that, throughout, the Federal Government was in possession of the advice consistently given by the permanent staff of the Law Ministry that assent was essential. The possibility of action *per incuriam* is ruled out conclusively.

The third great limb of the State is the Judicature, and as was brought out in the course of the argument, the question has been before superior Courts in Pakistan on three occasions. The first was in early 1950, in the Sind Chief Court, in the case *M. A. Khuhro* v. *The Federation of Pakistan*[1] decided on 20 March 1950. The plaintiff had been an original member of the Constituent Assembly of Pakistan, but by virtue of an order of disqualification made by the Governor-General under section 3 of the Public and Representative Offices (Disqualification) Act, 1949, he had been disqualified for three years for holding any political office, including membership of the Constituent Assembly. The other features of the case are not relevant for the purposes of the discussion. It will be sufficient to say that Mr M. A. Khuhro raised squarely the contention that the Act under which he had been disqualified was invalid because it had not been assented to by the Governor-General. The Federation of Pakistan met the contention squarely by asserting that no such assent was necessary because the Act was passed by the Constituent Assembly sitting as a Constitution-making body and not as Federal Legislature. The Judge (Hassanally Agha, J.) held that no assent was necessary, and with reference to the words in section 6 (3) 'the Governor-General shall have full power to assent in His Majesty's name [the last

[1] 1950–1 F.C.R. 24.

216

four words were deleted by the Constituent Assembly in 1950] to any law of the Legislature of the Dominion', he observed: 'All that this clause says is that in cases where the assent of His Majesty may be necessary, it shall be given in His Majesty's name.'

The attitude taken by the Federation of Pakistan in that case was the exact reverse of that presented before this Court. It was in complete accordance with the view of the Constituent Assembly with which, of course, the plaintiff Mr M. A. Khuhro, who had been disqualified for membership, could not be expected to agree.

The condition of the initiating party in the next case, viz. *Khan Iftikhar Hussain Khan of Mamdot* v. *The Crown*,[1] in this respect, was not productive of the same degree of antagonism. The case was decided on 19 May 1950. The Khan of Mamdot was an original member of the Constituent Assembly of Pakistan, and he too had been respondent in a case under the same Act as Mr M. A. Khuhro. At the stage at which he brought his case before the Federal Court, there had been an equal division among the Judges of the Lahore High Court who had tried the case, as to the question of guilt on several charges and a Full Bench of the same Court had decided that the matter should be referred to a third Judge for final decision. It was against the decision of the Full Bench that the Khan of Mamdot, who was still a member of the Constituent Assembly, appealed to the Federal Court, through a very senior and experienced Advocate, Dr Khalifa Shujauddin, barrister-at-law. The Federation of Pakistan was represented at the hearing. The question of assent to the Public and Representative Offices (Disqualification) Act, 1949, was raised in the following form, *viz.*:

The Act should have been passed, not by the Constituent Assembly, but by the Federal Legislature of Pakistan, and it should have received the assent of the Governor-General of Pakistan in accordance with the provisions of the Government of India Act. The Act, having been passed by the Constituent Assembly and not having received the assent of the Governor-General in accordance with the provisions of the Government of India Act, was void and *ultra vires*. . . .

The reply to the argument was that the Act was a 'constitutional law' and 'therefore, it fell within the purview of the words "for the purpose of making provision as to the Constitution of the Dominion", as they occur in sub-section (1) of section 8 of the

[1] P.L.D. 1950 Sind 49.

Independence Act, 1947'. This argument was accepted by the Federal Court in full, and the appeal was accordingly dismissed. There are no words in the judgment of Sir Abdul Rashid (then Chief Justice of Pakistan) which amount to formulation of the proposition for which the petitioner contends, but the proposition necessarily follows from the conclusion that the appeal must fail, although there was no assent by the Governor-General, because the law was a 'constitutional law'. The absence of assent being prominently before the Court, the sufficiency of the finding that the law was a 'constitutional law' to put the appellant out of Court, clearly leads to the inference drawn above.

The third case on the subject arose about four years later, also in the Federal Court. It is reported as *Ex-Major-General Akbar Khan and Faiz Ahmad Faiz* v. *The Crown*[1] and was decided on 21 December 1953. The appellants were two of the persons convicted in proceedings held under the Rawalpindi Conspiracy (Special Tribunal) Act, 1951, and were represented by an eminent English barrister with much experience of constitutional law cases, namely, Mr D. N. Pritt, Q.C. Here also the argument put forward was that the Act under which the appellants had been tried and convicted needed assent because it related to the sphere of Federal Legislation, and the latter contention being negatived, by reason of the presence of a provision having the effect of avoiding an appeal in the Federal Court, whose jurisdiction is a matter to be regulated by the Constitution, the appeal was dismissed. In both these cases, the argument that assent was necessary even to a constitutional law, which arose in the most obvious manner, was not taken, and the Court in dealing with the two-pronged argument that the decision of the Court below should be upset (1) because the law under which it was passed, was a law within the Federal sphere of legislation and (2) because the law had not received the assent of the Governor-General, thought that a reply sufficient to defeat the argument was that the law was a constitutional law. By clear implication, it was held that assent was not *sine qua non* for a constitutional law. [I should add here that since 1 March 1955, it has been laid down by this Court that it is not bound by its previous decisions; Criminal Appeal No. 50 of 1953, *Anwar and Nawaz* v. *The Crown*.]

[1] P.L.D. 1954 F.C. 87.

218

Thus, for the first seven years of Pakistan's existence, the three great limbs of this new 'autonomous community' exhibited complete harmony of view in regard to the point this Court is now called upon to decide. They had not reached their conclusions in any superficial way. Throughout there was awareness of the status of the country as a 'Dominion', and of the existence of the link with the British Crown. In the case of *Sarfaraz Khan*[1] it appeared, among the relevant facts, that the Governor-General's assent had been given to the Punjab Public Safety Act, 1949, in a form from which the words 'in His Majesty's name' had been scored out. Shortly after, the Constitution Act was amended by the Constituent Assembly, wherever necessary, to exclude these words from provisions relating to the grant of assent by the Governor-General and the Governors, thereby evincing an intention to retain the link at a purely nominal level.

These actions were plainly performed in compliance with a clearly-formed notion regarding the nature of the autonomy enjoyed by the country as an 'Independent Dominion'. They indicate a determination to manifest freedom from everything resembling control from without, and in that respect, they did no more than to confirm and continue that spirit which had inspired the people of the country in their struggle for independence which had achieved success in 1947. The autonomy of the country, its independent power to control its own affairs, both internal and external, was embodied in the three great agencies of the State, the Constituent Assembly, the Executive, and the Judicature, and all three were agreed that the country was independent in all but name, and that they were entirely free to adopt their own methods, in regard to matters such as legislation, without reference to any practice prevailing elsewhere, and without suffering from any sense of obligation, as the price of their continuing membership of the Commonwealth, to follow any methods, or assume any ideology, except such as was found suitable to their own requirements. True, they had undertaken to perform their tasks in accordance with the Indian Independence Act and the adapted Government of India Act, but that was the initial step only, for the Constituent Assembly had sovereign legislative power, including power to alter these instruments, which in relation to

[1] P.L.R. 1950 Lah. 658.

the Government of India Act, was repeatedly mentioned in the Indian Independence Act. The interpretation of the latter Act too was now a purely domestic matter, in which no outside interference, or sense of obligation to any outside person, or State, or organisation of States, could compel the autonomous State of Pakistan in favour of one view rather than of another.

I conceived that the settled and complete unanimity on the point now in dispute of the three major organs of the State, is most properly to be regarded, from this point of view, as a manifestation of their conception of the country's autonomy, in the particular sphere. Such a temper accorded with the still active demand for complete independence. In assuming such a temper, while accepting the appellation of an 'independent Dominion' Pakistan need not have feared to involve itself in any inconsistency, or any behaviour such as might bring about its expulsion from the Commonwealth. For it was a 'free association of free peoples', and the merest link with the British Crown was the sole *necessary* qualification for retention of membership. There was an example of a European nation, namely the people of the Irish Free State, who in 1947 continued to be accepted by the United Kingdom and the other Dominions as one of themselves despite having broken off, by unilateral act, nearly every possible link with the Crown. It could hardly have been expected, in the light of the views held at the time, that the great organs of the State of Pakistan, an Asiatic country, to which a degree of emancipation from every form of control exercisable by the British Sovereign or the British Parliament had been accorded which far transcended anything previously granted to any of the senior self-governing Dominions, should, in regard to the question of assent to constitutional laws made by its Constituent Assembly, assume an attitude less resistant to controls from the old masters than was evinced by Ireland.

On this point, moreover, they could find direct support in the practice of the great American Republic of the United States, a practice consistently followed since the year 1798. I refer once again to Cooley's *Constitutional Limitations*, 8th ed., at page 70, where the mode of amendment of the Constitution of the United States is dealt with, and it is said, in the simplest language: 'The submission of an amendment does not require the action of the President.'

Two cases are cited, namely *Hollingsworth* v. *Virginia*[1] and *Hawke* v. *Smith*.[2] A clear statement of the opinions expressed in both these judgments appears from the following paragraph which I extract from the latter judgment:

At an early day this court settled that the submission of a constitutional amendment did not require the action of the President, The question arose over the adoption of the Eleventh Amendment, *Hollingsworth* v. *Virginia*, 3 Dall. 378, 1 L. Ed. 644. In that case it was contended that the amendment had not been proposed in the manner provided in the Constitution, as an inspection of the original roll showed that it had never been submitted to the President for his approval in accordance with article 1, s. 7, of the Constitution. The Attorney-General answered that the case of amendments is a substantive act, unconnected with the ordinary business of legislation, and not within the policy or terms of the Constitution investing the President with a qualified negative on the acts and resolutions of Congress. In a footnote to this argument of the Attorney-General, Justice Chase said: 'There can surely be no necessity to answer that argument. The negative of the President applies only to the ordinary cases of legislation. He has nothing to do with the proposition, or adoption, of amendments to the Constitution'. The court by a unanimous judgment held that the amendment was constitutionally adopted.

The Constituent Assembly too was a supra-legal body, not acting in its constitution-making capacity within the Constitution. It was not to be presumed that, in this capacity, its proceedings and decisions were subject to the qualified negative of the Governor-General, who was a statutory authority, owing existence to the interim Constitution.

This, then, was the situation on 24 October 1954, and it was only thereafter that, for the first time, the Federal Government of Pakistan raised the plea that all constitutional Acts of the Constituent Assembly needed the Governor-General's assent. It is permissible, perhaps, at this stage, to refer to the argument *ab inconvenienti*, which arises naturally enough whenever a long course of legislative, administrative and judicial action has been based upon a certain view of law which is sought to be upset. Certain events have followed the pronouncement of the orders in this case, which necessitate the exercise of great caution in making these comments, lest they may influence and perhaps confuse the

---

[1] (1789), U.S.S.C.R. Ed., p. 644.
[2] (1919), U.S.S.C.R. 64, Ed., p. 871.

decision of matters already pending before other Courts. I will content myself with citing a few extracts from Cooley's *Constitutional Limitations*, and from Crawford's *Statutory Construction* (Thomas Law Book Co., St Louis, 1940).

At page 144 of Cooley's book, I find the following observations:

Indeed, where a particular construction has been generally accepted as correct, and especially when this has occurred contemporaneously with the adoption of the Constitution, and by those who had the opportunity to understand the intention of the instrument, it is not to be denied that a strong presumption exists that the construction rightly interprets the intention.

Three passages from Crawford's book are relevant. At page 388, he says:

Where the meaning of a statute is in doubt, the Court may resort to contemporaneous construction—that is, the construction placed upon the statute by its contemporaries, at the time of its enactment and soon thereafter—for assistance in removing any doubt. Similarly, resort may also be had to the usage or course of conduct based upon a certain construction of the statute soon after its enactment, and acquiesced in by the Courts and the legislature for a long period of time.

And, speaking of 'departmental construction' which means 'construction by the Executive Department', the learned author says at page 395 and page 399:

And where vested rights have grown up under the departmental construction, the Courts are justified in being more reluctant than in ordinary cases in adopting a construction which will destroy or disturb such rights. . . . Where the executive construction has been followed for a long time, an element of estoppel seems to be involved. Naturally, many rights will grow up in reliance upon the interpretation placed upon a statute by those whose duty it is to execute it.

The kind of case to which these observations, in their terms, apply is however of importance far below that of the present case. The present is not a case where a mere 'departmental construction', or even a judicial or legislative construction is put forward, as a caution against lightly disturbing that which has been accepted and acted upon as settled law for a period, leading to development of vested rights. The rule of *stare decisis* is altogether too small in its content to fit the case. Here, the greatest organs and agencies of the State have been consciously and unanimously holding a certain belief, and have been acting upon it in numerous respects affecting the most fundamental rights of the entire people. It is difficult to imagine a law which affects so large a proportion of the public as does a law designed to grant adult suffrage, and to determine the composition of Provincial Legislatures on that basis. The Delimitation of Constituencies (Adult Franchise) Act, 1951, was procured by the Federal Government, was passed by the Constituent Assembly, was put into operation by the combined labours of the Federal and Provincial Governments, and has borne fruit in the shape of new Legislative Assemblies, which have been busy ever since passing new laws and in other ways, regulating the lives of the people. It is beyond conception to tabulate all the vested rights and interests which have developed in consequence of this law. And there are many other laws which have produced extensive effects, which cannot possibly be ascertained with exactness. These circumstances should, in my opinion, furnish an argument of almost insuperable character, in favour of upholding what has been the practice hitherto in regard to assent to constitutional laws.

I now take up for examination the final argument for the appellants, namely, that assent of the Governor-General is rendered essential by the formula appearing in section 6 (3) of the Indian Independence Act, *viz.*: 'The Governor-General of each of the new Dominions shall have full power to assent to any law of the Legislature of that Dominion. . . .' The argument was supported by reference to section 5, which lays down that 'the Governor-General . . . shall represent His Majesty for the purposes of the government of the Dominions'. It was said that by this simple formula, His Majesty transferred all his Royal prerogatives to the Governor-General, including the prerogative of assent, which it thereafter became incumbent upon the Governor-General to employ, and upon the Legislature of the Dominion to seek. In my humble opinion, the argument is unsound, and for the following reasons. Assent is a matter which is *not* dealt with in any document issued to Governors-General of Dominions from His Majesty direct, except in relation to the question of reservation of Bills for His Majesty's own assent, when it finds place in the Instrument of Instructions. But in the Constitution of every Dominion, there are precise provisions relating to the presentation of Bills to the Governor-General for his assent, and for the action which he is to take thereon.

The Indian Independence Act, 1947, expressly deals with a field of legislation, *viz.* constitutional legislation, lying outside the scope of the Government of India Act, 1935, in which there was, as has been seen already, a specific provision relating to assent to Bills passed within the powers of the Federal Legislature. This provision was in the full terms already in use, since 1867, in relation to other Dominions. In 1947, when transferring additional legislative powers to the new Dominion, the British Parliament were aware that express provision for assent was necessary in relation to laws made in exercise of these powers, if such assent was to be prescribed. The provision would have been in the nature of conveyance of His Majesty's prerogative, which in this respect had been placed at the disposal of the British Parliament. That Parliament chose to make the provision in the terms reproduced above from section 6 (3). It is settled that when the British Sovereign parts with any of his prerogatives in the shape of a grant to a country with representative institutions, then unless there is an express reservation (which is not found here), the grant is final and cannot be revoked (*Sammut* v. *Strickland*[1]). Therefore, section 5 cannot be referred to for enlarging the power which the words of section 6 (3), Indian Independence Act, operate to convey.

I propose to examine the effect of those words in three parts, *viz.* firstly the words 'shall have full power', secondly the words 'any law' and lastly the words 'of the Legislature of the Dominion'.

It will not, I think, be disputed that the words 'shall have full power' convey no more than a power or capacity. I have already stated my opinion that the word 'full' signifies the withdrawal of pre-existing restraints, appearing in the original Government of India Act, 1935, and in the Instrument of Instructions, etc. Indirectly, it may also be thought to indicate a variation from, and an improvement upon, the limited powers conferred in the same respect by the Constitution Acts of the older Dominions. But I do not read it in any sense such as might impose obligations, besides conferring a capacity. It is one thing to enlarge a capacity to the utmost; it is quite another thing to convert it into a duty. These words purport plainly and unambiguously to convey a power.

[1] [1938] A.C. 678.

224

The circumstances in which such words occurring in an English statute may be construed to impose a duty have been considered and passed upon by the House of Lords in the case of *Julius* v. *Bishop of Oxford*.[1] Lord Cairns, L.C., stated the matter in the following terms regarding the meaning of the words 'It shall be lawful':

They are words merely making that legal and possible which there would otherwise be no right or authority to do. *They confer a faculty or power, and they do not themselves confer more than a faculty or power.* But there may be something in the nature of the thing empowered to be done, something in the object for which it is to be done, something in the conditions under which it is to be done, something in the title of the person or persons for whose benefit the power is to be exercised, which may couple the power with a duty, and make it the duty of the person in whom the power is reposed, to exercise that power when called upon to do so. .... And the words 'It shall be lawful' being according to their natural meaning permissive or enabling words only, it lies upon those, as it seems to me, who contend that an obligation exists to exercise this power, to show in the circumstances of the case something which, according to the principles I have mentioned, creates this obligation.

A little further on, the learned Lord Chancellor observed as follows:

... the cases to which I have referred appear to decide nothing more than this: that where a power is deposited with a public officer for the purpose of being used for the benefit of persons who are specifically pointed, and with regard to whom a definition is supplied by the Legislature of the conditions upon which they are entitled to call for its exercise, that power ought to be exercised, and the Court will require it to be exercised.

Similar views were expressed by the other three noble Lords who heard the case. Lord Penzance said:

The conclusion then, at which I arrive, is that the Appellant has not established his case. The words 'It shall be lawful' are permissive and enabling only. It devolved upon him to show that the legislature intended the exercise of the power, thus conferred, to be a duty, in the performance of which the Bishop was not intended to have any discretion. ....

And Lord Blackburn observed: 'The enabling words are construed as *compulsory whenever the object of the power is to effectuate a legal right.*'

[1] (1880), 5 App. Cas. 214.

I am not aware that the construction thus placed upon words which are, in themselves, merely potential, or permissive or enabling, i.e. words which create a mere faculty or power, has been varied or departed from in any judgment of equivalent authority. It therefore becomes necessary to examine why the same Parliament, which in relation to the other Dominions, and even to India, had, in this respect, always made the most precise and specific provision, requiring that Bills when passed should be submitted to the Governor-General, who should either assent in His Majesty's name, or withhold assent, or reserve the Bill for signification of His Majesty's pleasure, should on this occasion have elected to employ simpler language, conveying no more than a mere power of assent.

Two reasons stand out at once. The Constituent Assembly being designed to be a sovereign body and to exercise sovereign power, including power to alter the Constitution subject to which the Governor-General was intended to act, it would clearly be inconsistent with that design and purpose if the 'qualified negative' of assent by the Governor-General were imposed upon its constitutional laws. Secondly, it being within the complete power of the Constituent Assembly to determine the constitution of the 'Legislature of the Dominion', or Union Legislature, and to determine the scope of its legislature competency as well as the mode in which its laws should be enacted, the British Parliament could not affect to *prescribe* the requirement of assent, as an *essential* formality, in respect of the laws made by such a Legislature. This would be to usurp the functions of the Constituent Assembly. To impose such a requirement upon laws of a constitutional nature made by the Constituent Assembly would be a direct affront to the position and authority of that body. Hence the careful use of expressions in section 8, Indian Independence Act, to indicate that the necessary powers of legislation should be *exercisable by* the Constituent Assembly. The words signify the courtesy owed by one sovereign body to another. There was no direct imposition of obligations, but the need being indicated, it was indicated also that the Constituent Assembly, as previously agreed upon by the plenipotentiaries in the negotiations between the United Kingdom Government and the representatives of the Indian people, might fulfil the need.

I conceive that it was for these and possibly other similar reasons that a form of words was chosen which created no more than the power, without specifying the occasion and manner of its exercise. I do not agree that the words can mean that the British Parliament intended or assumed that assent was an essential requisite. I find it impossible to spell out of the words used any obligation upon any legislature, be it the Constituent Assembly acting as such or the 'Legislature of the Dominion', to present the laws made by them, for assent; that, in my opinion, must have been separately provided, to make it essential, and the absence of such provision, in the Indian Independence Act, when contrasted with its presence in the Government of India Act, 1935, and in the Constitutions of nearly all other British Possessions, having representative institutions, be they Dominions or merely Colonies or 'realms and territories', strongly inclines me to the view that such prescription was deliberately avoided by the British Parliament, in view of the special conditions created by the Indian Independence Act, and otherwise, at the time when Pakistan came into being.

On this view the conception of an obligation resting on the legislature in relation to the Governor-General cannot be thought to arise out of the terms of the section in the Indian Independence Act, whatever the condition might have been at a later date under the new Constitution, or under any provisions which the Constituent Assembly might have thought fit to make in respect of its constitutional laws. As has been pointed out above the Constituent Assembly, as early as May 1948, formally recorded its considered will that its constitutional laws should become operative with no more formality than (a) the President's signature on a copy of the Bill, by way of authentication, and (b) publication in the Federal Government's *Gazette* under the authority of the President. What right could then be thought to be effectuated by applying a compulsive effect to the disputed words of mere potentiality? The argument of the appellants seemed to be that the right inhered in the Governor-General by virtue of his being the representative of His Majesty, and from the fact that Pakistan was a Dominion.

I have already shown that section 5, Indian Independence Act, cannot operate to confer any right to grant assent beyond that conveyed by the relevant words in section 6 (3). Therefore, to draw the *right* of assent from section 5 seems to me to be impossible. Moreover, the position of the Governor-General was such that there was no power on earth which could compel him to exercise any power vested in him, unless it was or became coupled with a duty, as indicated in the case of *Julius* v. *Bishop of Oxford* (cited above), in which case recourse might perhaps be had to the Courts. For over seven years, the Governor-General had, despite advice being given by the permanent staff of the Law Ministry in the contrary sense, decided and acted on the basis that he did not possess any such right as that which was claimed for the first time in the present case. The sovereign body in the State, namely the Constituent Assembly, had declared to this effect, and the view was confirmed on three occasions by the highest courts in the land.

To derive the right or duty from the *idea* of Dominion Status seems to me an even more difficult operation. It may be entirely proper for a new member of a club to conform, as nearly as may be, to the manners and practices of the oldest and most influential members. That is the part of wisdom, if the new member sets a value upon his membership. But the sanction thus conceived is a social or communal sanction; it is entirely different from a legal sanction. Indeed, where the club is composed of 'autonomous communities', the entire conception of communal sanctions being applied, through legal process, to enforce any kind of obligation in the discharge of domestic functions of any one member, is fallacious. The question of assent by the Governor-General to constitutional laws was purely a domestic matter for Pakistan to settle for itself; and the three great limbs of the State had settled it, and were content with the settlement for seven years. No one in the club of Commonwealth countries had objected, or could object, to this practice. The club tolerated the greatest divergence of practice among its members and even of belief regarding the existence of any obligations whatsoever *inter se* among the members. When Pakistan, as a country whose people were intent upon securing their absolute independence, entered the club, there was among the members a country, namely Ireland, which had even renounced allegiance to the British Sovereign, and replaced the Governor-General by a President. Three years later, another republic, namely India, was allowed to continue its membership, on a slightly altered basis. There was apparently no limit to which the members could not go, in regard to what were habitually thought, not many years ago, to be the basic essentials, for acquiring and retaining Dominion Status, without incurring the least danger of forfeiting that status.

In these circumstances, was it unnatural that the State of Pakistan should evince, from the date of its admission to membership, a clear intention and determination to accept only the minimum possible obligations? If that be granted, it seems to me a very difficult proposition to suppose that the new State accepted, as a condition of membership, that *all* its laws would be subject to assent by the Governor-General. Such an inference is the precise opposite of the definitive opinion which the State, through its three great organs, displayed in all its relevant actions over the first seven years of its existence. What they had been given to run was an autonomous State, not an academy for the advancement of a particular school of political philosophy. It would be a denial of the autonomy of the State of Pakistan to declare that its opinion in this matter was wrong.

It seems to me that to enforce the right of assent in favour of the Federal Government would come clearly in conflict with the principle of 'approbation and reprobation'. To enforce it in the interest of the community of nations known as the Commonwealth would be absurd, because, firstly, it was not regarded as a necessary qualification for membership of the community when Pakistan was admitted, and, secondly, it conflicts with the clear principle of non-interference in the domestic affairs of an autonomous State. To enforce it, as an obligation arising out of the mere idea of Dominion Status, is to confer upon that idea a shape and a certitude which, if it ever existed, had quite definitely been blurred into vagueness by the toleration, at least since 1933, of widely variant practices and conditions among Dominion countries, in regard to the most essential features of their organisation.

The other two matters arising in respect of the relevant words in section 6 (3), Indian Independence Act, may be very briefly dealt with. The argument for the petitioner, Mr Tamizuddin Khan, that 'any law' meant only such instruments as had already acquired legal effect is plainly unacceptable. In the context, 'any law' must mean 'any law requiring assent for it to become operative', i.e. any Bill passed by the 'Legislature of the Dominion', which under any provision of law required to be presented to the Governor-

General for his assent, and to receive assent before it could become operative.

As for the term 'Legislature of the Dominion', I have already indicated my view that it cannot be, and was not intended to be, regarded as equivalent, at any time, to the Constituent Assembly. The mere provision, specific though it be, that certain powers stated in section 8 (1) of the Indian Independence Act to be powers of the 'Legislature of the Dominion' were to be *exercisable* by the Constituent Assembly cannot operate to produce any such identity even for the limited purpose of these powers. The further provision in this sub-section that 'reference to the Legislature of the Dominion shall be construed accordingly' must be confined in its meaning and application, by the earlier provision that the relevant powers were exercisable by another body. If the effect of section 8 (1) were to make the 'Legislature of the Dominion' and the Constituent Assembly identical in all respects, in relation to the power of constitution-making, there would be no reason whatsoever for providing in section 8 (3) that limitations on the power of the 'legislature of the Dominion' appearing in the Government of India Act should be deemed to have the same effect as similar limitations imposed by a law of the 'Legislature of the Dominion', *unless and until other provision is made by or in accordance with a law made by the Constituent Assembly of the Dominion in accordance with the provisions of sub-section (1) of this section.* The words in italic appear as they are in section 8 (3). I can only regard them as the clearest possible indication that the Constituent Assembly and the 'Legislature of the Dominion' were treated in the Act, and were intended by the British Parliament to be entirely distinct bodies. As I have pointed out already, one of the functions of the Constituent Assembly, in preparing the new Constitution, was expected to be to provide the country with a 'Legislature of the Dominion' if it was to remain a Dominion. An instance of a law of the British Parliament making the powers of one legislature exercisable by another and wholly distinct legislature, which the former was intended to replace in due time, may be found in section 316 of the original Government of India Act, 1935. The two legislatures in question were the Federal Legislature, for whose constitution specific provision was made under the Act of 1935, but which could not come into being until certain things were

the Legislature of the Dominion are required to be construed accordingly. Subject to laws thus made by the Constituent Assembly and the provisions of the Indian Independence Act, the government of the Dominion is to be carried on by virtue of sub-section (2), in accordance with the Government of India Act, 1935, and the Orders in Council, rules, etc., made thereunder, so far as applicable, with such adaptations and modifications as may be specified by the Governor-General under section 9 of the Act. The provisions requiring the Governor-General or any Governor to act in his discretion or in his individual judgment in respect of any matter, were to cease to have any effect, all control by His Majesty's Government was removed and the necessity of reserving Provincial Bills for the signification of His Majesty's pleasure was done away with. The powers of the Federal Legislature or Indian Legislature under the Government of India Act, 1935, as in force in relation to each Dominion, were, in the first instance, made exercisable by the Constituent Assembly, in addition to the powers referred to in sub-section (1) of section 8. The limitations placed by the adapted Government of India Act, 1935, on the legislative powers of the Dominion Legislature (which must be understood to mean the Federal or Indian Legislature in this context) were to have effect as a restrictive law of the Legislature of the Dominion, within the meaning of sub-section (6) of section 6 of the Indian Independence Act.

It is suggested on behalf of the respondent that sub-section (3) of section 6 of the Indian Independence Act should be so interpreted as to equate the expression 'Legislature of the Dominion' occurring therein, with the Federal Legislature functioning under the adapted Government of India Act, 1935, and that it should be held that the sub-section was merely intended to give the Governor-General plenary powers of assent within the limited legislative field of the latter Act.

The position seems to me to be untenable on several grounds. If that had been the sole object aimed at, it could have been effectively achieved without using the general words 'full power to assent to any law of the Legislature of that Dominion' in the first part of the sub-section and by merely enacting the subsequent part of the sub-section beginning with the words 'so much of an Act'. The argument raised imputes a redundancy to the

British Parliament without any apparent necessity. The interpretation contended for would cut down the generality of the words in the beginning of the sub-section and impose a limitation on them, to be imported from the latter part of the sub-section, a procedure not warranted by the context. Again, it should have been easy enough to use the words 'Federal Legislature' instead of the comprehensive expression 'Legislature of the Dominion' and thus to have ensured perfect clarity, if the intention sought to be read into this sub-section was the correct one.

It is clear that at the time of the passing of the Indian Independence Act or even on the appointed day, no Legislature of the Dominion, envisaged in section 6 of the Act, actually existed. Mr Chundrigar conceded at the Bar that the relevant expression occurring in this section would cover the future Legislature of the Dominion which, the framers of the Act anticipated, was likely to be set up under the new constitutional provision to be made by the Constituent Assembly under sub-section (1) of section 6 read with sub-section (1) of section 8 of the Act. It was further admitted, as is also apparent from the plain language of section 6, that such a Legislature would be competent to pass laws including constitutional laws and that if sub-section (3) was allowed to stand in its present form, the sub-section would subject all such laws to the necessity of assent by the Governor-General. For the interim period, however, while the provisional Constitution embodied in the adapted Government of India Act, 1935, and the Indian Independence Act, 1947, is in force, it was contended, the position was different *qua* the Constituent Assembly. The argument was raised that though sub-section (1) of section 8 made the constitution-making powers included in sub-section (1) of section 6 exercisable in the first instance (the phrase 'in the first instance' needs to be specifically emphasised in this connection) by the Constituent Assembly, the latter body was not identifiable with the 'Legislature of the Dominion' within the meaning of sub-section (3) of section 6. A similar formula contained in proviso (*e*) to sub-section (2) of section 8, makes the powers of the Federal Legislature or Indian Legislature, exercisable in the first instance by the same Constituent Assembly. After a comparison of sections 6 and 8, the inference seems to be irresistible that during the interregnum prior to the promulgation of a fresh constitution, the Constituent Assembly in fact functions as the Legislature of the Dominion. It is only thus that full meaning can be given to the words of sub-section (1) of section 8 'references in this Act to the Legislature of the Dominion shall be construed accordingly' and to the provision contained in sub-section (3) of section 8. The plenary law-making powers of the Legislature of the Dominion mentioned in section 6 had to be divided into two compartments for the transitional period, in order to keep the legislative machinery of the Government of India Act, 1935, in working order, with all its limitations, side by side with the enactment of a new Constitution. For the purpose of functioning as the Federal Legislature under the Government of India Act, 1935, the Constituent Assembly, as the Legislature of the Dominion, should be deemed to have placed the incident limitations on itself, under the provisions of sub-section (6) of section 6 read with sub-section (3) of section 8. I confess I am unable to follow the process of reasoning which seeks to give a different meaning to 'Legislature of the Dominion' occurring in sub-section (3) from that possessed by the expression in other sub-sections of section 6. The attempt seems to be directed towards investing the Constituent Assembly with all the powers under section 6, without attracting the restriction (if restriction it really be) regarding assent, provided for in the same section. The two submissions made that sub-section (3) is confined to the Federal Legislature functioning under the Government of India Act, 1935, and that the sub-section would also be applicable to laws passed by the future Legislature of the Dominion, appear to me to be mutually contradictory. The word 'law' or 'laws' used in sub-section (3) obviously includes laws of a constitutional character as a reading of the whole of section 6 shows and must clearly mean enactments passed by the Legislature and awaiting assent of competent authority.

The mere absence of an express provision included in the Indian Independence Act for Bills being presented to the Governor-General for assent, after being passed by the Constituent Assembly when sitting as the Legislature of the Dominion to frame the Constitution and the fact that discretion to withhold assent is not specifically mentioned, though provision to that effect exists in the Government of India Act, 1935, or in the

Constitutions of other Dominions, strike me as of no material significance. The words 'full power' amply connote discretion to give or withhold assent, besides indicating freedom from extraneous control, in full measure. The presumption is implicit in the sub-section that all such laws shall be submitted to the Governor-General for his assent.

It seems to me that the attitude adopted on behalf of the respondent rests on the fallacious premise that the prescription of the formality of assent for laws passed by the Constituent Assembly, would detract from the legislative sovereignty of that body, undoubtedly conferred on it by the Indian Independence Act. In the background of this attitude there appears to lurk the spectre of a full sovereignty, not merely in the legislative field but in all spheres, claimed for the Constituent Assembly, somewhat feebly, it is true, at one stage of the arguments. That the Constituent Assembly is not sovereign in the full sense of the term, it was later admitted. What was not realised was that the provision regarding assent should not be regarded as a clog on the legislative sovereignty of that body, in the context of an 'Independent Dominion' free from all control by His Majesty's Government in England. The Governor-General of such a Dominion is no doubt formally appointed by His Majesty but in effect the appointment rests with the responsible Ministry whose advice would, as a matter of settled convention, be accepted in all cases by the King or Queen. The Ministry would have the means, for the same reason, of arranging the recall of a Governor-General who intended to flout their wishes in any matter. This aspect of the case has been exhaustively dealt with in the judgment of my Lord the Chief Justice and I need not labour the point further.

A reference to the history of prerogative of the Crown in England would also lend support to the conclusion that the above interpretation of sub-section (3) of section 6 is correct. In my humble judgment, no other construction of that sub-section would be acceptable and I only wish to draw additional strength for this construction from a consideration of the constitutional history of England. Assent to legislation is one of the most important prerogatives of the Crown in England. There is also ample authority for the proposition that the prerogative of the Crown extends to the Colonies and Dominions of His Majesty beyond the Seas.

See Halsbury's *Laws of England*, 2nd ed. vol. VI, p. 445, para. 513; *New Brunswick Case*, [1892] A.C. 437 (at page 441) and *Re Bateman's Trusts*, L.R. 15 Eq. 355. Only express words or necessary intendment of a statute can take away a prerogative and the presumption would be against such a result. Reference in this connection may be made to *British Coal Corporation* v. *The King*, [1935] A.C. 500, and *Mayor of Weymouth's Case*, (1865), 6 B. & S. 22. I can discover nothing in the Indian Independence Act which could support the plea of express or implied abrogation of the prerogative of assent in the case of laws enacted by the Constituent Assembly sitting as the Legislature of the Dominion to frame the Constitution. On the other hand, a reading of sections 5 and 6 together, would lead to the inference that henceforth the prerogative of the Crown as respects assent, would, in the case of each new Dominion, be exercised by the Governor-General as representing His Majesty. Allegiance to the Crown, however tenuous the bond may in practice turn out to be, is an essential incident of Dominion Status. Nothing seems to turn in this connection on the form of the oath taken by the Governor-General or by members of the Provincial Legislatures in Pakistan or on the form of the Royal Style and Titles adopted in this country. This position would continue to hold good in Pakistan as long as it is a Dominion, albeit an 'Independent Dominion', unless of course it is altered by a proper constitutional provision. From the expression 'Independent Dominion', merely constitutional autonomy and not full political sovereignty in the legal sense can be spelt out, though the latter status would be potentially within the Dominion Legislature's grasp.

The doctrine of 'departmental construction' applied by American Courts to the interpretation of statutes, was also sought to be pressed into service on behalf of the respondent, to favour a particular construction of sub-section (3) of section 6 of the Indian Independence Act. Reliance was placed on rule 62 of the rules of procedure framed by the Constituent Assembly of Pakistan and the practice that has been followed hitherto, of not submitting laws passed by the Constituent Assembly to the Governor-General for his assent. These facts were, however, not advanced as raising the bar of estoppel against any party. Even in America the rule is not regarded as conclusive and is obviously available only to resolve doubts in cases where the language used in a statute is equivocal. The present does not appear to me to fall in that category of cases. As long ago as 1889, Lord Esher laid down the rule in *Sharpe* v. *Wakefield*, 22 Q.B.D. 239 (at p. 242), that an Act ought to be construed as it would have been the day after the Act was passed, unless some subsequent statute declares that another construction was to be adopted. It must follow as a corollary that the subsequent conduct of any functionaries in purported pursuance of an Act, would not be decisive of the interpretation to be placed on the statute. A practice in contravention of a constitutional provision contained in a statute, can never abrogate or repeal a rule of strict law, with which alone the Courts are concerned—see *Disallowance and Reservation References* (1938 S.C.R. 71), and *The Statute of Westminster and Dominion Status*, 1949 ed. by K. C. Wheare, pp. 18 and 292. It is doubtful if the practice or usage mentioned has hardened into an obligatory constitutional convention. Even if that were the position, it would require to be translated into or supplemented by a statute, if it is to be recognised by Courts (K. C. Wheare's book, p. 18 *et seq.*). As has been pointed out by my Lord the Chief Justice, rule 62 of the Constituent Assembly rules, is not really in conflict with the provisions of sub-section (3) of section 6 of the Indian Independence Act and in any case, it does not operate to effect the necessary constitutional amendment, even under the rules of that body, which prescribe a specific procedure for constitutional legislation.

Finally I am not impressed by the argument which seems to have found favour with some of the learned Judges of the Sind Chief Court that the omission to deal with the question of assent in earlier cases amounts to an indirect decision on that point. Every case is an authority for the point or points actually decided by it either expressly or by necessary implication and no more. The point was not expressly raised or decided in those cases and I can find little in them to support the theory of an implied decision. The only precedent which deals directly with the point is *Khuhro's* case, P.L.D. 1950 Sind 49, in which a learned Single Judge of the Sind Chief Court held that no assent was required under the law, for legislation passed by the Constituent Assembly. The *ratio decidendi* in that case was the assumption of unfettered legislative power possessed by the Constituent Assembly and the relevant provisions of the Indian Independence Act were not fully examined.

JUDGMENT

IN THE CASE OF

USIF PATEL AND TWO OTHERS

v.

THE CROWN

IN THE
FEDERAL COURT OF PAKISTAN
(APPELLATE JURISDICTION)

(On appeal from the judgment and order of the Chief Court of Sind at Karachi, dated 15 July 1954, in Criminal Miscellaneous Applications Nos. 127, 129 and 131 of 1954)

CONSTITUTIONAL CRIMINAL APPEAL
NO. 1 OF 1954, decided on 12 April 1955

Usif Patel and two others, appellants, v. *The Crown*, respondent

CRIMINAL APPEAL
NO. 63 OF 1954

Agha Muhammad, appellant, v. *The Crown*, respondent

and

CRIMINAL APPEAL
NO. 64 OF 1954

Syed Ali Shah alias *Thigri Shah*, appellant, v. *The Crown*, respondent
Present: Muhammad Munir, C.J., A. S. M. Akram, A. R. Cornelius, Muhammad Sharif and S. A. Rahman, JJ.

MUHAMMAD MUNIR, C.J.—This batch of appeals, Constitu- Judgment tional Criminal Appeal No. 1 of 1954, and Criminal Appeals Nos. 63 and 64 of 1954 by special leave, is being disposed of by one order because the determination of the constitutional question which is common to them all is sufficient for their disposal.

The appellants in these appeals were proceeded against by the District Magistrate of Larkana under the Sind Control of Goondas Act (Governor's) Act XXVIII of 1952. They were declared to be goondas, directed to furnish heavy security, and for their failure to give security confined to prison. Against their detention in prison the petitioners in the first-mentioned appeal made applications to the Chief Court of Sind under section 491 of the Code of Criminal Procedure, alleging that their imprisonment was wrongful and praying that they be set at liberty. The petitioners in the other two appeals moved revisions under section 17 of the aforesaid Act before the same Court. The Chief Court held that all the detentions were legal and rejected the applications.

The ground urged before the Chief Court on which their imprisonment was alleged to be illegal was that the Governor's Act under which action had been taken against them was invalid because it was passed by the Governor in exercise of the powers which were conferred on him by a Proclamation issued by the Governor-General under section 92 A of the Government of India Act, 1935, which section had been inserted in the Government of India Act by an order of the Governor-General under section 9 of the Indian Independence Act. It was contended that this action of the Governor-General was *ultra vires* of the provisions of the aforesaid section 9. The contention was repelled by the Chief Court.

Before this Court a fresh argument was advanced challenging the validity of section 92 A. It was pointed out that this action was taken after the expiry of the original date fixed by sub-section (5) of section 9 of the Indian Independence Act, for the making of orders under it. The date on or before which orders under section 9 of the Indian Independence Act could be made by the Governor-General was 31 March 1948, but this date was altered to 31 March 1949 by section 2 of the Indian Independence (Amendment) Act, 1948, passed by the Constituent Assembly. This Amendment Act, however, was never presented to the Governor-General for his assent. In *Mr Tamizuddin Khan's* case this Court has taken the view that the Governor-General's assent to laws made by the Constituent Assembly under sub-section (1) of section 8 of the Indian Independence Act is indispensable and that no Act making any provision as to the Constitution of the Dominion can become law unless it receives the assent of the Governor-General. The question involved in the present case therefore is whether the Indian Independence (Amendment) Act, 1948, by which the date mentioned in sub-section (5) of section 9 of the Indian Independence Act was altered to 31 March 1949, was law when on 19 July 1948, the Governor-General added section 92A to the Government of India Act, 1935. On the authority of *Mr Tamizuddin Khan's* case the answer to this question must be in the negative, with the result that the addition of section 92A to the Government of India Act, 1935, being unauthorised, the Sind Goondas Act, which was passed by the Governor of Sind in exercise of the authority derived by him from a Proclamation of the Governor-General under section 92A, must be held to be invalid and the proceedings taken thereunder void and inoperative.

To avoid the aforesaid result the learned Advocate-General of Pakistan relies on section 2 of Ordinance IX of 1955, which was promulgated by the Governor-General on 27 March 1955, after a Proclamation of Emergency under section 102 of the Government of India Act, 1935. That section of the Ordinance is in these terms:

Whereas none of the laws passed by the Constituent Assembly of Pakistan under the provisions of sub-section (1) of section 8 of the Indian Independence Act (10 & 11 Geo. VI, ch. 30), hereafter in this section referred to as the said Act, received the assent of the Governor-General in accordance with sub-section (3) of section 6 of the said Act, it is hereby declared and enacted that every law specified in column 1 of the Schedule to this Ordinance shall be deemed to have received the assent of the Governor-General on the date specified in column 2 of that Schedule, being the date on which it was published in the Official Gazette, and shall be deemed to have had legal force and effect from that date.

In the Schedule the date mentioned for the coming into force of the Indian Independence (Amendment) Act, 1948, is 19 March 1948, and clause (*a*) to sub-section (2) of section 2 of the Ordinance provides that the validity of any law to which sub-section (1) of section 2 applies shall not be questioned in any Court.

It could not possibly be contended by the learned Advocate-General of Pakistan that clause (*a*) can have the effect of divesting this Court of the jurisdiction conferred on it by section 205 of the Government of India Act to entertain, hear and determine an appeal if the High Court certifies that the case involves a substantial question of law as to the interpretation of the Government of India Act or the Indian Independence Act or if an appeal in a criminal matter is brought by special leave of this Court under the Privy Council (Abolition of Jurisdiction) Act, 1950. The two questions therefore that have to be determined in these appeals are : (1) whether the Governor-General could by an Ordinance validate the Indian Independence (Amendment) Act, 1948, and (2) whether the Governor-General can give assent to constitutional legislation by the Constituent Assembly with retrospective effect.

It is not disputed that the Amendment Act of 1948 was a constitutional provision. What is urged by the learned Advocate-General, however, is that the Ordinance was passed by the Governor-General in exercise of the powers given to him by section 42 of the Government of India Act read with the provisions of section 102 of that Act. The former section provides that the Governor-General's power of making Ordinances is subject to the like restriction as the power of the Federal Legislature to make laws, and that any Ordinance made under that section may be controlled or superseded by an Act of the Federal Legislature. Since the Governor-General's power to promulgate Ordinances is subject to the same restrictions as the power of the Federal Legislature to make laws, the true issue in the case is whether the Federal Legislature was competent to amend sub-section (5) of section 9 of the Indian Independence Act which the Constituent Assembly amended by the Amendment Act of 1948.

The rule hardly requires any explanation, much less emphasis, that a Legislature cannot validate an invalid law if it does not possess the power to legislate on the subject to which the invalid law relates, the principle governing validation being that validation being itself legislation you cannot validate what you cannot legislate upon. Therefore if the Federal Legislature, in the absence of a provision expressly authorising it to do so, was incompetent to amend the Indian Independence Act or the Government of India Act, the Governor-General possessing no larger powers than those of the Federal Legislature was equally incompetent to amend either of those Acts by an Ordinance. Under the Independence Act the authority competent to legislate on constitutional matters being the Constituent Assembly, it is that Assembly alone which can amend those Acts. The learned Advocate-General alleges that the Constituent Assembly has been dissolved and that therefore validating powers cannot be exercised by that Assembly. In *Mr Tamizuddin Khan's* case, we did not consider it necessary to decide the question whether the Constituent Assembly was lawfully dissolved but assuming that it was, the effect of the dissolution can certainly not be the transfer of its powers to the Governor-General. The Governor-General can give or withhold his assent to the legislation of the Constituent Assembly but he himself is not the Constituent Assembly and on its disappearance he can neither claim powers which he never possessed nor claim to succeed to the powers of that assembly.

On the question whether the Federal Legislature was competent to make the law sought to be validated there cannot be two opinions. Under section 102 of the Government of India Act the Federal Legislature on the Proclamation of Emergency has the power to make laws with respect to any matter not enumerated in any of the lists in the Seventh Schedule to that Act. The learned Advocate-General appeared to suggest that the scope of that section was wide enough to include legislation on constitutional matters. The suggestion is entirely erroneous and is the result not only of a misunderstanding of the scope of section 102 and of the history of the legislation by the Parliament by which the words 'or to make laws, whether or not for a Province or any part thereof, with respect to any matter not enumerated in any of the Lists in the Seventh Schedule to this Act' were added to that section but also of a misconception of the effect of section 8 of the Indian Independence Act.

During the second World War the Indian Legislature passed a law called the Defence of India Act empowering the Government of India to make rules on certain subjects. One of the rules made by that Government, Rule 75, empowered the Government to requisition property. In exercise of these powers the Government requisitioned a motor car from a person residing within the jurisdiction of the Bombay High Court. The owner brought a suit against the Government on the ground that the subject of requisitioning property was not included in any of the three Lists to the Seventh Schedule to the Government of India Act, and that therefore in the absence of a public notification by the Governor-General empowering the Federal Legislature to make laws on the subject of requisitioning property, Rule 75 of the Defence of India Rules was *ultra vires*. The matter went up to the Bombay High Court which upheld this contention of the plaintiff and the Government appealed to the Federal Court from the judgment of the High Court. Two other similar cases came up, one before the High Court of Calcutta and the other before the High Court of Madras, but both these Courts decided in favour of the Government holding that Rule 75 was *intra vires* the Federal Legislature. From one of these cases the plaintiff appealed to the Federal Court. These two appeals had not been determined by the Federal Court when the Government of India moved the Government of the United Kingdom to obtain from the Parliament legislation empowering the Federal Legislature to legislate retrospectively on matters which were not within any of the three Lists. Such legislation was considered to be necessary not only for the purposes of the aforesaid three cases of which two were still pending in the Federal Court but also to meet those cases where the Federal Legislature might have legislated or might wish to legislate on a subject not specifically included in the three Lists and as to which no public notification had been made by the Governor-General under section 104 of the Government of India Act. The result was the passing by Parliament of the India (Proclamations of Emergency) Act, 1946 (9 & 10 Geo. VI, ch. 23), the most important provisions of which were as follows:

1 In sub-section (1) of section one hundred and two of the Government of India Act, 1935 (which enables the Central Legislature, where a Proclamation of Emergency is in force, to make laws for a Province or any part thereof with respect to any of the matters enumerated in the Provincial Legislative List), after the words 'enumerated in the Provincial Legislative List' there shall be inserted the words 'or to make laws, whether or not for a Province or any part thereof, with respect to any matter not enumerated in any of the Lists in the Seventh Schedule to this Act'.

2 (1) Subject to the provisions of this section, this Act shall be deemed to have come into operation on the commencement of Part III of the Government of India Act, 1935.

(2) Where, before the passing of this Act, a High Court in British India has given a judgment or made a final order in any civil proceedings involving a question as to the validity of any law, ordinance, order, bye-law, rule or regulation passed or made in India, any party to the proceedings may, at any time within ninety days from the passing of this Act, apply

(*a*) where an appeal from the judgment or order has been decided by the Federal Court to the Federal Court; and

(*b*) in any other case, to the High Court,

for a review of the proceedings in the light of the provisions of this Act, and the Court to which the application is made shall review the proceedings accordingly and make such order, if any, varying or reversing the judgment or order previously given or made, as may be necessary to give effect to the provisions of this Act.

It is clear from the terms of this enactment that the words on which the learned Advocate-General places reliance were added to section 102 of the Government of India Act to meet not only a specific contingency but also certain possible contingencies. The object of adding these words to that section was to empower the Federal Legislature to make laws on subjects on which previously it could acquire authority to legislate only by a public notification of the Governor-General under section 104 of that Act. There were two objections to the adequacy of the machinery provided in section 104 where the Federal Legislature needed power to legislate on a residual subject, namely, a subject which was not covered by any of the items in the three lists in the Seventh Schedule to the Act. In the first place if the Governor-General made a public notification assigning a residual subject to the Provincial Legislature, it remained there until the Federal Legislature acquired power to legislate on it on the Proclamation of Emergency and in the second, even if such power could be given to the Federal Legislature it could not legislate on it retrospectively because the Governor-General by a mere notification could not confer on the Federal Legislature the power to legislate with retrospective effect. It was for the purpose of avoiding these inconveniences that the Parliament passed the Proclamations of Emergency Act, 1946, so that on the proclamation of an emergency under section 102 of the Government of India Act the Federal Legislature might be in a position at once to legislate on residual matters. The circumstance that sections 108 and 110 of the Government of India Act, 1935, have been omitted in the adaptations of that Act by Order XXII of 1947 has no relevancy. These two sections imposed certain restrictions on the legislative powers of the Federal Legislature and the Provincial Legislatures and because on Pakistan becoming an Independent Dominion all restrictions on the Legislature of the Dominion had to be removed, the sections which were restrictions on the competency of the legislature had to be deleted from the Act. Most of the matters mentioned in these sections are now for the Constituent Assembly to legislate upon when it functions as the Legislature of the Dominion under sub-section (1) of section 8 of the Indian Independence Act. When the Constituent Assembly functions as the Federal Legislature it necessarily functions under certain restrictions though it is always competent to remove these restrictions by making a law under sub-section (1) of section 8 of the Indian Independence Act. The omission of these sections proceeded on the same principle as led to the omission of sections 45 and 93 of the Government of India Act, 1935, which gave to the Governor-General and the Governors of Provinces certain powers in cases of emergency to assume to themselves the powers vested in or exercisable by other constitutional bodies or authorities and to exercise those powers in their discretion. While exercising these powers the Governor-General and the Governors were responsible, through the Secretary of State, to the Government in London and ultimately to the Parliament but because with the conferment of the status of an Independent Dominion on Pakistan the Parliament and the Government in London renounced their responsibility for the Government of the country, both these sections had to be omitted in the adaptations of the Government of India Act.

To assume that the words added by the Indian (Proclamations of Emergency) Act, 1946, to section 102 of the Government of India Act had the effect of investing the Federal Legislature with the power to legislate on constitutional matters is to overlook the broad schemes of both the Constitution Acts and the elementary principles of a Federal Constitution. The essence of a Federal Legislature is that it is not a sovereign legislature, competent to make laws on all matters; in particular it cannot, unless specifically empowered by the Constitution, legislate on matters which have been assigned by the Constitution to other bodies. Nor is it competent to remove the limitations imposed by the constitution on its legislative powers. The judgment of this Court in *Mr Tamizuddin Khan's* case attempted to put this position beyond doubt, as will appear from the observations at pages 112–14, 133 and 232–4. My own conclusion on this part of the case I stated in the form of the mathematical equation that the Federal Legislature is the Constituent Assembly plus the fetters to which it is subject under the Government of India Act, 1935. If that judgment was not understood as clearly laying down that the powers of the

Legislature of the Dominion for the purpose of making provision as to the constitution of the Dominion were exercisable in the first instance by the Constituent Assembly and that the Assembly when functioning as the Federal Legislature under Proviso (e) to sub-section (2) of section 8 was to be deemed to have imposed limitations on its powers as the Legislature of the Dominion, the time and labour expended on that judgment have been merely wasted. So that we may now be understood more clearly, let me repeat that the power of the Legislature of the Dominion for the purpose of making provision as to the constitution of the Dominion could under sub-section (1) of section 8 of the Indian Independence Act be exercised only by the Constituent Assembly and that that power could not be exercised by that Assembly when it functioned as the Federal Legislature within the limits imposed upon it by the Government of India Act, 1935. It is, therefore, not right to claim for the Federal Legislature the power of making provision as to the constitution of the Dominion—a claim which is specifically negatived by sub-section (1) of section 8 of the Indian Independence Act. If the constitutional position were otherwise, the Governor-General could by an Ordinance repeal the whole of the Indian Independence Act and the Government of India Act and assume to himself all powers of legislation. A more incongruous position in a democratic constitution is difficult to conceive, particularly when the Legislature itself, which can control the Governor-General's action, is alleged to have been dissolved.

This Court held in *Mr Tamizuddin Khan's* case that the Constituent Assembly was not a sovereign body. But that did not mean that if the Assembly was not a sovereign body the Governor-General was. We took pains to explain at length in that case that the position of the Governor-General in Pakistan is that of a constitutional Head of the State, namely, a position very similar to that occupied by the King in the United Kingdom. That position which was supported by Mr Diplock is now being repudiated by the learned Advocate-General and on the ground of emergency every kind of power is being claimed for the Head of the State. Let us say clearly if we omitted to say so in the previous case that under the Constitution Acts the Governor-General is possessed of no more powers than those that are given to him by those Acts. One of these powers is to promulgate Ordinances in cases of emergency but the limits within which and the checks subject to which he can exercise that power are clearly laid down in section 42 itself. On principle the power of the Governor-General to legislate by Ordinance is always subject to the control of the Federal Legislature and he cannot remove these controls merely by asserting that no Federal Legislature in law or in fact is in existence. No such position is contemplated by the Indian Independence Act, or the Government of India Act, 1935. Any legislative provision that relates to a constitutional matter is solely within the powers of the Constituent Assembly and the Governor-General is under the Constitution Acts precluded from exercising those powers. The sooner this position is realised the better. And if any one read anything to the contrary in the previous judgment of this Court, all that I can say is that we were grievously misunderstood. If the position created by the judgment in the present case is that past constitutional legislations cannot be validated by the Governor-General but only by the Legislature, it is for the Law Department of the Government to ponder over the resultant situation and to advise the Government accordingly. The seriousness of the implications of our judgment in the previous case should have been immediately realised and prompt steps taken to validate the invalid legislation.

The learned Advocate-General of Pakistan appeared to concede that so far as the validation part of section 2 of the Ordinance is concerned, it is *ultra vires* inasmuch as it seeks to validate a constitutional provision, namely, the Amendment Act of 1948, but he contends that since the Governor-General gave his assent to the Amendment Act by the Ordinance, the assent would act retrospectively and make the Act valid law from the date of its passing. The law relating to 'commencement' is contained in section 36 of the Interpretation Act, 1889, which applies to this case by reason of sub-section (2) of section 2 of the Provisional Constitution Order. That section is as follows:

36. 'Commencement.' (1) In this Act, and in every Act passed either before or after the commencement of this Act, the expression 'commencement', when used with reference to an Act, shall mean the time at which the Act comes into operation.

(2) Where an Act passed after the commencement of this Act, or

any Order-in-Council, warrant, scheme, letters patent, rules, regulations, or bye-laws made, granted, or issued, under a power conferred by any such Act, is expressed to come into operation on a particular day, the same shall be construed as coming into operation immediately on the expiration of the previous day.

The rule enacted in sub-section (2) of section 36 of the Interpretation Act merely provides that if an Act is expressed to come into operation on a particular day, the same shall be construed as coming into operation immediately on the expiration of the previous day. The word 'Act' in this sub-section, however, means an assented Act because unless assented to it is not an Act at all. The learned Advocate-General relies on the following passage at page 355 of Craies on Statute Law, 5th ed. :

It is sometimes specially enacted that a statute is to come into operation on some day prior to the day on which it receives the royal assent. Thus, in *Jamieson* v. *Att.-Gen.*[1] it was held that 11 Geo. 4 and 1 Will. 4, ch. 49, section 1, which enacted that certain duties should be levied from 15 March 1830, but did not receive the royal assent until 16 July 1830, operated from 15 March.

Referring to the case where a statute comes into force on some day prior to the day on which it receives the Royal assent the learned author cites the case of *R.* v. *Middlesex Justices*[2] and proceeds to make the following comment :

It is stated in Dwarris, p. 544, and also in Maxwell, 9th ed., p. 410, on the authority of *Burn* v. *Carvalho*[3] that 'where a particular day is named for its commencement, but the Royal assent is not given till a later day, the Act would come into operation only on the later day.' This rule is not borne out by the case cited, which merely decides that as the language of 3 & 4 Will. 4, ch. 42, section 30, is 'prospective only', it cannot apply to any proceeding which took place before the Act was passed. The Court said that the language of section 30 was very different from a question arising under section 21, the language of which was sufficiently comprehensive to include all actions brought by executors and administrators whether before or after the passing of the Act. In *Freeman* v. *Moyes*[4] a different decision was come to as to section 31 of the same Act, the language of that section not being in its terms prospective.

The aforesaid discussion relating to commencement has this essential feature that in all the cases in which the question arose

[1] (1883), Alcock & Nap. 37   [2] (1831), 2 B. & Ad. 818.
[3] (1835), 1 Ad. & E. 883.   [4] (1834), 1 Ad. & E. 338.

the statute itself had stated a particular date of its coming into operation. That discussion is therefore irrelevant to the present case because the Amendment Act of 1948 did not itself contain any provision relating to the date of its commencement. The law on this point is thus stated in paragraph 661 at page 510 of Halsbury's *Laws of England*, 2nd ed. vol. 31, 'The expression "commencement" used with reference to a statute means the time at which the statute comes into operation which, where no other time is provided, is the commencement of the day upon which it receives the Royal assent', and in footnote (*g*) at the same page it is stated:

In [the case of] *Burn* v. *Carvalho*,[1] it was pointed out that the Civil Procedure Act, 1833 (3 & 4 Will. IV, ch. 42), section 44, provided that it should commence and take effect on 1 June 1833, although it did not receive the Royal Assent until 14 August following. It is apprehended that the Act would be without statutory force until the later of the two dates, when it might have a retrospective operation, a result quite permissible in Acts regulating procedure, *Re Athlumney, Ex parte Wilson*.[2]

The latter part of the observation in the footnote is not applicable to the present situation because here the Amendment Act was not a procedural law and it did not enact that it shall come into force on a particular date. The only effect, in a case like the present, of giving assent later to an Act passed by the legislature can be that the statute comes into operation on the date that it is assented to and not before such date, all proceedings taken under that Act before assent being void unless they are subsequently validated by independent legislation.

For these reasons we are of the opinion that since the Amendment Act of 1948 was not presented to the Governor-General for his assent, it did not have the effect of extending the date from 31 March 1948, to 31 March 1949, and that since section 92A was added to the Government of India Act, 1935, after 31 March 1948, it never became a valid provision of that Act. Thus the Governor-General had no authority to act under section 92A and the Governor derived no power to legislate from a Proclamation under that section. Accordingly the Sind Goondas Act was *ultra*

---

[1] (1835), 1 Ad. & El. 883, 896.
[2] [1898], 2 Q.B. 547.

vires and no action under it could be taken against the appellants. That being so the detention of the appellants in gaol is illegal.

The Ordinance recites that the Governor-General had some other powers which enabled him not only to validate certain laws, but also temporarily to abolish the Federal Legislature, to amend the provisions to the Government of India Act, 1935, relating to Provinces and the High Courts and to make the future Constitution. In the arguments before us, however, the learned Advocate-General did not rely on any such powers, his entire argument having been confined to the powers of the Governor-General to promulgate Ordinances under section 42.

For these reasons we accept the appeal and order the appellants to be set at liberty.

One more observation before we conclude. During the course of arguments in *Mr Tamizuddin Khan's* case a question arose if the Constituent Assembly was dissolved or ceased to function, what would be the consequent constitutional position? The statement that Mr Diplock made in reply to the questions on this subject is reproduced below:

MR DIPLOCK: My Lords, it is important to note that in the Proclamation of the Governor-General he has said that the election will be held as early as possible. Having taken the first step to avert the disaster by dissolving the existing Constituent Assembly, elections will be held as early as possible. It was his intention, and I am instructed to inform Your Lordships that it is still his intention, to provide for the immediate election of fresh representatives to the Constituent Assembly by the Provincial Legislative Assemblies which was the method by which, Your Lordships would recall, the original members of the Constituent Assembly were elected. One hopes it would so act to provide as speedily as possible for direct elections. But nothing has been done by the existing Constituent Assembly to provide an election law or for the delimitation of constituencies for the election of the Central Legislature and such a provision for direct election would from the practical point of view take a minimum of 12 months or probably more.

CHIEF JUSTICE: And for indirect elections?

MR. DIPLOCK: Indirect election could be done within a period of a week or two. There are the Provincial Assemblies. They have got to be called together to select their representatives. Having regard to the fact about the practical difficulties for holding direct election, it may delay the matter.

In view of the delay as to the direct election, the Governor-General is anxious to adopt the quickest measure to have immediately an

Assembly which could be as nearly perfectly representative of the people as could be obtained at the present moment through indirect election.

CHIEF JUSTICE: So you agree that there is immediate need for a legislature.

MR DIPLOCK: Because the Governor-General has to act by proclamation. He is acting on the advice of his Ministers but without the assistance of the representatives of the people.

CHIEF JUSTICE: Will the Proclamation have the force of law?

MR DIPLOCK: The Governor-General's intention is to get into operation as quickly as possible an Assembly which is as nearly representative of the wishes of the people as can be obtained immediately. That is a matter which will necessarily be within the Governor-General's discretion.

MR JUSTICE RAHMAN: Have you been formally instructed to this effect to inform us?

MR DIPLOCK: Yes, My Lord, I have been instructed to tell Your Lordships that it was the intention of the Governor-General while making this proclamation and still is his intention to summon a fresh Constituent Assembly elected so far as the Provinces which have got Legislative Assemblies are concerned by members of those Assemblies.

As I said to Your Lordships it was the Governor-General's intention at the time that the Proclamation was made that steps for the reconstitution of the Constituent Assembly should be taken at once. It may be that he took the view at that stage on the advice which was given to him that it was within his powers under the Constitution to take the step which he has taken under the Proclamation. I am only saying that it is not for us to say that we are right; it is for Your Lordships to decide whether it was right. In those circumstances he thought it right, an immediate application having been made to the Sind Chief Court, to wait, unless the necessity became compelling, until the Court had said whether his interpretation of the law was right or not. My Lords, he took the view and I think whichever view is right as to construction: whether he is entitled to do it under the Act, as I submit he is, or whether he is entitled to do it in reliance on the maxim *salus populi suprema lex*. He took the view that so far as possible, although representative institutions are necessarily abrogated while he waited for the decision of the Court, it was undesirable, in addition to the abrogation of representative institutions which had already happened when the Constituent Assembly itself became unrepresentative, to abrogate that other essential feature of the democratic Constitution the rule of law, and to use force in order to prevent the matter coming before the Courts. My Lords, it may be, indeed it would have been, his duty, had circumstances so necessitated, to take those steps

254

without regard to the writ which had been issued, because *salus populi suprema lex*. Fortunately it has not been necessary at present to do so....

It was his intention in October last to set up a new Constituent Assembly. That is an action which he would have taken immediately after 24 October had this litigation not started and that is his intention still. I hope Your Lordships will not press me to say anything more than I can necessarily say about the matter.

It might have been expected that, conformably with the attitude taken before us by responsible counsel for the Crown, the first concern of the Government would have been to bring into existence another representative body to exercise the powers of the Constituent Assembly so that all invalid legislation could have been immediately validated by the new body. Such a course would have been consistent with constitutional practice in relation to such a situation as has arisen. Events, however, show that other counsels have since prevailed. The Ordinance contains no reference to elections, and all that the learned Advocate-General can say is that they are intended to be held.

Appeals allowed.

[The other learned judges concurred.]

REPORT

ON THE

SPECIAL REFERENCE

MADE BY

HIS EXCELLENCY
THE GOVERNOR-GENERAL
OF PAKISTAN

IN THE
FEDERAL COURT OF PAKISTAN
(ADVISORY JURISDICTION)

SPECIAL REFERENCE
NO. I OF 1955

(Reference by His Excellency the Governor-General under section 213 of the Government of India Act, 1935)

Present: Muhammad Munir, C.J., A. S. M. Akram, A. R. Cornelius, Muhammad Sharif, and S. A. Rahman, JJ.

MUHAMMAD MUNIR, C.J.—The situation presented by this Opinion *Reference* by His Excellency the Governor-General under section 213 of the Government of India Act, 1935, is that after experimenting for more than seven years with a constitution which was imposed on this country, with the consent of its leaders, by a statute of the Parliament of the United Kingdom, called the Indian Independence Act, 1947, we have come to the brink of a chasm with only three alternatives before us:

(i) to turn back the way we came by;
(ii) to cross the gap by a legal bridge;
(iii) to hurtle into the chasm beyond any hope of rescue.

It is not a long story to tell how we have come to this pass. Pakistan came into existence as an independent Dominion member of the British Commonwealth of Nations on 15 August 1947, with a provisional constitution of the federal pattern, under the Indian Independence Act, 1947. By that Act, until a new constitution was framed, the Government of Pakistan was to be carried on in accordance with the Government of India Act, 1935, with certain consequential adaptations and modifications. A Governor-General was to represent the Crown and the functions of the Legislature of the Dominion, including the making of a constitution, were to be performed by a Constituent Assembly which had also to

259

function as the Federal Legislature. The Assembly had not made any constitution when on 24 October 1954, it was dissolved by a Proclamation of the Governor-General, the ground of dissolution stated in the Proclamation being that the Assembly had lost the confidence of the people and could no longer function. The Proclamation also contained a promise of early elections to enable the people through their representatives to decide all issues including constitutional issues.

On 7 November 1954, Mr Tamizuddin Khan, the President of the Constituent Assembly, preferred a petition on the Extraordinary Special Jurisdiction side of the Chief Court of Sind, calling in question the Governor-General's power to dissolve the Assembly and praying for writs of mandamus and quo warranto. The jurisdiction to issue what in England are called prerogative writs had been conferred on the High Courts in Pakistan by section 223A, which was inserted in the Government of India Act, 1935, by an Act called the Government of India (Amendment) Act, 1954, passed by the Constituent Assembly on 16 July 1954. This Amendment Act, however, was never presented for assent to the Governor-General. The respondents to the petition were the Federation of Pakistan and certain Ministers of the Central Government including the Prime Minister. In their reply to the petition the respondents objected to the jurisdiction of the Sind Chief Court to issue the writs, on the ground that the Governor-General's assent to the Amendment Act, 1954, was indispensable and that since no such assent had been given to that Act the Chief Court had no jurisdiction to issue the writs. The Chief Court held that the Governor-General's assent to Acts passed by the Constituent Assembly, when it functioned as the Legislature of the Dominion under sub-section (1) of section 8 of the Indian Independence Act, 1947, was not necessary and that the Governor-General had no power to dissolve the Assembly. Accordingly the writs prayed for were issued.

The Federation and the Ministers appealed to this Court after obtaining a certificate under section 205 of the Government of India Act, 1935, from the Chief Court of Sind. It was contended on their behalf that the assent of the Governor-General to all legislation passed by the Constituent Assembly, whether as the Federal Legislature or as the Legislature of the Dominion, was necessary and that since the Amendment Act had not received such assent, section 223A of the Government of India Act, 1935, which conferred on the High Courts the jurisdiction to issue prerogative writs, was not a part of the law and that, therefore, the Chief Court had no jurisdiction to issue the writs. The dissolution of the Assembly by the Governor-General was sought to be defended on the ground that the power to dissolve was implicit in the wide terms of section 5 of the Indian Independence Act, 1947, which provides that the Governor-General shall represent His Majesty for the purposes of the government of the Dominion.

After hearing full arguments on the question of assent the majority of us came to the conclusion that all laws passed by the Constituent Assembly required the Governor-General's assent, and we determined the appeal on that issue alone. Our judgment in *Mr Tamizuddin Khan's* case was delivered on 21 March 1955, but reasons for it were given later on 3 April 1955.

It is a mistake to suppose that we were not aware of the far-reaching consequences of the decision in *Mr Tamizuddin Khan's* case. I referred to this aspect of the matter at pp. 136–40 of my judgment and concluded with the following observations:

I am quite clear in my mind that we are not concerned with the consequences, however beneficial or disastrous they may be, if the undoubted legal position was that all legislation by the Legislature of the Dominion under sub-section (3) of section 8 needed the assent of the Governor-General. If the result is disaster, it will merely be another instance of how thoughtlessly the Constituent Assembly proceeded with its business and by assuming for itself the position of an irremovable legislature to what straits it has brought the country. Unless any rule of estoppel require us to pronounce merely purported legislation as complete and valid legislation, we have no option but to pronounce it to be void and to leave it to the relevant authorities under the Constitution or to the country to set right the position in any way it may be open to them. The question raised involves the rights of every citizen in Pakistan, and neither any rule of construction nor any rule of estoppel stands in the way of a clear pronouncement[1].

On 27 March 1955, the Governor-General purporting to act under section 42 of the Government of India Act, 1935, and professing to exercise 'all other powers enabling him in that behalf' promulgated the Emergency Powers Ordinance, IX of 1955, by which he sought to validate and to give retrospective effect to 35

[1] *Ante*, p. 140.

Constitutional Acts which had been passed by the Constituent Assembly in exercise of its powers as the Legislature of the Dominion under sub-section (1) of section 8 of the Indian Independence Act, 1947, and which under the judgment of this Court in *Mr Tamizuddin Khan's* case had become invalid. By that Ordinance the Governor-General not only claimed the power of making by order such provisions as appeared to him to be necessary or expedient for the Constitution of Pakistan but he also repealed or amended certain provisions of the existing constitution relating to the Federal Legislature, the Annual Financial Statements, the Supplementary Statements of Expenditure, the Provinces and States and the High Courts and added a proviso to section 176 of the Government of India Act, 1935, forbidding the bringing of suits or other proceedings against the Government or any Minister or officer of the Government in respect of or arising out of anything done or omitted to be done by the Governor-General or by the Government or by any person under or in consequence of the Governor-General's Proclamation under section 102 of the Government of India Act, 1935, which had been issued simultaneously with the Ordinance. The question of the validity of section 2 of that Ordinance came up before us within a few days of our judgment in *Mr Tamizuddin Khan's* case, in *Usif Patel's* appeal. In that appeal the learned Counsel for the Crown relied on Ordinance IX of 1955 as having validated some of the constitutional laws which in consequence of our judgment in *Mr Tamizuddin Khan's* case had been supposed to have been declared invalid. We unhesitatingly repelled that contention and held that validation of constitutional legislation being itself legislation could only be effected by the Constituent Assembly under sub-section (1) of section 8 of the Indian Independence Act, 1947, and not by means of an Ordinance by the Governor-General promulgated under section 42 of the Government of India Act, 1935. In coming to that conclusion we did no more than repeat the finding of the Court in *Mr Tamizuddin Khan's* case.

Though it was recited in that Ordinance that the Constituent Assembly had been dissolved, that the Federal Court had declared all constitutional legislation by the Constituent Assembly to be invalid and that therefore the constitutional machinery had broken down, the powers professed to be exercised under the Ordinance were claimed under section 42 of the Government of India Act, 1935, and from some other sources not specified. In the arguments before us, however, none of the matters mentioned in the preamble was referred to and reliance was solely placed by the learned Advocate-General on the Governor-General's powers of promulgating Ordinances under section 42 of the Government of India Act. We repelled that contention on the short ground that that section did not enable the Governor-General to make by Ordinance any provision as to the constitution of the country. Since we had not so far recorded any finding that the constitutional machinery had broken down or that the Constituent Assembly had been rightly dissolved, and no legislative body to replace the Constituent Assembly as promised in the Proclamation of 24 October 1954, had yet been set up, the learned Advocate-General rightly did not rely on the inherent powers of the Governor-General to legislate in an emergency outside the purview of section 42 of the Government of India Act, 1935, and lost the Crown case simply on the ground that under the Constitution Acts the Governor-General could not exercise the powers claimed by him in the Ordinance.

On 15 April 1955, the Governor-General summoned a Constituent Convention for 10 May 1955, for the purpose of making provision as to the Constitution of Pakistan, and on the following day issued a Proclamation assuming to himself until other provision was made by the Constituent Convention such powers as were necessary to validate and enforce the laws that were needed to avoid a breakdown in the constitutional and administrative machinery of the country or to preserve the State and maintain the Government of the country in its existing condition, and in exercise of those powers retrospectively validated and declared enforceable the laws mentioned in the Schedule to the Emergency Powers Ordinance, 1955. These powers were exercised by the Governor-General subject to the opinion of this Court on certain questions which had in the meantime been referred to it under section 213 of the Government of India Act, 1935. The Proclamation was accompanied by two Ordinances, No. XIII of 1955, to validate Acts enacted by the Governors of the Provinces of East Bengal, Punjab and Sind, and No. XIV of 1955, precluding the Courts from questioning the validity of any Act passed by the

Provincial Legislatures or of any order made, decision taken or other acts done in pursuance of any such Act, on the ground that any law passed by the Constituent Assembly had not received the assent of the Governor-General. The questions originally referred were:

1. What are the powers and responsibilities of the Governor-General in respect of the Government of the country before the new Constituent Convention passes the necessary legislation?

2. The Federal Court having held in *Usif Patel's* case that the laws listed in the Schedule to the Emergency Powers Ordinance could not be validated under section 42 of the Government of India Act, 1935, nor retrospective effect given to them, and no legislature competent to validate such laws being in existence, is there any provision in the Constitution or any rule of law applicable to the situation by which the Governor-General can by order or otherwise declare that all orders made, decisions taken and other acts done under those laws shall be valid and enforceable and those laws which cannot without danger to the State be removed from the existing legal system shall be treated as part of the law of the land until the question of their validation is determined by the new Constituent Convention?

Subsequently as suggested in the course of this Court's order, dated 18 April 1955, the following further questions were also referred for opinion:

3. Whether the Constituent Assembly was rightly dissolved by the Governor-General?

4. Whether the Constituent Convention proposed to be set up by the Governor-General will be competent to exercise the powers conferred by sub-section (1) of section 8 of the Indian Independence Act, 1947, on the Constituent Assembly?

Question no. 4 was later modified and in the form in which it has now to be answered is: Whether the Constituent Convention proposed to be set up by the Governor-General will be competent to exercise the powers conferred by section 8 of the Indian Independence Act, 1947, on the Constituent Assembly.

Dissolution: (a) Power to dissolve not absolute

The fundamental question in the *Reference* is whether the action of the Governor-General in dissolving the Assembly was legal. The Proclamation of 24 October 1954, which is relied upon as the order dissolving the Assembly, stated that the constitutional machinery had broken down; that a state of emergency had been declared throughout Pakistan; that the Constituent Assembly, as

264

then constituted, having lost the confidence of the people, could no longer function; and that the Prime Minister had accepted the invitation to reform the Cabinet with a view to giving the country a vigorous and stable administration. The question whether in acting in the manner that he did, the Governor-General acted in his discretion, does not arise because the acceptance of the invitation by the Prime Minister must, on the strength of several constitutional precedents in the Commonwealth, be taken as assumption by him of the responsibility for dissolution. This, however, does not solve the issue because, whether the Governor-General was acting with the advice of the Prime Minister or without his advice, some authority, express or implied, must be found in the Constitution Acts to make the action of the Governor-General legal; though if the power to dissolve be found to exist, the Court will not enquire into the propriety or impropriety of the exercise of that power, nor go into the question whether the action was or was not backed by Ministerial advice. Such action by the constitutional Head of the State always gives rise to two issues, one of which is purely legal and the other, political or constitutional, by the word 'constitutional' being meant whether the action was consistent with the practice and usages of the Constitution. The first issue is for the courts to determine; and if the Court finds that the power claimed existed in law, it is not concerned with the question whether the power was exercised in accordance with the conventions or unwritten traditions of the Constitution. This position is recognised by sub-section (4) of section 10 of the Government of India Act, 1935, which prohibits a court from inquiring into the question 'whether any and, if so, what advice was tendered by Ministers to the Governor-General'. Therefore the word 'rightly' in the question whether the Constituent Assembly was rightly dissolved by the Governor-General can only mean 'lawfully' or 'legally' because the political propriety or impropriety of a dissolution is not a question of law that can be referred by the Governor-General or answered by this Court under section 213 of the Government of India Act, 1935.

It was the case of Mr Faiyaz Ali, the learned Advocate-General of Pakistan, and of Mr Diplock in *Mr Tamizuddin Khan's* case that the Governor-General had an unqualified legal right to dissolve the Constituent Assembly at any time he liked and that the act of dissolution was not a justiciable issue in courts of law. This power was claimed in that case for the Governor-General and is still being claimed for him by Mr Faiyaz Ali, though Mr Diplock, as will be mentioned later, has slightly altered his position, on the following grounds:

(i) that the power to dissolve was as much a prerogative of the Crown as the power to prorogue and summon; and that it was vested in the Governor-General to be used unreservedly by him as representative of the Crown under section 5 of the Indian Independence Act, 1947;

(ii) that the setting up of the Constituent Assembly being an executive act, it could be performed by the Governor-General, in supersession of the earlier act, under sub-section (3) of section 19 of the Indian Independence Act, 1947, read with sub-sections (1) and (2) of section 32 of the Interpretation Act, 1889, the argument being that the power to set up a new Assembly necessarily implies the power to dissolve an existing Assembly.

Having given anxious thought to these grounds I find myself unable to find the Governor-General as the repository of the wide and unqualified powers which are claimed for him.

In *Mr Tamizuddin Khan's* case I had the occasion to explain at length the profound constitutional changes that were brought about by the Indian Independence Act, 1947. The changes that are relevant to the present *Reference* were:

(i) that a Governor-General was to represent His Majesty for the purposes of the government of the Dominion—section 5;

(ii) that the Legislature of the Dominion was given full and unqualified powers to make laws, of whatever kind, for the Dominion, the exercise of those powers being subject to the Governor-General's assent—section 6;

(iii) that the Assembly set up or about to be set up at the date of the passing of the Act under the authority of the Governor-General, was to be the Constituent Assembly for Pakistan—section 19, sub-section (3) (*b*);

(iv) that the powers of the Legislature of the Dominion conferred on that Legislature by section 6 were, in so far as they related to the making of provision for the constitution of the Dominion, 'exercisable in the first instance' by the Constituent Assembly; and

(v) that the powers of the Federal Legislature under the adapted Government of India Act, 1935, were also to 'be exercisable' 'in the first instance' by the Constituent Assembly.

The Act contained no express provision for the dissolution of the Constituent Assembly, nor did it prescribe any time limit within which it was to frame the Constitution or to function as the Federal Legislature. As dissolution of the Assembly, if it performed the duty assigned to it, was not contemplated, the Act made no provision for the election of a new Constituent Assembly. Similarly as the Constituent Assembly was to function as the first Federal Legislature, the provisions relating to the oaths of members, vacation of seats, disqualification for membership, which occurred in sections 24 to 27 of the Government of India Act, 1935, and the provisions in the First Schedule to that Act relating to the composition of the Federal Legislature, were omitted. It seems to me to be perfectly clear from this scheme of the Indian Independence Act, 1947, and the adapted Government of India Act, 1935, that the absolute and unqualified prerogative right of the Crown and of the Governor-General as representative of the Crown to dissolve the Assembly was taken away. If the intention had been to transfer to the Governor-General, as representative of the Crown, the prerogative right of summoning, proroguing and dissolving the Constituent Assembly, the elaborate constitutional structure that was built upon the Indian Independence Act, 1947, and the adapted Government of India Act, 1935, could have been pulled down by the Governor-General, with or without the advice of the Prime Minister, on the very day he assumed his office and before the Constituent Assembly had even commenced to function.

This possibility was certainly excluded by and is clearly inconsistent with the intention of the Indian Independence Act, 1947, particularly sub-section (1) of section 8 according to which the powers of the Legislature of the Dominion were to be exercised in the first instance by the Constituent Assembly and proviso (e) to sub-section (2) of that section which similarly declared that the powers of the Federal Legislature under the adapted Government of India Act, 1935, were to be exercisable in the first instance by the same Assembly. If this be the correct interpretation of the Indian Independence Act, 1947, then two of the principles which were developed by Mr Diplock in a full day argument in *Mr Tamizuddin Khan's* case would be applicable but would produce a result entirely contrary to what is contended by him. The operation of the principle that the prerogatives of the Crown in an overseas Dominion can be taken away by a statute, whether of the United Kingdom or of the Dominion itself, by express words or necessary intendment, would negative an unqualified power on the part of the Governor-General to dissolve the Assembly because the Indian Independence Act, 1947, by providing that the powers of the Legislature of the Dominion for the purpose of making a Constitution and of the Federal Legislature under the adapted Government of India Act, 1935, were to be exercised in the first instance by the Constituent Assembly, would take away the unqualified prerogative of the Crown to dissolve the Assembly; and the principle that the Crown may delegate its prerogative in whole or in part to the Governor-General of an overseas Dominion and that it is a question of construction of the relevant statute or instrument to determine the extent to which the prerogative has been delegated would produce the result that, on this interpretation of the Indian Independence Act, the prerogative to dissolve, though delegated by the Crown, was not intended to be exercised by the Governor-General so long as the Constituent Assembly continued to function within the intention of the Indian Independence Act, 1947. Mr Diplock has not questioned the correctness of the House of Lords' decision in *Attorney-General* v. *De Keyser's Royal Hotel*,[1] on which the learned Judges of the Sind Chief Court had relied in support of the proposition that where a prerogative matter has been legislated upon, the prerogative as to that matter must be deemed to have been merged in the statute to the extent that it has been legislated upon. In that case in May 1916, the Crown purporting to act under the Defence of the Realm Regulations took possession of an hotel for the purpose of housing the headquarters personnel of the Royal Flying Corps and denied the legal right of the owners to compensation. The owners yielded up possession under protest and without prejudice to their rights, but by a petition of right asked for a declaration that they were entitled to compensation under the Defence Act, 1842. It was held by the House of Lords that Regulation 2 of the Defence of the Realm Regulations issued under the Defence of the Realm Consolidation Act, 1914, when read with sub-section (2) of section 1 of the Act, conferred no new powers of acquiring

[1] [1920] A.C. 508.

land but authorised the taking possession of land under the Defence Act, 1842, while impliedly suspending the restriction imposed by that Act upon acquisition and user of land; that the Crown had no power to take possession of the suppliants' premises in right of its prerogative *simpliciter*; and that the supplicants were entitled to compensation in the manner provided by the Act of 1842. While considering the question to what extent prerogative can be considered to have been taken away by statute, Lord Dunedin said at p. 526 of the report:

None the less it is equally certain that if the whole ground of something which could be done by the prerogative is covered by the statute, it is the statute that rules. On this point I think the observation of the learned Master of the Rolls is unanswerable. He says: 'What use would there be imposing limitations if the Crown could at its pleasure disregard them and fall back on prerogative?'

The prerogative is defined by a learned constitutional writer as 'the residue of discretionary or arbitrary authority which at any given time is legally left in the hands of the Crown'. Inasmuch as the Crown is a party to every Act of Parliament, it is logical enough to consider that when the Act deals with something which before the Act could be effected by the prerogative, and specially empowers the Crown to do the same thing, but subject to conditions, the Crown assents to that, and by that Act, to the prerogative being curtailed.

To a similar effect were the observations made by Lord Atkinson, who said at p. 539:

It is quite obvious that it would be useless and meaningless for the Legislature to impose restrictions and limitations upon, and to attach conditions to, the exercise by the Crown of the powers conferred by a statute, if the Crown were free at its pleasure to disregard these provisions, and by virtue of its prerogative do the very thing the statute empowered it to do. One cannot in the construction of a statute attribute to the Legislature (in the absence of compelling words) an intention so absurd. It was suggested that when a statute is passed empowering the Crown to do a certain thing which it might theretofore have done by virtue of its prerogative, the prerogative is merged in the statute. I confess I do not think the word 'merged' is happily chosen. I should prefer to say that when such a statute, expressing the will and intention of the King and of the three estates of the realm, is passed, it abridges the Royal Prerogative while it is in force to this extent: that the Crown can only do the particular thing under and in accordance with the statutory provisions and that its prerogative power to do that thing is in abeyance. Whichever mode of expression be used, the result intended

269

to be indicated is, I think, the same—namely, that after the statute has been passed and while it is in force, the thing it empowers the Crown to do can thenceforth only be done by and under the statute, and subject to all the limitations, restrictions and conditions by it imposed, however unrestricted the Royal Prerogative may theretofore have been.

And another noble lord, Lord Sumner, remarked at p. 561:

The Legislature, by appropriate enactment, can deal with such a subject-matter as that now in question in such a way as to abate such portions of the prerogative as apply to it. It seems also to be obvious that enactments may have this effect, provided they directly deal with the subject-matter, even though they enact a *modus operandi* for securing the desired result, which is not the same as that of the prerogative. If a statute merely recorded existing inherent powers, nothing would be gained by the enactment, for nothing would be added to the existing law. There is no object in dealing by statute with the same subject-matter as is already dealt with by prerogative, unless it be either to limit or at least to vary its exercise, or to provide an additional mode of attaining the same object.

The principle so clearly enunciated, though in different words, by each of the noble lords speaking on this case is, that where restrictions or limitations are imposed by statute on a prerogative matter, the prerogative is abridged or taken away to the extent of the restriction or limitation. Applying that principle to the present case it must be held that sub-section (1) of section 8 of the Indian Independence Act, 1947, took away from the Crown by necessary implication the prerogative of dissolution to this extent, that the Crown was bound to give to the Constituent Assembly a reasonable opportunity to frame the Constitution.

The instances of the power to dissolve, unqualified in law but strictly restricted by conventions, which vests in the Governors-General of the other Dominions are not relevant for the purpose of inferring a similar power for the Governor-General of Pakistan, because that power is expressly recognised by the Constitutions of those Dominions. Thus under the British North America Act, 1867, section 50, the House of Commons is to continue for five years (subject to be sooner dissolved by the Governor-General) and no longer. Similarly under section 28 of the Commonwealth of Australia Constitution Act, 1900, the House of Representatives continues for three years but may be sooner dissolved by the

Governor-General. Under the South Africa Act, 1909, section 20, the Governor-General could dissolve the Senate and the House of Assembly simultaneously or the House of Assembly alone. Section 15 of the Ceylon (Constitution) Order-in-Council, 1946, which continues by virtue of the Ceylon Independence Act, 1947, and the Ceylon Independence (Commencement) Order-in-Council, 1947, provides that the Governor-General may by proclamation summon, prorogue or dissolve Parliament. In the New Zealand Constitution Act, 1852, the relevant provision is section 44 which empowers the Governor-General at his pleasure to prorogue or dissolve the General Assembly. Similar power is given to the Governors of the Colonies by the instruments appointing them or by the Constitutions of those Colonies. In the case of Pakistan, the Indian Independence Act, 1947, contains no express provision empowering the Governor-General to dissolve the Assembly; nor is any express reference to this power to be found in the warrant of his appointment, though one of the prerogatives, namely that of granting pardon and reprieves, etc., to persons convicted, has been specifically mentioned because by reason of section 259 of the Government of India Act, 1935, this prerogative had expressly to be delegated to the Governor-General to be exercised on His Majesty's behalf. Of course the warrant refers to the Indian Independence Act, 1947, and to the powers and duties of the Governor-General under that Act as well as to the powers, rights, privileges and advantages belonging or appertaining to the office of Governor-General.

In *Mr Tamizuddin Khan's* case the learned Judges of the Sind Chief Court inferred from the adaptation of sub-sections 18 and 19 of the Government of India Act, 1935, that the power to dissolve the Federal Legislature was impliedly taken away from the Governor-General because while his power to summon and prorogue was kept intact, that to dissolve the Federal Legislature was omitted in the adaptations. In its original form section 18 of the Government of India Act, 1935, had provided that the Federal Legislature was to consist of His Majesty, represented by the Governor-General, and two Chambers to be known respectively as the Council of State and the House of Assembly which was referred to in the Act as the Federal Assembly. The Council of State was to be a permanent body not subject to dissolution while the Federal Assembly, unless sooner dissolved, was to continue for five years. By the Provisional Constitution Order this section was substituted by the following provision:

The powers of the Federal Legislature under this Act shall, until other provision is made by or in accordance with a law made by the Constituent Assembly under sub-section (1) of section 8 of the Indian Independence Act, 1947, be exercisable by that Assembly, and accordingly references in this Act to the Federal Legislature shall be construed as references to the Constituent Assembly.

The substituted section was bodily taken from clause (e) of the proviso to sub-section (2) of section 8 of the Indian Independence Act, 1947, with only this exception, that the words 'in the first instance' were omitted and the words 'and accordingly references in this Act to the Federal Legislature shall be construed as references to the Constituent Assembly', added. Section 19 in its original form dealt with the summoning of the Chambers or either Chamber, prorogation of the Chambers and dissolution of the Federal Assembly, and gave to the Governor-General, in his discretion, the power to do any of these acts. The Provisional Constitution Order omitted the words 'in his discretion' and substituted 'Federal Legislature' for the words 'Chambers or Chamber', and while retaining the Governor-General's power to summon or prorogue the Federal Legislature omitted clause (c) of sub-section (2) of the section, which had given to the Governor-General the power to dissolve the Federal Assembly. On the basis of these adaptations it is argued by Mr Chundrigar and Mr Pritt that the omission of the power to dissolve the Federal Assembly, and not making any provision for the dissolution of the Federal Legislature, must be taken to imply the taking away of the power of dissolution of that legislature from the Governor-General while preserving his power to summon and prorogue. It is, however, contended before us both by Mr Faiyaz Ali and Mr Diplock that there are two obvious explanations for removal of the provision relating to the dissolution of the Federal Assembly and not substituting for it any provision as regards the dissolution of the Federal Legislature. Firstly, since the Federal Assembly disappeared under the adapted Constitution, all provisions relating to it including clause (c) of sub-section (2) of section 19 of the

Government of India Act, 1935, had necessarily to be omitted. Secondly, the provisions relating to dissolution could, under that Act, only relate to dissolution of the Federal Legislature and not of the Legislature of the Dominion if by Legislature of the Dominion was meant the Constituent Assembly in its capacity of the body charged with the duty of making provisions as to the constitution of the Dominion. The power to dissolve the Constituent Assembly, it is contended, having been included in the delegation of the King's prerogatives to the Governor-General under section 5 of the Indian Independence Act, it did not require any specific delegation. The argument is good so far as it goes but does not repel the implications that arise from the omission of the provision relating to the dissolution of the Federal Legislature. If a provision relating to the dissolution of the Federal Legislature had been enacted, as it could quite properly have been enacted in the Provisional Constitution Order, the result would have been that the Governor-General would in that case have acquired an unqualified power to dissolve the Federal Legislature which would have been inconsistent with clause (*e*) of the proviso to sub-section (2) of section 8 of the Indian Independence Act, 1947, which had provided that the powers of the Federal Legislature shall, in the first instance, be exercisable by the Constituent Assembly. Since, therefore, the intention was that not only the duty of making a Constitution but the functions of the Federal Legislature were in the first instance to be performed by the Constituent Assembly, no provision relating to the dissolution of the Federal Legislature was inserted in the adapted section 19. This conclusion is strengthened by the fact that in the adaptations the First Schedule to the Government of India Act, 1935, which dealt with the composition of the Federal Legislature, was completely omitted. If the possibility of a dissolution of the Federal Legislature at all times and of new members being chosen to it had been contemplated, some provision relating to elections should certainly have found place in the adaptations. The fact therefore that the First Schedule was omitted and no provision relating to dissolution of the Federal Legislature was enacted and the only provision relating to dissolution of the Federal Assembly was omitted, shows quite clearly that the expert who adapted the Government of India Act, 1935, by an order under section 9 of the

Indian Independence Act, 1947, thought that within a reasonable time the Constituent Assembly would complete the work assigned to it and dissolve itself when the new Constitution came into force. I accept Mr Diplock's contention that nothing that was done by an order under the Indian Independence Act, 1947, is relevant to a true interpretation of that Act because the adaptations merely represented the personal view of the adapter and the implications that arise from them are not conclusive of a particular construction; but the whole scheme of that Act appears to me to suggest that the Constituent Assembly was to make a Constitution under sub-section (1) of section 8 of the Act as well as to exercise the powers of the Federal Legislature under the adapted Government of India Act, because the words 'in the first instance' on which considerable emphasis was laid by Mr Diplock in another connection and which occur both in sub-section (1) and clause (e) of the proviso to sub-section (2) of that section are unmistakably indicative of the intention that the Constituent Assembly, if it functioned according to the true intent of the Constitution Acts, was in neither capacity to be dissolved. A dissolution is no more than an appeal to the electorate, and it is admitted that neither under the Indian Independence Act, 1947, nor under the adapted Government of India Act, 1935, there exists any provision relating to fresh elections to the Legislature of the Dominion or the Federal Legislature. This, in my opinion, being the correct interpretation of the Indian Independence Act, 1947, no unqualified delegation of the prerogative of dissolution can be read in section 5 of the Indian Independence Act, 1947, or in the warrant of Governor-General's appointment.

Mr Faiyaz Ali and Mr Diplock also attempted to justify the dissolution under clause (a) of sub-section (1) and clause (b) of sub-section (3) of section 19 of the Indian Independence Act, 1947, read with sub-section (2) of section 32 of the Interpretation Act, 1889. Clause (a) of sub-section (1) provides that references in the Act to the Governor-General shall in relation to any order to be made or other act done on or after the appointed day, be construed, where the order or other act concerns only one of the new Dominions, as references to the Governor-General of that Dominion; while clause (b) of sub-section (3) declares that in relation to Pakistan references in the Act to the Constituent Assembly are to be read as references to the Assembly set up or about to be set up at the date of the passing of the Act under the authority of the Governor-General, as the Constituent Assembly for Pakistan. Sub-section (2) of the Interpretation Act says that where an Act passed after the commencement of that Act confers a power or imposes a duty on the holder of an office, as such, then, unless the contrary intention appears, the power may be exercised and the duty shall be performed by the holder for the time being of the office. The Indian Independence Act, 1947, was passed on 18 July 1947, but on that day no Constituent Assembly had in fact been set up. The personnel of the Constituent Assembly was announced by the Governor-General on 26 July 1947, that is to say, after the passing of the Act. It is argued that since there was a possibility of the composition of the Constituent Assembly not being completed before the appointed day, i.e. 15 August 1947, the act of setting up the Assembly on a subsequent date could only be done by the Governor-General of Pakistan under clause (*a*) to sub-section (1) of section 19 and that in that case the references in the Act to the Constituent Assembly could only have been meant as references to the Constituent Assembly to be set up by the Governor-General of Pakistan. The whole argument is based on the words 'about to be set up at the date of the passing of this Act under the authority of the Governor-General' and we know that the Governor-General on the date of the passing of the Indian Independence Act, 1947, was Lord Louis Mountbatten who had practically taken all necessary steps for the setting up of the Constituent Assembly. The intention to set up a Constituent Assembly had been announced in paragraphs 5–7 of the Statement of His Majesty's Government of 3 June 1947. Paragraph 14 of that statement had also detailed the manner in which the members of the Constituent Assembly were to be chosen, and paragraph 15 had provided that the representatives of the various Provinces which were divided for the purposes of election were, in accordance with the mandate given to them, to decide whether they were to join the existing Constituent Assembly or form a new Constituent Assembly. On 10 June 1947, the Governor-General, in pursuance of paragraph 21 of that statement, had issued an order directing a certain procedure to be followed for the purpose of giving effect to paragraphs 5–8 of the statement. By this announcement the constituencies whose representatives were to form part of the Legislative Assemblies of those Provinces for the purpose of taking the decision referred to in paragraphs 6–8 of the Statement were specified. The procedure relating to the District of Sylhet was announced in the Statement of 16 June 1947, while the announcement, dated 21 June 1947, detailed the procedure for holding fresh elections in Bengal and a referendum in Sylhet. The procedure for fresh elections in the Punjab was announced on 23 June 1947, that for holding a referendum in North-West Frontier Province on 23 June 1947, and that for ascertaining the wishes of British Baluchistan on 24 June 1947. The announcement of cessation of membership of Sind members came on 27 June 1947, that of membership of representatives of British Baluchistan on 30 June 1947, and that of cessation of membership of the representatives of North-West Frontier Province on 21 July 1947. Fresh elections in Assam and East Bengal were announced on 22 July 1947. The final composition of the Constituent Assembly of Pakistan, with the exception of the representatives of Sylhet District whose names were announced a few days later (4 August 1947), was announced on 26 July 1947. The Indian Independence Act, 1947, received the Royal assent on 18 July 1947. It is, therefore, clear that references to the Constituent Assembly of Pakistan in the Indian Independence Act, 1947, could only have been meant as references to the Constituent Assembly whose composition was finally completed on 4 August 1947, and not to any other Constituent Assembly to be set up by the Governor-General of Pakistan after 15 August 1947. If Mr Diplock's argument be accepted, it would mean that the words in clause (*b*) of sub-section (3) of section 19 of the Indian Independence Act, 1947, 'Assembly set up or about to be set up at the date of the passing of this Act' (18 July 1947), are comprehensive enough to include an Assembly set up at any time after 15 August 1947—even today. I cannot accept this result as reasonably possible or agree to any such construction of section 19 of the Indian Independence Act, which was drafted by the best legal brains in the United Kingdom, as would lead to a conclusion so ludicrous. I am, therefore, of the view that the statutory provisions relied on are not an authority for the Governor-General of Pakistan to set up a new Constituent Assembly in supersession of the original

Constituent Assembly and that if any such authority exists it lies elsewhere in the Act.

Mr Diplock in the early stages of the arguments in this *Reference* seemed materially to qualify the position taken by him in *Mr Tamizuddin Khan's* case by conceding that until the Constituent Assembly had had a reasonable opportunity to frame a Constitution, the Governor-General had no power to dissolve it. But while attempting to construe sub-section (1) and proviso (e) to sub-section (2) of section 8 of the Indian Independence Act, 1947, so as to mean that the Governor-General can create another Constituent Assembly, he finally took up the position that the Governor-General's right to dissolve the Assembly was excluded only as long as the Constituent Assembly did not make any provision as to the Constitution of the Dominion and that as soon as that Assembly exercised the right of making any such provision the Governor-General's right to dissolve re-asserted itself. On this argument the moment the Constituent Assembly passed its first constitutional Act, namely, the Indian Independence (Amendment) Act, 1948, the condition laid down in sub-section (1) of section 8 of the Indian Independence Act, 1947, of making provision as to the constitution of the Dominion, in the first instance, was fulfilled and immediately thereafter the Governor-General acquired the legal right to dissolve the Assembly. I find it impossible to accept this construction of sub-section (1) and having considered the argument in all its implications and the words of the statute on which it is based I am perfectly clear that the contention has unhesitatingly to be rejected. In my opinion the words in that sub-section and proviso (e) say no more than that the Constituent Assembly was the first Legislature of the Dominion to exercise the powers, in so far as those powers related to the making of provision as to the constitution of the Dominion, conferred on it by section 6, as well as the first Federal Legislature competent to exercise the powers of that Legislature under the adapted Government of India Act, 1935. Neither of these provisions is capable of the interpretation that the moment the Constituent Assembly exercised either of these powers, in however inchoate or imperfect a form, the Governor-General's right to dissolve it in the capacity in which it exercised those powers was revived. The only reasonable meaning that can be given to

277

sub-section (1) of section 8 of the Indian Independence Act, 1947, is that the powers of the Legislature of the Dominion in making provision as to the constitution of the Dominion were to be exercisable in the first instance by the Constituent Assembly, that is to say, the Constituent Assembly was invested with the right of making such provision as to the constitution of the Dominion as would bring into existence another Legislature of the Dominion, whether that Legislature had the form of a representative legislature of a single person legislature responsible to nobody being immaterial so that the new legislature could take the place of the Constituent Assembly. The words are certainly not capable of the construction that if the Constituent Assembly made even a single law in the constitutional sphere, it discharged its function and became liable to dissolution by the Governor-General.

(b) Power to dissolve conditional — I now proceed to reply to the two basic questions in the *Reference* which are allied and mixed up with each other, namely, whether in the circumstances stated in the *Reference* the Governor-General had the legal authority to dissolve the Constituent Assembly and to constitute another Constituent Assembly. But before doing that it is necessary to make a preliminary observation and that is that the answers have to be given in the context in which and on the assumptions on which the questions have been formulated. The *Reference* states:

(i) that though the Constituent Assembly functioned for more than seven years, it was unable to carry out the duty of providing a Constitution, and for all practical purposes assumed the form of a perpetual legislature;

(ii) that the Constituent Assembly was dissolved by the Governor-General because by reason of repeated representations from and resolutions passed by representative public bodies throughout the country, he formed the opinion that the Assembly had become wholly unrepresentative of the people, and

(iii) that the Constituent Assembly from the very beginning asserted the claim that the laws passed by it under sub-section (1) of section 8 of the Indian Independence Act, 1947, did not require the assent of the Governor-General.

Thus the assumptions of fact on the basis of which this Court's opinion is asked are:

(a) the Constituent Assembly's inability to provide a Constitution and its assumption of the powers of a perpetual legislature;

(b) its wholly unrepresentative character which it had gradually acquired during the seven years of its existence; and

(c) its claim that it was itself competent to make provisions as to the constitution of the Dominion without obtaining to those provisions the assent of the Governor-General.

It is here necessary to dispose of some objections which have been taken by Mr Pritt to the manner in which the *Reference* has been made. I have already mentioned that the word 'rightly' in question No. 3 must be taken to mean 'lawfully' or 'legally' because the question whether, if the Governor-General had the authority to dissolve the Constituent Assembly, it was properly dissolved, is not a legal but a political issue which cannot be referred to this Court for opinion. Mr Pritt, however, contends that the question must be answered in the form in which it has been framed and that the Court should go into the facts on which the propriety or impropriety of the dissolution may depend. He has, therefore, referred to the affidavits which were filed on behalf of the Government and the counter-affidavits that were put in by Mr Tamizuddin Khan, in an endeavour to show that the dissolution was not justified on the facts and that it was ordered with some ulterior motives. We cannot, on this *Reference*, undertake this enquiry or record any findings on the disputed questions of facts because any such course would convert us into a fact-finding tribunal, which is not the function of this Court when its advice is asked on certain questions of law. The answer to a legal question always depends on facts found or assumed and since we cannot try issues of fact the *Reference* has to be answered on the assumption of fact on which it has been made. The Privy Council also has, under section 4 of the Act of 1833 (3 & 4 Will. IV, ch. 41), similar advisory jurisdiction but no precedent from that Board or from the Federal Court has been shown to us where a reference was ever made to ascertain a legal position after a trial of facts by the advisory Court. We consider that there is nothing improper or peculiar about the manner in which the *Reference* has been made. The Governor-General has taken the responsibility of asserting certain facts and has merely asked us to report to him what the legal position is if those facts are true.

Mr Pritt also appeared to complain that in the *Reference* there are certain facts which were not mentioned in the Proclamation of 24 October 1954, by which the Constituent Assembly was dissolved. But the Proclamation cannot be treated to have been a plaint or a written statement in a suit in which all facts which led the Governor-General to dissolve the Assembly should have been exhaustively mentioned. Even if some facts or some legal position were not present to the mind of the Governor-General when he dissolved the Assembly, there is nothing to preclude him from asking this Court whether the dissolution could be defended on the additional facts and the subsequently discovered legal position. The question relating to the necessity of assent to legislation by the Constituent Assembly under sub-section (1) of section 8 of the Indian Independence Act, 1947, was not mentioned in the Proclamation as a ground for the dissolution of the Assembly but this was probably due to the fact that the legal position as to this was still uncertain. The point, however, was prominently mentioned in the Chief Court of Sind and since this Court in *Mr Tamizuddin Khan's* case upheld the objection, I think the Governor-General is justified in asking whether the Constituent Assembly by asserting the claim that its constitutional laws did not require the Governor-General's assent, had not begun to function as an unconstitutional body which could have been dissolved. I am, therefore, of the view that for the purposes of this *Reference* we shall have to assume the facts mentioned therein and to give our opinion on that assumption.

Thus the precise issue to be determined in relation to the question of dissolution is whether, if the facts be as postulated in the *Reference*, the common law right of the Crown to dissolve a Dominion Legislature can be said to have been excluded by the Indian Independence Act, 1947. It cannot be doubted that the power to summon, prorogue and dissolve is a prerogative of the Crown, well recognised by the common law. It is equally plain, and not disputed by anyone, that a prerogative of the King may be created, abridged or completely taken away by an Act of Parliament or of an Independent Dominion. The true question in the case, therefore, is whether the Indian Independence Act took away the King's prerogative right to dissolve the Constituent Assembly, and if so, was this taking away absolute or qualified? If that right had been taken away by the Indian Independence Act for ever, it could not be delegated to the Governor-General, and the Governor-General, being merely a representative of the King, could not exercise it. On the other hand, if that right was taken away only for a specific purpose, and that purpose was not fulfilled, the right would still vest in the Governor-General, having been delegated to him by the King under section 5 of the Indian Independence Act, 1947.

This position was indicated by me in my opinion in *Mr Tamizuddin Khan's* case. Dealing with the prerogatives of the King in a colony I said [above, p. 91]:

Thus in every question which arises between the King and his colonies respecting the prerogative, the first consideration is the Charter granted to the inhabitants. If that be silent on the subject, it cannot be doubted that the King's prerogatives in the colony are precisely those prerogatives which he may exercise in the mother country. Where the colony charter affords no criterion or rule of construction, the common law of England with respect to the rule of prerogatives is the common law of the country.

Thus the real question that has to be determined in the present case is whether the King's prerogative right to dissolve the Constituent Assembly was taken away for ever or only on the condition that the Assembly was to function for a certain purpose and in a particular manner. If the legal position be that the taking away was not absolute but only qualified, the reply to the question referred would depend upon whether in the circumstances presented by the *Reference* the case fell outside the qualifying conditions. The matter may also be looked at in the light of principles 2 and 3, stated by Mr Diplock in *Mr Tamizuddin Khan's* case, the correctness of which was admitted by Mr Pritt, principle 2 being that the prerogative of the Crown in an overseas Dominion can be taken away by a statute, whether of the United Kingdom or of the Dominion, by express words or necessary intendment, and principle 3 that the Crown may delegate its prerogative, in whole or in part, to the Governor-General of a Dominion and that the extent of the delegation is a matter of construction of the statute or instrument of delegation. It is not disputed, and is otherwise plain, that under the common law the Crown has the right to dissolve a representative legislative assembly. This right is exercised by him in the United Kingdom when under Ministerial advice he dissolves the House of Commons before the expiry of its term. In the overseas Dominions that right is exercised by the Governor-General, as representative of the King, under the Constitution Acts of those Dominions or the Commission of his appointment. 'Of the legal power of the Crown', says Forsey at p. 3 of *The Royal Power of Dissolution of Parliament in the British Commonwealth*,

in this matter there is of course no question. Throughout the Commonwealth (except in Eire, where there is no longer any representative of the Crown), the King or his representative may in law grant, refuse or force dissolution of the Lower House of the Legislature. In the Commonwealth of Australia, the Union of South Africa, Southern Rhodesia, Victoria and South Australia, he may, in defined circumstances, dissolve both Houses. In legal theory the discretion of the Crown is absolute (though of course any action requires the consent of some Minister), but the actual exercise of the power is everywhere regulated by conventions.

And Maitland at p. 42 of his book, *Constitutional History of England*, 1950 ed., observes: 'The King's power of summoning, proroguing and dissolving Parliament is very large.'

At pp. 271-2 of vol. I of Chalmers' *Opinions of Eminent Lawyers* is stated the opinion of Ryder and Murray that the King has the prerogative right of dissolving a popular Legislative Assembly in a Colony.

Now if it be once found that the prerogative to dissolve is a common law right of the King or his fully accredited representative in an overseas Dominion, the short question on which the legality or otherwise of dissolution of the Constituent Assembly will depend is whether the statute, namely, the Indian Independence Act, 1947, expressly or by necessary intendment excludes the exercise of that prerogative in the circumstances stated in the *Reference*. Ever since common law began to come in competition with statute law, the rule of decision has always been that where a statute makes provision for a particular situation, it excludes the common law; but if the situation be entirely outside the contemplation of the statute, it is governed by the common law. Stated more concisely, the principle is *casus provisus* (case provided), the statute rules; and *casus omissus* (case omitted), the common law retains the field. The issue, therefore, is whether the common law right to dissolve has in the circumstances stated in the *Reference* been ousted by the Indian Independence Act, 1947.

According to the announcement on behalf of His Majesty, both in the House of Lords and the House of Commons, at the time of the passing of the Indian Independence Act, 1947, His Majesty had placed his prerogatives and interests at the disposal of the Parliament only 'so far as concerned the matters dealt with by the Bill'. If, therefore, the matter raised by this *Reference* has been dealt with, and the prerogative of dissolution taken away, expressly or by necessary intendment, by the Act, then the prerogative having been utilised by the Parliament it must be deemed to have been surrendered by the King and therefore not to have been delegated by section 5 to the Governor-General. Now if we look at the language of sub-section (1) of section 8 of the Indian Independence Act it becomes perfectly clear that because the power of making provision as to the constitution of the Dominion had been given to the Constituent Assembly, the prerogative to dissolve that Assembly was taken away if that Assembly did exercise its powers to make provision as to the constitution of this country. It is, however, equally clear that the provisional constitution granted to Pakistan by the Indian Independence Act, 1947, and the adapted Government of India Act, 1935, was, until its nature was altered by a law made by the Constituent Assembly, a democratic constitution, and it cannot possibly be contended that the Constituent Assembly had been given the power to function as long as it liked and assume the form of a perpetual or indissoluble legislature. The only reasonable construction of sub-section (1) of section 8 of the Indian Independence Act, 1947, is that that sub-section gave to the Constituent Assembly an opportunity to frame a working or functioning constitution for the country within a reasonable time and not the right to go on with constitution–making indefinitely. The prerogative to dissolve, therefore, must be taken to have been taken away by the Act only if the Constituent Assembly performed the duty assigned to it by the Act, and if the Act did not intend to install that Assembly as a perpetual legislature, the prerogative of dissolution which was in abeyance must be held to have revived when it became apparent to the Governor-General that the Constituent Assembly was unable or had failed to provide a constitution for the country. It could certainly not be the intention of the Indian Independence Act that in the guise of a constitution-making body the Constituent Assembly could function as the Legislature of the Dominion indefinitely until it became necessary to remove it by a revolution. And if that was not the intention of the Act, it must follow that the common law prerogative to dissolve was not taken away by the Act in that contingency. The words 'in the first instance' in sub-section (1) of section 8 of the Indian Independence Act, 1947, appear to me to indicate quite clearly that an indefinite life for the Assembly was not intended and that the prerogative right to dissolve it was excluded only if the Assembly performed the duty assigned to it, within a reasonable time. Therefore if the Assembly was unable or refused to perform the function assigned to it, and on the contrary assumed the form of a perpetual legislature, the right in that event to dissolve it was not taken away by the Act. Of course, if the Act can be construed as making the Constituent Assembly a permanent Legislature of the Dominion, then the prerogative right to dissolve must be held to have been taken away from the King's representative for ever, but I am quite clear in my mind that that was not the intention of the Indian Independence Act. The framers of that Act had before them the experience of other Constituent Assemblies in the world and inserted sub-section (1) of section 8 in the Act in the belief that both the Constituent Assemblies would complete the work assigned to them within approximately the same time as other Constituent Assemblies had done. They never imagined that in this respect the Constituent Assembly for Pakistan would beat the world record, and for seven long years would not even be able to introduce the draft constitution for enactment. In *The Select Constitutions of the World*, a book which was prepared for presentation to Dáil Eireann, there is some interesting information of the activities of Constituent Assemblies or Constituent Conventions and of the time taken by them in the preparation and adoption of constitutions. The following abstract from the publication will be found interesting:

Name of the Constituent Assembly or Convention	Date of election or first meeting	Date of completion or adoption of the constitution	Total time taken (not including days)
1	2	3	4
1. Kingdom of Serbs, Croats and Slovenes	November 1920	28 June 1921	About 7 months
2. Polish Republic	21 January 1920	17 March 1921	1 year and 2 months
3. Republic of Austria	15 February 1919	1 October 1920	1 year and 7 months
4. The Esthonian Republic	7 April 1919	15 June 1920	1 year and 2 months
5. The Czechoslovak Republic	14 November 1918	19 February 1920	1 year and 3 months
6. German Reich	19 January 1919	31 July 1919	6 months
7. Russian Socialist Federal Soviet Republic	18 January 1918	10 July 1918	About 6 months
8. United States of Mexico	February 1856	5 February 1857	About 1 year
9. Kingdom of Denmark	January 1848	5 June 1849	1 year and 5 months
10. Union of South Africa	12 October 1908	June 1909 (Constitution enacted by the British Parliament on 20 September 1909)	About 9 months
11. Commonwealth of Australia			
(a) (First Convention called the Sydney Convention)	March 1891	9 April 1891 (On which date it was dissolved)	1 month
(b) (Second Constituent Convention, called the Adelaide Convention)	23 March 1897	20 January 1898 (Constitution enacted by the British Parliament on 9 July 1900)	About 10 months
12. French Republic	November 1873	16 July 1875 (The three constitutional laws passed during this period formed the foundation of the subsequent French Constitution)	1 year and 7 months
13. Swiss Confederation:			
(a) Constitution of 1842			Less than a year
(b) Revision of 1842 constitution in 1874			Ditto
14. The Dominion of Canada	1 September 1864	Convention's resolutions approved by the Canadian Parliament in 1865	Ditto
The Maritime Union	(Became Constituent Convention in October)	British North America Act passed by the British Parliament in March 1867	
15. Kingdom of Belgium	10 November 1830	January 1831	3 months
16. Kingdom of Norway			Less than a year
17. Kingdom of Sweden (Constitution of 1809)			Ditto
18. United States of America	25 May 1787	4 March 1789 (Ratification by other States 26 July 1788)	1 year and 9 months
19. Ireland	6 December 1921	25 October 1922 (Constitution enacted by the U.K. Parliament on 5 December 1922)	1 year
20. India	15 August 1947	26 November 1949	2 years and 10 months

Thus when the Constituent Assembly for Pakistan was set up, the longest time ever taken by any Constituent Assembly had been one year and nine months. Citing the instance of the Constituent Convention of Australia, Mr Pritt alleged that that Convention took about ten years to complete its work but he is clearly wrong there because the Sydney Convention which he links up with the Adelaide Convention in calculating the period of ten years completed its work in about a month's time and then formally dissolved itself, and the subsequent Convention, the Adelaide Convention, was called six years later.

If there was a clear assumption in the Indian Independence Act that the Constituent Assembly would frame a constitution for the country and then dissolve itself, and the whole structure of that Act was built upon that assumption, then it is obvious that for more than seven years the Assembly having made no constitution for the country and on the contrary having assumed the form of a Legislature for an indefinite period, its dissolution was in further-ance and not in contravention of the intention of the Act. While explaining the fundamental principles of a democratic constitution in my opinion in *Mr Tamizuddin Khan's* case I had pointed out that an irremovable legislature was the worst calamity that could befall a people. I said there [above, at pp. 85–6]:

The basic principle is that no representative body can continue indefinitely and that its composition must admit of change from time to time by means of an appeal to the people. An irremovable legislature is the very antithesis of democracy and no democratic constitution is known in the world where elections are for life or for an indefinitely long time. . . .

This is what Sir William Blackstone said in 1765 about a perpetual Legislature: 'Lastly, a Parliament may be dissolved or expire by length of time. For if either the legislative body were perpetual; or might last for the life of the Prince who convened them, as formerly; and were so to be supplied, by occasionally filling the vacancies with new representatives; in these cases, if it were once corrupted, the evil would be past all remedy; but when different bodies succeed each other, if the people show cause to disapprove of the present, they may rectify its faults in the next' (*Commentaries on the Laws of England*, bk. I, ch. 2, p. 189).

The requirement of periodic accountability of a representative As-sembly to the electors is so basic that in the United Kingdom the Crown, which since long has ceased to exercise its discretion in opposition to the advice of the Ministry, will be considered to be justified in exercising its reserve powers of withholding assent or directing dissolution if Parliament ever attempted to prolong its own life indefinitely. The reason for it is that in a democratic constitution the ultimate or political sovereignty resides in the people, while the popular assembly, where the constitution does not impose any limitations on its powers, exercises legislative sovereignty only during its term. Since sovereignty as applied to States imports the supreme, absolute, uncontrollable power by which a State is governed, and democracy recognises all ultimate power as resting in the people, it is obvious that in the case of a conflict between the ultimate and legal sovereign, the latter must yield. An irremovable legislature, therefore, is not only a negation of democracy but is the worst calamity that can befall a nation. . . .

Referring to a self-dissolving Parliament, Blackstone at p. 162 of the first volume of his *Commentaries on the Laws of England* says:

If nothing had a right to prorogue or dissolve a Parliament but itself, it might happen to become perpetual, and this would be extremely dangerous if at any time it should attempt to encroach upon the executive power; as was fatally experienced by the unfortunate King Charles I, who, having inadvisably passed an Act to continue the Parliament, then in being, till such time as it should please to dissolve itself, at last fell a sacrifice to that inordinate power which he himself had consented to give them. It is, therefore, extremely necessary that the Crown should be empowered to regulate the duration of these assemblies under the limitations which the English Constitution has prescribed; so that, on the one hand, they may frequently and regularly come together for the despatch of business and redress of grievances; and may not on the other, even with the consent of the Crown, be continued to an inconvenient or unconstitutional length.

Mr Pritt maintained that the dissolution of the Assembly could only be brought about by itself by its bowing to the force of public opinion or by revolution. So far as public opinion is concerned, there was abundance of it before the Governor-General in the form of resolutions and representations by the provincial legislatures and other representative bodies which showed that the Assembly had become indifferent to the public opinion, and as regards its dissolution by a revolution, it is sufficient to say that revolutions are not in the contemplation of those who frame constitutions.

In my view it cannot reasonably be contended that the intention of the Indian Independence Act was to foist a perpetual legislature on this country, and if that was not the intention but the Constituent Assembly did become in fact a perpetual legislature, the purpose of the Act could only be served by ordering its dissolution. The demand for Pakistan was formulated for the first time in 1940, and by the middle of August, 1947, the new State had come into being. The highly complicated legal formalities necessary to establish that State took hardly three months. But though the Constituent Assembly sat for more than seven years it failed to make provision for the future constitution of the State. And seven years is a long period in the history of a people, particularly a new people. If the task of constitution-making was proving too formidable and the difficulties in its accomplishment appeared to be insurmountable, the Assembly could have dissolved itself or created the necessary mechanism to bring another Assembly into existence. Its omission to take any such step or to provide a working constitution for the country was, in my opinion, a sufficient ground for the Governor-General to hold that the Assembly had failed to perform the function assigned to it by sub-section (1) of section 8 of the Indian Independence Act. And if he came to that conclusion, the prerogative power of dissolution must be held to have been revived.

The second ground for the dissolution stated in the *Reference* is the unrepresentative character of the Assembly. This ground is not materially distinguishable from the first since the Assembly is alleged to have lost its representative character by lapse of time. Here again if the intention of the Indian Independence Act, 1947, was, as I think it was, to give a representative Assembly to the new Dominion, the Assembly if it lost that character could not function as the Assembly intended by the Act, and could under the prerogative right be lawfully dissolved. It is stated in the Reference that the public opinion was unanimously in favour of the dissolution of the Assembly and that repeated representations from and resolutions passed by public bodies were received by the Governor-General against the unrepresentative character of the Assembly. Probably the reference here is to the resolutions passed by the various Provincial Legislatures and the Corporation of the City of Karachi, copies of which were filed with affidavits in *Mr Tamizuddin Khan's* case. We cannot, however, enter upon a discussion of the truth or otherwise of those affidavits or the counter-affidavits of Mr Tamizuddin Khan because, as I have already mentioned for the purposes of the present *Reference* it will have to be assumed that the Governor-General dissolved the Assembly because in view of repeated representations from and resolutions passed by various representative public bodies throughout the Country he was satisfied that the Assembly had become wholly unrepresentative of the people of Pakistan and ceased to be responsible to them. In my opinion in *Mr Tamizuddin Khan's* case I thus expressed myself as to the necessity of a popular Assembly retaining its representative character:

The second and by far the most important requirement of a democratic constitution is the need for periodic accountability of the representatives to their electors. In modern times within a few years political events of great and unanticipated importance may happen in a country and the mental horizon of the whole people may change by a sudden international or domestic event, the importance and implications of which may not have been present to the minds of the people when elections were held. It is, therefore, necessary that old representatives should seek re-election either because of their having ceased to reflect in the legislature the progressive or changing outlook of the people or because of their having ceased to represent the views of the people on a particular issue. The principle, therefore, is fundamental that in every democratic constitution there must exist a provision for holding elections after a few years, so that the House may continue to be representative of the varying aspirations and needs of the people.

Therefore dissolution on the ground that the Assembly had become unrepresentative can be held to be illegal only if it be found that the intention of the Indian Independence Act, 1947, was to retain the Assembly as the Legislature of the Dominion, however unrepresentative of the people it became by the efflux of time. Since I am unable to read any such intention in the Act, it follows that the prerogative right to dissolve was not excluded by the Act in the circumstances mentioned. And the reason for the dissolution of an unrepresentative Constituent Assembly is that since the constitution made by it, if it makes one, cannot be acceptable to the people, the Assembly becomes incapable of discharging the duty assigned to it by the statute. Here again it is obvious that if the Assembly cannot function in furtherance of the intention of the Act, the case is one of *casus omissus*, in the sense that the prerogative of dissolution cannot be held to have been ousted by the Act.

It should not be overlooked that dissolution does not in any way adversely affect the rights of the members of the Assembly. If their claim that they are in the Assembly by the consent of the people and as their representatives and not merely because of a statutory provision is good, they can seek re-election to the new Constituent Assembly, there being no disqualification attaching to them from being chosen as members of that Assembly. If they receive a fresh electoral mandate, they can return to the Assembly with greater popular acclamation and thus disprove the allegation that they represent nobody except themselves.

The third ground for the dissolution is that 'though under the Indian Independence Act, 1947, all legislation passed by the Constituent Assembly required the assent of the Governor-General, the Assembly took up the position that no assent was needed to its legislation under sub-section (1) of section 8 of the Indian Independence Act, 1947'. This Court has held in *Mr Tamizuddin Khan's* case that the Governor-General's assent to laws made by the Assembly under sub-section (1) of section 8 of the Indian Independence Act, 1947, is necessary to give them validity, and therefore if the Assembly claimed that it could give laws to the country without the assent of the Governor-General, it must be held that it was functioning outside the Constitution and was liable to removal on the short ground that it was an illegal legislative body. A further illegality that tainted the composition of the Assembly was the addition of six members to its personnel by the Increase and Redistribution of Seats Act, 1949, without obtaining the assent of the Governor-General to that Act. Thus, on the date that it was dissolved, the Constituent Assembly was not functioning as the Constituent Assembly for Pakistan as defined by section 19 (3) (*b*) of the Indian Independence Act, but as an illegal legislature whose removal by the Governor-General was not only legal but the performance of a clear constitutional obligation. The existing legal confusion is solely due to the Assembly's claim to function as the sole constituent of the legislature, a claim which has brought the whole legal system of the country, on which the State itself depends, literally to ruination. In *Sammut* v. *Strickland*,[1]

[1] [1938] A.C. 678.

the Privy Council has held that the dictum of Lord Mansfield in *Campbell* v. *Hall*[1] to the effect that the King's prerogative to legislate for a ceded or conquered territory to which representative legislative institutions have been granted is excluded applies only if such institutions continue to exist. The principle of this Privy Council decision is in my opinion applicable to a situation like the present where a representative legislature begins to function illegally, i.e. in a manner different from the one in which it was intended to function. For this reason alone, it seems to me that the Constituent Assembly never functioned as it was intended by the Indian Independence Act, 1947, to function, with the result that the prerogative to dissolve all along remained with the Governor-General.

The fourth question, namely, 'whether the Constituent Convention proposed to be set up by the Governor-General would be competent to exercise the powers conferred by section 8 of the Indian Independence Act, 1947, on the Constituent Assembly' is not separable from the question relating to the Governor-General's power to dissolve the Assembly because in a democratic constitution of the British type such as is envisaged by the Indian Independence Act, 1947, and the adapted Government of India Act, 1935, the power to dissolve a representative legislative institution implies the right to convene another, the power exercised in both cases being a prerogative power. Here again the matter is governed by the principle that where the prerogative has not been excluded by the statute, the common law applies. *Casus omissus et oblivioni datus dispositioni communis juris relinquitur* (a case unprovided for in a statute and given to oblivion must be disposed of according to common law). Under the Indian Independence Act, 1947, there is no provision relating to the convention or composition of a fresh Constituent Assembly. It follows therefore that the Governor-General must, as representative of the Crown, exercise the same powers as were exercised by the Governor-General in 1947 on behalf of the Crown, the only difference between the two cases being that whereas in 1947 the Governor-General exercising the powers was responsible to His Majesty's Government in the United Kingdom, the present Governor-General having been appointed to represent the King for the purposes of the

[1] (1774), Cowp. 204.

291

government of the Dominion, is not responsible to any agency outside the Dominion, though in law the source of the authority in both cases is the Crown. The dissolved Constituent Assembly was set up by an executive order and not under any law and the new Constituent Assembly also can be set up by a similar order.

Before elections were regulated in England by law, the King exercised his prerogative right under the common law to convene the Parliament. The number of knights, citizens and burgesses summoned and the counties, cities and boroughs that were to return them were both determined by the King and all election disputes were settled by the King-in-Council. This was the position under the common law though later it began gradually to be regulated by statute. Referring to this right Maitland in the *Constitutional History of England*, 1950 ed. says at p. 239:

But this was by no means all: the king, we remember, had exercised the power of conferring on boroughs the right to send members. Hitherto this power had not been extensively used for the purpose of packing parliament and Henry VIII used it but very sparingly: he gave the right to but five boroughs. Under Edward VI the power was lavishly used for political purposes: he thus added forty-eight members, Mary twenty-one, Elizabeth sixty, James twenty-seven. The number of burgesses in the lower house was thus vastly increased, and with it the power of the Crown. When a new borough was created, and when a new charter was granted to an old borough, care was generally taken to vest the right of election not in the mass of the burgesses, but in a small select governing body—a mayor and council—nominated in the first instance by the crown, and afterwards self-elected.

The learned author reverts to this subject and goes on to say at p. 289:

The numbers of the House of Commons have grown. In the first Parliament of James there were 467 members. In the Long Parliament (1640), 504. In the Parliament of 1661, 507; in 1679, 513. The causes of the increase have been various. In 1672 a statute admitted two knights for the County Palatine of Durham, and two citizens for the city. Except in this respect the representation of the counties remains unaltered. We have seen that under Edward VI, Mary, Elizabeth and James, the number of borough members was increased by royal charter —thus it was hoped that a House favourable to the Crown might be returned. Charles I added, or restored, I think, eighteen borough members. Charles II exercised this prerogative but once, he gave Newark two members. . . . The representation of the two Universities is due to James I. The prerogative of increasing the number of borough members was never taken away—but it was last exercised in favour of Newark in 1677—and after the Restoration the House of Commons would have resented its exercise : though it is curious to observe that the excellent whig, John Locke, agreed that if the House would not reform itself, the king might reform it.

In his opinion reported at pp. 188–9 of *Opinions of Eminent Lawyers*, by George Chalmers, vol. I, Mr Fane described the King's power of calling an assembly in the colony of New York as 'an undoubted right, which the Crown has always exercised, of calling, and continuing, the assembly of the colony, at such times, and as long, as it was thought necessary for the public service'. Similarly, Mr Raymond, the Attorney-General, is reported at pp. 267–9 of the same book to have thought that in the absence of an Act the King had the power, in point of law, to empower a new county to send representatives to the colonial representative assembly and to restrain a town which had enjoyed the right of sending representatives to such assembly from sending such representatives. At pp. 271 and 272 of the book are the opinions of two other lawyers, Ryder and Murray, to the effect that where 'the right of sending representatives was founded originally on the commissions and instructions, given by the Crown to the Governors of New Hampshire (Colony), His Majesty lawfully may extend the privilege of sending representatives to such new towns, as His Majesty shall judge to be, in all respects, worthy thereof'.

I have gone so far back in English history merely to illustrate the simple point that in the absence of a statute the representation of the Realm in Parliament was in the discretion of the King though the repetition of similar writs addressed to the Sheriff of the same county from time to time tended to create in the shires, cities and burgesses of the county expectations which gradually developed into rights in Common Law. The order of 1947 constituting the Constituent Assembly for Pakistan was merely a surrender of this prerogative right by the Crown which the Parliament utilised in the statute of independence. That being the legal position, it follows that Pakistan being a Dominion and the Governor-General here representing the King for the purposes of the Government of the Dominion, he is possessed in this matter of the same powers as in the absence of a statute were or are exercisable by the King. Since eight years have expired since the dissolved Constituent Assembly was set up, it is obvious that in setting up the new Constituent Assembly the Governor-General is not only entitled but is bound to take cognisance of the altered conditions, the new issues, the views of the different political parties and the measure of agreement among them. The dissolved Constituent Assembly was chosen on an issue which has been replaced by more burning issues and it cannot possibly be contended that the executive order constituting the Assembly of 1947 is a part of the law which must determine the composition of the new Assembly. The mode in which representation of the country is to be secured, namely, whether elections should be direct or indirect, whether there should be equal distribution of seats between East Pakistan and West Pakistan, how backward area or areas in which there are no representative legislatures should be represented are not legal issues but political controversies which should be raised not in courts but elsewhere. The only legal requirement in setting up a new Assembly is that it should be a representative body, but in attaining that object time, practicability, and agreement between various political leaders are as much relevant factors as they were in the Cabinet Mission's Plan of 16 May and His Majesty's Government's announcement of 3 June 1947. I am therefore of the view that under the Indian Independence Act, 1947, the Governor-General had the authority to issue the Constituent Convention Order, 1955, and that subject to the observations in the three succeeding paragraphs, the convention called by that Order will have all the powers of the Constituent Assembly.

In law the new assembly can only be a Constituent Assembly, the term Convention being misleading and not known to the Indian Independence Act. Since the Governor-General cannot assume to himself powers which are not expressly or by necessary implication given to him by the Indian Independence Act, 1947, it follows that he cannot derive the power to dissolve the new Assembly from the Constituent Convention Order which is his own creation. That power must still depend on the Indian Independence Act, 1947, unless by a properly assented Act the new Assembly makes some other provision as to it. The same observations apply to the power to summon and prorogue after the Assembly has commenced to function.

As regards the right of the Governor-General to nominate particular persons to the new Assembly, it is admitted by Mr Diplock that the duty of the Governor-General being to bring into existence a representative Assembly, he has no right to nominate members, though consistently with the all-important principle of representation of the people and areas on as wide a basis as possible he may determine the manner in which members are to be chosen.

With respect to the representation of States and tribal areas, the matter is governed by the Indian Independence Act itself. Under the proviso to sub-section (3) of section 19 of that Act, arrangements for the representation of these territories have to be made by the Constituent Assembly and not by the Governor-General.

In approaching Questions 1 and 2 the circumstances in which they came to be referred must be borne in mind. The *Reference* thus states these circumstances: Emergency powers: validation

In the *Federation of Pakistan* v. *Moulvi Tamizuddin Khan*, the Federal Court decided that the legislation referred to in paragraph 5 (legislation under sub-section (1) of section 8 of the Indian Independence Act, 1947) did require the Governor-General's assent.

It was found that 44 Acts passed by the Constituent Assembly had not received the assent of the Governor-General and that under them hundreds of orders had been issued and judicial decisions taken. Thus the consequences which seemed to follow were:

(1) All actions taken under orders made after 31 March 1948, under section 9 of the Indian Independence Act, 1947, as amended by the Indian Independence (Amendment) Act, 1948, were invalid. In particular, section 92 A of the Government of India Act, 1935, and hundreds of Acts made by the Governors of East Bengal, the Punjab (which in law should be called 'West Punjab'), and Sind were not and never had been part of the law. Further, the criminal law and procedure of Pakistan had never been applied to those parts of Baluchistan which had not been part of British India.

(2) The executive and judicial government of Karachi had apparently no legal foundation.

(3) All laws passed after 1950 by the Constituent Assembly functioning as Federal Legislature under sub-section (2) of section 8 of the Independence Act, 1947, were probably invalid because the Assembly had purported to change its composition by laws which had not received the Governor-General's assent.

(4) All laws passed by the Provincial Legislatures since the last

general elections were presumably invalid because the Assembly had purported to amend the fifth and sixth schedules to the Government of India Act, 1935, under which the Provincial Assemblies were elected and constituted.

(5) All laws passed by the Provincial Legislature of East Bengal after 14 March 1953, were invalid because the Provincial Assembly had no legal existence after that day.

(6) Other branches of the civil, criminal and revenue law were in large part invalid because they had been enacted by the Constituent Assembly either under sub-section (1) of section 8 of the Indian Independence Act, 1947, or under sub-section (2) of that section in accordance with amendments to the Government of India Act, 1935, made under sub-section (1) of the section.

By the Emergency Powers Ordinance, 1955, the Governor-General sought to validate *ab initio* 35 of the laws passed by the Constituent Assembly under sub-section (1) of section 8 of the Indian Independence Act, 1947, but in *Usif Patel's* case the Federal Court held that the Governor-General could not validate those laws by an Ordinance promulgated under section 42 of the Government of India Act, 1935.

On 15 April 1955, the Governor-General issued a Proclamation and Order for the meeting of a new Constituent Assembly, designated Constituent Convention, to exercise the powers of the Legislature of the Dominion for the purpose of making provision as to the constitution of Pakistan. The members representing the Governor's Provinces will be elected by the persons elected to the Provincial Assemblies. The members representing the other parts of Pakistan will be nominated by the Governor-General. This Convention is required to meet on 10 May 1955, and it is hoped that it will take the earliest opportunity of validating invalid and questioned laws.

Until the situation could be regularised by the Convention, it became necessary for the Governor-General in order to avoid a possible breakdown in the constitutional and administrative machinery of the country to assume to himself all such powers as may be requisite to validate certain of the invalid laws needed to preserve the State and to maintain the *status quo*. The Governor-General therefore issued a Proclamation dated 16 April 1955, vesting such powers in himself, and validating (subject to the report of the Federal Court on the basis of this Reference) the laws mentioned in the Schedule to the Emergency Powers Ordinance, 1955, and all acts done and orders made under those laws. This Proclamation would, of course, cease to operate as soon as the appropriate legislation had been enacted by the Constituent Convention.

The questions formulated are:

(1) What are the powers and responsibilities of the Governor-General in respect of the government of the country before the new Constituent Convention passes the necessary legislation?

(2) The Federal Court having held in *Usif Patel's* case that the laws listed in the Schedule to the Emergency Powers Ordinance could not be validated under section 42 of the Government of India Act, 1935, nor retrospective effect given to them, and no legislature competent to validate such laws being in existence, is there any provision in the Constitution or any rule of law applicable to the situation by which the Governor-General can by order or otherwise declare that all orders made, decisions taken and other acts done under those laws shall be valid and enforceable and that those laws which cannot without danger to the State be removed from the existing legal system shall be treated as part of the law of the land until the question of their validation is determined by the new Constituent Convention?

In order to appreciate the urgency and importance of these questions the following facts have to be remembered:

(i) that if the Governor-General had not validated the laws after assuming to himself the powers to validate them the constitutional and administrative machinery of the country would have broken down;

(ii) that the power to validate the laws has been assumed in order to preserve the State and to maintain the *status quo*;

(iii) that a new Constituent Assembly has been called and the validation is merely an emergency measure which would last till the new Constituent Assembly decides the question of validation.

There is, therefore, this fundamental difference between the situation as existing at the time of this Court's decision in *Usif Patel's* case and the situation that exists now, that whereas the Ordinance the validity of which was considered in *Usif Patel's* case made no reference to a new Constituent Assembly and claimed for the Governor-General the power not only of permanently validating invalid constitutional legislations, but also the right of framing a constitution for Pakistan, the validation by the present Proclamation of Emergency is only temporary and the power has been exercised with a view to preventing the State from dissolution and the constitutional and administrative machinery from breaking down before the question of validation of these laws has been decided upon by the new Constituent Assembly. Thus the issue raised refers to the extraordinary powers of the Governor-General during the emergency period and not to powers which vest in the Governor-General during normal times when the vital organ of the Constitution, namely, the legislature is functioning, and the question that we have to consider is whether there is any provision in the Constitution governing such a situation or any other legal principle within, outside or above the Constitution Acts which entitles the Governor-General to act in case of necessity of such a nature.

Law of necessity   The point that arises, and I am not aware if it has ever arisen before in this acute form, is whether in an emergency of the character described in the *Reference* there is any law by which the Head of the State may, when the Legislature is not in existence, temporarily assume to himself legislative powers with a view to preventing the State and society from dissolution. In seeking an answer to this question resort must necessarily be had to analogies and first principles because the law books and reported precedents furnish no direct answer to the precise question which today confronts the judiciary of Pakistan. The Governor-General claims in the Proclamation that he has acted in the performance of a duty which devolves on him as Head of the State to prevent the State from disruption, and the preliminary question that has to be considered is whether when we speak of rights and duties in the matter of preservation of States or their creation, foundation and dissolution, we are still in the field of law or in a region out of bounds to lawyers and courts. Having anxiously reflected over this problem I have come to the conclusion that the situation presented by the *Reference* is governed by rules which are part of the common law of all civilised States and which every written constitution of a civilised people takes for granted. This branch of the law is, in the words of Lord Mansfield, the law of civil or State necessity.

The law of natural necessity is a part of the statute law of our country but the law of civil or State necessity is as much a part of the unwritten law as the law of military necessity, instances of which are adjudged cases and authorities. On this part of the case Mr Diplock has addressed us an eager and anxious argument claiming for the Governor-General, as representative of the King or as Head of the State, certain powers which entitle him in the interests of the State temporarily to act outside the limits of the written constitution. He has relied in this connection on the maxim cited by Bracton at folios 93E and 247A of his Treatise, 'De legibus et consuetudinibus Angliae' (Of the laws and customs

298

of England), 'id quod alias non est licitum, necessitas licitum facit' (that which otherwise is not lawful, necessity makes lawful), and the maxims *salus populi suprema lex* (safety of the people is the supreme law) and *salus reipublicae est suprema lex* (safety of the State is the supreme law) and certain authorities where one or more of these maxims or the principle underlying them was treated as part of the law. The best statement of the reason underlying the law of necessity is to be found in Cromwell's famous utterance: 'If nothing should be done but what is according to law, the throat of the nation might be cut while we send for someone to make a law.' Broom at p. 1 of the 10th ed. of his *Legal Maxims* says that the phrase *salus populi suprema lex* is based on the implied agreement of every member of society that his own individual welfare shall, in cases of necessity, yield to that of the community; and that his property, liberty, and life shall, under certain circumstances, be placed in jeopardy or even sacrificed for the public good. *In re an Arbitration between Shipton, Anderson & Co. and Harrison Brothers & Co.*[1] Darling, J., described the maxim *salus populi suprema lex* as not only a good maxim but 'essential law'. In that case, by a contract in writing, made in September, 1914, the owner of a specific parcel of wheat in a warehouse in Liverpool sold it upon the terms 'payment cash within seven days against transfer order'. Before delivery and before the property passed to the buyer the wheat was requisitioned by and delivered to His Majesty's Government under the powers of an Act passed before the date of the contract. It was held by the Court of the King's Bench Division that delivery of the wheat by the seller to the buyer having been rendered impossible by the lawful requisition of the Government, the seller was excused from the performance of the contract. The act of requisition was described both by Lord Reading, C.J., and Lush, J., as 'an act of State'. Referring to that act Darling, J., said:

It must be here presumed that the Crown acted legally, and there is no contention to the contrary. We are in a state of war; that is notorious. The subject-matter of this contract has been seized by the State acting for the general good. *Salus populi suprema lex* is a good maxim and the enforcement of that essential law gives no right of action to whomsoever may be injured by it.

[1] [1915] 3 K.B. 676.

In *Attorney-General* v. *De Keyser's Royal Hotel*[1] Lord Moulton
dealing with the Crown's prerogative in taking possession of land
for the defence of the Realm observed:

To decide this question one must consider the nature and extent of
the so-called Royal Prerogative in the matter of taking or occupying
land for the better defence of the realm. I have no doubt that in early
days, when war was carried on in a simple fashion and on a smaller
scale than is the case in modern times, the Crown, to whom the defence
of the realm was entrusted, had wide prerogative powers as to taking
or using the lands of its subjects for the defence of the realm when the
necessity arose. But such necessity would be in general an actual and
immediate necessity arising in face of the enemy and in circumstances
where the rule *salus populi suprema lex* was clearly applicable.

Nor have I any doubt that in those days the subjects who had suffered
in this way in war would not have been held to have any claim against
the Crown for compensation in respect of the damage they had thus
suffered. . . .

There are some interesting observations on the Crown's right
to take the subjects' property in an emergency at pp. 176–180 in
the 6th ed. of Chalmers and Hood Phillips' *Constitutional Law*.
The purport of the precedents cited there including the *Saltpetre
Case*, (1607), 12 Co. Rep. 12 and the *Shipmoney Case, R.* v.
Hampden[2], is that in times of war the King, acting out of military
necessity, may take the subjects' property and that this rule is a
rule of common law. Referring to the right of the executive to
act in contravention of the law in an emergency Dicey says at
pp. 412–13 of the 9th ed. of his *Law of the Constitution*:

There are times of tumult or invasion when for the sake of legality
itself the rules of law must be broken. The course which the government
must then take is clear. The Ministry must break the law and trust for
protection to an Act of Indemnity. A statute of this kind is (as already
pointed out) the last and supreme exercise of Parliamentary sovereignty.
It legalises illegality; it affords the practical solution of the problem
which perplexed the statesmanship of the sixteenth and seventeenth
centuries, how to combine the maintenance of law and the authority of
the Houses of Parliament with the free exercise of that kind of discretionary power or prerogative which, under some shape or other,
must at critical junctures be wielded by the executive government of
every civilised country.

[1] [1920] A.C. 508.
[2] (1637), 3 St. Tr. 825.

Commenting on this passage, Chalmers and Hood Phillips, at p. 177 of their book cited above, remark:

What Dicey calls convention, Darling, J., appears in one case (*Shipton, Anderson and Co.* v. *Harrison Brothers and Company*) to treat as law: '*Salus populi suprema lex* is a good maxim, and the enforcement of that essential law gives no right of action to whomsoever may be injured by it.' The unbiased opinion of Darling, J., appears to tally with the so-called corrupt judgment in *Bates's Case* :[1] 'The power of the King is both ordinary and absolute. Ordinary power, which exists for the purpose of civil justice, is unalterable save by consent of Parliament. Absolute power, existing for the nation's safety, varies with the royal wisdom.'

It is true that most of the cases mentioned above relate to the acquisition of the subjects' property for the defence of the realm in times of war, but it seems to me that the same principle must be applicable, and as I shall presently show, has been applied where the State is in danger of a collapse due to other factors.

Chitty in the 1820 ed. of his book, *Prerogatives of the Crown*, states at p. 68 'that the King is the first person in the nation . . . being superior to both Houses in dignity and the only branch of Legislature that has a separate existence, and is capable of performing any act at a time when the Parliament is not in being'. At the same page referring to two memorable instances in which Parliament had assembled in an illegal manner, i.e. without the authority of the King, the reference being to the Parliament which restored Charles II and the Parliament of 1688 which disposed of the British Crown to William III, that learned author says, 'that in both these instances the necessity of the case rendered it necessary for the Parliament to meet as they did, there being no King to call them together and necessity supersedes all law'. Maitland at pp. 283–6 of the 1950 ed. of his *Constitutional History of England* makes some interesting observations as to the legality of what happened when William, Prince of Orange, became the King of England and as to the validity of legislation after James dissolved the Parliament and fled from London on 11 December 1688, dropping the Great Seal into the Thames. The Prince, who was then not King, invited an Assembly which advised him to summon a Convention of the States of the Realm. In accordance with this advice he invited Lords to come and the

[1] (1606), 2 St. Tr. 371.

counties and boroughs to send representatives to a Convention which met on 22 January 1689. On 25 January the Commons resolved that King James had abdicated the government and that William and Mary should be proclaimed King and Queen. The crown was accepted and thereupon the Convention passed an Act declaring itself to be the Parliament of England notwithstanding the want of a proper writ of summons. This Parliament, known as the Convention Parliament, passed many important Acts, including the Bill of Rights and was dissolved early in 1690. A new Parliament which was duly summoned by writs of the King and Queen met on 22 March 1690, and it proceeded to declare by statute that the King and the Queen were King and Queen and that the statutes made by the Convention 'were and are laws and statutes' of the Kingdom. Commenting on this episode in English history Maitland says:

Now certainly it was very difficult for any lawyer to argue that there had not been a revolution. Those who conducted the revolution sought, and we may well say were wise in seeking, to make the revolution look as small as possible, to make it as like a legal proceeding, as by any stretch of ingenuity it could be made. But to make it out to be a perfectly legal act seems impossible. Had it failed, those who attempted it would have suffered as traitors, and I do not think that any lawyer can maintain that their execution would have been unlawful. The convention hit upon the word 'abdicated' as expressing James's action, and, according to the established legal reckoning, he abdicated on 11 December 1688, the day on which he dropped the Great Seal into the Thames. From that day until the day when William and Mary accepted the Crown, 13 February 1689, there was no king of England. Possibly the convention would better have expressed the truth if, like the parliament of Scotland, it had boldly said that James had forfeited the Crown. But put it either way, it is difficult for a lawyer to regard the Convention Parliament as a lawfully constituted assembly. By whom was it summoned? Not by a king of England, but by a Prince of Orange. Even if we go back three centuries we find no precedent. The parliaments of 1327 and 1399 were summoned by writs in the King's name under the Great Seal. Grant that parliament may depose a king, James was not deposed by parliament; grant that parliament may elect a king, William and Mary were not elected by parliament. If when the convention met it was no parliament, its own act could not turn it into a parliament. The act which declares it to be a parliament depends for its validity on the assent of William and Mary. The validity of that assent depends on their being king and queen; but how do they come to be king and queen?

As a matter of strict law the Convention Parliament not having been summoned by the King was not a lawful Parliament, with the result that William was not a king and that being so, the Act of Settlement which regulated the succession to the throne was not a valid piece of legislation and none of the sovereigns who succeeded to the throne under the Act of Settlement was a legal sovereign and none of the laws to which they gave assent was a valid law. The only ground on which all that was illegal can be held to have been legal was, as Chitty observes, the necessity of the situation.

In *Opinions of Eminent Lawyers* by George Chalmers several opinions are quoted where what was apparently illegal was supposed in case of necessity to have been legal. At pp. 29 and 30 is cited the opinion of Lord Chief Justice Holt on the forfeiture of Lord Baltimore's charter of Maryland and the grant of it to another Governor. The question in that case was whether, before Lord Baltimore's forfeiture of his charter was adjudged, Maryland could be granted to another Governor. Giving his opinion the Lord Chief Justice said, 'I think it had been better, if an inquisition had been taken, and the forfeiture committed, by the Lord Baltimore, had been therein found, before any grant be made to a new governor; yet, since there is none and it being in a case of necessity, I think the king may by his commission constitute a governor, whose authority will be legal, though he must be responsible to Lord Baltimore for the profits.' The opinion of the Attorney- and Solicitor-Generals, Northey and Harcourt, at pp. 30–2 that the Queen may resume a government granted under a royal charter that has been abused proceeded on the same ground. They both agreed 'that by an extraordinary exigency happening through the default or neglect by a proprietor or of those appointed by him, or their inability to protect or defend the province under their government and the inhabitants thereof in times of war, or imminent danger, Your Majesty may constitute a Governor of such province, or colony, as well for the civil as military part of government, and for the protection and preservation thereof and of your Majesty's subjects there.' The opinion of the Attorney- and Solicitor-Generals, Ryder and Murray, which appears at pp. 186–8 was asked on the King's right to establish a government in Georgia upon the surrender of the trustees and it was to the effect that 'if the surrender of the charter, by the trustees, cannot be postponed, and the present government there kept up, till a new method of administering the new government can be settled, the proper way for authorising the present magistrates and officers to continue in the exercise of their respective offices, in the meantime, will be, for His Majesty to issue a proclamation for that purpose, under the great seal of Great Britain to be published in Georgia'. There is one feature which was common to all the instances I have mentioned above—immediate necessity—and that circumstance was supposed to have rendered legal what otherwise appeared to be illegal.

The powers and responsibilities of the Head of a State in preserving the State and Society during an extraordinary emergency and preventing from disruption the constitution and government of the country are analogous to the powers which an Army Commander has during Martial Law. That is so because the law of civil necessity and that of military necessity are both founded on a common principle. The nature and extent of the powers of an army commander were fully discussed by me in the full bench case of *Muhammad Umar Khan* v. *The Crown*[1] where referring to the dicta of Willies, J., in *Phillips* v. *Eyre*[2] I said:

... there may be occasions in which the necessity of the case demands prompt and speedy action for the maintenance of law and order at whatever risk, and where the governor may be compelled, unless he shrinks from the discharge of paramount duty, to exercise *de facto* powers which the legislature would assuredly have confided to him if the emergency could have been foreseen, trusting that whatever he has honestly done for the safety of the State will be ratified by an Act of indemnity and oblivion.

I held on the authority of that case and the observations in *Tilonko* v. *Attorney-General of Natal*[3] that where civil authority is paralysed by tumult, all acts done by the military which were dictated by necessity and done in good faith will be protected even if there be no bill of indemnity. Of course the duty of an army commander arises where there is a revolt, insurrection or disturbance of the public order, but the principle which permits, and occasionally demands, the exercise of emergency powers is

[1] 1953 P.L.R. Lahore 825. [2] (1870), 6 Q.B. 1.
[3] [1907] A.C. 93.

304

not limited to those cases and equally governs a situation where the Head of the State is required to act in a case of necessity when the Legislature is not in being. This result follows from the address of Lord Mansfield in the Proceedings against *George Stratton and others* (21 Howell's St. Tr. 1046) which had started against them on an information filed by His Majesty's Attorney-General for a misdemeanour in arresting, imprisoning and deposing Lord Pigot, Commander-in-Chief of the Forces in Fort St George and President and Governor of the Settlement of Madras in East Indies. The defence to the information was that Lord Pigot had violated the constitution of the government of Madras with regard to the Governor and Council in whom the whole power was vested by the East India Company and that the defendants had acted under necessity in order to preserve the constitution. In his address to the jury, Lord Mansfield thus dealt with the law of civil necessity, as distinguished from the law of natural necessity (at p. 1224):

I cannot be warranted to put you any case of civil necessity that justifies illegal acts, because the case not existing, nor being supposed to exist, there is no authority in the law books, nor any adjudged case upon it. Imagination may suggest, you may suggest so extraordinary a case as would justify a man by force overturning a magistrate and beginning a new government, all by force, I mean in India, where there is no superior nigh them to apply to; in England it cannot happen; but in India you may suppose a possible case, but in that case, it must be imminent, extreme, necessity; there must be no other remedy to apply to for redress; it must be very imminent, it must be very extreme, and in the whole they do, they must appear clearly to do it with a view of preserving the society and themselves, with a view of preserving the whole. . . . Then you must see, the Company's settlements are preserved by it. For if there is a struggle of a faction, it will be upon an illegal act. If the governor does twenty illegal acts, that will not be a justification of it; it must tend to the dissolution of society, and the intervention must tend to the preservation of it. . . .

But the only question for you to consider is this.—Whether there was that necessity for the preservation of the society and the inhabitants of the place as authorises private men (for when they are out of the Council till a Council is called they are private men . . .) to take possession of the government; and to take possession of the government to be sure it was necessary to do it immediately. . . .

If you can find that there was that imminent necessity for the preservation of the whole, you will acquit the defendants.

In another version of the same case Lord Mansfield is reported to have said (21 St. Tr. at p. 1230):

... to amount to a justification, there must appear imminent danger to the government and individuals; the mischief must be extreme, and such as would not admit a possibility of waiting for a legal remedy. That the safety of the government must well warrant the experiment. . . . The necessity will not justify going further than necessity obliges: for though compulsion takes away the criminality of the acts, which would otherwise be treason, yet it will not justify a man in acting farther than such necessity obliges him or continuing to act after the compulsion is removed.

The principle clearly emerging from this address of Lord Mansfield is that subject to the condition of absoluteness, extremeness and imminence, an act which would otherwise be illegal becomes legal if it is done *bona fide* under the stress of necessity, the necessity being referable to an intention to preserve the constitution, the State or the Society and to prevent it from dissolution, and affirms Chitty's statement that necessity knows no law and the maxim cited by Bracton that necessity makes lawful [that] which otherwise is not lawful. Since the address expressly refers to the right of a private person to act in necessity, in the case of Head of the State justification to act must *a fortiori* be clearer and more imperative.

This being the position regarding individual acts, the next question is whether the Head of the State can, in the circumstances postulated, legislate for the society. This Court has held in *Usif Patel's* case that the Governor-General has no power to make such laws as are mentioned in sub-section (1) of section 8 of the Indian Independence Act, 1947, but that decision was expressly limited to the Governor-General's powers under section 42 of the Government of India Act, 1935, no other source for the power to pass such laws having been claimed for him in that case. If it once be conceded that the power to act in an emergency of the nature just indicated exists, the conclusion is inescapable that the act may be done by a general order, which, as admitted by Mr Pritt, would amount to legislation. If the law, as stated by Chitty, that the Crown is the only branch of legislature that is capable of performing any act at a time when Parliament is not in being is correct, legislative powers of the Crown in an emergency are a necessary corollary from that statement, and the same result flows from Dicey's statement that the free exercise of a discretion or prerogative power at a critical juncture is essential to the executive government of every civilised country, the indispensable condition being that the exercise of that power is always subject to the legislative authority of Parliament, to be exercised *ex post facto*. The manner in which such power is exercised, whether in individual cases or by positive directions or restraint orders of a general character, is essentially a question of method and detail, not affecting the main principle. The emergency legislative power, however, cannot extend to matters which are not the product of the necessity, as for instance, changes in the constitution which are not directly referable to the emergency.

The disaster that stared the Governor-General in the face, consequent on the illegal manner in which the Constituent Assembly exercised its legislative authority, is apparent from the results described in the *Reference* as having followed from this Court's decision in *Mr Tazimuddin Khan's* case and the subsequent case of *Usif Patel*. The Governor-General must, therefore, be *held* to have acted in order to avert an impending disaster and to prevent the State and society from dissolution. His proclamation of 16 April 1955, declaring that the laws mentioned in the Schedule to the Emergency Powers Ordinance, 1955, shall be retrospectively enforceable is accordingly valid during the interim period, i.e. until the validity of these laws is decided upon by the new Constituent Assembly. Needless to say that since the validity of these laws during the interim period is founded on necessity, there should be no delay in calling the Constituent Assembly.

I would, therefore, reply to the questions referred as follows:

Question No. 3. Whether the Constituent Assembly was rightly dissolved by the Governor-General.

Opinion. That on the facts stated in the *Reference* namely (1) that the Constituent Assembly, though it functioned for more than 7 years, was unable to carry out the duty to frame a constitution for Pakistan to replace the transitional constitution provided by the Indian Independence Act, 1947; (ii) that in view of the repeated representations from and resolutions passed by representative bodies throughout the country, the Constituent Assembly, in the opinion of the Governor-General, became in course of time wholly unrepresentative of the people of Pakistan and ceased to be responsible to them; (iii) that for all practical purposes the Constituent Assembly assumed the form of a perpetual legislature; and (iv) that throughout the period of its existence the Constituent Assembly asserted that the provisions made by it for the constitution of the Dominion under sub-section (1) of section 8 of the Indian Independence Act, 1947, were valid laws without the assent of the Governor-General, the Governor-General had under section 5 of the Indian Independence Act, legal authority to dissolve the Constituent Assembly.

Question No. 4. Whether the Constituent Convention proposed to be set up by the Governor-General will be competent to exercise the powers conferred by sub-section (1) of section 8 of the Indian Independence Act, 1947, on the Constituent Assembly?

Opinion. That subject to this—

(i) that the correct name of the Constituent Convention is Constituent Assembly;

(ii) that the Governor-General's right to dissolve the Assembly can only be derived from the Indian Independence Act;

(iii) that the arrangements for representation of States and Tribal Areas can, under the proviso to sub-section (3) of section 19 of the Indian Independence Act, be made only by the Constituent Assembly and not by the Governor-General; and

(iv) that the Governor-General's duty being to bring into existence a representative Constituent Assembly he can only nominate the electorate and not members to the Constituent Assembly, the new Assembly, constituted under the Constituent Convention Order, 1955, as amended to date, would be competent to exercise all the powers conferred by the Indian Independence Act, 1947, on the Constituent Assembly including the powers under section 8 of that Act.

Question No. 1. What are the powers and responsibilities of the Governor-General in respect of the government of the country before the new Constituent Convention passes the necessary legislation?

Opinion. That this question is too general and need not be answered.

Question No. 2. The Federal Court having held in *Usif Patel's* case that the laws listed in the Schedule to the Emergency Powers Ordinance could not be validated under section 42 of the Government of India Act, 1935, nor retrospective effect given to them, and no legislature competent to validate such laws being in existence, is there any provision in the Constitution or any rule of law applicable to the situation by which the Governor-General can by order or otherwise declare that all orders made, decisions taken, and other acts done under those laws shall be valid and enforceable and those laws which cannot without danger to the State be removed from the existing legal system shall be treated as part of the law of the land until the question of their validation is determined by the new Constituent Convention?

Opinion. That in the situation presented by the *Reference* the Governor-General has, during the interim period, the power under the common law of civil or state necessity of retrospectively validating the laws listed in the Schedule to the Emergency Powers Ordinance, 1955, and all those laws, until the question of their validation is decided upon by the Constituent Assembly are, during the aforesaid period, valid and enforceable in the same way as if they had been valid from the date on which they purported to come into force.

Before I conclude, I should like to dispel the impression, which this opinion may produce on the mind of a layman, that while seeking in common law the origin of a jurisdiction exercisable in Pakistan, I have assigned to the Governor-General of this country a position analogous to that of English Kings in the Middle Ages. Nothing that I have said here in any way affects the independence of Pakistan or is inconsistent with the constitutional position of the Governor-General described at length by me at pp. 96–100 and 143–6 of my opinion in *Mr Tamizuddin Khan's* case. The words 'Crown', 'King', 'Queen', 'His Majesty', 'Her Majesty', 'Prerogative', etc., are mere legal abstractions and do not in any manner imply the subordination of Pakistan to any outside power. Thus, to explain my point, when after winning independence for Pakistan the Qaid-i-Azam, while taking the oath of office as the first Governor-General of Pakistan, promised to be 'faithful to His Majesty King George the Sixth, His Heirs and Successors, in the office of Governor-General of Pakistan' no one could suppose, and none can suppose now, that he was swearing allegiance to the laws of another country or to a subordinate and dependent position for Pakistan or was acknowledging the right of the British Crown to govern or interfere with the affairs of this country. Though appointed by the Crown, the Governor-General is in fact a representative of this country and not of any outside power, and the authority that he exercises flows from the laws of this country.

AKRAM, J.—For the reasons given by the learned Chief Justice I agree in the opinions expressed by him in the *Special Reference No. 1 of 1955.*

CORNELIUS, J.—In this note, I proceed to state the reasons underlying the opinions on the referred questions which I delivered in open Court on 10 May 1955.

Each of the four questions referred to this Court rests basically upon the fundamental question of *vires* in the Governor-General of Pakistan, in relation to acts performed or proposed to be performed by him. Therefore, a proper answer to the questions requires an examination of the following fundamental questions, *viz.*—

(i) What is the status of the State of Pakistan?

(ii) What is the status of the Constituent Assembly referred to in the Indian Independence Act, 1947?

(iii) What is the status of the Governor-General of Pakistan under the existing constitutional instruments, and what are the powers which he can exercise, in the relevant respects?

Each of these questions has been examined and pronounced upon in greater or less detail in the judgments delivered by this Court on 3 April 1955 in the case of *Moulvi Tamizuddin Khan.* The sole question which was decided in that case was whether constitutional laws passed by the Constituent Assembly of Pakistan required the assent of the Governor-General in order to be effective in law. I had the misfortune of adhering to a point of view which varied greatly from that which found favour with my Lord the Chief Justice and the other learned Judges. Proceeding on what I thought was the true construction of the constitutional instruments, I came to the conclusion that Pakistan was an independent Dominion, and in that status, it enjoyed a sufficient degree of autonomy to justify the three great limbs of State, namely, the Constituent Assembly, the Executive (i.e. the Governor-General acting with his Ministers), and the Judiciary (i.e. the superior courts) in holding unanimously for a period of seven years, that constitutional laws passed by the Constituent Assembly became laws in accordance with a rule made in that respect by the Constituent Assembly, viz., upon the Bill as passed being authenticated by the signature of the President, and thereafter being published in the Government *Gazette* under the authority of the President. I expressed the opinion that to say that the State of Pakistan as operating through the three great organs mentioned above was wrong in adopting this mode of passing constitutional laws, was in effect to deny the autonomy of Pakistan.

Having been overruled in this respect, however, it is my duty loyally to accept the view expressed by the majority of the Full Bench, and I proceed to reproduce below extracts from the other judgments delivered in the case, which set out with clarity what must now be regarded as the law of the land in this particular respect. In the leading judgment of my Lord the Chief Justice, the expression 'Independent Dominion' applied by section 1 of the Indian Independence Act was elaborately analysed and the principal features were set out in the following words:

Thus Pakistan became independent because:

(i) in law, on the midnight of the 14 August 1947, the Constituent Assembly made a law and the Governor-General assented to it, it could secede from the Commonwealth and become a completely independent State, its citizens owing no allegiance to the Crown and not being British subjects; and

(ii) it was not subject, as Canada and Australia were, to any disability to change its constitution. It could have any constitution or form of government it liked, having no connection with the Commonwealth or the Crown or the Governor-General as the representative of the Crown.

But so long as it did not secede from the Commonwealth, it was a Dominion because:

(a) it was linked with the Commonwealth by allegiance to a common Crown;

(b) its citizens were internationally British subjects;

(c) its laws needed the assent of His Majesty or his representative, the Governor-General;

(d) the King's prerogative existed here except to the extent that it was utilized by Parliament in the Indian Independence Act because the King had placed his prerogatives and interests at the disposal of Parliament only 'so far as concerned the matters dealt with by the bill'; and

(iii) it could make any law it liked, constitutional or otherwise, and no law of the dominant country was to extend to it.

In a discussion of the meaning of the expression 'Dominion'

under the sub-heading 'Allegiance to the Crown', the following observations occur:

But though independent in the sense just explained, Pakistan is a Dominion and therefore certain incidents attach to it by reason of that status. The first feature that is common to the Dominions which are members of the British Commonwealth of Nations is common allegiance to the Crown.

But so long as either of them remains a Dominion, assent to its legislation is necessary both under the common law doctrine and the statutory provision in sub-section (3) of section 6. So strict is this rule that even if a Dominion intended to secede from the Commonwealth and repudiate allegiance to the Crown, it could do so only by an extra-legal act. But if it intended to proceed constitutionally such secession would itself require the assent of the Queen or her representative, or legislation by the Parliament of the United Kingdom. Such assent was given when Burma became independent under the Burma Independence Act, 1947. And though in the case of India no such assent seems to have been requested or given, the connection between India and the United Kingdom had to be recognised by a statute of the British Parliament, India (Consequential Provisions) Act, 1949, to retain India as a member of the Commonwealth.

Earlier in the judgment, in a discussion of the requirement of assent in respect of laws passed under the Government of India Act, 1935, my Lord the Chief Justice observed as follows:

The restrictions are, therefore, illustrative of the constitutional position that assent to the Dominion legislation by the Crown or its representative is indispensable and has in no instance ever been dispensed with by the Crown.

My brother Muhammad Sharif expressed his full concurrence with the views contained in the judgment of my Lord the Chief Justice.

In the separate judgment of my brother Akram, reference is made to the fact that His Majesty's Government by their declaration of 3 June 1947, announced their decision 'to introduce legislation during the current session for the transfer of power this year on a Dominion Status basis to one or two successor authorities according to the decisions taken as a result of this announcement'. After reproducing the description of the Dominions contained in the declaration of the Imperial Conference held in London in 1926, Akram, J., proceeded to observe as follows:

Thus the effect of conferring a Dominion Status was that certain rights and liabilities as between the Dominion and the United Kingdom came into existence, for instance, if the Dominion by its legislation negated allegiance to the Crown or severed connection with it, such a legislation perhaps could not be considered as legally valid or justified. The expression 'Independent Dominion' has, therefore, been purposely used in the Independence Act in order to give to the Dominion a freedom of choice either to remain or to refuse to remain within the British Commonwealth of Nations. . . . It is clear that by the Independence Act the intention was to give a constitutional form of government modelled on the pattern of the British government pending the setting up of a final constitution by the Dominion itself. According to English constitutional theories, the sovereign, who is the Executive Head of the State, is always a constituent part of the supreme legislative power and as such has the legal right not only of giving assent but also of refusing assent in case he considers a provision to be inexpedient or injurious. . . . Such being the English constitutional theories, it would be a strange supposition to make that the British Parliament, while framing an interim Constitutional Act for Pakistan, acted in a manner contrary to its own principles and traditions and deprived the Executive Head of the Dominion of power to give or to withhold assent as respects constitutional laws.

I understand my learned brother to be saying in the passages reproduced above that by the Indian Independence Act a constitution modelled on the British pattern was provided as an interim measure for Pakistan, and the incidents of constitutional laws as applicable to His Majesty's Government in the United Kingdom apply also in relation to the State of Pakistan. In a number of passages cited from authoritative sources, my learned brother has referred to the prerogative powers of the King in relation to legislation, in particular the prerogative of assent and one of these passages contains reference also to the power of the King to dissolve Parliament.

From the separate judgment of my brother S. A. Rahman, I extract the following passages:

Assent to legislation is one of the most important prerogatives of the Crown in England. There is also ample authority for the proposition that the prerogative of the Crown extends to the Colonies and Dominions of His Majesty beyond the Seas. . . . Only express words or necessary intendment of a statute can take away a prerogative and the presumption would be against such a result. . . . I can discover nothing in the Indian Independence Act which could support the plea of express or implied abrogation of the prerogative of assent in the case of laws

313

enacted by the Constituent Assembly sitting as the Legislature of the Dominion to frame the Constitution. On the other hand, a reading of sections 5 and 6 together, would lead to the inference that henceforth the prerogative of the Crown as respects assent, would, in the case of each new Dominion, be exercised by the Governor-General, as representing His Majesty. Allegiance to the Crown, however tenuous the bond may in practice turn out to be, is an essential incident of Dominion Status. . . . This position would continue to hold good in Pakistan as long as it is a Dominion, albeit an 'Independent Dominion', unless of course it is altered by a proper constitutional provision. From the expression 'Independent Dominion', merely constitutional autonomy and not full political sovereignty in the legal sense, can be spelt out, though the latter status would be potentially within the Dominion Legislature's grasp.

The observations reproduced above from the judgments of my Lord the Chief Justice and my brothers Akram and Rahman are addressed to the existence or otherwise of the prerogative of assent, but they are based upon a view of the status of Pakistan which, I say so with all respect, is expressed in sufficiently general terms to found an inference regarding the cognate prerogative of dissolution as well. That dissolution falls within the Royal prerogative in the United Kingdom admits of no doubt. I reproduce here, merely for convenience of statement, the following passages from the monograph on the subject of Parliament in vol. 24 of Halsbury's *Laws of England*, 2nd ed.:

295. The two Houses of Parliament are summoned, prorogued, and dissolved by the Sovereign by the exercise of his Royal Prerogative, and his assent must be given to any Bill passed by the Lords and Commons before it can have the force of law.

490. A new Parliament can be called together for the transaction of business only by the Crown. It is summoned by means of the King's writ, issued by the direction of the Lord Chancellor from the office of the Clerk of the Crown in Chancery with the advice of the Privy Council and in pursuance of a Royal proclamation.

513. A session of Parliament can only be brought to an end by the exercise of the Royal Prerogative. Parliament is prorogued at the end of a session either by the Sovereign in person or by a commission appointed for the purpose by letters patent under the Great Seal.

518. Parliament can be dissolved at any time by the Crown by the exercise of the Royal Prerogative, but its duration is limited by statute to a period of five years from the day on which by the writ of summons it was appointed to meet.

It is clear on general principle as well as authority that the prerogatives of the Crown extend to all British possessions and Dominions overseas and that they are exercisable subject to certain qualifications based upon the relevant statute or instrument of appointment, by the Governor or Governor-General, in each such possession or Dominion. The point has been placed beyond doubt in the leading judgment in the case of *Moulvi Tamizuddin Khan*, in the paragraph reproduced below:

The Governor-General of Pakistan is appointed by the King or Queen and represents him or her for the purposes of the Government of the Dominion (section 5 of the Indian Independence Act). The authority of the representative of the King extends to the exercise of the Royal prerogative in so far as it is applicable to the internal affairs of the Member State or Province, even without express delegation, subject to any contrary statutory or constitutional provisions.

The primary question in the present case is whether the Governor-General had power to dissolve the Constituent Assembly, and the decision of this question must, in the light of the conclusions reached in *Moulvi Tamizuddin Khan's* case by my Lord the Chief Justice and my learned brothers, turn upon the question whether there is anything in the statutes or other relevant instruments which operates either expressly or by necessary intendment to curtail the prerogative of dissolution in this respect.

The second question which I have posed above, admits of an answer after the same fashion as the first. With reference to the relevant provision in the Indian Independence Act, 1947, the view which I held in *Moulvi Tamizuddin Khan's* case was that the Constituent Assembly was not at any time from its establishment onwards, capable of being regarded as the Legislature of the Dominion. It was given a capacity, by express provisions, to exercise certain powers which were stated to be powers of the Legislature of the Dominion, as well as to exercise the powers of the Federal Legislature under the Government of India Act, 1935. In the view which I took, the 'Legislature of the Dominion' was and is still to be set up, in accordance with a law made by the Constituent Assembly, and the provisions mentioned above relating to the powers of two other Legislatures being *exercisable* by the Constituent Assembly did not appear to me to have the effect of making the Constituent Assembly identical with the Legislature of the Dominion (or, for that matter, with the Federal Legislature).

In this respect also, mine was a minority view, as my Lord the Chief Justice and two of my learned brothers were clearly of the opinion that as from the date on which Pakistan became a separate State, the Constituent Assembly of Pakistan was the Legislature of the Dominion. The following extract from the leading judgment contains the views of my Lord the Chief Justice and my brother Muhammad Sharif on this point:

Under the temporary constitution provided by section 8 a Federal Legislature had to come into existence and some one from the appointed day had to exercise its functions under that constitution. Proviso (c) to sub-section (2) of section 8 therefore declares that the powers of the Federal Legislature or the Indian Legislature under the Government of India Act, 1935, as in force in relation to each of the Dominions, shall, in the first instance, be exercisable by the Constituent Assembly of the Dominion in addition to the powers exercisable by that Assembly under sub-section (1) of that section. Thus the Constituent Assembly became on 15 August 1947, not only the Legislature of the Dominion for the purposes of section 6, fully competent to make provision as to the constitution of the Dominion but also the first Federal Legislature under the scheme outlined in the Government of India Act, 1935, which with necessary adaptation came into force on the same date. Accordingly the position of the Constituent Assembly is that it is the Legislature of the Dominion when it makes laws for the constitution of the Dominion and the Federal Legislature when it functions under the limitations imposed upon it by the Government of India Act, 1935.

The views of my brother S. A. Rahman appear from the following extract:

The argument was raised that though sub-section (1) of section 8 made the constitution-making powers included in sub-section (1) of section 6, exercisable in the first instance (the phrase 'in the first instance' needs to be specifically emphasised in this connection) by the Constituent Assembly, the latter body was not identifiable with the 'Legislature of the Dominion' within the meaning of sub-section (3) of section 6. A similar formula contained in proviso (e) to sub-section (2) of section 8 makes the powers of the Federal Legislature or Indian Legislature exercisable in the first instance by the same Constituent Assembly. After a comparison of sections 6 and 8, the inference seems to be irresistible that during the interregnum prior to the promulgation of a fresh constitution, the Constituent Assembly in fact functions as the Legislature of the Dominion.

The point was not specifically pronounced upon in the separate judgment of my brother Akram who was content to observe that 'the Constituent Assembly which in the first instance is to make provision for the constitution of the Dominion is to exercise the power of the Legislature of the Dominion for that purpose'. Since, however, the majority of the Full Bench were clearly of the opinion that the Constituent Assembly was in fact the Legislature of the Dominion in the period prior to the promulgation of a new Constitution, I must accept that view as being the law of the land. It serves to determine the status of the Constituent Assembly as well as to place it in a well-defined position in relation to the Governor-General of the Dominion having regard to the conception of Dominion Status as accepted by the majority of the Full Bench.

Three members of the Full Bench including my Lord the Chief Justice were indeed of the opinion that the Governor-General was to be regarded as a part of the Legislature of the Dominion. The following extracts from the leading judgment are relevant:

The power to make all laws was given to the Legislature of the Dominion while the power to give assent to those laws was given to the Governor-General, who thus became a constituent part of the legislature and was to occupy the same position as the Sovereign in the United Kingdom in respect of the prerogative of giving or withholding assent.

The Crown is a constituent part of Parliament in the United Kingdom and of all Dominion Legislatures either because it is expressly so stated in the constitutional statutes or because the Crown appoints the Governor-General who is empowered to give or withhold assent to the legislation of the Dominion.

Similarly the provisions in the Government of India Act which give to the Governor-General the right to withhold assent from legislation do not confer on, or create a new right in, the Crown; on the contrary, they implicitly recognise such right and regulate the manner in which it is to be exercised. It is for this reason that the fiction of making the Crown a constituent of the legislature is resorted to, because neither the King nor his representative, the Governor-General, is a member of the legislature like other members. The King or the Governor-General is a part of the legislature only in the sense that all bills passed by the legislature are presented to him, so that he may exercise his right of giving or withholding assent. Thus sub-section (3) of section 6 produces the same result by giving to the Governor-General full power to assent in His Majesty's name to any law of the Legislature of the Dominion.

It makes the Governor-General a constituent part of the legislature inasmuch as the right to give assent necessarily includes in it the right to withhold assent.

It (i.e. the Constituent Assembly) had, of course, legislative sovereignty as the legislature of the Dominion but then the Governor-General was a constituent part of the Legislature.

In the judgment of my brother Akram, there is direct reference to the English constitutional theory under which the Sovereign 'who is the executive head of the State is always a constituent part of the supreme legislative power' and in arriving at the conclusion that the Governor-General had the power of giving or withholding assent as respects constitutional laws, the judgment refers to him as the 'Executive Head of the Dominion', in a passage already quoted.

The exact position of the Governor-General of the Dominion, under the existing constitutional instruments, did not receive the same attention in the judgment in *Moulvi Tamizuddin Khan's* case which it is necessary to apply to the matter in the present *Reference*. In the leading judgment, the following observations occur which are helpful in the present context:

From the fact that the Governor-General is the head of the State, it must not be inferred that in matters of legislation his position is either that of a nodding automaton or that of an autocrat. He is appointed by the King and represents the King for the purposes of the Government of the Dominion, but that does not mean that he is an unrestrained autocrat, and purporting to act on behalf of the King, can in normal times take an active part in the actual administration of the country. Since the Imperial Conference of 1926 he has generally been a man of the Dominion and a representative of that Dominion just as the Prime Minister is. As a constitutional functionary, it is his duty to give his assent to all reasonable and necessary legislation by the legislature.

For the purposes of the present *Reference*, it is necessary to examine the matter at some length. The position of the Governor (or the Governor-General) of a Dominion is one of the highest importance. It is not my purpose here to deal exhaustively with every aspect of his powers and responsibilities. That is indeed not necessary for the purposes of the matter in hand. In Dr Berriedale Keith's *Responsible Government in the Dominions*, 2nd ed., 1928, the status, privileges, powers and responsibilities of the Governor are considered in six separate Chapters under the heading 'The Executive Government'. He is described as the chief Executive officer and is appointed by the Crown. The following observation in Chapter II is relevant:

The office of Governor is now normally constituted by letters patent under the Great Seal of the United Kingdom, and this instrument is accompanied and supplemented by royal instructions under the sign manual and signet. It is important to note that the act of constituting the office is a prerogative action, resting on the authority of the Crown to exercise executive authority in so far as no other provision is made by legislation.

The extent of a Governor's authority to exercise the royal prerogative must be held to be determined by the pronouncement on the subject contained in the leading judgment in *Moulvi Tamizuddin Khan's* case, for the purposes of the Dominion of Pakistan. It is, however, useful and it may be valuable to reproduce certain observations regarding the Governor's exercise of prerogative power from Dr Keith's Chapter on the Powers of the Governor, in section 2. The learned writer refers to the judgment of the Privy Council in *Musgrave* v. *Pulido*[1] where the Judicial Committee emphatically asserted that—

The Governor of a colony in ordinary cases cannot be regarded as a Viceroy, nor can it be assumed that he possesses general sovereign power. His authority is derived from his commission and limited to the powers thereby expressly or impliedly entrusted to him.

Commenting on this judgment, the learned writer observes that there can be no doubt of the doctrine of the Privy Council, and that a Governor has no special privilege like that of the Crown. He is under the necessity of showing in respect of his acts that they are covered by authority in law, and in order to do this, he must show not only that the Crown possesses the power to do the act, but also that he had the authority to do the act. The general conclusion is then reached that—

apart from statutory powers, the Governor has a delegation of so much of the executive power as enables him effectively to conduct the Executive Government of the territory.

At the conclusion of the same section, the learned writer refers to views favouring a larger authority in a Governor expressed by

[1] (1879), 5 App. Cas. 102.

other writers, and cites the following statement from a book by Sir H. Jenkyns:

There is no doubt that a Governor will be always held to have had all the power necessary for meeting any emergency which may have required him to take immediate action for the safety of the Colony. If he acts in good faith and having regard to the circumstances reasonably, he will be held harmless.

As regards this dictum Dr Keith has the following observation to offer—

This is doubtless unsound doctrine, if it suggests that there is any special privilege in the case of a Governor or that mere reasonable action in good faith will cover any act. Every member of the executive may violate in case of emergency ordinary laws, but the Governor, like every other officer, runs the risk of finding that a Court of law may conclude that the emergency was not such as to justify his action despite its good faith and apparent reasonableness.

In the case of Pakistan, the question of satisfying a Court may be thought to be partially excluded by section 306 of the Government of India Act, 1935, but it is to be observed that both in the present proceedings, as well as in the arguments in *Moulvi Tamizuddin Khan's* case it was conceded by Senior Counsel appearing for the Federation of Pakistan that the Court had jurisdiction to examine whether the impugned action was justified by the nature of the emergency that was declared by the Governor-General of Pakistan. But as regards the opinion of Dr Keith on this point, I consider that it is unexceptionable, particularly in the case of a Dominion such as Pakistan which is provided with a most elaborate constitution contained in the Indian Independence Act, 1947, and the Government of India Act, 1935. By these instruments, all the powers of government are distributed in detail among the several authorities of the Centre and the Provinces. This Constitution, which was well adapted to the requirements of a great country with a population of some 350 millions, was operated successfully for ten years before the Partition, some six of these years being covered by the period of the Second World War, in a most successful manner, without resort by the Chief Executive to any powers other than those expressly provided by the British Parliament in the Government of India Act and certain other statutory instruments of a temporary nature. Prior to the coming into operation of the Government of India Act, 1935, the country had been governed for some twenty-two years under the previous Constitution Act, viz. the Government of India Act, 1915, whose provisions differed from those of the 1935 Act in two main respects, *viz.* that powers were mainly concentrated in the hands of the Executive, and legislative institutions were as yet embryonic and were provided with only limited scope. Yet even in that earlier period, when responsibility for the safety and welfare of the State devolved so much more heavily upon the Executive heads at the Centre and in the Provinces, it was never found necessary to invoke any powers in relation to British India except such as were derived clearly from express statute. Consequently, it is in my opinion entirely fair to say, in relation to the Governor-General of Pakistan, what Dr Keith has said generally with reference to the Governor of a Dominion, that he possesses no special privilege to act in excess of the powers afforded to him by the written constitution, and by his Commission of appointment, and that he cannot affect to act as Viceroy or to assume that he possesses general sovereign power.

The instruments which govern the matter in the case of the Governor-General of Pakistan are as follows. By section 5 of the Independence Act, the Governor-General is 'appointed by His Majesty and shall represent His Majesty for the purposes of the government of the Dominion'. This formula has been held to attract all the prerogatives of the Crown as exercisable in the United Kingdom, except to the extent that they may have been excluded expressly or by necessary intendment. Then there is the Commission issued to the Governor-General upon his appointment by His Majesty which confers upon him 'all the powers, rights, privileges and advantages to the said Office belonging or appertaining'. The Governor-General is further authorised, empowered and commanded to exercise and perform powers and duties conferred and imposed upon him by the constitutional instruments. He is invested with authority to grant pardons in the exercise of the Royal Prerogative. The remaining provisions contained in the Commission are not relevant for the present purpose, but it is of advantage to note that the Oath which the Governor-General takes is one of 'true faith and allegiance to the

Constitution of Pakistan as by law established' and secondly, to be faithful to the British Sovereign.

There is also conferred upon the Governor-General by section 7 of the Government of India Act, 1935, general authority in the following words: ' Subject to the provisions of this Act, the executive authority of the Federation shall be exercised by the Governor-General, either directly or through officers subordinate to him.'

One major question which will require answer in the present *Reference* is, whether the Governor-General can make constitutional laws under any conditions. It seems obvious that he cannot affect to do so under the Government of India Act, 1935. In the context of that Act, he is a statutory authority and plainly it would be contrary to principle and good reason to allow that a statutory authority has power to interfere with the very statute under which it purports to act, and from which it derives its entire power to act. Nothing in the Commission of appointment or the oath of office can be construed so as to confer a power of this kind. On the other hand, the oath of true faith and allegiance to the Constitution of Pakistan and the direct injunction by the British Sovereign to carry out the duties and exercise the powers conferred by the Indian Independence Act, 1947 (which by express reference imports all the powers and duties dealt with in the Government of India Act, 1935), afford the strongest possible indication of limitation of the Governor-General's powers. The fact of the Governor-General being made the representative of His Majesty by section 5 of the Indian Independence Act, 1947, has been deemed to invest him with all the available Royal Prerogatives as exercisable in the United Kingdom but it is not suggested, and in my view it cannot be suggested that the Royal Prerogative anywhere in the British Commonwealth extends to interference with Constitutions granted by the British Parliament. Consequently, it seems entirely correct to say of the Governor-General what has been said by Dr Keith concerning a Governor of the Dominion, viz. 'manifestly the Governor has not the Royal Prerogative of constitution-giving being merely himself a part of the Constitution'.

On this point indeed, the law has been stated as recently as 12 April 1955, by this Court, sitting in Full Bench, in the case of *Usif Patel*,[1] in the following terms:

[1] P.L.D. 1955 F.C. 387.

This Court held in *Mr Tamizuddin Khan's* case that the Constituent Assembly was not a sovereign body. But that did not mean that if the Assembly was not a sovereign body the Governor-General was. We took pains to explain at length in that case that the position of the Governor-General in Pakistan is that of a constitutional Head of the State, namely, a position very similar to that occupied by the King in the United Kingdom.

This is a convenient point at which I should perform the duty of explaining an expression I have employed in my opinion on the fourth question referred to this Court. That question will be reproduced later at its proper place. Here I need only reproduce the particular expression which is as follows: 'the exercise of any political initiative outside the constitutional instruments'.

I can best elucidate this phrase by means of illustrations from the proceedings which immediately preceded the passing of the Indian Independence Act, 1947. It is, of course, perfectly clear that when the conqueror of a country is pleased to grant representative institutions to that country, he exercises what may, in the context of constitutional law as applicable to representative institutions, be truly said to be sovereign political power. The step which he takes is one which involves a sharing of power between himself, the conqueror, and the people whom he has conquered. Such a step may, in my opinion, be truly described as a political initiative. As the governmental processes are liberalised, and the rule of the people is extended over increasingly large areas included in the governmental field, further instances are afforded of the exercise of political initiative. It is not my purpose to enumerate every such step taken by the British Sovereign in the long term of years which elapsed between the assumption of complete sovereignty over India by the British Sovereign, and the grant of Dominion Status coupled with a Constituent Assembly which was expressly empowered, if it thought fit, to withdraw the country from every form of attachment to or association with the British Crown. It will be sufficient to accept the position as it was in May 1946 when, after lengthy negotiations between representatives of His Majesty's Government in the United Kingdom on the one hand, and representatives of the major Indian political parties on the other, a very marked political initiative was taken by His Majesty's Government in the United Kingdom, which was embodied in the Plan of 16 May 1946. This document is replete with political initiative as exercisable only by a Sovereign. Remembering that the Constitution of India, by which must be understood that instrument under which the powers of absolute sovereignty over the country vested in the King were distributed among authorities in the United Kingdom and subordinate authorities in India, viz. the Government of India Act, 1935, it is evident that any new scheme for transfer of responsibility from the United Kingdom to India was not competent, at any rate on the very great scale appearing in the Plan of 16 May 1946, under that Constitution. In other words, the Plan was, in relation to the law in force in India, a supra-legal constitutional initiative taken by the absolute political Sovereign of India, namely, His Majesty's Government in the United Kingdom. I select for mention a few instances of the exercise of such political initiative embodied in that Plan. There was first a declaration that the function of providing a Constitution for India was not to be discharged by the British Parliament any longer, but His Majesty's Government as the political sovereign had determined 'to set in motion machinery whereby a constitution can be settled by Indians for Indians'. The objective was one entirely outside the Government of India Act, 1935. It was a conception which far transcended the scope of the Constitution provided by the latter Act. To give shape to this conception, the Plan furnished details of the constitution-making machinery which was proposed to be set up. This was to be on what has been described as the three-tier basis. The Provinces of India were divided into three groups whose representatives were to meet separately and settle their own provincial constitutions, including the question whether any group constitution should be set up for those Provinces. For settling the Union Constitution, representatives of Provinces and States were to assemble together at a later stage.

In paragraph 18 His Majesty's Government in the United Kingdom set out with great clarity the basic principles upon which representatives were to be returned to the Union Constituent Assembly from the provinces of British India. Declaring that for the purpose of deciding a new constitutional structure, the first problem was 'to obtain as broad-based and accurate a representation of the whole population as is possible' they regretted that the optimum method, namely, election based on adult franchise would involve 'wholly unacceptable delay' and consequently that it is necessary to accept the only practicable alternative, viz. 'to utilise the recently elected Provincial Legislative Assemblies as elective bodies'. It was then pointed out that to grant representation to the Provinces in proportion to the numerical strength of their respective Legislative Assemblies would, owing to the existing conditions, not secure accurate representation of the whole population. The strengths of the Legislative Assemblies bore no uniform proportion to the population, and further source of difficulty lay in the fact that weightage had been given to minorities on account of what is described as the 'Communal Award'. (This was a further political initiative taken at a much earlier stage, prior to the passing of the Government of India Act, 1935, by means of which a compromise was worked out by His Majesty's Government in the United Kingdom, between strongly conflicting views held in India regarding the representation of the various communities in the Legislatures. In order to secure uniform representation of the whole population, which was declared by the Plan to be a requisite of 'any Assembly to decide a new constitutional structure', it was found necessary by the then political Sovereign to ignore the political compromise represented by the Communal Award.) To overcome these difficulties, the following decision was taken which obviously represents a political initiative of the utmost importance:

After a most careful consideration of the various methods by which these points might be corrected, we have come to the conclusion that the fairest and most practicable plan would be

(a) to allot to each Province a total number of seats proportional to its population, roughly in the ratio of one to a million, as the nearest substitute for representation by adult suffrage;

(b) to divide this provincial allocation of seats between the main communities in each Province in proportion to their population;

(c) to provide that the representatives allotted to each community in a Province shall be elected by the members of that community in its Legislative Assembly.

We think that for these purposes it is sufficient to recognise only three main communities in India: General, Muslim, and Sikh, the 'General' community including all persons who are not Muslims or Sikhs. As the smaller minorities would, upon the population basis, have little or no representation since they would lose the weightage which

325

assures them seats in the Provincial Legislatures, we have made the arrangements set out in paragraph 20 below to give them a full representation upon all matters of special interest to minorities.

As regards representation of the smaller minorities, the decision taken by the political sovereign was that at a preliminary meeting of the Constituent Assembly proposed to be set up in pursuance of the Plan, an 'Advisory Committee on the rights of citizens, minorities and tribal and excluded areas' should be set up. Then, in paragraph 20 of the same Plan the following provision was made:

The Advisory Committee on the rights of citizens, minorities, and tribal and excluded areas should contain due representation of the interests affected, and their functions will be to report to the Union Constituent Assembly upon the list of Fundamental Rights, clauses for protecting minorities, and a scheme for the administration of the tribal and excluded areas, and to advise whether these rights should be incorporated in the Provincial, Group, or Union constitutions.

With reference to the administration of the country while constitution-making was in progress, the Plan declared that a Government having popular support was necessary and that the Viceroy hoped 'to form an interim Government in which all the portfolios, including that of War Member, will be held by Indian leaders having the full confidence of the people'. Nothing being said to indicate that there was to be a change in the status of the country or in the mode of Government under the Government of India Act, 1935, which was then in force, it seems clear that the interim Government was to operate under the Government of India Act, 1935. The statement containing the Plan closed with an appeal to the Indian people to implement the Plan which was intended 'to enable you to attain your independence in the shortest possible time and with the least danger of internal disturbances and conflict'. The hope was, however, expressed that the new independent India might choose to remain a member of the British Commonwealth. In pursuance of this Plan, a Constituent Assembly was set up in December 1946, but the refusal of the Muslim League Party to join this Constituent Assembly obliged His Majesty's Government in the United Kingdom to reconsider the situation, and eventually, a new Plan was announced on 3 June 1947 after further lengthy negotiations with the leaders of major political parties. The necessity for the new Plan appears from the following sentence contained in its first paragraph:

His Majesty's Government had hoped that it would be possible for the major parties to co-operate in the working out of the Cabinet Mission's Plan of 16 May 1946, and evolve for India a constitution acceptable to all concerned. This hope has not been fulfilled.

In other words the political initiative taken outside the then Constitution by the political sovereign had failed and the circumstances forced the political sovereign to continue its efforts to transfer political sovereignty to the Indian people on an altered basis. Again, it became incumbent upon the political sovereign to exercise political initiative at the highest level. The eventual result was the partition of India into two countries, namely, India and Pakistan. This document of 3 June 1947 furnishes another example of political initiative being taken practically in every sentence. Declaring once again that the intention of the political sovereign was that political power should be transferred in accordance with the wishes of the Indian people themselves, and that the framing of the ultimate Constitution for Indians was a matter for the Indians themselves, the Plan expressed the intention of the political sovereign to ascertain the wishes of the people on the question of partition of the country, which would involve the setting up of two separate Constituent Assemblies, through resolution of the Provincial Legislative Assemblies of Bengal, the Punjab and Sind, and by means of referenda in the North-West Frontier Province and in the district of Sylhet in Assam. The expression of views by these Muslim majority areas was declared to be the factor which would determine whether there were to be two countries or only one, two Constituent Assemblies or only one. It was declared that as regards the Indian States, the decision in the earlier Plan of 16 May 1946 remained unchanged. Finally, a most important announcement was made concerning the administrative arrangements during the period that constitution-making was in progress. It is contained in the following words:

The major political parties have repeatedly emphasised their desire that there should be the earliest possible transfer of power in India. With this desire His Majesty's Government are in full sympathy, and they are willing to anticipate the date June 1948 for the handing over of power by the setting up of an independent Indian Government or

327

Governments at an even earlier date. Accordingly, as the most expeditious, and indeed the only practicable way of meeting this desire, His Majesty's Government propose to introduce legislation during the current session for the transfer of power this year on a Dominion Status basis to one or two successor authorities according to the decisions taken as a result of this announcement. This will be without prejudice to the right of the Indian Constituent Assemblies to decide in due course whether or not the part of India in respect of which they have authority will remain within the British Commonwealth.

This last decision furnishes a most forcible illustration of the 'exercise of political initiative outside the constitutional instruments in force'. Dominion Status was not conceivable within the constitutional instrument which then was in force in India, namely, the Government of India Act, 1935. To grant Dominion status it was necessary that the political sovereign should perform an act of the highest political initiative, not in any legal field, but in the unfettered field of sovereign power.

The foregoing expositions of the principles which are, in my opinion, the governing principles by which any question regarding powers of the Governor-General under the existing Constitution must necessarily be gauged, enables me now to approach the final task of explaining the answers which I have proposed to the questions referred to this Court. The order in which the questions are placed is chronological but by no means logical. The fundamental question is Question 3 which is in the following terms: 'Whether the Constituent Assembly was rightly dissolved by the Governor-General?'

To this the answer which I have returned is in the following terms:

In view of the decision of the majority of the Judges in *Moulvi Tamizuddin Khan's* case, the Constituent Assembly as mentioned in the Indian Independence Act, 1947, is the 'Legislature of the Dominion' for the purposes of that Act, which also provides for the Governor-General to be the representative of Her Majesty for the purposes of the government of the Dominion. The majority of the Judges have also held that the Governor-General is invested with all the Royal prerogatives, except where barred by express words or necessary intendment. The prerogative of dissolution of the Legislature is recognised to exist in all representative institutions in the British Commonwealth of Nations, and there are no words in the relevant instruments, taking away,

328

expressly or by necessary intendment, this prerogative power in relation to the 'Legislature of the Dominion'. Consequently, the Governor-General must be held to possess the prerogative to dissolve the Constituent Assembly.

The indications to the contrary contained in the Government of India Act, 1935, affect the Federal Legislature, which, in the precise context, is not the same body as the 'Legislature of the Dominion'.

The exercise of a prerogative power is not a justiciable matter. Therefore, the question whether the act of dissolution was 'rightly' performed does not arise within this Court's jurisdiction, and the enquiry must be limited to the legality of the action.

In view of the answer to Question 4, viz. that after dissolving the Constituent Assembly, the Governor-General has the duty and the corresponding power to convene it afresh, the consideration that the Indian Independence Act, 1947, provided for the Constituent Assembly to perform a certain function' in the first instance' imports no restraint upon the exercise of this prerogative power, in point of time.

It is not necessary for me to explain any further the conclusion which I have reached that the power of dissolution of the Constituent Assembly arises from the circumstance that it is, as held in *Moulvi Tamizuddin Khan's* case, the Legislature of the Dominion, and that the Governor-General of the Dominion possesses all prerogatives of His Majesty, among which must necessarily be included the power of dissolving the principal Legislature of the Dominion. It was urged that the Indian Independence Act and the constitutional instruments which preceded it should be understood as laying down that there was to be only one Constituent Assembly, namely that set up by Lord Mountbatten for Pakistan on 26 July 1947, and that this Constituent Assembly should continue to exist and function until it has discharged its duty of providing a new Constitution for the country. Support was sought for this point of view from a speech of the Prime Minister of Pakistan made in the Constituent Assembly on 20 March 1954 in which the following passages occur:

The Members of this Assembly were given a mandate by the Federation to frame a Constitution for Pakistan. They must carry out that mandate. . . . They must continue as Members of the Constituent Assembly till the duty for which it was set up has been accomplished.

329

Reference was also made to the fact that a provision for the dissolution of the Federal Legislature contained in the Government of India Act, 1935, had been deliberately omitted at the adaptation of that act effected in advance of the transfer of power on 14 August 1947. It was pointed out also that a very powerful provision intended for employment in case of breakdown of the constitutional machinery as affecting the Federal Government, namely section 45, Government of India Act, had also been omitted from the Act. This provision enabled the Governor-General in cases of emergency to suspend the constitution and to govern the country if he so chose, without the aid of the Federal Legislature. By section 8, subsection (2) of the Indian Independence Act, it was declared that the powers of the Federal Legislature should be exercisable in the first instance by the Constituent Assembly. The inference was sought to be drawn from the omission of the power of dissolution of the Federal Legislature, and the omission of section 45 from the Government of India Act, 1935, that the Governor-General was to have no power of dissolution of the Constituent Assembly, or to interfere in any way with its working. If the position were that during the interim period, the Legislature of the Dominion was not yet in existence, it would in my opinion have been necessary to give serious consideration to this argument but, as it has now been held that from 14 August 1947 onwards, the Constituent Assembly was the Legislature of the Dominion, these considerations do not carry the same weight. For there is a strong presumption that the prerogative of dissolution of the Legislature of the Dominion vests in the Governor-General and if this presumption is to be dislodged, there must be either express provision to that effect, or the relevant instruments must, by necessary intendment, produce the same result. The Federal Legislature is not in the context of the existing constitutional instruments identical with the Legislature of the Dominion. Therefore, references in the Government of India Act which save the operation of the Federal Legislature cannot be extended to produce the same result in relation to the Legislature of the Dominion. It is clear that the prerogative of dissolution in relation to the Legislature of the Dominion is not excluded by express words.

Since the exercise of a prerogative power is not a justiciable matter, whether it is rightly or wrongly exercised is not a matter of law, and therefore not a suitable subject for expression of opinion by this Court. The use of the word 'rightly' in the question was necessitated by the circumstance that it was conceded in the present case and had been conceded in *Moulvi Tamizuddin Khan's* case as well that if the power of dissolution was available only outside the constitutional instruments, then the maxim *'fraus omnia corrumpit'* was applicable, and the validity of the action could be challenged on the ground of *mala fides*. It is, in my opinion, a source of satisfaction that as a result of the decision in the earlier case, the power of dissolution can be found to lie within these strictly legal limits of the prerogative. For otherwise, it would have been necessary to enter into questions of justification for the Governor-General's action, and in that connection to refer to a number of statements by the Head of the Government, namely the Prime Minister, of which the earliest in point is dated 1 April 1954 and the latest was made on 23 October 1954 about twelve hours before the issue of the Governor-General's Proclamation which declared that the Constituent Assembly could no longer function. Briefly, the statements operate to convey ample justification of the functioning of the Constituent Assembly. In the earliest statement it was said that the Constituent Assembly could not be dissolved nor could its Members resign until its specific task of framing a constitution for the country was accomplished, and that it would proceed with this task from 5 April onwards without interruption. The delay which had already occurred was justified on the ground that the Constituent Assembly had been at pains to secure the willing consent of all the Units of Pakistan to its proposals. Then, in a speech made on 15 September 1954 and a broadcast on 1 October 1954, reference was made to the fact that the Constituent Assembly was proceeding with its work with all possible speed, and that the first and the most important phase of constitution-making had been completed on 21 September 1954 when the House adopted the Report of the Basic Principles Committee. The final phase remained, namely, that of considering and passing the Draft Constitution Bill, and it was hoped that this would be completed by 25 December 1954. On 23 October 1954, it was publicly stated that the Constituent Assembly would pass the Constitution by that date.

The finding that the power of dissolution lies within the

prerogative relieves the Court of the duty of considering these undoubtedly weighty pronouncements with reference to Question 3.
All that I need add for the complete elucidation of my answer to
this question is that since it was conceded that the Governor-
General could not dissolve the Constituent Assembly unless he
had the power to re-convene it, the continued life of the Constituent Assembly until it had accomplished its task of providing a
working Constitution for the country which could operate after
the abolition of the Constituent Assembly, was assured. Therefore,
it cannot be urged that since by section 8 of the Indian Independence Act, 1947, certain powers are said to be exercisable 'in the
first instance' by the Constituent Assembly, there is any duty
upon the Governor-General not to exercise his power of dissolution for any period. So long as the Constituent Assembly does
not provide for the setting up of a 'Legislature of the Dominion'
its necessity for the operation of the existing Constitution remains.
But, once it has set up a Legislature of the Dominion, which will
by expression have the power of making provision as to the
constitution of Pakistan, the Constituent Assembly can, without
detriment to the country, eliminate itself as soon as the new
Legislature of the Dominion is complete. Until that time, it
seems to me that the Governor-General cannot be said, in law,
not to possess the power of dissolving the Constituent Assembly.
I do not concern myself with the consideration of particular
circumstances in which he may or may not dissolve the Constituent Assembly, in the *proper* exercise of his powers. That is a
matter within the Governor-General's discretion, and is subject
to recognised conventions. But it is no part of the duty of this
Court to advise upon matters of convention.

Question 4 is in the following terms : 'Whether the Constituent
Convention proposed to be set up by the Governor-General is
competent to exercise the powers conferred by sub-section (1) of
section 8 of the Indian Independence Act, 1947, on the Constituent Assembly?'

I have returned the following answer :

The powers conferred by Section 8 of the Indian Independence
Act, 1947, on the Constituent Assembly, can only be exercised
by a successor body, of the same name, summoned by the
Governor-General, in the discharge of a duty so to do, which

arises out of, and is complementary to, his order dissolving the Constituent Assembly. The duty of summoning does not involve, and cannot include, the exercise of any political initiative outside the constitutional instruments in force. It must be performed in accordance with the basic principles which were expressly followed in the setting up of the Constituent Assembly of 1947. These basic principles are stated with clarity in paragraph 18 of the Statement of the Cabinet Delegation and His Excellency the Viceroy and Governor-General of India, issued on 16 May 1946.

This answer obviously proceeds upon the basis that by the Proclamation of 24 October 1954, the Governor-General has acted, not to abolish the Constituent Assembly, but has merely exercised his prerogative of dissolving the Legislature of the Dominion, which for the time being is the Constituent Assembly. It is perfectly clear that for the Governor-General to continue the Federal Government without a Legislature is entirely contrary to the letter and spirit of the existing constitutional instruments by which he is himself governed. Therefore having dissolved the Constituent Assembly, it is his duty to reconvene it. So much was conceded by the Senior Counsel appearing for the Federation of Pakistan. Therefore, it is clear that what is to be convened is the Constituent Assembly, and this is essential for the working of the existing Constitution, viz. the Indian Independence Act, 1947. Consequently, the Assembly which the Governor-General is proposing to convene must be called the Constituent Assembly, if it is to be that body which alone has been entrusted with legislative powers by the existing constitution. It is immaterial that it may be called by another name or names as well, but it is essential that it should be called the Constituent Assembly.

It is with some regret that I find myself at variance with my Lord the Chief Justice and my learned brothers in regard to the manner adopted by the Governor-General for reconvening the Constituent Assembly. I find, however, that I am supported by the majority in relation at least to the validity of the proposal that the Governor-General should nominate a number of members to the new Constituent Assembly. I base my objection to this proposal upon the comprehensive basis that, in adopting this particular mode of securing representation for certain areas, the Governor-General is exceeding the limits of his power as a constitutional head, working within the relevant constitutional instruments. He is not a political sovereign, and political initiative outside the existing constitutional instruments must, in my opinion, be denied to him. It was urged with great force that the Plans of 16 May 1946 and 3 June 1947 are not law, and therefore do not provide an electoral law binding upon the Governor-General in relation to the reconvening of the Constituent Assembly. The view which I prefer to take is this. The original Constituent Assembly was elected upon the basis of these two instruments, and I therefore look to these two instruments for the electoral law which governed the constitution of that Constituent Assembly. No other electoral law having been passed in the meantime and it being now necessary to reconvene the Constituent Assembly in the absence of any enactment by the Constituent Assembly providing for its own reconstitution I can see no alternative for a constitutional head like the Governor-General, but to repeat as nearly as may be, with the minimum of adaptation necessary to provide for the changed circumstances, the process by which the first Constituent Assembly was constituted by the then Governor-General, expressly in pursuance of the Plans mentioned above.

In one respect, the Governor-General is clearly exceeding his legal authority, and that is in making provision for representation of the States and tribal areas. By the proviso to section 19, subsection (3), Indian Independence Act, 1947, it is clearly made a function of the Constituent Assembly to provide for the representation of the States and the tribal areas. The Governor-General's assumption of power to appoint persons to represent these areas is therefore clearly *ultra vires*. But in my opinion, it is no less clearly an excess of his power, if he departs from the basic principles set out in paragraph 18 of the Plan of 16 May 1947 in convening the Constituent Assembly afresh. The relevant extract from paragraph 18 has already been quoted above, and I need therefore say no more on this subject.

Question 1 is in the following terms: 'What are the powers and responsibilities of the Governor-General in respect of the government of the country before the new Constituent Convention passes the necessary legislation?'

The answer I have returned is as follows:

'The powers and responsibilities of the Governor-General during the period in question are those defined and delimited

334

by the Indian Independence Act, 1947, as in force on 24 October 1954.'

It is obviously impossible to return a detailed answer, enumerating all the powers and responsibilities in question. In the view which I take, the Governor-General, as a constitutional head, is obliged to find his powers in the existing constitutional instruments, and to employ them for the discharge of his responsibilities under that constitution.

Question 2 is in the following terms:

The Federal Court having held in *Usif Patel's* case that the laws listed in the Schedule to the Emergency Powers Ordinance could not be validated under section 42 of the Government of India Act, 1935, nor retrospective effect given to them, and no legislature competent to validate such laws being in existence, is there any provision in the Constitution or any rule of law applicable to the situation by which the Governor-General can by order or otherwise declare that all orders made, decisions taken, and other acts done under those laws shall be valid and enforceable and those laws which cannot without danger to the State be removed from the existing legal system shall be treated as part of the law of the land until the question of their validation is determined by the new Constituent Convention?

The answer which I have returned is as follows:

(*a*) There is no provision in the Constitution and no rule of law applicable to the situation, by which the Governor-General can, in the light of this Court's decision in the case of *Usif Patel*, by proclamation or otherwise, validate the laws enumerated in the Schedule to the Emergency Powers Ordinance, 1955, whether temporarily or permanently.

(*b*) The expression 'laws which cannot without danger to the State be removed from the existing legal system' is altogether vague, and therefore no answer can be offered to the second part of the question.

The legislative powers of the Governor-General under the existing Constitution are confined within the terms of section 42, Government of India Act, 1935. Those powers are sufficient to enable the Governor-General to stay all proceedings in courts other than the Federal Court, in which the legal provisions referred to are called in question, pending such action as the proposed Constituent Convention (Constitutional Assembly) may see fit to take in respect thereof.

In this answer I have indicated that any embarrassment caused through multiplicity of legal proceedings which have arisen in consequence of the decision of this Court in *Moulvi Tamizuddin Khan's* case may be avoided by the exercise of certain powers which the Governor-General possesses in relation to the jurisdiction of all courts other than the Federal Court. (In view of certain existing proclamations under section 102, Government of India Act, it seems plain that the powers of the Governor-General in this respect can be construed as covering all the three legislative lists in the Seventh Schedule to the Government of India Act.) This suggestion, it must be admitted, is of a speculative nature and necessarily so on account of the failure to provide in the reference, any indication of the nature of the inconvenience which the Federal Government was concerned to avoid.

But on the general question, I am in no doubt whatsoever, that the Governor-General is confined by his Commission and the existing constitutional instruments within the powers that he can derive from these documents. As is stated by Dr Keith in his book *Responsible Government in the Dominions* at p. 84, 'the Governor is charged with the duty of obeying the law himself and of encouraging obedience to it in others'. The learned writer speaks of occasions when the Governor in a Dominion may be justified in breaking the law in the exercise of extraordinary powers, but in a lengthy chapter upon this subject, the only occasions which are enumerated by him to illustrate these powers are those upon which it became necessary to declare martial law and certain other occasions where the requirement arose in relation to public order. Such extraordinary powers are generally confined to matters affecting the property and the persons of individual subjects. The existence of an emergency, say a state of war or a large-scale disturbance, may justify the executive in making an order commandeering all private motor vehicles. Similar circumstances may justify entry by officers of the executive upon privately owned premises which are, in the eye of the ordinary law, inviolable. In a more stringent emergency, the services of members of the public may be requisitioned for the purposes of carrying out works or otherwise offering resistance to check a calamity or offering resistance to an enemy.

This is well understood to be the condition in the United

Kingdom and in the countries of the British Commonwealth. In the United States of America also, the operation of the maxim 'necessity knows no law' is recognised but only in relation to matters falling within the *police powers of the State*. In the words of Blackstone, these powers may be defined as including 'the due regulation and domestic order of the Kingdom whereby the inhabitants of a State, like members of a well-governed family, are bound to conform their general behaviour to the rules of propriety, good neighbourhood, and good manners, and to be decent, industrious, and inoffensive in their respective stations'.

That is a sufficiently comprehensive statement, but it is clearly very far removed from the powers of interference with constitutional instruments. On this subject, it seems to me that it is unnecessary to attempt a fresh exposition of the legal position. That has already been given by a Full Bench of this Court as recently as 12 April 1955 in the case of *Usif Patel* (cited above). A few preliminary facts may be stated with advantage before I reproduce the relevant extracts from the judgment. The appellants in that case were held in custody in pursuance of an Act which had been made by the Governor of Sind purporting to act under powers derived from section 92A, Government of India Act. This section had been inserted in the said Act by an order made under section 9 of the Indian Independence Act, 1947, by the Governor-General. This power of the Governor-General under section 9 of the Indian Independence Act, 1947, in its original shape was expressed to expire on 31 March 1948, but this date was altered to 31 March 1949 by section 2 of the Indian Independence (Amendment) Act, 1948, passed by the Constituent Assembly, to which the assent of the Governor-General had not been obtained. As a result of this Court's decision in *Moulvi Tamizuddin Khan's* case, the extension of the date by one year became invalid without the Governor-General's assent, and consequently all action taken by the Governor-General under section 9 of the Indian Independence Act, 1947, after 31 March 1948, and all consequential action by other authorities, became invalid. A great many other laws and executive action thereunder were affected in the same way, and to meet the difficulty, the Governor-General issued an Ordinance No. IX of 1955 entitled the Emergency Powers Ordinance, 1955. This Ordinance was expressed to be made 'in exercise of the powers conferred by sub-section (1) of section 42 of the Government of India Act, 1935 (26 Geo. 5 ch. 2) and of *all other powers enabling him in that behalf*. The following provision was contained in section 2 (1) of this Ordinance:

2. Validity of certain laws, etc. (1) Whereas none of the laws passed by the Constituent Assembly of Pakistan under the provisions of sub-section (1) of section 8 of the Indian Independence Act, 1947 (10 & 11 Geo. 6 ch. 30), hereafter in this section referred to as the said Act, received the assent of the Governor-General in accordance with sub-section 3 of section 6 of the said Act, it is hereby declared and enacted that every law specified in column 1 of the Schedule to this Ordinance shall be deemed to have received the assent of the Governor-General on the date specified in column 2 of that Schedule, being the date on which it was published in the official *Gazette*, and shall be deemed to have had legal force and effect from that date.

The question was raised that in purporting to give assent to constitutional legislation by the Constituent Assembly with retrospective effect, the Governor-General was acting beyond his authority. In view of the last words of the sub-section quoted above, namely that the laws in question 'shall be deemed to have had legal force and effect from that date', it is clear that what the Governor-General purported to do was to legislate in the constitutional field with effect from a date in the past. This Court in the most emphatic terms declared that the Governor-General had no power to do so. I may state here, having been a member of the Bench which heard that case, that the Advocate-General, when questioned on the precise point, declared that the Governor-General had made the Ordinance under section 42, Government of India Act only, and no claim was made regarding the existence of any 'other powers enabling him in that behalf'.

The relevant observations of this Court appear in the judgment of my Lord the Chief Justice, with whom each of the other four Judges agreed, and are as follows:

The rule hardly requires any explanation, much less emphasis, that a Legislature cannot validate an invalid law if it does not possess the power to legislate on the subject to which the invalid law relates, the principle governing validation being that validation being itself legislation you cannot validate what you cannot legislate upon. Therefore if the Federal Legislature, in the absence of a provision expressly authorising it to do so, was incompetent to amend the Indian Independence

338

Act or the Government of India Act, the Governor-General possessing no larger powers than those of the Federal Legislature was equally incompetent to amend either of those Acts by an Ordinance. Under the Independence Act the authority competent to legislate on constitutional matters being the Constituent Assembly, it is that Assembly alone which can amend those Acts. The learned Advocate-General alleges that the Constituent Assembly has been dissolved and that therefore validating powers cannot be exercised by that Assembly. In *Mr Tamizuddin Khan's* case, we did not consider it necessary to decide the question whether the Constituent Assembly was lawfully dissolved but assuming that it was, the effect of the dissolution can certainly not be the transfer of its powers to the Governor-General. The Governor-General can give or withhold his assent to the legislation of the Constituent Assembly but he himself is not the Constituent Assembly and on its disappearance he can neither claim powers which he never possessed nor claim to succeed to the powers of that assembly. . . .

. . . So that we may now be understood more clearly, let me repeat that the power of the Legislature of the Dominion for the purpose of making provision as to the constitution of the Dominion could under sub-section (1) of section 8 of the Indian Independence Act be exercised only by the Constituent Assembly and that that power could not be exercised by that Assembly when it functioned as the Federal Legislature within the limits imposed upon it by the Government of India Act, 1935. It is, therefore, not right to claim for the Federal Legislature the power of making provision as to the constitution of the Dominion—a claim which is specifically negatived by sub-section (1) of section 8 of the Indian Independence Act. If the constitutional position were otherwise, the Governor-General could by an Ordinance repeal the whole of the Indian Independence Act and the Government of India Act and assume to himself all powers of legislation. A more incongruous position in a democratic constitution is difficult to conceive, particularly when the Legislature itself, which can control the Governor-General's action, is alleged to have been dissolved.

This Court held in *Mr Tamizuddin Khan's* case that the Constituent Assembly was not a sovereign body. But that did not mean that if the Assembly was not a sovereign body the Governor-General was. We took pains to explain at length in that case that the position of the Governor-General in Pakistan is that of a constitutional Head of the State, namely, a position very similar to that occupied by the King in the United Kingdom. That position which was supported by Mr Diplock is now being repudiated by the learned Advocate-General, and on the ground of emergency every kind of power is being claimed for the Head of the State. Let us say clearly if we omitted to say so in the previous case that under the Constitutional Acts the Governor-General is possessed of no more powers than those that are given to him by those Acts. One of these powers is to promulgate Ordinances in cases of emergency but the limits within which and the checks subject to which he can exercise that power are clearly laid down in section 42 itself. . . . Any legislative provision that relates to a constitutional matter is solely within the powers of the Constituent Assembly and the Governor-General is under the Constitution Acts precluded from exercising those powers. . . . If the position created by the judgment in the present case is that past constitutional legislations cannot be validated by the Governor-General, but only by the Legislature, it is for the Law Department of the Government to ponder over the resultant situation and to advise the Government accordingly.

After the pronouncement of the judgment in *Usif Patel's* case, the Governor-General issued a Proclamation on 16 April 1955 which, after a series of preliminary recitals, contained the following operative provisions:

(1) The Governor-General assumes to himself until other provision is made by the Constituent Convention such powers as are necessary to validate and enforce laws needed to avoid a possible breakdown in the constitutional and administrative machinery of the country and to preserve the State and maintain the government of the country in its existing condition.

(2) For the purposes aforesaid it is hereby declared that the laws mentioned in the Schedule to the Emergency Powers Ordinance, 1955, shall, subject to any report from the Federal Court of Pakistan, be regarded as having been valid and enforceable from the dates specified in that Schedule.

Comparison of the provision in paragraph 2 above with that contained in section 2, sub-section (1) of the Emergency Powers Ordinance, 1955, will show that the Governor-General has purported to do once again, but on this occasion, 'subject to any report from the Federal Court of Pakistan', what had been held in *Usif Patel's* case to be in excess of his powers. On this occasion, no reference has been made to any powers conferred by any statute which the Governor-General is purporting to exercise. It has been argued that the action thus taken is one taken in an extreme emergency, to save the State from dissolution, and is relatable to powers derived from the maxim *salus populi suprema lex*.

The scope and content of this maxim were fully canvassed before the Court in the earlier case of *Moulvi Tamizuddin Khan*, by the Senior Counsel for the Federation of Pakistan. It was possible for the Advocate-General of Pakistan, who attended the proceedings in *Moulvi Tamizuddin Khan's* case throughout, to have relied upon the powers derived from this maxim, when he was asked in *Usif Patel's* case to refer the Court to the specific sources from which the Governor-General derived power to make constitutional law with retrospective effect. (For the validation of such law with retrospective effect undoubtedly is tantamount to making such law.) No reliance was placed by the Advocate-General of Pakistan at that stage upon the maxim *salus populi suprema lex*, but the argument, based upon this maxim, that the Governor-General possessed powers over and above those contained in the constitutional instruments in force which he was competent to exercise in an emergency, was fully present to the mind of the Court. This appears clearly from several passages in the extracts from the judgment in *Usif Patel's* case which I have reproduced above. It was said for instance that the Advocate-General of Pakistan was repudiating a position previously supported by Mr Diplock, and 'on the ground of emergency every kind of power is being claimed for the Head of the State'. The effect of that judgment is, in my opinion, to make it clear that in relation to the very situation which the Proclamation of 16 April 1955 is intended to remedy, this Court was emphatically of the view that the Governor-General could not invoke any powers except such as were available to him under the constitutional instruments in force. To that opinion, I steadfastly adhere, and nothing which has been said in the arguments in the *Reference* affords, in my view, sufficient justification for varying that finding, which constitutes law declared by this Court under section 212, Government of India Act, 1935.

The case might have been different if the Governor-General were not, as must be held on the authorities, a mere constitutional head. If he were a political sovereign, he might have claimed such powers as, for instance, the King of England was advised that he could exercise:

(i) in 1723, in relation to the colony of New Jersey in America, to determine the electoral right by prescribing the qualifications of electors, and varying constituencies, in the absence of a local electoral law;

(ii) in 1747, in relation to the colony of New Hampshire in America, to increase the number of constituencies;

(iii) in 1690, by appointment of a Governor for Maryland, in

341

America, in respect of which Lord Baltimore had incurred forfeiture of the charter held by him, in advance of the forfeiture being enforced; or

(iv) in 1752, in relation to the colony of Georgia in America, upon surrender of the charter, to authorise magistrates and other public officers by proclamation under the Great Seal, in advance of the establishment of a new system of administration.

As I am clearly of the opinion that similar special powers are not available to the Governor-General, I will not further lengthen this opinion by discussing the value of these opinions which have been made available from Chalmers, *Opinions of Eminent Lawyers*, whether categorically or intrinsically. Nor is it of advantage, from the viewpoint which seems to me to be the only correct viewpoint, to discuss the applicability of the *Shipmoney Case*. These affairs belong to periods when, and to territories where, the power of the King was, in fact, supreme and undisputed. The records of these affairs are hardly the kind of scripture which one could reasonably expect to be quoted in a proceeding which is essentially one in the enforcement and maintenance of representative institutions. For they can bring but cold comfort to any protagonist of the autocratic principle against the now universal rule that the will of the people is sovereign. In the case of North America, the territory was lost eventually to the British Crown through the maintenance of just such reactionary opinions, as those which Senior Counsel for the Federation of Pakistan has been pleased to advance for acceptance by the Court. And in the English case, the fate of the King, and the Judges who delivered the opinion favouring absolute power in the King, stands for all time as a warning against absolutism, and as a landmark in the struggle for the freedom and eventual sovereignty of the people.

It is perfectly clear, in my opinion, that in respect of the exercise of political initiative outside the constitutional instruments in force, the position since the Partition has been exactly the same as in regard to variation of the existing constitutional instruments, viz. that the power vests exclusively in the Constituent Assembly, and that the Governor-General can claim no share in the positive exercise of that power.

MUHAMMAD SHARIF, J.—At the time of her start as an independent Dominion on 15 August 1947 Pakistan was to be

342

governed under the Indian Independence Act, 1947, and in accordance with sub-section (2) of section 8 of this Act. It is as follows:

(2) Except in so far as other provision is made by or in accordance with a law made by the Constituent Assembly of the Dominion under sub-section (1) of this section, each of the new Dominions and all Provinces and other parts thereof shall be governed as nearly as may be in accordance with the Government of India Act, 1935; and the provisions of that Act, and of the Orders in Council, rules and other instruments made thereunder, shall, so far as applicable, and subject to any express provisions of this Act, and with such omissions, additions, adaptations and modifications as may be specified in orders of the Governor-General under the next succeeding section, have effect accordingly.

The omissions, additions, etc., were made by the Governor-General of the united India by virtue of the authority given to him under section 9 of the Indian Independence Act. As a result, the Government of India Act, 1935, was brought into conformity with the letter and spirit of the Indian Independence Act and the Act so adapted was to be considered the Government of India Act, 1935, from 15 August 1947 onwards. It established a federal form of Government. The above Constitution Act could only be changed or amended by the Constituent Assembly exercising the powers of the Legislature of the Dominion for the purpose of making provision as to the constitution of the Dominion (see sub-section (1) of section 8 of the Indian Independence Act). Section 6 details the plenitude of the powers of the Legislature of the Dominion to make laws of the Dominion to which the Governor-General 'shall have full power to assent' under sub-section (3) of this section. In other words, the laws were to be made by the Legislature of the Dominion and the Governor-General's assent would render them operative. Thus the Governor-General was only a constituent part of his legislative machinery and none of the parts could independently perform the functions of the Legislature of the Dominion. Both must conjoin and act together to produce the result. At p. 18 of his *Constitutional Law*, 7th ed., Professor Keith observes: 'The case of *Stockdale* v. *Hansard*[1] is instructive as showing that neither House can by its own

[1] (1839), 9 Ad. & E. 1.

343

resolution negative the effect of an Act of Parliament, nor make any new law.'

The powers of the Governor-General to promulgate Ordinances during the recess of the Federal Legislature are described in section 42 of the Government of India Act. The relevant portion reads as follows:

42 (1) The Governor-General may, in cases of emergency, make and promulgate ordinances for the peace and good government of Pakistan or any part thereof, and any ordinance so made shall have the like force of law as an Act passed by the Federal Legislature, but the power of making ordinances under this section is subject to the like restrictions as the power of the Federal Legislature to make laws, and any ordinance made under this section may be controlled or superseded by any such Act.

. . .　　. . .　　. . .

(3) An ordinance promulgated under this section after the thirty-first day of December 1949, shall be laid before the Federal Legislature and shall cease to operate at the expiration of six weeks from the re-assembly of the Legislature, or, if before the expiration of that period a resolution disapproving it is passed by the Legislature, upon the passing of that resolution.

On the making of a proclamation by the Governor-General under section 102 of the Government of India Act, 1935, that a grave emergency exists whereby the security or economic life of Pakistan or any part thereof is threatened by war or internal disturbance or circumstances arising out of any mass movement of population from or into Pakistan, the Federal Legislature shall have power to make laws for a Province or any part thereof with respect to any of the matters enumerated in the Provincial Legislative List, or to make laws, whether or not for a Province or any part thereof, with respect to any matter not enumerated in any of the Lists in the Seventh Schedule to this Act. Sub-section (5) of this section reads as follows:

(5) A Proclamation of Emergency declaring that the security or economic life of Pakistan is threatened by war or internal disturbance or circumstances arising out of any mass movement of population from or into Pakistan may be made before the actual occurrence of war or disturbance or circumstances if the Governor-General is satisfied that there is imminent danger thereof.

It means that, where an emergency has been proclaimed, the Federal Legislature can also trespass into the Provincial field, from

344

which it is ordinarily kept out, or legislate on the other matters referred to in section 102, but the Federal Legislature would still be acting within the framework of the Government of India Act, 1935, of which it is the creation. It can in no circumstances transcend the boundaries of the statute itself. Consequently, the Governor-General, acting under section 42 of the Government of India Act, could not do better or exercise greater powers than the Federal Legislature. On the other hand, while the Governor-General is so acting, there must be in existence the Federal Legislature or, if it is under dissolution, its successor must be in sight. To think that the Governor-General can govern without the Federal Legislature is a notion wholly repugnant to the Government of India Act.

Section 42 is the only provision in the Government of India Act which empowers the Governor-General to legislate under exceptional circumstances and its limitations have been defined above. There used to be section 45 where the Governor-General was invested with extraordinary powers in the case of failure of constitutional machinery and he could assume to himself all or any of the powers vested in or exercisable by any Federal body or authority. The only check imposed was that the Governor-General could not assume to himself any of the powers vested in or exercisable by the Federal Court to suspend, either in whole or in part, the operation of any provision of the Act relating to the Federal Court. This section, however, was omitted by the adaptations made under section 9 of the Indian Independence Act and could not, therefore, be availed of after 15 August 1947.

It must follow from the above that in an emergency, howsoever grave it might be, the Governor-General could not legislate on matters which fell beyond the purview of the Federal Legislature. It has been shown above that the amendment of the existing constitution can only be made by the Constituent Assembly, acting under sub-section (1) of section 8 of the Indian Independence Act. In the recent case of *Usif Patel* v. *The Crown*, decided by this Court on 12 April 1955, it was laid down that

under the Constitution Acts the Governor-General is possessed of no more powers than those that are given to him by those Acts. One of these powers is to promulgate Ordinances in cases of emergency but the limits within which and the checks subject to which he can exercise

345

that power are clearly laid down in section 42 itself. On principle the power of the Governor-General to legislate by ordinances is always subject to the control of the Federal Legislature and he cannot remove these controls merely by asserting that no Federal Legislature in law or in fact is in existence. No such position is contemplated by the Indian Independence Act, or the Government of India Act, 1935. Any legislative provision that relates to a constitutional matter is solely within the powers of the Constituent Assembly, and the Governor-General is under the Constitution Acts precluded from exercising those powers. The sooner this position is realised the better. And if any one read anything to the contrary in the previous judgment of this Court, all that I can say is that we were grievously misunderstood. If the position created by the judgment in the present case is that past constitutional legislation cannot be validated by the Governor-General but only by the Legislature, it is for the Law Department of the Government to ponder over the resultant situation and to advise the Government accordingly.

Earlier, in the same judgment, it was observed:

The rule hardly requires any explanation, much less emphasis, that a Legislature cannot validate an invalid law if it does not possess the power to legislate on the subject to which the invalid law relates, the principle governing validation being that validation being itself legislation you cannot validate what you cannot legislate upon. Therefore if the Federal Legislature, in the absence of a provision expressly authorising it to do so, was incompetent to amend the Indian Independence Act or the Government of India Act, the Governor-General possessing no larger powers than those of the Federal Legislature was equally incompetent to amend either of those Acts by an Ordinance. Under the Independence Act the authority competent to legislate on constitutional matters being the Constituent Assembly, it is that Assembly alone which can amend those Acts.

There is thus left no room for doubt that on constitutional matters the Governor-General is not competent to legislate and cannot, therefore, by his own act make valid laws which he himself could not enact. Realising this difficulty, the learned counsel for the Government had recourse to dicta like 'salus populi suprema lex' and 'necessity makes lawful what is otherwise unlawful'. These have been sometimes invoked in times of war or other national disaster to infringe private rights or commandeer private property, but we have not been referred to any authority or reported case where, under the stress of circumstances created by some interpretation of law, these were extended to embrace

346

changes in constitutional law. It might on occasions lead to dangerous consequences if in any real or supposed emergency of which the head of the State alone must be the judge, the constitutional structure itself could be tampered with. It has a sanctity of its own which is not to be violated. My answer, therefore, to Question No. 2 is that it is beyond the authority of the Governor-General, both under the Constitutional and the general law, to do even for a short period what the Constituent Assembly alone could do.

S. A. RAHMAN, J.—I respectfully concur in the answers proposed to be returned by my Lord the Chief Justice to the questions as finally formulated in this *Reference* and agree generally with the reasoning by which they are supported. I venture to add in respect of the answer to Question 2 that while accepting the validity and applicability of the supreme principle of necessity embodied in the maxim '*salus populi suprema lex*' to the constitutional impasse to which the country had been reduced, I was nevertheless anxious that no more than the minimum of powers requisite to meet this special contingency ought to be conceded in favour of the Governor-General. I was, therefore, at first inclined to hold that a power in the Governor-General to declare a sort of judicial moratorium so as to prevent all Courts from going on with proceedings or cases in which the validity of the relevant laws was canvassed, till such time as the new Constituent Assembly could provide legal cover for those laws, might be regarded as the judicially recognisable desideratum; some doubt, however, existed whether such an order passed by the Governor-General would be effective to save all such laws from the onslaught of forensic ingenuity during the interregnum. I was, therefore, persuaded that in the special circumstances envisaged in the *Reference* there was no alternative to recording the finding, consistently with the supreme law of necessity, that the Governor-General could exercise temporarily the powers of validation with retrospective effect, so as to prevent a constitutional breakdown.

Question No. 1.   What are the powers and responsibilities of the Governor-General in respect of the government of the country before the new Constituent Convention passes the necessary legislation?

Answer.   That this question is too general and need not be answered.

Question No. 2.   The Federal Court having held in *Usif Patel's* case that the laws listed in the Schedule to the Emergency Powers Ordinance could not be validated under section 42 of the Government of India Act, 1935, nor retrospective effect given to them, and no legislature competent to validate such laws being in existence, is there any provision in the Constitution or any rule of law applicable to the situation by which the Governor-General can by order or otherwise declare that all orders made, decisions taken, and other acts done under those laws shall be valid and enforceable and those laws which cannot without danger to the State be removed from the existing legal system shall be treated as part of the law of the land until the question of their validation is determined by the new Constituent Convention?

Answer.   That in the situation presented by the *Reference* the Governor-General has during the interim period the power under the common law of civil or state necessity of retrospectively validating the laws listed in the Schedule to the Emergency Powers Ordinance, 1955, and all those laws, until the question of their validation is decided upon by the Constituent Assembly, are during the aforesaid period valid and enforceable in the same way as if they had been valid from the date on which they purported to come into force.

Question No. 3.   Whether the Constituent Assembly was rightly dissolved by the Governor-General.

Answer.   That on the facts stated in the *Reference*, namely, (i) that the Constituent Assembly, though it functioned for more than 7 years, was unable to carry out the duty to frame a constitution for Pakistan to replace the transitional constitution provided by the Indian Independence Act, 1947; (ii) that in view of the repeated representations from and resolutions passed by representative bodies throughout the country the Constituent Assembly, in the opinion of the Governor-General, became in course of time wholly unrepresentative of the people of Pakistan and ceased to be responsible to them; (iii) that for all practical purposes the Constituent Assembly assumed the form of a perpetual legislature; and (iv) that throughout the period of its existence the Constituent Assembly asserted that the provisions made by it for the constitution of the Dominion under sub-section (1) of section 8 of the Indian Independence Act were valid laws without the consent of the Governor-General, the Governor-General had, under section 5 of the Indian Independence Act, legal authority to dissolve the Constituent Assembly.

Question No. 4. Whether the Constituent Convention, proposed to be set up by the Governor-General, is competent to exercise the powers conferred by sub-section (1) of section 8 of the Indian Independence Act, 1947, on the Constituent Assembly.

Answer. That subject to this:

(i) that the correct name of the Constituent Convention is Constituent Assembly;

(ii) that the Governor-General's right to dissolve the Assembly can only be derived from the Indian Independence Act;

(iii) that the arrangements for representation of States and Tribal Areas can, under the proviso to sub-section (3) of section 19 of the Indian Independence Act, be made only by the Constituent Assembly and not by the Governor-General; and

(iv) that the Governor-General's duty being to bring into existence a representative legislative institution he can only nominate the electorate and not members to the Constituent Assembly;

the new Assembly, constituted under the Constituent Convention Order, 1955, as amended to date, would be competent to exercise all the powers conferred by the Indian Independence Act, 1947, on the Constituent Assembly including those under section 8 of that Act.

JUDGMENT

IN THE CASE OF

FEDERATION OF PAKISTAN

v.

ALI AHMAD HUSSAIN SHAH AND THE UNION OF INDIA

IN THE
FEDERAL COURT OF PAKISTAN
(APPELLATE JURISDICTION)

CIVIL APPEAL
NO. 14 OF 1953

(On appeal from the judgment and decree of the High Court of Judicature at Lahore, dated 23 January 1946, in Regular First Appeal No. 286 of 1943)

Federation of Pakistan, appellant, v. *Ali Ahmad Hussain Shah*, son of *Sayed Muhammad Allah Wasaya Shah*, plaintiff, *Union of India*, respondents.

Present: Muhammad Munir, C.J., A. S. M. Akram, A. R. Cornelius, Muhammad Sharif, and S. A. Rahman, JJ.

MUHAMMAD MUNIR, C.J.—I concur in the order proposed by my brother Cornelius to be made in this appeal, and in the view that the appeal is a Pakistan appeal. But on the main point in the case, I regret, I differ from him.

In *Special Reference No. 1 of 1955*, by the Governor-General under section 213 of the Government of India Act, 1935, this Court has recently expressed the opinion that the Increase and Re-distribution of Seats Act, 1949, by which the Constituent Assembly added six members to its personnel without obtaining to that Act the assent of the Governor-General was invalid, and that therefore the Constituent Assembly, after the addition of these six members, ceased to be the Constituent Assembly for Pakistan, as defined in section 19 (3) (b) of the Indian Independence Act, 1947. This result must follow unless, contrary to this Court's decision in *Moulvi Tamizuddin Khan's* case, we are prepared to hold that the Constituent Assembly could, without a properly assented Act, add any number of persons to itself. The general rule is that if a legislature illegally adds to its members and the persons so added take part in discussion and voting, the

23—C.P.P.   353

laws passed by it are void. In the case of companies and statutory bodies, like municipal corporations, the rule is well settled that the proceedings of such bodies are vitiated by strangers taking part in and voting at their meetings. Section 66 of the Government of India Act, 1935, which provides that the Provincial Legislature shall have power to act notwithstanding any vacancy in the membership thereof, and that any proceedings in that legislature shall be valid notwithstanding that it is discovered subsequently that some person who was not entitled so to do, sat or voted or otherwise took part in the proceedings, is an express departure from that general principle. This section was intended to provide that the laws passed by a Provincial Legislature are valid, even though a vacancy be subsequently filled, or some person who took part in the proceedings was subsequently unseated as the result of an election petition. There was a similar provision, section 23, in the Government of India Act, 1935, for the Federal Legislature, but it was omitted in the adaptations, because elections to the Constituent Assembly as defined by section 19 (3) (b) of the Indian Independence Act, 1947, were not at that time contemplated and since that Constituent Assembly was also to function as the Federal Legislature, no question of any member being subsequently unseated or being disqualified on an election petition was considered to be possible.

Section 19 (3) (b) of the Indian Independence Act, 1947, contains an exact definition of the Constituent Assembly of Pakistan and it is that Assembly, as altered by any action taken under the proviso to sub-section (3) of section 19, alone which was competent to pass constitutional laws under sub-section (1) of section 8 of that Act. And since the Privy Council (Abolition of Jurisdiction) Act, 1950, was passed not by the Constituent Assembly as defined by section 19 (3) (b), but by that Assembly with six illegally added members, it was not a valid law, having been passed by an illegally constituted legislature of the Dominion. The question then is whether that Act can at present be held to be valid on any other ground. If my view about the illegal constitution of the Assembly be correct, then it is unnecessary to discuss the question whether the subsequent assent of the Governor-General to the Act would make it valid, because the Governor-General, unless it be a case of necessity, has no authority

354

to give assent to laws which are not passed by a properly constituted legislature. The Act is one of those Acts which have been validated by the Governor-General by his Proclamation of Emergency of 16 April 1955. In the *Special Reference* mentioned above this Court has held that, in the circumstances existing at the time of that Proclamation, the Governor-General under the law of civil necessity had the authority temporarily and retrospectively to validate those Acts. The correctness of that opinion is accepted by learned counsel on both sides. If we were to hold that the Abolition of Jurisdiction Act has not been properly validated and is not law today, the consequences would be:

(i) that hundreds of persons will have lost their right of appeal to the Privy Council;

(ii) that hundreds of judgments of this Court are void;

(iii) that persons whose capital sentences were confirmed by the High Courts, but who were acquitted by this Court, will have to be hanged;

(iv) that hundreds of persons whose sentences of imprisonment were set aside by this Court will have to go back to jail;

(v) that judgments relating to property and other civil rights, by which this Court interfered with the judgments of the High Courts, are void, and that such property and rights have been illegally affected.

These results follow specifically from the invalidity of only one law. In the aforesaid *Special Reference* the result which followed from the invalidity of constitutional laws consequent on the judgment of this Court in *Moulvi Tamizuddin Khan's* case was stated to be that forty-four constitutional Acts passed by the Constituent Assembly to which the assent of the Governor-General was not obtained had become invalid, and in consequence:

(i) all action taken after 31 March 1948 in pursuance of orders made under section 9 of the Indian Independence Act, 1947, was invalid, including the insertion of section 92A to the Government of India Act, 1935, and hundreds of Acts made by the Governors of East Bengal, the Punjab and Sind, together with the orders made under those Acts;

(ii) the criminal law and procedure of Pakistan which had been applied to those parts of Baluchistan which had not been part of British India had never been a part of the law of that area;

(iii) the executive and judicial government of Karachi had no legal foundation;

355

(iv) all laws passed after 1950 by the Constituent Assembly functioning as Federal Legislature were invalid;

(v) all laws passed by the Provincial Legislatures since the last general elections were invalid;

(vi) all laws passed by the Provincial Legislature of East Bengal after 14 March 1953 were invalid; and

(vii) other branches of civil criminal and revenue laws were in large part invalid.

This result was stated more generally and forcefully by my brother Cornelius in *Moulvi Tamizuddin Khan's* case in support of the *ab inconvenienti* argument. He observed:

The rule of *stare decisis* is altogether too small in its content to fit the case. Here, the greatest organs and agencies of the State have been consciously and unanimously holding a certain belief, and have been acting upon it in numerous respects affecting the most fundamental rights of the entire people. It is difficult to imagine a law which affects so large a proportion of the public as does a law designed to grant adult suffrage, and to determine the composition of Provincial Legislatures on that basis. The Delimitation of Constituencies (Adult Franchise) Act, 1951, was procured by the Federal Government, was passed by the Constituent Assembly, was put into operation by the combined labours of the Federal and Provincial Governments, and has borne fruit in the shape of new Legislative Assemblies, which have been busy ever since passing new laws and, in other ways, regulating the lives of the people. It is beyond conception to tabulate all the vested rights and interests which have developed in consequence of this law. And there are many other laws which have produced extensive effects, which cannot possibly be ascertained with exactness. These circumstances should, in my opinion, furnish an argument of almost insuperable character, in favour of upholding what has been the practice hitherto in regard to assent to constitutional laws.

Now if the undoubted position be that justification for the validity of a large body of the law which has become inextricably wedged into the whole system has to be found, does it really matter whether such justification is founded on the *ab inconvenienti* argument as my brother Cornelius seems to have thought or on the maxim *id quod alias non est licitum necessitas licitum facit* on which this Court based its opinion in the *Special Reference*. In the desire to preserve the integrity of the legal system of the State, my brother Cornelius in *Moulvi Tamizuddin Khan's* case proceeded on the doctrine of *ab inconvenienti*, which the majority of us held that that doctrine was not applicable where the constitutional provision in question was not ambiguous and the usurpation of power and the consequent infraction of the Constitution was clear. Thus there is no difference of substance in the result arrived at by my brother Cornelius in *Moulvi Tamizuddin Khan's* case and by the majority of the Court in the aforesaid *Special Reference* as regards the necessity of validation of the invalid laws, the difference being confined only to the question whether those laws are valid on the *ab inconvenienti* argument or on the maxim *id quod alias non est licitum necessitas licitum facit*. It is obvious that any argument *ab inconvenienti* must include in its scope all cases of necessity because what is absolutely necessary must cause inconvenience if it has to be separated. Where, therefore, the issue is, as it admittedly is in this case, whether society should survive or perish because of the integration or disintegration of its legal system, does it really matter what Latin phrase is used to discover the justification for its preservation and for the prevention of its dissolution? And where the constitutional provision is not ambiguous, is not the argument *ab inconvenienti* as much outside the letter of the Constitution as the law of civil or military necessity? I, therefore, adhere to the opinion which I expressed in the *Special Reference* that the Governor-General has the authority temporarily and retrospectively to validate the laws whose invalidity followed from the judgment of this Court in *Moulvi Tamizuddin Khan's* case. And since the Privy Council (Abolition of Jurisdiction) Act, 1950, is one of the laws thus validated by the Governor-General, it is a part of the law today. The quintessence of the law of civil necessity is that it has the effect of making legal what otherwise is illegal and this law is implicit in the constitution of every civilised community. This law in no way interferes with or affects the sovereignty of, the legislature, nor does it put the executive in a position of independence from the legislature or give it absolute and arbitrary powers because in the last resort the action of the executive has got to be validated by the legislature. In *Usif Patel's* case we held validation by the Governor-General to be illegal because by the validating Ordinance the Governor-General claimed for himself the power to validate without any reference to, and in the absence of, the legislature, whereas in the present case the validation is only provisional and subject to legislation by the Constituent Assembly. For these reasons, I think, the Governor-General's Proclamation of 16 April 1955, by which he validated certain laws which were supposed by the judgment of this Court in *Moulvi Tamizuddin Khan's* case to have been declared invalid was legal, in the sense that the power to validate temporarily and retrospectively was, in the circumstances, lawfully exercised. The Privy Council (Abolition of Jurisdiction) Act therefore is at present valid.

AKRAM, J.—I agree in the order made. In the *Special Reference No. 1 of 1955*, we expressed the opinion that the Governor-General has power under certain circumstances to validate temporarily and retrospectively laws found to be defective and ineffectual.

CORNELIUS, J.—The order under appeal in this case is one by a Divisional Bench of the Lahore High Court made on 23 January 1946. On that date, a further appeal lay to the Privy Council. On 11 June 1947, the Privy Council granted special leave to the defendant (the Governor-General-in-Council) to appeal against the decree of the High Court. The partition of the Indian Empire took place on 14 August 1947, and in subsequent proceedings before the High Court it was directed on 17 March 1949 that both the resulting Dominions, namely, the Dominions of India and Pakistan should be brought on the record in place of the Governor-General in Council, and after due proceedings, on 5 May 1949, a formal order was made to this effect. On 20 July 1951, an application was made to the effect that 'the title of the appeal be so changed as to make the Federation of Pakistan the sole appellant and Syed Ali Ahmad Hussain Shah and the Union of India respondents, Nos. 1 and 2 respectively, without prejudice to the contention of the petitioner as to liability'. An order to this effect was accordingly made by a learned Judge of the Lahore High Court on 17 December 1951.

It may conveniently be mentioned here that the contention in regard to liability was that the decree which had been awarded in favour of the respondent Ali Ahmad Hussain Shah was exclusively a liability of the Indian Dominion by virtue of Article 8 (1) of the Indian Independence (Rights, Property and Liabilities) Order, 1947, by which certain rights, property and liabilities had been apportioned between the two Dominions. It will be necessary in the course of this judgment to adjudicate upon this contention.

Before the date of the last mentioned order of the Lahore High Court, this appeal had, by virtue of the Privy Council (Abolition of Jurisdiction) Act, 1950, been received in the Federal Court for disposal. That Act was expressed to come into force on 1 May 1950, by section 1 (2) thereof.

A question has been raised as to the competency of the appeal in this Court, and it has been argued for the respondent Ali Ahmad Hussain Shah that the appeal lies before the Privy Council, by virtue of two decisions recently given by this Court. In Constitutional Civil Appeal No. 1 of 1955, *The Federation of Pakistan* v. *Moulvi Tamizuddin Khan*, this Court decided on 21 March 1955 that all laws of a constitutional nature passed by the Constituent Assembly required the assent of the Governor-General and without such assent such laws were not valid. The Privy Council (Abolition of Jurisdiction) Act, 1950, was a law amending certain provisions of the Government of India Act, 1935, in relation to the jurisdiction of the Privy Council as well as of the Federal Court, and, under the practice prevailing in April, 1950 (see Rule 62 of the Rules of Procedure of the Constituent Assembly), when this law was passed by the Constituent Assembly it was deemed to have become law upon authentication of a copy of the Bill as passed, and publication of such Bill in the Government *Gazette*, under the authority of the President of the Constituent Assembly. It did not receive the assent of the Governor-General. In consequence of the decision of this Court pronounced on 21 March 1955, this law became ineffective until such time as it should receive the assent of the Governor-General. On 27 March 1955, the Governor-General made and promulgated an Ordinance No. IX of 1955, called the Emergency Powers Ordinance, 1955, by section 2 of which provision was made for the validation of certain laws enumerated in a schedule to the Ordinance. The operative words in sub-section (1) of section 2 are as follows:

It is hereby declared and enacted that every law specified in column 1 of the Schedule to this Ordinance *shall be deemed to have received the assent of the Governor-General* on the date specified in column 2 of that Schedule, being the date on which it was published in the official *Gazette*, and *shall be deemed to have had legal force and effect from that date*.

The Privy Council (Abolition of Jurisdiction) Act, 1950, appears in column 1 of the said schedule against the date 22 April 1950.

On 12 April 1955, in Constitutional Criminal Appeal No. 1 of 1954 *Usif Patel and Others* v. *The Crown*, this Court declared that the provisions of section 2 of the Emergency Powers Ordinance, 1955, were inoperative in so far as they purported, of their own force, to give retrospective effect to constitutional laws passed by the Constituent Assembly. In other words, the Governor-General's assent could only be effective from a date in the present. The case of a law which does not provide a specific date for its commencement, and would therefore under the ordinary law be deemed to commence from the date on which assent is given is, however, distinguishable from the case of a law which itself fixes the date of its commencement. The Privy Council (Abolition of Jurisdiction) Act, 1950, does fix the date of its commencement, namely 1 May 1950. This provision is part of the law as made by the Constituent Assembly, and becomes valid upon the law receiving the assent of the Governor-General, whenever that may be accorded. Consequently, if the words which have been reproduced above from section 2 of the Emergency Powers Ordinance, 1955, can be construed to have the effect of granting assent upon the date of the Ordinance, viz. 27 March 1955, it would clearly follow that jurisdiction in respect of the present appeal vests in this Court, and has vested in this Court, ever since the 1st day of May, 1950. This result seems to me to follow from the principle of section 5 (1), General Clauses Act, 1897, which is in the following terms: 'Where any Central Act is not expressed to come into operation on a particular day, then it shall come into operation on the day on which it receives the assent of the Governor-General.' I say 'principle', because by definition, the Constituent Assembly, when enacting constitutional laws, was not the equivalent of the 'Indian Legislature' of the 'Federal Legislature' acting under the Government of India Act, 1935. (See section 8 (1), Indian Independence Act, 1947, and the definitions of 'Central Act' and 'Central Legislature' in section 3, General Clauses Act, 1897.) The Constituent Assembly's own rule on the subject, viz. Rule 62 which has been referred to already, has been held by the majority of the Judges in *Moulvi Tamizuddin Khan's* case, to be *ultra vires*, and not to have the effect of law. I conceive it to be my duty, when the validity of a legislative act of high importance is involved, and particularly, a statute which invests this Court with jurisdiction in relation to the bulk of the cases coming before it, to construe the relevant instruments in accordance with such principle as shall operate, to the maximum extent, without contravening any law, written or otherwise, to preserve at the same time the jurisdiction of this Court and the validity of the law from which it is derived.

The argument is however raised that the formula adopted by the Governor-General under section 2 of the Emergency Powers Ordinance, 1955, does not have the effect of granting assent in the present but merely directs that it shall be assumed, contrary to the fact, that *inter alia*, the Privy Council (Abolition of Jurisdiction) Act, 1950, received assent on 22 April 1950. As a result of this Court's decision in the case of *Usif Patel* (cited above), these words which are intended to operate so as to give retrospective effect to the statute are to be regarded as void and of no effect. If these words, and the words 'shall be deemed to have had legal force and effect from that date' be eliminated, the section would become void of any expression purporting to accord assent.

The argument in reply by Mr Abdul Haq was that this Court should presume that the Governor-General has actually accorded assent separately to the Act here in question, because this would be done in the ordinary course of business.

Such a presumption can hardly be made in view of the clear proof provided by section 2 of the Emergency Powers Ordinance, 1955, that the Governor-General has chosen to act in respect of a large number of laws in a composite manner, and by a formula designed to give effect to these laws from a date in the past. But that does not mean that effect should not be given to the formula as a declaration of grant of assent in the present, if the language employed, and the intention expressed permit of such an interpretation. It is clear that section 2 of the Ordinance is a remedial law. So much is clear from the preamble of the Ordinance as well as from the opening words of section 2 (1), viz. 'whereas none of the laws passed by the Constituent Assembly of Pakistan— received the assent of the Governor-General'. The language employed certainly has the effect of doing something in the past, but the intention equally certainly is to produce an effect in the

361

present. Since the thing which was to be deemed to have been done in the past was a thing having continuing effect, it is inconceivable that an intention of producing a present effect should have been absent. It is a recognised rule of interpretation applicable to remedial statutes that the construction adopted should be that which accords with the express or manifest intention of the statute, and that giving full effect to the language employed, the remedy should be held to extend to all cases within the mischief aimed at. In so doing, the courts do not offend against any recognised canon of interpretation, if they extend the meanings of important words beyond their ordinary etymological sense. The principle is stated with clarity in the following passage from Maxwell's *Interpretation of Statutes*, 10th ed., at p. 275:

... that sense of the words is to be adopted which best harmonises with the context and promotes in the fullest manner the policy and object of the Legislature. The paramount object, in construing penal as well as other statutes, is to ascertain the legislative intent, and the rule of strict construction is not violated by permitting the words to have their full meaning, or the more extensive of two meanings, when best effectuating the intention. They are, indeed, frequently taken in the widest sense, sometimes even in a sense more wide than etymologically belongs or is popularly attached to them, in order to carry out effectually the legislative intent, or, to use Lord Coke's words, to suppress the mischief and advance the remedy.

In the present case, the sense in which the words 'shall be deemed to have received the assent' coupled with the words 'shall be deemed to have legal force and effect from that date' should properly be construed, includes, in my opinion, a declaration that the desired effect is to be produced in the present as well. Accordingly I would hold that by section 2 of the Emergency Powers Ordinance, 1955, and the relevant entry in the schedule, the Privy Council (Abolition of Jurisdiction) Act, 1950, received the assent of the Governor-General on 27 March 1955 and that, subject to objection on one or other ground, which I shall consider immediately, the assent thus given rendered the law valid as from the first day of May 1950.

The second objection to the validity of the Act is this. By an Act of the Constituent Assembly, entitled the Constituent Assembly for Pakistan (Increase and Redistribution of Seats) Act, 1949, provision was made for the addition of six seats to the

362

Constituent Assembly and for the distribution of such seats between the Muslims of West Punjab and the Muslims of Sind. The Act did not receive the Governor-General's assent, and has not been assented to yet. The argument is that by the addition of these seats, which is an act found in the case of *Moulvi Tamizuddin Khan* to be invalid, the constitution of the Constituent Assembly was rendered illegal, and all its acts thereafter were invalid. The Advocate-General of Pakistan, on the other hand, has contended that on the principle embodied in section 23 (2)—repealed at the adaptation of 1947—and section 66 (2), Government of India Act, 1935, the addition of these seats, though invalid, did not vitiate the Constituent Assembly, whose acts as a representative body could not be called in question merely by reason of the presence of these six members from 1949–50 onwards. At that time, and until 21 March 1955, their membership was believed to be completely legal, and there is no suggestion of *mala fides*, as the Prime Minister of Pakistan and all senior members of his Cabinet participated in the proceedings of 1949. Even the Governor-General at that time, was a member of the Constituent Assembly, though not in his official capacity. The Advocate-General, however, conceded that in the commentary by Rajagopala Iyengar under section 23 (2), Government of India Act, 1935, it has been said that the general law in relation to municipal corporations and companies is that the presence of strangers vitiates their proceedings. He thought the special provision in section 23 (2) relating to the Federal Legislature—which is in the same terms as the similar provision in section 66 (2) in respect of the Provincial Legislature—viz. that 'its proceedings shall be valid notwithstanding that it is discovered subsequently that some person who was not entitled to do so, sat and voted or otherwise took part in the proceedings', constituted a departure from the ordinary law, for which statutory provision is necessary, and there being none in relation to the Constituent Assembly, the saving was not available for the Act in question.

With respect to the learned commentator on the Government of India Act, 1935, his comment regarding the *general law* applicable to municipal corporations and companies is not correct. There is no indication furnished where this general law is to be found. On the other hand, the principle is perfectly clear that, as a juristic person, a corporation is distinct from the corporators, and certainly, it cannot be right to think that the acts of such a juristic person are vitiated *ex post facto* because of the discovery made subsequently that some of the corporators, who participated in the acts of the corporation perfectly *bona fide*, lacked the necessary qualification or were otherwise not validly appointed or included as corporators. I quote here, with respect, from a judgment of a Divisional Bench of the Lahore High Court consisting of Shadi Lal, C.J., and Zafar Ali, J., viz. *Devi Ditta Mal* v. *Standard Bank of India*,[1] the following short passage: 'It is beyond dispute that a director invalidly appointed cannot, in the absence of a provision in the articles of association, bind the shareholders, *unless the defect is unknown at the time.*'

On the other hand, the statute law in England, as well as here, clearly saves the acts of a director in the given circumstances. Section 86, Companies Act, 1913, provides as follows for Pakistan:

The acts of a director shall be valid notwithstanding any defect that may *afterwards* be discovered in his appointment or qualification: Provided that nothing in this section shall be deemed to give validity to acts done by a director after the appointment of such director has been shown to be invalid.

The relevant law in England is found in the Companies Act, 1862, in section 67, the operative words being:

. . . all appointments of directors, managers or liquidators shall be deemed to be valid, and all acts done by such directors, managers or liquidators shall be valid, notwithstanding any defect that may afterwards be discovered in their appointments or qualifications.

British Medical etc. Association v. *Jones*[2] is an authority of Pollock, B., to the effect that this provision saves a call for share money made by directors appointed at a meeting which was convened after notice which was shorter than that required by law.

As regards municipal corporations also, the statute law in India and Pakistan seems clearly to disprove the dictum of the learned commentator. Among a great many similar Acts which are available for reference, I select for mention two, namely the Bombay City Municipalities Act, 1925, and the City of Lahore Corporation Act, 1941. Section 57 of the Bombay Act provides as follows:

[1] A.I.R. 1927 Lahore 797.   [2] 61 L.T. 384.

(1) No disqualification of, or defect in the election or appointment of any person acting as councillor—shall be deemed to vitiate any act or proceeding of the municipality—in which such person has taken part, whenever the majority of persons, parties to such act or proceeding, were entitled to act.

[The strength of the Constituent Assembly was, I believe, raised to 77 after the addition of 6 members in 1949.]

Section 32 of the Punjab Act is in almost precisely the same terms as those quoted above. These instances should, in my opinion, suffice to show that, at any rate, where the defect is of subsequent discovery, and the inclusion and participation of the affected members is entirely *bona fide*, their presence cannot operate to vitiate either the constitution of the corporation or the acts of such corporation.

On the analogy of the British Parliament, the Constituent Assembly was undoubtedly a corporation. The following short quotation from Halsbury's *Laws of England*, 2nd ed. in the monograph on 'Corporations', paragraph 29 will place this matter beyond doubt: 'Parliament is a corporation aggregate by the common law, consisting of the Crown (the head), the Lords Spiritual and Temporal, and the Commons.' Further, in the absence of a statutory bar, the autonomy of a corporation extends to the addition of members and to the renewal of members, if need arises.[1] Consequently, there is no question of *ultra vires*, and the only defect in the addition of the six members was the absence of assent by the Governor-General, which defect did not come to light until the decision of this Court in the case of *Moulvi Tamizuddin Khan* some six years later.

I am therefore clearly of the opinion that the second objection too is devoid of validity in law, and consequently hold that the Privy Council (Abolition of Jurisdiction) Act, 1950, is good and valid law since 1 May 1950, and therefore that this Court has full jurisdiction to hear the present appeal. I regret that I should be placing this conclusion upon a basis different from that which has appealed to my Lord the Chief Justice and my learned brothers. I must not be thought to be expressing any view in this appeal concerning the opinion expressed by them in the answer to Question 2 of the Governor-General's *Reference* recently dealt

[1] Bagchi, *Principles of the Law of Corporations*, 1928 ed.

with by this Court, even though my own opinion on the same question was materially different. The answer, favouring power in the Governor-General under the common law of civil or state necessity, of retrospectively validating constitutional laws, including the Privy Council (Abolition of Jurisdiction) Act, 1950, expressly imposes two conditions, viz.

(i) that the existence of the power is conditional upon the existence of *necessity* arising out of the 'situation presented by the Reference';
(ii) that the power is exercisable in the interim period, until the validity of these laws 'is decided upon by the Constituent Assembly'.

It is, in my opinion, desirable that I should avoid going into matters of detail, to illustrate the dangers to which the justiciable nature of certain vital matters of fact, which are embodied in these conditions, are apt to give rise. It will suffice to say that I prefer to place my decision, affecting the jurisdiction of this Court, on a basis free from precariousness. In adopting the principles upon which I have proceeded to my conclusion, I am not conscious of having acted otherwise than for the maintenance and preservation of a number of laws 'which cannot without danger to the State be removed from the existing legal system', in furtherance of the maxim *ut res magis valeat quam pereat*.

It will be convenient now to deal with an argument raised on behalf of the respondent Ali Ahmad Hussain Shah that this Court is not competent to deal with the present appeal because it is not 'a Pakistan appeal' within the meaning of section 2 of the Privy Council (Abolition of Jurisdiction) Act, 1950. The contention appeared to be that since by virtue of Article 8 of the Indian Independence (Rights, Property and Liabilities) Order, 1947, the liability in the case was exclusively that of the Dominion of India, and the last decision in the case was that of the Lahore High Court, delivered prior to the Partition of India, therefore, the subject-matter of the case not being a concern of the State of Pakistan, the appeal could not be regarded as a 'Pakistan Appeal'. The definition of the expression 'Pakistan Appeal' as it appears in section 2 aforesaid is an 'appeal from or in respect of any judgment, decree or order of any court or tribunal (other than the Federal Court) in Pakistan'. The cause of action in this suit is an order of dismissal from public service made by the Divisional Superintendent of the N.W. Railway, Multan Division, in respect of the plaintiff Ali Ahmad Hussain Shah who was then a permanent way inspector posted at Lodhran in the Multan Railway Division. Lodhran and Multan are now in Pakistan. The suit was instituted in the Court of the Senior Sub-Judge, Multan, and was decided by a First Class Sub-Judge of that place. As already stated, the appeal was heard and decided by the Lahore High Court, which, since the Partition, is a court in Pakistan. *Ex facie*, therefore, the appeal pending before the Privy Council on 1 May 1950, from the order of the Lahore High Court, was a Pakistan appeal and it would therefore appear that this Court has jurisdiction to dispose of it. This jurisdiction is not affected by the consideration that the satisfaction of any decree in favour of the plaintiff which this Court may be pleased to award, might in the result prove to be a liability of the Dominion of India. By section 3 of the Indian Independence (Rights, Property and Liabilities) Order, 1947, it was provided that the provisions of that Order 'relate to the initial distribution of rights, property and liabilities consequential on the setting up of the Dominions of India and Pakistan and shall have effect subject to any agreement between the two Dominions or the Provinces concerned and to any award that may be made by the Arbitral Tribunal'.

Accordingly this Court may proceed in the assurance that machinery exists whereby effect can be given to any orders which it may make, whether the liability be that of the Federation of Pakistan, or of the Indian Dominion (now Republic).

The facts of the case which are necessary for disposal of the remaining points arising in this appeal may be briefly stated as follows. The plaintiff Ali Ahmad Hussain Shah was serving as a permanent way inspector when on 15 July 1939 he was suspended from service and subsequently on 10 August 1940 he was dismissed from the service of the N.W. Railway by an order made by the Divisional Superintendent of the Multan Division. He contended that this order was *ultra vires* because it had been made by an authority lower than the authority by which he had been appointed, viz. the Chief Mechanical Engineer N.W. Railway. For this, reliance was placed on a provision in the constitution of the country, viz. section 240 (2) of the Government of India

367

Act, 1935. Claiming that his right to receive salary was unaffected by the order of dismissal, the plaintiff sued for a decree for Rs. 9240 as pay and for interest thereon, in addition to a declaration that the order of dismissal was void.

The first court granted a decree as prayed with costs. There was an appeal by the Governor-General in Council and the High Court maintained the declaration regarding the order of dismissal, but reduced the monetary decree by the amount of interest only. In the concise statement furnished by the appellant in this Court, the reliefs claimed are firstly that no decree for arrears of salary should be made and secondly the liability in respect of the decree should be declared to be exclusively that of the Indian Dominion (now Republic).

The ground on which the High Court on 17 March 1949 directed that both Dominions should be impleaded in place of the Governor-General in Council was that the cause of action in the suit lay not so much in contract, as 'in respect of an actionable wrong other than breach of contract' to which Article 10 of the Indian Independence (Rights, Property and Liabilities) Order, 1947, in its terms applied. By Article 10, the provision was made that liabilities of the Governor-General in Council based upon actionable wrongs other than breaches of contract should be distributed as between the two Dominions according as the cause of action arose wholly within the territories of the one Dominion or the other. Where it could not be determined that the cause of action arose wholly within the territories of one of the two Dominions, the liability was to be a joint liability. It is not clear, and it is not necessary to determine whether, even if this Article be applied, the liability could *prima facie* be said to attach to both the Dominions. It is conceded on behalf of the plaintiff respondent that at least in part, the suit does lie in contract. It is obvious that it cannot lie wholly in tort, for in that case it would be liable to dismissal on the short ground that no action in tort can lie against the Crown. Therefore as was said by the Judicial Committee in the case of *Mr I. M. Lall*,[1] the present suit must be held to proceed either on the basis of contract or upon a right of action conferred by statute.

It is in my opinion reasonable to hold that the relationship between the Governor-General in Council and the plaintiff which

[1] A.I.R. (35), 1948 P.C. 121.

was created by the agreement concluded between them at the time of his permanent appointment to service was a contract of service, of which certain of the incidents were prescribed by specific provisions in the Constitution Act, which provisions it was not necessary to mention in the agreement of service of which a copy has been exhibited on the record as Ex. P.W. 1/16. Viewing this agreement as a contract of service, it seems that the case must fall clearly within the provisions of Article 8 of the aforesaid Order which provides in its first sub-section that, with the exception of contracts which are 'for purposes which as from that day (i.e. the day of Partition) are exclusively purposes of the Dominion of Pakistan', all contracts made on behalf of the Governor-General in Council should as from the date of Partition be deemed to have been made on behalf of the Indian Dominion. In the present case, the contract of service was terminated, by unilateral act of the Governor-General in Council, on a date seven years in advance of the date of Partition. It is impossible to regard the contract as being exclusively for the purposes of the Dominion of Pakistan after the date of Partition, since it was not subsisting on that day. It therefore becomes clear that the liability in the present case must fall on the Indian Dominion, in the first in-stance, subject to any agreement which might be made between the two countries as to the source from which the liability is to be met.

As regards the money part of the decree, representing arrears of salary, the contention on behalf of the appellant is that the plaintiff is entitled only to a declaration that on 10 August 1940 and thereafter until the date when he was validly dismissed, by an order which he has not thought fit to challenge, he was still in service, and his further remedy was by petition to the Government in the appropriate department.

Reliance was placed for this proposition upon the decision of the Judicial Committee in the case of *Mr I. M. Lall* (cited above). In that case, the agreement of service was embodied in a covenant which gave the servant no right to pay, and was mainly concerned with the duties he was to discharge. The Privy Council, dealing with the prayer of Mr I. M. Lall for arrears of pay from the date of the purported order of dismissal up to the date of action, quoted from the well-known case of *Mulvenna* v. *The Admiralty*,[1] a

[1] (1926), S.C. 842.

passage to the effect that there is a rule of public policy applicable to every public servant which prevents them from suing the Crown for their pay, on the assumption that their only claim is on the bounty of the Crown and not for a contractual debt, and consequently 'their only remedy under that contract lies in an appeal of an official or political kind'. The prayer was disallowed.

In the present case, there is an undertaking to pay salary to the servant so long as he remains in service (paragraph 8 of contract of service, Ex. P.W. 1/16), which is relied upon by Mr Anwar for the respondent, for the purpose of distinguishing the *I. M. Lall* case. On the other hand, there is the fact that the respondent was duly dismissed by an order made some time after 10 August 1940, which subsequent order the respondent has not challenged. The respective rights and liabilities as between the employer and the employee, as respects the period between the date of his suspension and the date of his dismissal in proper form, are subject to express provisions contained in the Civil Service Rules and the fundamental Rules. No ground appears why the operation of these provisions should be interfered with. In the circumstances it seems to me that the relief to be awarded to the plaintiff should be confined to a declaration that on 10 August 1940 he was still in the service of the N.W. Railway.

In the result, the appeal succeeds on both points. I would accordingly direct that the decree of the Courts below should be amended so as to make it a decree for a declaration against the Indian Dominion (now Republic) to the effect that the order dated 10 August 1940 passed by the Divisional Superintendent, N.W. Railway, Multan, dismissing the plaintiff from service is *ultra vires* and that on that date, he was still in the service of the N.W. Railway. In all the circumstances, I would direct that the parties shall bear own costs throughout.

MUHAMMAD SHARIF, J.—I agree that the appeal be accepted to the extent that a decree for declaration be granted to the plaintiff-respondent and the parties be left to bear their own costs throughout.

S. A. RAHMAN, J.—I agree with my Lord, the Chief Justice, and have nothing to add.

INDEX

Ab inconvenienti, argument, 138, 221–2, 356

Act of Parliament,
application to Dominions, 14
application to Pakistan, 107
commencement, 250
and see repugnancy of laws

act of State, 299

advice to Governor-General, not to be inquired into, 265

advisory opinion,
application for, 5
questions asked, 264
submissions for, 263–4

affidavits, 73

Agha, J., 79, 158, 216

Akbar Khan, 5, 36, 41, 46, 47, 178, 218

allegiance,
bond of servitude, 180
Dominion status and, 237
in Eire, 184
inconsistent with freedom, 180
generally, 19–20, 115, 151–3
maintenance of, 312
not owed by Governor-General, 174
in Pakistan, 185
removal of, 311

Anson, Sir William, 119

appointed day, 13

argument *ab inconvenienti*, 138, 221–2, 356

assent,
in Canada, 189
in colonies, 92, 120
in Dominions, 100, 116, 120, 151–3
in English law, 119–20
Federal Legislature and, 24
full power, meaning of, 13, 28, 29, 125, 161, 204, 224–9, 236
generally, 25–37
history of, 117–18
inconsistent with independence, 175
not inconsistent with independence, 236
in India before partition, 103–4, 121–2, 192
informal, 38, 57, 140
inherent in Crown, 123
invalid laws, 52, 355
merchant shipping, 130–1
necessity of, 128, 160
opinion of Law Ministry, 24
power not transferred to Governor-General, 223
power to, includes power to refuse, 129

prerogative power, 118
procedure for, 38, 57, 118–19, 140
provincial bills, 26, 110, 125–6
purpose of, 187–8
question raised, 4, 13, 14
refusal of, 118, 129, 146
retrospective, 250, 360
secession, 128
under Statute of Westminster, 17–18
statutes regulate form, 123

Atkinson, Lord, 269

Australia, 18, 28, 29, 72, 89, 92, 96, 115, 151, 152, 153, 181, 188, 189–90, 192, 196, 202, 270–1, 282, 311

Azad Moulana, 8

Bagchi, 365

Bahadur Khan, Khan Sardar, 135

Bakhsh, J., 29, 35–7, 59, 64, 65, 124, 159

Balfour Declaration, 93

Baltimore, colony of, 303

Baluchistan, invalid laws in, 39, 136

bills, provincial, assent to, 26, 110, 125–6; *and see* assent, laws

Bill of Rights, power to enact, 16

Blackstone, Sir William, 85, 163–4, 286, 287, 337

Bracton, Henry de, 298–9, 306

Breakdown of constitutional machinery, 70, 71, 80, 116; *and see* Emergency

British Commonwealth of Nations, as club, 228
common allegiance in, 151–3
Conference, 20, 151
Head of, 174; *and see* Crown, Dominions
links in, 311
nature of, 180–8
qualified freedom within, 188

British India, division of, 15

British subjects, 116

Brohi, A. K., 178

Broom, 299

Burke, E., 118

Burma, 153, 312

Cabinet Mission, 7, 63, 162–3, 275, 323–8, 333, 334

Canada, 18, 28, 29, 72, 89, 92, 96, 115, 151; 152, 153, 155, 181, 188–9, 191, 192, 196, 202, 270, 311

24*

Canning, Lord, 101
casus omissus, 282, 291
Ceylon, 15, 16, 18, 24, 28, 68, 151, 153, 271
Chalmers, George, 282, 293, 303, 342
charter, binding character of, 91
  forfeiture of, 303
Chitty, J., 301, 303, 306
citizenship, 19–20; *and see* nationality
civil necessity, 348, 355
colony,
  acquisition of, 89–90
  assent in, 92, 120
  charter, binding character of, 91; forfeiture of, 303
  conquered or ceded, 55, 60, 90
  definition of, 89
  dissolution of Assembly in, 282
  settled, 90–1
commencement of Act, 250
commission, Governor-General's, 195
Commonwealth, *see* British Commonwealth
Commonwealth (Civil War),
  assent during, 119
  legislation during, 56
  Rule of Law in, 51
Commonwealth Conference, 20, 151
Communal Award, 325
conquered and ceded territories,
  legislation in, 55, 90
  prerogative in, 60
Constantine, C. J., 31–2, 64, 65, 68, 79, 158
Constituent Assembly,
  above Governor-General, 213
  absolute autonomy of, 208
  abuse of powers by, 73
  assent to laws of, *see* Assent
  "as such", 23
  attempted to function outside the Constitution, 139
  attitude towards Dominion status, 20
  bills, authentication of, 136; *and see* assent
  not bound by law, 206
  casual vacancies, 110
  composition of new, 294; intention to summon, 48; nominated members in, 295, 333; name of, 333; States' representatives in, 295, 334; tribal representatives in, 295, 334
  constituent powers of, 20–1, 109, 112
  as corporation, 365
  not created by Parliament, 205
  created by will of people, 205
  Crown and, 28; *and see* Crown
  dissolution of, 3, 57–75; *and see* dissolution
  establishment of, 3, 275–6
  examples of time taken by, 284–5
  extra-territorial legislation, 13, 15, 107
  as Federal legislature, 23; *and see* Federal Legislature
  formation of, 3, 275–6
  functions of, traditional interpretation, 23
  government in, 123
  Governor-General and, 28, 213; *and see* Governor-General
  illegal body, 290, 353
  improper constitution of, 38, 57
  interim powers of, 21
  as irremovable legislature, 86
  not bound by law, 206
  legislative powers of, 15, 20, 109, 112; *and see* Federal Legislature, Legislature of the Dominion
  as Legislature of the Dominion, 127, 160, 171, 235, 316, 328
  not Legislature of the Dominion, 230
  limitations on, 21, 109
  lived in a fool's paradise, 139
  mathematical formula, 114, 248
  meaning of, 63, 110, 274–7
  monopoly over constitutional laws, 249
  origin of, 10–11
  not a perpetual legislature, 283
  possible misuse of powers by, 73, 147
  power to dissolve and summon, 6
  powers of, generally, 3, 112, 205
  prerogative powers vested in, 34–5
  President of, 3
  proceeded thoughtlessly, 140
  proceedings invalidated by strangers, 354
  repeal of Public and Representative Offices (Disqualification) Act, 148
  rules of procedure, 23, 58, 134–6, 159, 210–2
  sovereignty of, 7, 8–9, 22, 23, 30, 33–4, 36, 67, 108, 139, 143–4, 172, 201, 213, 226, 236, 249, 339; fear of full sovereignty, 236
  States representation in, 110, 295, 334
  summoning of, 23, 51
  supra-legal body, 221
  tribal areas represented in, 110, 295, 334
  unconstitutional, 38, 57
  undertaking to summon new assembly, 253–4
  Union, boycott of, 9–10; composition of, 325–6; establishment of, 7, 326; meeting of, 9–10; Muslim League and, 8–10, 326; Objectives Resolution, 9–10; separation of, 327–8
  unrepresentative, 288

372

Constituent Convention,
  name wrong, 333
  summoning of, 5, 6, 52, 53, 54, 75, 263
  unknown to law, 294
constituent powers, 16, 20–1, 109, 112
constitution,
  essentials of democratic, 84–6
  functions of a, 84
  suspension of, 51
constitutional law, distinction from ordinary law, 35–6
constitutional lawyers, reduced to makeshifts, 119
constitutional machinery, breakdown of, 70, 71, 80, 116
constitutional monarchy, 87–8
contemporaneous exposition, 136–9, 212, 220–1
conventions,
  courts and, 88
  Dominion status, 96–100
  irrelevance of, 182
  laws and, 141
Convention Parliaments, 51, 56, 301
Cooley, quoted, 137, 138, 212, 220, 222
coronation oath, 154
coup d'état, legal conception of, 70, 85
Craies, quoted, 211, 212, 251
Crawford, quoted, 137, 222
criminal law, invalidity of, 42
Cromwell, Oliver, 300
Crown,
  allegiance to, 19–20, 115, 151–3
  assent to bills, 13, 14; and see Assent
  authority in India, 102
  colonies held of the, 90
  disallowance of laws by, 14, 21; and see disallowance
  dissolution by, 86, 172; and see dissolution
  Dominions, position in, 95
  Head of the Commonwealth, 174, 187
  legislative powers of, 29, 55, 60, 90–1
  Pakistan and the, 19–20
  part of legislature, 28, 124, 169, 174
  part of Parliament, 117
  prerogatives, see prerogatives
  prosecutions in the name of, 156
  reservation of laws for assent of, 14; and see reservation of laws
  rights of, generally, 29
  royal style and titles, see royal style and titles
  services of, 156
  suspension of laws for assent of, 14
  suzerainty of, over States and tribal areas, 19
  symbol of free association, 170

symbol, mere, 188
  territories not held in right of, 90
  as ultimate constitution, 72

Darling, J., 299
defence, 214
democracy, meaning of, 83
democratic constitutions, 84–6
departmental construction, 222, 237–8
diarchy, in India, 101
Dicey, A. V., 16, 118, 120, 300, 307
diplomatic representation, 68, 155–6
disallowance of laws, 14, 17–18, 29–30, 107, 201
  Imperial Conference on, 93
  India before 1947, 192
  provincial Acts, 21
Disraeli, B., 118
dissolution,
  appeal to the people, 87
  argument on, 54–5
  colonial assemblies, 282
  power of, claimed, 4, 57–75, 85–6, 328–9; not unlimited, 267; prerogative, 59–60, 171, 280; responsibility for, 265
  United Kingdom, in, 314
Dominion,
  assent in, 120
  characteristics of, 115–6
  conventions as to, 96–100
  Crown in, 95
  Governor-General in, 96–100
  independent of control, 150, 170
  not independent of control, 173, 182
  meaning, 150
  Pakistan, not so blessed as, 206
  responsible government in, 92–3
  not sovereign State, 181
Dominion legislation, Conference on operation of, 94–5
Dominion status,
  allegiance and, 237
  conventions and, 96–100
  effects of, 313
  equals independence, 150, 170
  generally, 89–92
  Imperial Conference and, 92–4
  incidents of, 311–2
  not independence, 173, 182
  no legal sanction, 288
  technical meaning, 163
draft constitution of Pakistan, 3
Dunedin, Lord, 269
Dwarris, quoted, 251

East Bengal, elections in, 3
East India Company, 100–1
Eire, 183, 282
elections, periodical necessity of, 85
Elizabeth II, accession of, 20
emergency,
  alternative solutions, 50–1

373

emergency—(*cont.*)
legislation for, 38–56
nature of the, 39–40
ordinances in case of, 42
powers to deal with, 45–6, 47, 72–3, 298–307
proclamation of, 4, 41, 53
Emergency Powers Ordinance, 4, 5, 41, 45–8
Emperor of India, title, 19–20, 108, 153
estoppel, 70, 138, 140, 158
Evatt, H. V., 97, 98, 99
executive, responsibility of, 86–7
extra-territorial legislation, 13, 15, 107

Fane, quoted, 293
Federation of India, three-tiered, 7
Federal Court,
appeal to, 4
advisory opinion sought, 5
not bound by own decisions, 218
stare decisis, 218
stop order, 5
Federal Legislature,
assent to bills of, 24, 26
composition before 1947, 193–4
Constituent Assembly as, 23
creation of, 15
dissolution of, 171
extra-territorial legislation by, 15
Governor-General part of, 122
invalid laws, 38, 58
Legislature of the Dominion, included in, 15; not included in, 329
meaning of, 31
non-sovereign body, 32–3
powers of, 21, 109, 114, 248; not constituent, 245
repugnancy of laws of, 16–17
rules of procedure, 23
summoning of, 23, 62
form of government, 115
Forsey, E., 282
fraus omnia corrumpit, 331
full power, meaning, 13, 28, 29, 32, 125, 161, 204, 224–9, 236

Game, Sir Philip, 98
Georgia, colony of, 303, 342
Governor,
acts of, invalid, 39, 295
discretionary powers, 21, 109
individual judgment, 21, 109
Governor-General,
advice about appointment, 145
advice to, not to be questioned, 265; acts on, 123
adaptation of Government of India Act by, 15, 22, 110
allegiance to Crown, 174

appointment of, 13, 40, 98, 107, 110, 197, 236
as constitutional monarch, 97, 100, 249
assent by, 13–14, 25–37, 107, 120, 146
autocrat, not an, 146, 318
Constituent Assembly and, 28, 245
dissolution of Assembly by, 3, 328–9
emergency action by, 4–5, 17, 38–56, 72–3, 298–307
individual judgment of, 21, 109
instructions to, 143
meaning of, 63, 274–5
not a nodding automaton, 146, 318
oath taken by, 20, 154, 173, 186, 321–2
orders of, adapting Government of India Act, 15, 22, 110
ordinances enacted by, 17, 42, 72–3, 298–307
part of Federal Legislature, 122
part of Legislature of the Dominion, 129, 139, 317–8
political initiative by, 323–8
position of, 309; in Dominions, 93, 95–100
powers of, 107, 318–23, 339; none over constitutional laws, 322; delegation of, to, 64; discretionary, 21, 109; in India, 102–4; treaty-making, 68; none for validation of laws, 347 (*and see* invalid laws)
prerogatives exercised by, 223, 321, 328
proclamation of dissolution, 80
recall of, 98, 128, 144, 236
representative of the Crown, 80; of the Dominion, 145; of the people, 147–8
sovereignty not vested in, 249
stay of proceedings by, 335
not a viceroy, 65, 319

Habeas corpus, 41
Hanover, 152
Harcourt, Solicitor-General, 303
Head of the Commonwealth, 174, 187
historical materials, use of, for interpretation, 6–7
Holt, L.C.J., 303
Hore-Ruthven, Sir Alexander, 98

Ilbert, Sir Courtenay, 118
Imperial Conference of 1926, 92–4, 120, 146, 151, 163, 180
Imperial Conference of 1930, 95–6
imperialism, tradition of, 24
independence,
assent does not clog, 236
assent inconsistent with, 175
characteristics of, 106, 115, 150–1
freedom from British yoke, 185

Independent Dominion,
assent consistent with, 236
assent inconsistent with, 175
Canada, Australia or South Africa
not, 191
characteristics of, 106, 150–1, 195–7
different from Dominion, 173, 191
establishment of, 13
free from British yoke, 185
manifestations of, 219
meaning of, 149, 170, 311
Pakistan as, 110
India,
annexation of, by Crown, 101
attitude to United Kingdom, in,
24–5
Crown's authority in, 102
dependence of, before 1947, 191–2
diarchy in, 101
federal scheme for, 104–5
general position of, before 1947,
105–6
government of, after 1935, 102–3
as independent Dominion, 173
Montague-Chelmsford reforms, 101
partition of, 7–8, 10–11
provincial government in, 104
as republic, 151, 185
repugnancy of laws in, 105
royal title in, 101
'Indiae Imperator', 108, 153
Indian Legislature,
assent to Bills of, 26
functions of, 15, 21, 109
Indian National Congress, 7, 8–10,
18, 24
Indian States,
representation in Constituent Assembly, 110
suzerainty over, 19, 108
instructions to Governor-General, 143
Interim Government, 8, 326
interpretation,
ab inconvenienti, 138, 221–2, 356
casus omissus, 282, 291
contemporaneous exposition, 136–9,
212, 220–1
departmental construction, 222,
237–8
golden rule, 162
quotation of parliamentary debates,
7, 125, 126, 127, 149–51
stare decisis, 218, 222, 356
use of historical material, 6–7
invalid laws, 4, 36, 38–9, 58, 295–6,
354
assented to, 52
consequences of, 295–6, 355
criminal law and, 42
federal legislation, 38
Governors' Acts, 39
passed by illegal Assembly, 354
Indian laws as amended, 40

proclamation as to, 263, 296
provincial, 39, 52
stop to litigation over, 53
validation of, by ordinance, 4–5,
42–3, 48, 244, 338–9; by necessity, 298; impossible, 335; invalid, 396; no power for, 347;
provisional only, 357; temporary,
5, 53, 297, 307
Irish Free State, 17, 89, 92, 142, 181,
183, 220, 228
Iyengar, Rajagopala, 363

Jenks, Edward, 99, 164
Jenkyns, Sir Henry, 320
Jennings, Sir Ivor, 142
Jinnah, Muhammad Ali (Qaid-i-
Azam), 9, 12, 23, 24, 25, 30, 135,
141, 172, 173, 186, 199, 210, 213,
309

Karachi, invalid laws, 29
Keith, A. Berriedale, 152, 164, 318,
319, 320, 321, 322, 336, 343

Lacuna, Indian Independence Act,
69, 116
Law Ministry, advice on assent by, 24
Law Officers, advice on assent, 158
law of civil necessity, 298; and see
civil necessity
laws,
assent to, 14, 17–18, 24–6, 107;
and see assent
authentication of, 136
constitutional, 13, 14, 235; and see
Constituent Assembly
conventions and, 141
declaration of, 159
disallowance of, 14, 17–18, 29–30,
107, 201; Imperial Conference
on, 93; Provincial Acts, 21; in
India before 1947, 192
Dominion, disallowance of, 93;
legislative competence in, 93;
reservation, 93
extra-territorial operation of, 13, 15,
107
in force in Pakistan, 14
invalid, 4, 36, 38–9, 58, 295–6, 354;
assented to, 52; consequences of,
295–6, 355
limiting future legislature, 14
meaning of, 29–30, 35, 129, 132,
133, 159, 229–30
practices and, 141
Provincial, 21, 26
repugnancy of, 13, 16, 107; in
India, 105
reservation of, for royal assent, 14
17–18, 30, 107, 201; in India
before 1947, 192
suspension of, 14, 17–18, 30, 107, 201

legal sovereignty, 86
Legislature,
Crown included in, 28
irremovable, 85
Legislature of the Dominion,
Constituent Assembly equivalent to, 127, 133, 160, 171, 235, 316, 328; not equivalent to, 230
constituent powers of, 16, 20–1, 109, 112
Crown not included in, 174
dissolution of, 280
Federal Legislature included, 15; not included, 329
future legislature only, 201
Governor-General, a part of, 129, 317–18
laws limiting future action, 14, 21
legislative sovereignty in, 139, 146, 158
meaning of, 111, 230–1
powers of, 13–16, 20–1; legislative, 13, 14; plenary, 16, 139, 146, 158
prorogation of, 280
repugnancy of laws of, 13
sovereignty of, 16
summoning of, 280
and see Constituent Assembly
Locke, John, 293

Madras, president of, 305
Maitland, F. W., 282, 292, 301, 302
Man, Isle of, 30
mandamus, 3, 25, 81
mandate, the, 88, 290
Mansfield, Lord, 305, 306
martial law, 73, 304–5, 336
Maryland, colony of, 341–2
'mathematical formula', 114, 248
maxims,
casus omissus dispositioni communis juris relinquitur, 282, 291
fraus omnia corrumpit, 331
necessitas licitum facit, 299, 346, 356, 357
necessity makes law, 54–6, 70–1, 299, 346, 348, 355, 356
plain words, plain meaning, 162
salus populi suprema lax, 45, 47, 73, 172, 254, 299, 300, 340, 341, 346, 347
ut res magis valeat quam pereat, 366
Maxwell, quoted, 251, 362
Merchant Shipping Act, assent for, 130–1
ministerial responsibility, 87–8, 265
Ministers,
appointment of, 166; valid, 40
quo warranto against, 4
minorities, protection of, 8, 326
monarchy, 117; and see Crown

Mountbatten, Lord, 3, 10, 11, 12, 17, 22, 23, 24, 29, 61, 64, 67, 72, 75, 150, 198, 275
Muhammad, Ghulam, 186, 213; and see Governor-General
Munir, C. J., 38, 71, 79
Murray, Solicitor-General, 282, 293, 303; and see Mansfield, Lord
Muslim League,
defeat of, in East Bengal, 3
Interim Government and, 9
Union Constituent Assembly and, 326

Napoleon, Louis, 51, 71
nationality, 19–20, 116, 155
natural law, 73
Nazimuddin, Khwaja, 213
Nehru, Jawaharlal, 8, 12, 24
Newfoundland, 18, 68, 89, 92, 181
New Hampshire, colony of, 293, 341
New Jersey, colony of, 341
New York, colony of, 293
New Zealand, 18, 28, 29, 89, 92, 96, 151, 152, 153, 181, 271
Nishtar, Sardar Abdur Rab Khan, 135
North-West Frontier Province, 10
Northbrook, Lord, 101
Northey, Attorney-General, 303

oath of Governor-General, 20, 154, 173, 186, 321–2
Ogg, F. A., 118
oligarchy, 86
Orders in Council, 14, 18–19, 107
ordinances, 17, 42; and see Emergency Powers Ordinance in Table of Enactments

Pakistan,
citizenship, 19–20, 155
Constitution of, 60–1
creation of, 9–10
Crown in, 19–20; and see Crown, Governor-General
Interim Constitution of, 21
laws applying to, 14
nationality in, 19–20, 155
proposal for, rejected, 7
secession of, see secession
transfer of power to, 23
pardon, 196
Parliament of the United Kingdom,
legislation by, for Pakistan, 107
legislative control of, 90, 91
sovereignty of, 56, 105
summons and dissolution of, 55
parliamentary debates, quotation of, 7, 125, 126, 127, 140–51
partition of India, 9–10
people, creation of Constituent Assembly by will of, 205
Phillips, G. Godfrey, 151, 164

Phillips, O. Hood, 300, 301
Phipson, quoted, 137
Pigot, Lord, 305
plain words, plain meaning, 162
political initiative, not vested in Governor-General, 332–3
political sovereignty, 86
practices, laws and, 141
prerogatives of the Crown, 20, 34–5
  abridgment of, 268–70
  assent to legislation, 118
  definition of, 269
  delegation of, to Governor-General, 64, 223, 281, 321, 328
  dissolution of legislature, 171, 267, 280
  in Dominions, 116, 155
  emergency, 300
  extension of, to Pakistan, 311, 313
  extension of, to territories overseas, 91, 236, 315
  as Head of the Commonwealth, 187
  limitable by statute, 268–70
  martial law, 304–5
  pardon, 196
  placed at disposal of Parliament, 205–6
  prorogation, 280
  statutory powers and, 268–70, 280
  summons and dissolution of legislature, 55, 280, 292–3
prerogative writs, 71
Prime Minister,
  appointment of, 166
  reconstruction of Cabinet by, 3
  statements of, relevant to interpretation, 329; not relevant, 331
Privy Council, appeals to, 6, 40, 354
proclamations of emergency, 41, 263, 296, 307, 340
prorogation, prerogative power, 280
provincial laws,
  assent to, 26, 110, 125–6
  invalidity of, 4–5, 39, 52, 295
  reservation of, 21
  suspension of, 39
provincial legislatures, improperly composed, 38–9, 48, 57–8
public order, extraordinary powers for, 336

Qaid-i-Azam, see Jinnah, Muhammad Ali
Queen Elizabeth, accession of, 187
Quit India, 185
quo warranto, 4, 25, 80

Rahman, J., 40
Rashid, C.J., 218
Raymond, Attorney-General, 293
reductio ad absurdum, 143
representative government, 84
republic, power to provide for, 17

repugnancy of laws, 13, 16, 42, 96, 105, 107
reservation of bills, 14, 17–18, 30, 107, 201
  provincial, 21
  Imperial Conference on, 93
  in India before 1947, 192
responsible government, 86–7
revolution, legal concept of, 70, 85
Rhode Island, colony of, 71
royal assent, see assent
royal prerogative, see prerogatives of the Crown
royal style and titles, 19, 101, 108, 151, 153–4, 173, 187
rule of law, 51
rules of procedure, 23, 58, 134–6, 159, 210–2
Ryder, Attorney-General, 282, 293, 303

Salisbury, Marquis of, 101
salus populi suprema lex, 45, 47, 73, 172, 254, 299, 300, 340, 341, 346, 347
secession from Commonwealth, 17, 115, 128, 144, 152, 311, 312
sign manual, 195, 196, 197
Sind Chief Court, jurisdiction of, 3, 4, 152
Smuts, General, 152
South Africa, 17, 18, 28, 29, 89, 92, 151, 153, 155, 181, 188, 190–1, 196, 202, 271, 282
South Australia, 282
Southern Rhodesia, 30, 282
sovereignty, Constituent Assembly and, 7, 8–9, 22–3, 30, 33–4, 36, 67, 108, 139, 143–4, 172, 201, 226, 249, 339
  not vested in Governor-General, 249
  legal, 86
  legislative, 21
  limitations on, 16, 106–7
  political, 86
Special Reference,
  facts cannot be enquired into, 279
  submission of questions for, 264
stare decisis rule,
  inapplicable to Federal Court, 218
  too small to fit the case, 222, 356
State Bank of Pakistan, legislation relating to, invalid, 39
States, representation in Constituent Assembly, 110, 295, 334
Statute of Westminster,
  amendment of, 17
  assent under, 17–18
  lacuna in, 18–19
  origins of, 95
  repeal of, 17
statutory instruments, application to Pakistan, 14

statutory powers, prerogatives and, 268–70, 280
Stephen, J., 164
Stephen, Leslie, 146
stop order, 5
Strickland, Sir Gerald, 99
Sumner, Lord, 270
suspension of laws, 14, 17–18, 30, 107, 201
Sylhet, referendum in, 10

Taylor, quoted, 137
three-tier federation, 324
throne, succession to, 151
treaty-making power, 68
tribal areas,
    agreements for, 108
    representation in Constituent Assembly, 110
    suzerainty over, 19

United Kingdom,
    government of, control by, 20, 21;
    no responsibility for Pakistan, 20, 21, 108, 109; no right to interfere, 150
Parliament of, application of enactments of, 14; repugnancy of laws of, 13, 16–17; and see Act of Parliament
United Kingdom and Colonies, citizenship of, 155
ut res magis valeat quam pereat, 366

Vellani, J., 32–5, 64, 65, 79, 159
Viceroy, powers of, 65
Victoria,
    Queen, 152
    State of, 282

Wade, E. C. S., 120, 151, 164
war, declaration of, 68
Wavell, Lord, 10
Wheare, K. C., 141, 238
writ procedure, 3–4, 25
    discretionary remedy, 158
    jurisdiction remedy, 158
    jurisdiction over, 116–17, 165–6